Serious Games

Ralf Dörner · Stefan Göbel
Wolfgang Effelsberg · Josef Wiemeyer
Editors

Serious Games

Foundations, Concepts and Practice

 Springer

Editors
Ralf Dörner
Department of Design, Computer Science
and Media
RheinMain University of Applied Sciences
Wiesbaden
Germany

Stefan Göbel
Multimedia Communications Lab - KOM
Technische Universität Darmstadt
Darmstadt
Germany

Wolfgang Effelsberg
Lehrstuhl für Praktische
Informatik IV
University of Mannheim
Mannheim
Germany

Josef Wiemeyer
Institut für Sportwissenschaft
Technische Universität Darmstadt
Darmstadt
Germany

ISBN 978-3-319-82137-5   ISBN 978-3-319-40612-1   (eBook)
DOI 10.1007/978-3-319-40612-1

Printed on acid-free paper

This Springer imprint is published by Springer Nature
The registered company is Springer International Publishing AG Switzerland

Preface

Entertainment, fun, challenge, motivation, excitement, and interest: These are some of the positive associations people have when they think about computer games. Recent developments—from powerful graphic processing units, smartphones and other mobile devices, to novel interaction devices such as 3D cameras or VR glasses—all increase the chances that the next generation of digital games will be able to strengthen these positive associations. This makes it even more tempting to think about how to use digital games for purposes other than "just" playing. Who would not want to use software, e.g., for learning that is entertaining, fun, challenging, motivating, exciting, and interesting? Who would not want to develop such software? Who would not want to provide such software to others?

A *serious game* is a name given to computer software that tries to achieve just that. While some people think that *serious games* and *games for learning* are synonymous, digital games can be used for "serious" purposes other than learning. Serious games can be used for motivating people to exercise more. Serious games can be used for medical treatment. Serious games can be used as a marketing tool. These are just a few examples, and we will illustrate various application areas with many actual serious games in this book.

Much practical work and much research have already been carried out in the field of serious gaming. The field is leaving its infancy. This book does not report the latest research results and insights, but strives to consolidate what has been achieved so far. This book is a textbook that aims to provide an introduction to the fundamentals of serious games and an initial guide to this fascinating field. As serious games differ considerably from computer games that are meant for pure entertainment, this textbook focuses on the former.

Computer games are truly multidisciplinary, with computer scientists, artists, user interface designers, game designers, psychologists, and musicians contributing to their development. Given the large number of potential application areas for serious games, the number of disciplines that might be involved in their development is even higher. Chemists, sport scientists, teachers, journalists, marketing experts, historians, medical doctors—they could all provide a valuable contribution to a serious game. We editors have enlisted the support of over 50 authors in order to gather all the competencies necessary to write this book. Among the authors are not only researchers in various disciplines whose expertise lies in serious games, but also persons who have actually designed, created, and evaluated serious games.

As this book is meant for introduction and guidance, we editors took great care that the book hides the fact that it was written by many authors. Our task was to ensure that this book is not an incoherent collection of articles about serious games, but is well structured, easily understandable, and highly consistent.

Undergraduate and graduate students from various disciplines who want to learn about serious games are one target group of this book. They can use it as an accompanying textbook to a lecture or as background reading, e.g., for a seminar. In Chap. 1, we provide some teaching suggestions for how this book can be used in both courses that are dedicated to serious games, and courses about game-based learning or entertainment computing.

Students are not the only ones interested in serious games. Another target group is prospective users of serious game technology. The book provides them with a solid basis for judging the advantages, limitations, and application areas of serious games. This book also discusses resources and other economic aspects. Readers will be able to develop an understanding for the production process and to judge its complexity. Moreover, they will be provided with a methodology of how to assess if a serious game actually meets its goals.

Prospective developers of serious games are another target group of this book. If they are already familiar with the development of games for pure entertainment, they can use the book for self-study in order to learn about distinctive features of serious game design and development.

To cater to this heterogeneous readership and wide range of interests, we made this book flexible to use. We expect all readers to read Chap. 1, as it provides some basics, e.g., a terminology, that will be used in all other chapters of the book. Readers can then choose the chapters they find particularly interesting, and work through those chapters in any order. Teachers can select chapters and a sequence that is most suitable for their course or seminar. The book contains suggestions for courses such as "Introduction to Serious Games", "Entertainment Technology", "Serious Game Design", "Game-based Learning", or "Applications of Serious Games". Moreover, the book can serve as additional literature in a course (e.g., about game development or eLearning) that touches on the subject of serious games. The book's chapters can also serve as introductory texts for student assignments on original literature in the research field of serious games and entertainment computing.

The eleven chapters that follow Chap. 1 cover the creation of serious games (design, authoring processes and tools, content production), the runtime context of a serious game (game engines, adaptation mechanisms, game balancing, game mastering, multi-player serious games), the effects of serious games and their evaluation (player experience, assessment techniques, performance indicators), and serious games in practice (economic aspects, cost benefit analysis, serious game distribution). A description of many practical examples for serious games can be found in the last chapter of the book.

More specifically, the chapters of this book are clustered into four parts. The first part focuses on the creation of serious games. This is an interdisciplinary effort requiring skills in areas such as computer science, art and design, psychology, didactics, and storytelling. The basics that are fundamental for interdisciplinary collaboration are laid in Chap. 2. In the following chapters, the design of serious games (Chap. 3), authoring processes and tools (Chap. 4), and the content of serious games and its production (Chap. 5) are addressed.

The second part examines the phase when the finished serious game is played. Important aspects are game engines (Chap. 6) that are the backbone during runtime. Peculiar for serious games is the need for personalization and adaptation; Chap. 7 deals with adaptation mechanisms, game balancing, and dramaturgy. Game mastering in serious games is often application-dependent. In game-based learning, for instance, the game master may have the role of a tutor or instructor at the same time; Chap. 8 discusses game mastering together with social aspects of serious games, especially in multi-player games.

The third part takes a look at the effects of serious games and their evaluation. Chapter 9 discusses the goal to entertain and shows how the game experience can be measured. It also introduces the concept of player experience. In addition, evaluation techniques that are vital for games in general (such as the evaluation of the game's usability) are addressed. Chapter 10 focuses on the assessment of how far the goals pursued with the serious game are met. In this chapter, evaluation techniques are presented, and indicators for the performance of a serious game are identified.

Finally, the fourth part discusses serious games in practice. A collection of 37 examples of serious games is contained in Chap. 12. Each set of examples highlights different purposes of serious games: training and simulation, learning and education, health, societal and public awareness, heritage and tourism, and marketing. As a basis for the discussion, Chap. 11 addresses economic aspects of serious games such as budgeting, cost benefit analyses, and serious game distribution.

We editors would like to thank all authors involved in this book project: Without their competence, their enthusiasm, and their dedication, this book would not have been possible. We also thank Springer, our publisher. Special thanks go to Ralf Gerstner from Springer, Carolyn Gale for proofreading, and Rolf Kruse who was responsible for all the illustrations in this book.

Darmstadt, Wiesbaden   Ralf Dörner
March 2016   Stefan Göbel
                                                                    Wolfgang Effelsberg
                                                                      Josef Wiemeyer

Contents

6   Game Engines 127

Jonas Freiknecht, Christian Geiger, Daniel Drochtert,
Wolfgang Effelsberg and Ralf Dörner

11   Serious Games—Economic and Legal Issues   303

Stefan Göbel, Oliver Hugo, Michael Kickmeier-Rust
and Simon Egenfeldt-Nielsen

12   Serious Games Application Examples   319

Stefan Göbel

Introduction

1

Ralf Dörner, Stefan Göbel, Wolfgang Effelsberg
and Josef Wiemeyer

Abstract

This chapter introduces the basic subject of this book: serious games. Besides a
definition of the term serious game, related fundamental concepts and terms such
as gamification, gaming, and playing or game mechanics are detailed. Reasons
for using serious games and for delving into this subject are discussed. To better
understand a serious game and its context, a reference scenario is provided.
Moreover, as a frame of reference, the development process of a digital game is
sketched, and the peculiarities of serious games development are highlighted.
A short history of serious games provides some background on the subject. This
is followed by some general hints for how to use this book. Suggestions are
provided for different target groups (e.g., prospective developers or prospective
users) for how to best utilize this textbook. Finally, as in every chapter of this
book, a summary is given, accompanied by a set of questions for self-assessment
and recommendations for further reading.

R. Dörner (✉)
RheinMain University of Applied Sciences, Wiesbaden, Germany
e-mail: ralf.doerner@hs-rm.de

S. Göbel · J. Wiemeyer
Technische Universität Darmstadt, Darmstadt, Germany

W. Effelsberg
University of Mannheim, Mannheim, Germany

© Springer International Publishing Switzerland 2016
R. Dörner et al. (eds.), *Serious Games*, DOI 10.1007/978-3-319-40612-1_1

1.1 What Are Serious Games?

People love being entertained. People love playing games. Human history indicates that games have been played in all societies. Some ancient board games such as *Go* or *Backgammon* are still in use today, although they have predecessors that date back more than 5,000 years. Games can be considered a specific form of playing behavior, with characteristics such as rules and an identifiable outcome. For example, while it may be entertaining to try to hit a target with a ball, this is just playing with a toy—not a game. If a set of rules is obeyed by the players (e.g., the target is a hoop 46 cm in diameter and is mounted 3 m above the ground) and points are awarded according to rules making quantifiable who is in the lead, this playing activity is said to be a game (basketball).

Balls, dice, cards, and other artifacts have been used for playing games. Given the fondness of humans for gameplay, it is no wonder that the computer as a technical artifact has also served as a basis for games.

> Games that use some kind of computing machinery (e.g., a personal computer, a smartphone or a piece of electronics dedicated for playing games such as a video game console) are called *digital games*.

Digital games have been immensely successful. Computer game software has wide user demographics ranging from toddlers to users well advanced in years, encompassing all social groups. More than 50 % of all households in the U.S., for instance, own a video game console (Ipsos Media CT 2013). This success is also reflected in the market volume of digital games. According to one study (Gartner Inc. 2013), the worldwide marketplace for digital games is estimated to be $93 billion USD in 2013, with a growth rate of more than 17 % over 2012. This mass market, and investments in the industry, fuel a dynamic development in game technology. For example, Microsoft's Kinect depth camera for the Xbox game console provides 3D sensing technology that is not only an acceptable alternative to similar products used in non-gaming applications, but also because of the economies of scale more affordable, costing an order of magnitude less. So, why not use game technology for non-gaming applications? Why not take advantage of the success of digital games in application areas beyond entertainment?

It is not only the technological advances that make digital games attractive for pursuing objectives different from pure entertainment. Sophisticated methodologies have been developed for digital games. For instance, game designers acquired skills that can be used to emotionally involve players in a digital game (Freeman 2003). Digital game methodologies have also become an area of research. Researchers were able to identify important factors for game enjoyment besides the technical capacity, such as aesthetic presentation or narrativity (John and Srivastava 1999).

Digital games can also be intrinsically motivating (Wong et al. 2007). They are even capable to put players into the mental state of flow (Csikszentmihalyi 1990), where they feel fully immersed in, and absorbed by, an activity. Would it not be desirable to use a digital game to put learners into this flow state, where they would be highly focused on their learning activity? Would it not be advantageous to employ digital games in order to turn learning into an enjoyable experience where time flies by?

Television is an example of a new medium where a while after its introduction the applicability for purposes such as learning has been explored (e.g., by producing television formats such as Sesame Street). Why not do the same with digital games? Traditional games have been used for more serious purposes than entertainment. For example, the board game *Monopoly* was created with the intention to serve as a tool to teach the negative effects of monopolies on the economy (Orbanes 2006). Sport games such as basketball can be played not only for a fun experience, but also because players strive to increase their fitness and improve their health. If traditional games are able to serve other purposes than entertainment, why should digital games lack this ability? We call a digital game that possesses this ability a *serious game,* and define the term as follows:

> A *serious game* is a digital game created with the intention to entertain and to achieve at least one additional goal (e.g., learning or health). These additional goals are named *characterizing goals.*

Today, the term serious game is somewhat vague because no universally accepted definition exists. In other definitions, serious games are not characterized by the intention of the developer, but by the intention of the player. Thus, a digital game such as the ego-shooter *Doom* would become a serious game if the player uses it not only for entertainment, but also to train motor skills or to improve reaction time. Moreover, some definitions distinguish serious games from other games by requiring that they are played not in a formal educational setting, but voluntarily in the player's leisure time. In our definition, there are no demands made that the serious game actually meets its goals. The mere intention of the developers is sufficient to categorize a game as a serious game. This is not the case in other definitions of the term. Michael and Chen (2006) define a serious game as a game that does not have entertainment, enjoyment, or fun as their primary purpose. In our definition, the goals of a serious game are not ranked by their importance. While we require a serious game to be a digital game, others specify the term more generally and apply it to all types of games. In fact, Abt (1970) coined the term *serious games* with only board and card games in mind.

Serious games are not a particular game genre. For instance, a serious game could be an action adventure, a strategy game, or a sports game. Serious games also need to be distinguished from gamification. *Gamification* is the transfer of game methodologies or elements to non-game applications and processes (Deterding et al. 2011).

For example, the sports apparel manufacturer Nike uses badges, achievements, challenges, and rewards in their customer loyalty program—concepts typically found in games. Thus, the result of gamification is not necessarily a game.

Often, serious games are intended for learning. For example, *Jetset* (Persuasive Games LLC 2014) is a mobile game that allows travelers to keep up to date with current security regulations at 100 international airports. Players not only learn whether they have to take their shoes off at a particular airport, but they can also strip search other virtual travelers for fun and obtain virtual souvenirs. In addition to learning simple facts, serious games can also pursue more complex goals such as the acquisition of specific skills. Disney's *Minnie explores the land of Dizz* (The Walt Disney Company Ltd. 2014) is an example of a serious game where small children can develop problem solving skills. The simulation game *INNOV8* from IBM (IBM Corp. 2014) provides learning opportunities for IT and business professionals to grasp the effects of business process management.

Learning is not the only characterizing goal of serious games. There is a whole range of other characterizing goals. *America's Army* (Knight 2002) provides a soldiering experience of basic training and is used as a tool for recruitment. *Re-Mission* (HopeLab 2014) is a serious game for young cancer patients where they have to control a nanobot to fight cancer and infections in the human body. The game intends to inform patients about cancer treatments and to positively change their attitude (in this case, towards a strict adherence to chemotherapy treatments). *SnowWorld* (Hoffman 2000), a first-person shooter with snowballs, is a serious game that tries to distract burn victims from pain during wound treatment by immersing them in a virtual world.

Serious games can be divided into categories according to their characterizing goals. For example, *exergames* encourage people to become physically active and sustain a healthy lifestyle, whereas *advergames* are used for marketing purposes or recruiting and may raise the players' awareness of certain topics. The characterizing goals of today's serious games also include lifestyle behavior change, medical diagnosis, enterprise management, decision support, development of social skills, analysis of causal mechanisms, creation and defense of arguments, development of conflict resolution strategies, arousal of fantasy, elevation of civic engagement, promotion of ethical values, persuasion and recruitment to causes, campaigning in politics, and many more.

1.2 Motivation

There are many motivations for those interested in creating a serious game and pursuing goals beyond entertainment with it. First, creators want to provide the users with a fun experience: the sensory pleasure (e.g., nice visuals and sounds) of a well-made game can contribute to making the software enjoyable to use. An interesting narration is another factor that can increase the enjoyment.

Second, it is difficult to increase user motivation, and games can provide a tool to accomplish this. For example, a joyful experience can motivate users and generate interest or curiosity. Factors inherent in many games such as achievement and control have been shown to contribute to motivation.

Third, software creators aim to reach users on an emotional level. Good gameplay should be able to evoke challenge, suspense, thrill, relief, empathy with characters, or caring for an environment. This can foster active engagement. Game creators intend to have their users lean forward and not lean back when using the software. As a result, the users may be more committed or invest higher levels of endurance and effort. This can be highly supportive to achieve the intended goals of a serious game.

Fourth, the level of goal achievement with serious games might be higher than with other means. For instance, there are reports that serious games foster sustained learning (Michael and Chen 2006). The advantages of using a narrative (e.g., quicker comprehension and better remembrance, Graesser and Ottati 1996) can be exploited in narrative serious games, which are unique in the sense that the user is able to interactively influence the development of a story, in contrast to other media for narratives such as books or videos. The *SnowBall* game was reported to be as effective in achieving the goal of pain reduction as morphine, while avoiding the adverse effects of the drug (Hoffman 2000).

Fifth, serious games offer immediate feedback and adaptability. As games have a quantifiable result, players are immediately able to assess their progress. Since assessment is accomplished by an anonymous system, players might perceive the assessment to be less stressful or embarrassing. Based on the assessment, the game software can adapt parameters—for example, the difficulty level—to the individual player. As a result, serious games are capable of providing users with a cognitive, emotional, or physical challenge that is neither too easy nor too difficult.

Sixth, serious games can be a smart tool to achieve a certain goal where there are simply no equivalent alternatives. For example, serious games are capable of engaging a user in a simulated hypothetical world, where contradictions or anomalies are integrated to induce problem-solving strategies and increase their self-efficacy in case of success.

These are six of the major reasons to explore and employ serious games as a tool for achieving a variety of goals. Additionally, there are other reasons to concern oneself with serious games, such as taking advantage of market opportunities or fostering social experiences by using multiplayer game technology.

However, employing serious games may not only have positive consequences. The term serious game itself is an oxymoron—a game that is serious appears to be a contradiction. Indeed, players might be demotivated to play a game simply because it is labeled to be serious. Players might perceive a serious game as a feeble attempt to wrap something that is not pleasant in a nice box—and find serious games as appealing as chocolate-coated spinach. Just because something is a game does not mean that it is fun (Wong et al. 2007). Serious games have the inherent tradeoff, where they are trying to achieve more than one goal. If the goal to entertain is neglected, the playing experience might be negative. Even worse, players might fear that they are manipulated by a serious game. In his science fiction novel *Ender's Game,* Card (1985) describes a serious game where an action game is used to trick children to fight a real war where they take ruthless decisions because they assume that it is only a game. Games in general have not only positive traits, for example, there is the problem that games might be addictive or have adverse effects on the player's well-being. Examples are eyestrain, headaches, and even injuries in exergames).

Thus, there are interesting perspectives but also pitfalls in using serious games. Persons who like to either use or create a serious game face many difficult issues. How can a serious game be made enjoyable? How can it be motivating? How can it be engaging on an emotional level? What mechanisms can be used to adapt the game to an individual user? Which goals can be targeted with a serious game? To which degree does a serious game really achieve the intended goals? How does it compete successfully with other leisure time activities? What can expertise in pedagogy, psychology, computer science, art, design, economics, or social sciences contribute to the development of a serious game? How is a serious game produced? How does the development process differ from the production of an entertainment game? How costly is the production? In order to answer these questions, this textbook compiles insights from research, experiences from developing and using serious games, and many best practice examples. The aim of the book is to lay a solid foundation on top of which the reader can assess, create, use or research serious games.

1.3 Terminology

There are many terms associated with serious games. In this section, some of the basic terminology of serious games is introduced. Important terms are defined and explained to provide a common conceptual basis for all chapters of this book. Further terms that are relevant to serious games will be defined in subsequent chapters. Figure 1.1 provides an overview of the basic terms defined in this section.

The definition of the term *serious game* was already presented in Sect. 1.1. As has been mentioned there, the term should be clearly distinguished from the term *gamification.* Taken literally, the term gamification means "making a game of something that is not a game." According to Deterding et al. (2011), *gamification* is an "informal umbrella term for the use of video game elements in non-gaming systems to improve user experience (UX) and user engagement." In particular, game-based concepts and/or elements are used to "gamify" existing non-game applications. Typically, but not necessarily, this is less than a full serious game.

Games with a purpose (GWAP) can be considered as a kind of complement of the term *gamification.* The term *GWAP* denotes games deliberately designed to employ players in order to serve a particular non-game purpose (von Ahn 2006). Ideally, GWAP provide incentives for people to participate in efforts such as large-scale problem solving, picture tagging or finding appropriate textual description of images. GWAP are a motivating and attractive means to exploit the

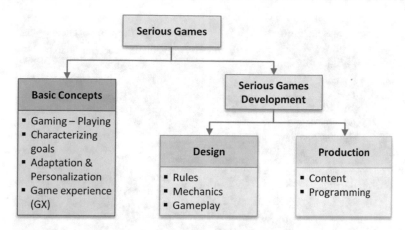

Fig. 1.1 Terminology of serious games—overview of basic terms

potentials of crowdsourcing or citizen science, e.g., (Quinn and Bederson 2011). In citizen science, for example, scientific problems are transformed into a comprehensive game to be solved by a community of non-scientists (Hand 2010). Successful examples are *Galaxy Zoo* (Raddick et al. 2010, 2013), *Foldit* (Khatib et al. 2011; Cooper et al. 2010), and *Phylo* (Kawrykow et al. 2012).

> *Gamification* means to add game elements to a non-game area, whereas *games with a purpose* denote games designed to exploit crowdsourcing in order to achieve a non-game purpose.

In order to distinguish other digital games from serious games, we introduce the term *entertainment game*.

> An *entertainment game* is a digital game that has exclusively the goal to entertain the player. A digital game is either an entertainment game or a serious game.

Figure 1.2 shows that terminology in serious games is concerned not only with serious games themselves, but also with their basic concepts. Here, two activities have to be distinguished on a fundamental level: Play(ing) and Gaming.

- According to George Herbert Mead, a well-known philosopher and social psychologist, *play* is an activity in human development where a child imitates the roles of others in the sense of role playing (Mead 2009). In a broader sense, playing means a *purposeless, intrinsically motivated activity with no explicit rules*

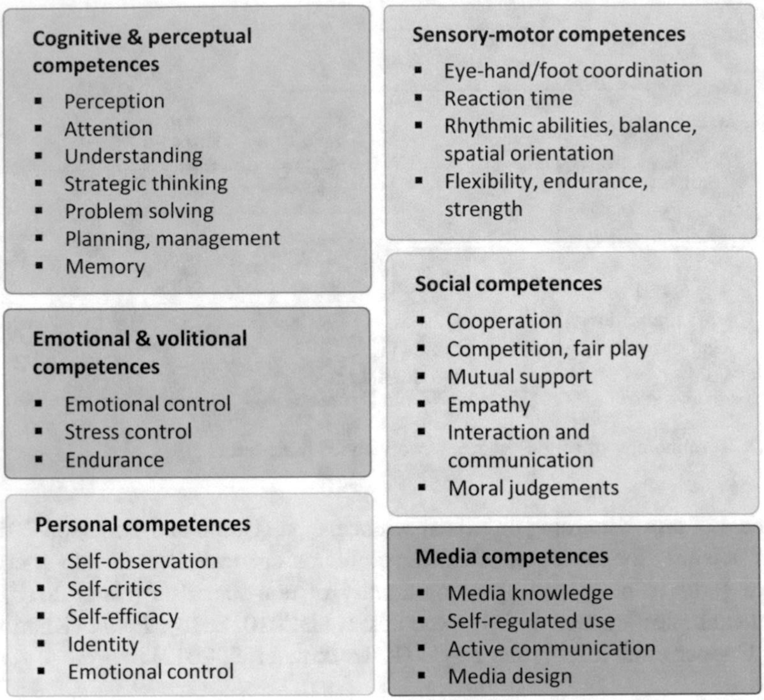

Cognitive & perceptual competences	Sensory-motor competences
• Perception • Attention • Understanding • Strategic thinking • Problem solving • Planning, management • Memory	• Eye-hand/foot coordination • Reaction time • Rhythmic abilities, balance, spatial orientation • Flexibility, endurance, strength

Emotional & volitional competences	Social competences
• Emotional control • Stress control • Endurance	• Cooperation • Competition, fair play • Mutual support • Empathy • Interaction and communication • Moral judgements

Personal competences	Media competences
• Self-observation • Self-critics • Self-efficacy • Identity • Emotional control	• Media knowledge • Self-regulated use • Active communication • Media design

Fig. 1.2 Six examples of competence domains specifying the characterizing goals of serious games according to Wiemeyer and Hardy (2013)

(as opposed to gaming). Rather, the activity of playing emerges and progresses according to the implicit dynamic interaction of the players and the situation. For example, players may change a game feature and watch what happens; based on the result they may change the game feature again to experience the effect. This cycle may continue, without being determined by explicit rules.

- *Gaming* (as the second stage of identity development) is an organized rule-based group-play with structured roles (Mead 2009). Again, in a broader sense, gaming can be considered a *purposeless, intrinsically motivated activity according to explicit rules*. Examples would be to play basketball or table tennis. In these games, certain rules—i.e., passing, serving and returning of the ball—determine players' activities.

Playing is a purposeless, intrinsically motivated human activity without explicit rules, whereas *gaming* is a purposeless, intrinsically-motivated human activity based on explicit rules.

As mentioned above, another basic concept of a serious game is its characterizing goal. It is important, as it characterizes the serious game and can be used to classify serious games into several categories. The characterizing goal can pertain to several competence or skill domains, e.g., Wiemeyer and Kliem (2012) or Wiemeyer and Hardy (2013):

- Cognitive and perceptual competences/skills
- Emotional and volitional competences/skills
- Sensory-motor competences/skills
- Personal competences/skills
- Social competences/skills
- Media competences/skills

Figure 1.2 illustrates examples for these competence domains.

> The characterizing goals of serious games can be matched to *competence domains*, e.g., cognition and perception, emotion and volition, sensory-motor control, personal characteristics, social attitudes, and media use.

Serious games can be classified according to various competence domains. It is less common to distinguish serious games based on their target group within specific application contexts. One example is a *corporate game* that is targeted at the employees of a company. Sometimes, there is a distinction made between serious games for (formal) education and serious games for (informal) training and simulation, as it is assumed that they cater to different target groups and application contexts, respectively (e.g., university students vs. company employees).

> *Educational games* denote a subgroup of serious games, tackling the formal educational sector from elementary schools to higher education, vocational training, and collaborative workplace training. Whereas *learning games* address primarily informal learning, *educational games* focus on formal learning in dedicated educational institutions.

Besides the characterizing goal, the competence domain, and the target group, serious games can be categorized by application area. According to the *Serious Game Classification System* provided by Ludoscience (2014) or the serious games directory provided by the Serious Games Association (2014), among the most common serious games categories are corporate games for training and simulation purposes, educational games, health games, and advergames. Further categories include social awareness games, games for architecture and planning, and games for tourism and cultural heritage. Training and simulation represent a large application area for serious games that is also commercially relevant. Popular examples are numerous flight simulators. Other examples are *TechForce*, a game-based training and learning environment for trainees in the field of electro and metal industries, or game modifications of the popular entertainment games *Civilization* or *Oblivion* that are employed to teach history or geography in higher education. Due to increasing demands on the health system, *health games* have become more and more popular. These games address several health-related aspects such as nutrition and physical activity. To support therapy, numerous *rehab games* have been developed, e.g., in neurorehabilitation (Wiemeyer 2014). The genre of *persuasive and public/social awareness games* tackles issues such as energy, e.g., *EnerCities* (Enercities consortium 2014), climate, e.g., *Imagine Earth* (Serious Brothers GbR 2014), security awareness games, e.g., quiz-based games such as *ID Theft Faceoff* from OnGuardOnline (Johnson 2014), and religion, e.g., *Global Conflicts: Palestine* (Serious Games Interactive 2014).

Adaptation and personalization are basic concepts of serious games (see Fig. 1.2). Entertainment games as well as serious games are usually played by a wide variety of players having quite different characteristics. Furthermore, players show more or less progress in the competences mentioned above during and after playing. Therefore, one of the most important requirements for good games is to fit as closely as possible to the characteristics of the player in order to be both attractive and effective. This means that the game should be *adaptive and adaptable* to the personal characteristics of the player as well as to the requirements for reaching the characterizing goal. There are many options to ensure adaptability—from designing one's own avatar to choosing an appropriate game level. On the other hand, adaptivity means that the game adapts itself more or less automatically to the specific situation. There are also many options for adaptivity, for example, presenting easier or more difficult tasks, providing support (e.g., hints to the solution), or switching to a new scenario. For adaptivity to be effective, a valid *in-game assessment* of relevant aspects like emotional or cognitive state of the player or emerging difficulties is required. Kickmeier-Rust et al. (2011) introduced the concepts of micro and macro adaptation. *Micro adaptation* is a specific fine tuning *whereas macro adaptation* comprises traditional techniques such as adaptive presentation, navigation, curriculum sequencing, and problem solving support based on static learner characteristics. Due to the challenge that game adaptation must not compromise gaming experience, a dynamic in-game (or "stealth") real-time assessment of cognitive, perceptual-motor, emotional, and motivational states is indispensable in order to provide appropriate non-disruptive micro adaptations, i.e., non-invasive adaptations like adaptive hinting, adaptive feedback, or an adaptive adjustment of the environment.

> *Personalization* means that games can be tailored to the individual characteristics of the playing person. The game can be either adapted by an external person like the player, teacher, or therapist (*adaptability*) or adapt itself based on in-game assessment (*adaptivity*).

Due to their dual mission, serious games have to be both attractive and effective: They have to achieve the characterizing goal without compromising game experience. Therefore, the term *game experience* (GX) is central to the claim of serious games to elicit experiences that are characteristic for games. GX denotes complex and dynamic psychic phenomena while playing games. The concept of GX includes several dimensions like fun, challenge, flow, immersion, presence, tension, positive and negative emotions, curiosity, fantasy, self-efficacy, and motivation. GX can be measured at three levels: behavior, physiology, and subjective experience.

> *Game experience* (GX) is a subjective experience of "true gaming," having fun, being challenged, being immersed and involved in the game, feeling emotions, and being absorbed by the game. The concept of GX can be subdivided into numerous dimensions. One of the most important dimensions is *game flow*.

Game flow is another basic concept. Game flow is an experience during gaming characterized by exclusive concentration on the game, feeling control over the game, being immersed in the game, facing clear goals and getting immediate and consistent feedback, e.g., Sweetser and Wyeth (2005). Game flow occurs when there is an appropriate fit of task difficulty and player skills. Sinclair (2011) introduces the concept of *dual flow*, i.e., a balance of attractiveness and effectiveness. Figure 1.3 illustrates the idea to influence both attractiveness (i.e., good GX) and effectiveness (i.e., achievement of the characterizing goal) by establishing and maintaining an appropriate balance of task difficulty and skill level.

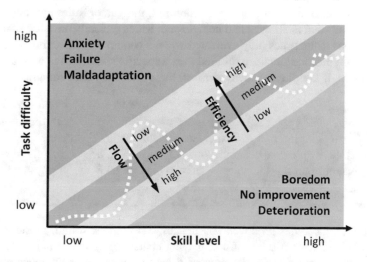

Fig. 1.3 Dual flow as a balance of task difficulty and skill level

The concept of *dual flow* is characteristic of, and unique to, serious games. The appropriate balance of task difficulty and skill level ensures that the double mission of serious games is accomplished: being both effective and attractive.

As depicted in Fig. 1.1, a second major branch in the terminology of serious games is concerned with serious games development.

Serious games development consists of two main components: game design and game production. *Game design* comprises all aspects relevant to the internal structure and external appearance of a game, whereas *game production* comprises all aspects of building the game.

Game mechanics, gameplay, and rules are important aspects of game design. These elements are explained in the following.

Game mechanics denotes "methods invoked by agents for interacting with the game world" (Sicart 2008). In other words, game mechanics signifies the ways to interact with a game according to the implemented rules and the specific situation, i.e., a scenario or game level. Examples include jumping on platforms or hitting a ball.

Gameplay is a term that is very similar to game mechanics. In a narrow sense, game mechanics denotes the internal management of interactions, whereas gameplay denotes the external process that develops between the player and the game while the game is played. Examples are controlling the dancing movements of an avatar by waving the arms or eliciting jumps by pressing a button.

Rules are regulations or settings constraining the game. Rules can contain regulations about what is allowed and not allowed. Rules typically have the shape of *if-then relations* (sometimes only evaluated when a certain *event* occurs). This means that if certain preconditions are fulfilled then a specific consequence will take place. For example, if the player moves too fast, the avatar may start running.

Game mechanics denotes the way the players can interact with the game. It focuses on the internal management of interactions, whereas *gameplay* denotes the external appearance of interactions. *Rules* are regulations and settings constraining the game. They typically take the form of if-then relations.

Moreover, game design covers 2D images, 3D models, sound, music, art, avatars, the behavior description of non-playing characters (NPCs), and level design. All tangible or perceivable elements of a game, including their appearance and behavior (e.g., images, textures, 3D models, sounds, scripts), are called *game assets*. The game design is specified in a *game design document*. For the design of serious games, the entertainment part has to be combined with the characterizing goals of the serious part. In other words, game design principles need to match the requirements and characterizing goals of a serious game. This starts with the game idea and ends with the production of appropriate game assets fitting to the nature of a serious game application domain and the targeted user groups.

As mentioned above, game production is the implementation of game design, i.e., the building of the game. Two important components of game production are *asset production* (also called *content production*) and *game programming*. To actually produce a serious game, methods, concepts, and technologies are used analogous to the development of entertainment games. However, these concepts, technologies, and principles are enhanced with further information and communication technologies (ICT) as well as domain-specific methodologies and technologies with regard to the characterizing goals of the serious game. These are applied in different application domains of serious games (see Sect. 1.5).

> *Game production* comprises content production and game programming. *Content and assets* are produced combining domain-specific knowledge and game technology. *Game programming* denotes adequate hardware and software arrangements including sensors, interfaces and multimedia components as well as relevant algorithms and programming concepts.

1.4 A Reference Scenario for Serious Games

What does the lifecycle of a serious game look like? What are the typical steps and phases that are encountered from the wish to have a serious game to players actually playing it? Who participates in this process? Who are the stakeholders? In this section, we provide a prototypical reference scenario and illustrate it with two application examples: (1) development and deployment of a serious game for corporate training—initiated and financed by a corporation, and (2) a game-based mobile guide for the elderly to access cultural heritage—initiated and financed as a publicly funded research project.

The lifecycle of a serious game begins with a *preparation phase*, followed by a *development phase* (with a number of iterations) and a *deployment phase*, as shown in Fig. 1.4. Similar to book editions, the overall process might be restarted again (and again), resulting in several editions of the serious game. Reasons for that might include new research and technology achievements, as well as an extended spectrum of targeted user groups or further developments in the application domain. For instance, improved domain knowledge with new therapeutic approaches or new sensor technologies might lead to improved game design concepts. With respect to

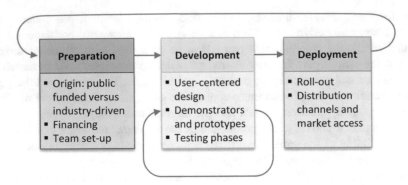

Fig. 1.4 Lifecycle and iterations of a serious game—preparation phase, user-centered iterative development phases and deployment phase

the extension of targeted user groups, corporate training environments might not only address employees of the company, but also applicants for recruiting programs. Similarly, a game-based mobile guide originally planned for the elderly might be also adopted for younger users, providing slightly modified user interfaces and age-appropriate interaction principles.

The preparation phase is the first step towards the development and introduction of a serious game, and initializes the lifecycle of a serious game (see Fig. 1.4). As outlined in Sect. 1.2, the basic motivation to create and introduce a serious game is usually the same. Serious games are seen as a promising mechanism or "tool" to fulfill a specific goal in the different application areas, e.g., serving as a corporate training instrument, or a mobile assistant for playful access to cultural heritage for the elderly. Although there is the common motivation to use a serious game as a tool to fulfill characterizing goals, this commonality does not extend to its origin, preparation, development, and deployment. In fact, those differ considerably in concrete application contexts. Whereas public awareness games, educational games, or cultural heritage games typically originate from and are financed in the context of publicly funded projects with an overall focus beyond serious games, the starting point in the commercial sector is often different.

In the case of publicly-funded projects, a serious game is often a byproduct. It is not the ultimate goal of the surrounding project, but serves as a showcase to demonstrate what the key objective of the funding scheme might be, for example, the working principles of new ICT mechanisms, new learning paradigms, or new concepts for ambient assisted living and mobility support for elderly people. On the other hand, in industry-driven serious games, typically decision makers of corporations look for a good solution for a concrete problem (e.g., all employees need to be trained for a new product or process), and they might have heard of the potential of serious games, e.g., as a training instrument. The reason for a decision maker to choose a serious game over other means might be that there are either no alternatives, or that the alternatives (e.g., classical eLearning solutions) are assumed to be less effective, less innovative, less promising, or too expensive.

In the second step of the preparation phase, the market for existing serious games is checked. However, in most cases there are no commercial off-the-shelf serious games available matching the concrete situation and particular needs of the company. Hence, the decision maker searches for appropriate serious game providers (i.e., game developer studios or other research and technical development (RTD) providers with profound knowledge of serious games development). In an optimal case, a game developer studio or RTD provider for serious games can reference similar solutions with related evaluation studies that have proved the effects of a serious game (both in terms of fun and user/game experience, and effects towards the characterizing goal). This also serves as an internal argument for the project initiator and decision maker for necessary investments. And this indicates one dilemma of serious games: Unfortunately, only a few reference examples with singular evaluation studies exist proving their benefit in dedicated application contexts. Therefore, the majority of serious game development projects are based on a trial and error strategy. Apart from pure economic or scientific considerations, many corporations are fully convinced of the potential of game-based mechanisms and serious games in principle. Being among the first in their field to use these innovative new media concepts, they strive to obtain a status as an early adopter. This is particularly true if they have digital natives or digital immigrants among their employees or customers (i.e., people who grew up being surrounded by or fascinated with digital games and highly interactive technologies).

The third step of the preparation phase includes the development team's composition, consisting of the customer side (management level and technical level) and the development side (game designer, game programmer, etc., see Sect. 1.5.6). In contrast to entertainment games, further domain experts (e.g., educators, psychologists, marketing experts) complement the development team. In our two examples, doctors, therapists, or subject matter experts for corporate training or personalized tourism need to be involved. Then the actual development can begin.

The development phase represents the main part of the overall development process of a serious game (in terms of development duration per edition, neglecting phases from one edition to another). It typically follows a *user-centered design* approach involving users (e.g., trainees or employees in the first application example, or elderly people in the second example) from the beginning. User involvement may even have already started in the preparation phase.

The development phase begins with gathering information about the characteristics, needs and interests of the target user group and of the customer such as a training department of a corporation. This is the basis for writing the game design document and functional requirements of a serious game. Simple paper mockups or tinkered devices might be developed in order to provide a first impression about the envisioned serious game scenario and practical outcomes to the end users.

Based on the first round of user feedback, a set of initial use cases is defined in collaboration with the customer, the development team, and the targeted end users. This step is extremely important with regard to goal-oriented evaluation studies. These studies will be carried out to prove both the effects and the benefit of serious games, both in concrete situations and application contexts in later stages of the development process. Again, mockups or early technical demonstrators providing the principle functionality of the serious game are developed to receive valuable feedback from the end user side. Similar to classical software engineering processes, the game design document and functional requirements are then translated into game scenarios (including game environments and game content, e.g., game assets), gameplay, and technical specifications (including game mechanics). This process typically results in a prototype that provides full functionality of the serious game, which is tested in detail by a broader number of end users.

After taking user feedback into account, game production begins. This results in fully integrated prototypes of the serious game or specific parts—such as a game level for a thematic area in the corporate training scenario, or a sightseeing point for the mobile guide scenario. These prototypes are tested and evaluated within user studies following the use case scenarios. During this process, different software engineering methods are often used, ranging from classical methods, (e.g., the *waterfall model*) to more recent *agile software development methods* such as *SCRUM* (software engineering concepts will be described in more detail in Sect. 4.4). Agile methods focus on iterative development and improvement of smaller parts of a game with much shorter development cycles that are called *sprints*. This approach to software development is well known and widespread in the game development community. Sprints typically take only a few days up to some weeks—which is much less compared to classical software development projects following the waterfall model. For instance, in publicly funded research projects, two to three development cycles are common in a project of 3 years. As soon as a stable version accepted by the end users is available, the roll-out of the serious game begins.

The third major phase in the serious game lifecycle is the deployment phase. Here, the serious game is rolled out to as many end users as possible from the target user group. In our two application examples, this includes all employees who need to take corporate training, or all elderly people who are visiting a city and might be interested in a game-based mobile guide to playfully explore it. The corporate scenario rollout is much easier, since employees are accessible via traditional hierarchies and can be easily reached via a corporate intranet. Furthermore, corporate training is usually free for employees, so there are no obstacles caused by cost issues. For the second example, the mobile city might be offered for free via a web portal from the city's marketing agencies or associations of elderly people. The practical question is how to access the market and reach as many customers a possible. Distribution platforms and channels such as *Steam* (Steam 2014) that are widespread in both the entertainment games industry and in the gamer communities seem to be inappropriate for serious games. Also, the principle of cross-platform publishing of entertainment games (on different game consoles or as PC, browser or mobile versions) is not widespread for serious games yet.

The introduction of a serious game into existing corporate processes typically takes at least 6 months. Depending on the complexity of the content, it may take up to a year, or even more. This duration is comparable with the introduction of a Web-based training module when eLearning was introduced.

From an economics perspective, a challenge for both commercial and publicly funded projects is the limited development budget for serious games, especially compared to the budgets available for entertainment games. This may lead to a discrepancy between the expectations of the end users and the necessary budgets to create a convincing, successful serious game that is both entertaining and fulfilling its characterizing goal. Especially members of the generation born after the mid 1980s, sometimes called "digital natives," who are familiar with entertainment games providing a convincing gameplay, excellent graphics, etc. have similarly high expectations for serious games even in case they are aware that these serious games have a lower budget. This problem of a limited development budget is most apparent when it comes to the conceptualization and production of personalized, adaptive serious games. In contrast to entertainment games created for the mass market, the primary goal for the field of serious games is to provide adaptive games that match the characteristics and needs of individual users or smaller user groups. The particular requirements for the development of personalized, adaptive serious games will be described in Chap. 7. Compared to traditional learning and training systems such as classical Web-based training or eLearning arrangements, the cost of digital games are much higher. This often causes wrong assumptions and expectations by end users who expect to get high-end games for a similar budget as traditional eLearning arrangements.

1.5   Overview of the Development Process of Serious Games

There are established development processes for digital games described in the literature, e.g., in Rabin (2009). These processes were developed with entertainment games in mind. The development process of serious games, however, is not identical to the one for entertainment games. In serious games, there are one or more specialists from an application area involved. For instance, a health game needs medical and health-related competence right from the beginning. A second example is an educational game about the nourishment for babies requiring pediatricians, behavioral scientists and experts in the field of didactics. One or more of the application area specialists may provide an application-specific game behavior. For example, a didactic expert might introduce didactic elements into the game.

Figure 1.5 shows a framework for the development of serious games. In the center, game design methods, concepts and principles are used in analogy to the development and design of entertainment games. These concepts, technologies and principles are supported by further information and communication technologies (ICT) as well as domain-specific methodologies and technologies with regard to the characterizing goal of the serious game) Typical ICT technologies include mechanisms of artificial intelligence (AI) for the planning, automated generation and intelligent behavior of virtual characters, aspects of human-computer interaction (HCI), usability features, usage of game controllers and I/O devices, multimedia aspects (computer graphics, audio, etc.) as well as sensor technology to retrieve and

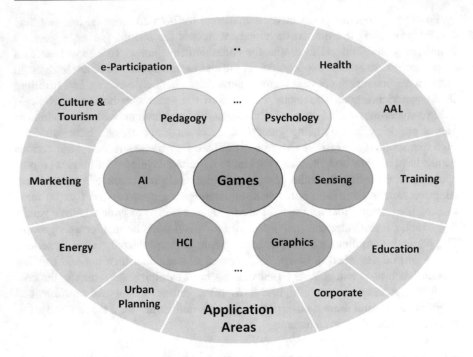

Fig. 1.5 Serious games—game design combined with further concepts, technologies and disciplines, applied in a broad range of application domains

monitor context information. Domain-specific methodologies include aspects such as psychosocial, didactic, and pedagogic concepts for educational settings, ranging from kindergarten to collaborative workplace training, or psychophysiological mechanisms to monitor the vital status in healthcare applications.

In the following, we briefly introduce key aspects of the game development process: game idea and game design, game architecture and game production, game adaptation mechanisms, game platforms, game engines, and the game development team.

1.5.1   Game Idea and Game Design

At the heart of a good game design is always a creative team and a good game idea. The better the idea, the more fun the game is usually to play, and the more useful it might be for achieving the goal to entertain and to reach the characterizing goals. A creative atmosphere in the development company is helpful for good game design (Fullerton 2008). Creativity can also be stimulated using creativity techniques, books (e.g., Csikszentmihalyi 2009), and seminars.

A game idea that is developed from scratch is rare. As no model exists to predict how well a game idea will be received by the intended audience, the use of best practices is fundamental. Thus, game designers often rely on previous experiences. They often analyze existing games and stick to working formulas, reducing the risk of a game being a failure. This is also a reason why sequels of successful games are common. One problem with serious games is that not as much experience has been gathered as with entertainment games.

A fundamental task of game design is to create the game experience. However, game experience cannot be designed directly but only indirectly by specifying game rules, game mechanics, and other features of the game (e.g., the design of game assets). The game experience emerges from these design choices. In serious games, the game designers also have to take into account that the players not only have a positive game experience but that the characterizing goals are met. As there can be a tradeoff between achieving all these goals, game designers need to compromise. In order to achieve this, there needs to be a close cooperation of the area specialists with the game designers and game engineers. Often, creative ideas come from both sides. The area specialists might have plenty of initial ideas that they would like to see in the game, the engineers have to find ways how to implement them. Gradually both game designers and game engineers learn more and more about the characterizing goal. This allows them to have their own implementable, creative ideas (Ritterfeld et al. 2009). On the other hand, the area specialists gradually understand what is feasible in software, and that steers their ideas into the right direction.

As described above, a basic approach of game designers is to work iteratively. Initial choices are tested. Then these test results are analyzed, and modifications to the game are made. This is repeated in order to fine-tune the game design. An example is the balancing of the game rules. If the game emerging from the initial rules is too difficult, the players will become frustrated. If it is too easy the players will be bored (see Fig. 1.3). A good approach is thus that the game designers start with an initial set of rules, test the emerging game and use the test results for modifying the rules.

To complicate matters, the players change when playing the game: they become more experienced and hone their skills. Thus, game designers need to design a mechanism that maintains the challenge for the player at the right level. In his landmark paper, Csikszentmihalyi (1990) describes a diagonal corridor in a two-dimensional graph, where the players should find themselves; the two dimensions are the degree of difficulty of the game and the level of skill of the players (see Fig. 1.4 for a version adapted to serious games). For achieving this, the game designers have several game design methods, for instance, the concept of *levels*. Novice players start at level 0 where they have to accomplish simple tasks. When they do that well, the players are elevated to higher levels where the tasks become more difficult.

Another task for the game designers is to motivate players to continue playing. Motivating aspects are of particular importance in serious games. Game designers can also use several game design methods for this. One method is again to use levels and motivate players by giving them a sense of progress or by making them curious about the next levels. Another game design concept is *in-game awards*. A player who has accomplished a task gets awarded an in-game bonus. In the simplest case, this bonus consists of points, and a ranked list of the players with their points is displayed when the game is over. This might motivate players to try their best to end up high on that *high-score list*. Other awards can consist of more powerful weapons, desirable objects or additional lives for the player. In serious games, those awards could refer to the purpose of the game.

1.5.2 Game Architecture and Game Production

The game design describes a serious game on a conceptual level. In order to be playable as a digital game, the game design needs to be implemented in a software system. This is the task of the game production. Beside software development, the game production also comprises the creation of the game assets (e.g., generating 3D models of game objects, animating game characters, drawing textures, or recording a soundtrack).

Developing a game software system can be challenging task, as these systems can be highly complex. *Divide et impera*, i.e., breaking down a complex problem into smaller problems, is a software design paradigm that has been successfully employed in the past to deal with complexity. Thus, to make the production task manageable, the game software system is often broken down into subsystems. A *game architecture* describes which subsystems are present in a game and how they are assembled to form the entire digital game. The architecture of a game is depicted in Fig. 1.6.

The game architecture is structured into many components interacting with each other. The *hardware* layer can be a PC, smartphone, game console, etc. As usual in any computer system, we have the *operating system* on top of the hardware. On general-purpose computers, such as PCs or smartphones, it supports many applications in parallel. In contrast, on game consoles, it is tailored to enable gaming efficiently.

On top of the operating system comes the game runtime environment. It is based on a *platform independence* layer that shields the *core* of the game engine from the details of the operating system so that it can run on many different hardware platforms. At the heart of the core is the *main loop*. Here, a timer controls the execution of all those components that require periodic updating; examples include the game's artificial intelligence (AI), the physics (e.g., simulation of gravity), collision detection and many more. If the game has a multiplayer mode, the *multiplayer management* component allows connecting to other players, typically via a central server, and often game mastering is also supported. A *resource manager* maintains the *asset database* of the game, including materials and textures, fonts, the skeletons of avatars, and sounds. In contrast to the assets, the *game data manager* stores information about the state of the game and the players, e.g., the points they currently have and the level at which they last played. As its name says the *output generator* creates the visual output for the display and the audible output for the speakers or earphones; sometimes haptic output is also provided, for example, force feedback on a steering wheel. And the *input handler* deals with all

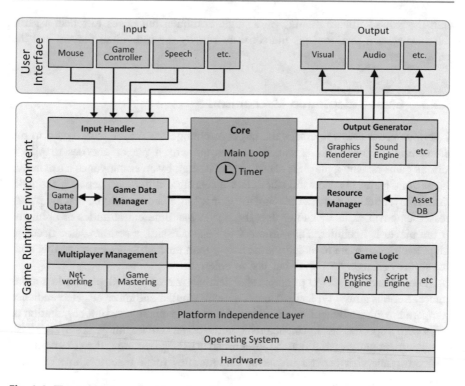

Fig. 1.6 The architecture of a game at runtime

kinds of user input, such as mouse input, game controller input, camera input from a Kinect device or speech input. The game architecture is simplified here; more details will be discussed in Chap. 6 on game engines.

The game architecture of multiplayer games is more complicated than that of single-player games. There are two main reasons for that. First, the network causes a delay for the communicated actions of the players, causing temporal inconsistencies. Second, the global common state of the game must be maintained somewhere. Although several research papers were written propagating peer-to-peer games without a central server (Hu and Liao 2006; Bharambe et al. 2008; Lehn et al. 2011) experience shows that a central server is the most reasonable solution to run a multiplayer game efficiently: the players are connected to that server, the server receives action messages from them and reflects those in the centrally maintained global state. Updates to that state are then periodically forwarded to the machines of the players. Inconsistencies are still possible. For example, when two networked players shoot at each other within a short time period (say, 100 ms), both expect the other player getting killed because they do not see him shoot in time. The game server has to resolve that inconsistency, deciding which player was quicker than the other. The two local displays at the players are then updated to reflect that new global state. As a result, the game architecture is not only concerned with the game software running on a single computer but needs to reflect a game software system that contains the software run by the individual players and the game server.

1.5.3   Game Adaptation Mechanisms

A serious game always pursues the target to change the player with regard to the characterizing goal. This is usually the reason why a player chooses to play a serious game or why a player is asked to play it, e.g., by an employer or a teacher. If the serious game is successful, there is a discernible difference between the individual player before and after playing the game. Differences could be that the player possesses novel skills or knowledge, the player has different attitudes or opinions, or the player is healthier. Thus, in order to be successful, a serious game needs to adapt itself even more to an individual player than an entertainment game that does not seek to change the player but just to entertain.

There is another reason to emphasize personalization and adaptation in serious games. Serious games typically address a much smaller and more targeted audience compared to entertainment games. Examples include employees of a corporation or users with a specific health characteristic in the context of health games. In contrast, entertainment games are produced for a broader user group, e.g., the community of hardcore gamers in general or player communities for a specific game or game genre.

Hence, the aim of personalized, adaptive serious games is to match the individual needs and characteristics of a small user group as well as possible. This adaptation must happen automatically, without manual intervention. Figure 1.7 provides a conceptual model for the development and control of adaptive serious games. The model consists of four major components and four phases: First, within the sensing phase, the current player behavior is collected and recorded via sensing technology. This ranges from simple logging of game events and contextual information about the setting, time and place to the measurement of psychophysiological data of users during the play. In a second phase, this information is aggregated and stored in a knowledge base. There, the dynamically acquired, user-centered data is combined and aligned with the static information, such as the user profile, domain model (e.g., training programs for health games), or game patterns and interaction templates. The analysis and interpretation might take place either automatically (i.e., algorithmically according to predefined rules), in real-time during play, or manually by subject matter experts such as doctors, therapists or sport scientists familiar with cardio training programs. The results of the analysis and interpretation phase are the input parameters for the adaptation component. For instance, in the application context of a cardio training game, a very high heart rate of the player triggers a rule to reduce the resistance of an ergometer. Further adaptation concepts include an automatic content creation and difficulty adaptation for individual users as well as adaptation rules for the gameplay. For example, the training intensity might be varied by a higher or lower frequency of appearance of

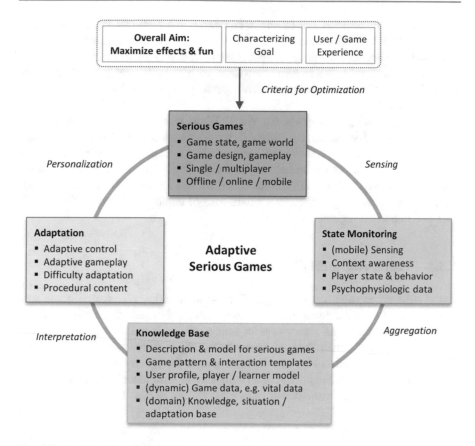

Fig. 1.7 A pattern for adaptation in serious games

objects to be collected by the player. Finally, in the personalization phase, the result of the adaptation process is presented to the player. More details about the underlying concepts of the adaptation and personalization process for serious games will be presented in Chap. 7.

1.5.4   Game Platforms

Game software alone is not sufficient to play a game. We also need hardware that runs the software. The hardware comprises processors, graphics hardware, memory, storage, input devices (e.g., a keyboard or specific game controllers), and output devices (e.g., a smartphone display or loudspeakers). This hardware together with basic software (e.g., device drivers or an operating system such as iOS or Microsoft Windows) forms a platform supporting the game software. Nowadays, we have many game platforms to choose from: a standard PC, a game console connected to a TV set, a mobile game device, and a smart phone are just examples. Each platform has typical characteristics. For example, compared to a high-end PC, a smartphone is mobile and has more sensors that can be integrated into a game (e.g., GPS, touchscreen, acceleration sensors)—but it also has a very small screen and inferior graphics performance. While some platforms such as tablets or PCs are multipurpose, other platforms are geared towards gaming or only support games (e.g., a Nintendo 3DS).

A special gaming platform is the World Wide Web. With the software of the Web browser and standardized content descriptions such as HTML, an additional layer of abstraction is put above the hardware layer. This allows abstracting from different peculiarities of the underlying hardware. Digital games in general that use the Web as their gaming platform are called *browser games*. They are especially attractive for marketing applications where ease of deployment and no cost for the user are important arguments.

1.5.5   Game Authoring Environment

Game software is often not developed from scratch; either an existing game software is modified, or a game authoring environment is used. Since many mechanisms exist in much the same ways in many games, it makes sense to develop generic software for their support. Game authoring software that helps the game developer is illustrated in Fig. 1.8. Its main part is the game engine.

The most important component of an authoring environment is the *game runtime environment*. Its architecture has already been shown in Fig. 1.6.

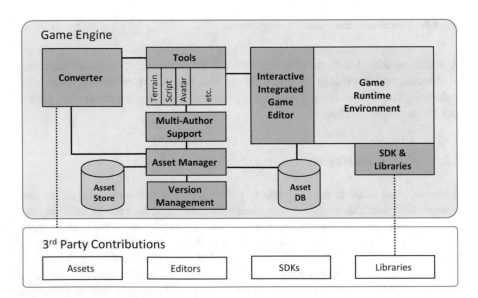

Fig. 1.8 Game engine and game authoring environment

When a game is developed, the game developers have prefabricated assets at their disposition from an *asset store*, managed by the *asset manager*. It is possible to fill the asset database for the game runtime environment either by importing assets via the asset manager from the asset store, or by creating assets with editors or third-party tools. In order to be usable within the game engine, converters are necessary to import and export data. Authoring tools provided by the game engine usually allow editing terrains, levels, game scripts, avatars, materials, textures, etc. In some game engines, there is an *integrated interactive game editor* that offers sophisticated editing capabilities, which makes it feasible to assemble the game from the assets, define the game logic, etc. Often, this editor allows the game to run while editing is in progress.

In addition, the game engine offers a *version control subsystem* for different versions of the game, *performance analysis tools* for optimizing the game, and *support for multiple authors* working in parallel. It may also provide a *software development toolkit* (SDK) that allows extending the pre-fabricated functionality of the tools or the runtime environment. Game engines can also be open source, or they can offer a set of software libraries in different programming languages that can serve as a foundation for a customized game software development. Likewise, third-party software libraries can be used to alter a game engine (e.g., integrating or replacing a physics engine), and other 3rd party tools may offer SDKs to customize them and integrate them better into the authoring workflow.

A large number of proprietary game engines exist, which have been developed by game companies. Almost all the big game studios have their own: Some are commercially available, e.g., Unity (Unity3d 2014), and others are in the public domain, e.g., OGRE 3D—Object-oriented Graphics Rendering Engine (OGRE 2014). In recent years, the licensing policy for game runtime environments has changed. Today, inexpensive or even free versions are available in order to get game developers or small game companies hooked to a specific product. Usually, these inexpensive versions do not offer full functionality, but can be upgraded for an additional fee. They are especially popular in both academic environments and with casual developers of smartphone games. For example, based on this licensing model, the Unity 3D game engine has won more than 3.3 million users by 2014. In this book, Chap. 6 is devoted to game engines.

1.5.6 The Game Development Team

A typical game development team consists of several persons with different skills and different duties who are not necessarily involved during all phases of game development. Key roles are game designer, game engineer/game programmer, artist, quality assurance experts and expert for the serious part.

Game designers are the heart of the game; their ideas determine the success of the game, both in terms of the fun while playing and of the characteristic (serious) component. Game designers can work at different levels: at the basic level, the goal and the levels of the game are designed. At an intermediate level, specific areas in the game world or specific levels of the game are designed. At the detailed level, game rules are fine-tuned. In larger teams, a *game design manager* ensures that game designers work together in a consistent manner.

Game engineers (sometimes called *game programmers*) are responsible for software development. They are often computer scientists, and they design and implement the game software. Some development studios distinguish between tool developers writing game engine software, with game programmers writing the game-specific code, and game engineers who are responsible for the software engineering process.

Artists are responsible for the artwork; they design the landscape, the objects in the game, and the avatars. The audio components are often designed by *sound artists*.

QA experts are responsible for the quality assurance of the game. They not only test the game software for its software quality (e.g., its robustness or performance), but also they conduct user tests to assess the game experience and the degree to which the characterizing goals are reached. The QA experts recruit test players and organize play tests.

Experts for the characterizing goal (also called *area specialists*) contribute knowledge that is essential to achieve the serious goal. For example, if the game is for medical rehabilitation, the experts must have a medical background.

Sometimes there exist additional roles, e.g., the *IT support engineer* responsible for the technical infrastructure (such as backups and software maintenance), the *project manager* responsible for organizing and running the development project, the *project controller* responsible for monitoring the projects' finances, the *producer* responsible for providing the resources for production (in particular the financial resources), and the *customer* responsible for specifying the characterizing goals. Key roles in the development process can be supported by secretaries or assistants.

1.6 A Short History of Serious Games

An introduction to serious games would not be complete without taking a look at their history. Although it is possible to also consider classic (non-electronic) games that have a serious purpose, we focus here on the history of digital games.

Early work on serious games was done in the US military. For example, Abt (1970) describes a game for training officers developed as early as 1961. The term became really popular with two events in 2002: Sawyer and Rejetski (2002) published their white paper *Serious Games: Improving Public Policy through Game-based Learning and Simulation*, and the game *America's Army* appeared in the market (Knight 2002). The latter is a military game engaging the player in realistic combat situations. It was developed by the US army in order to support the recruiting of young people. It features realistic weapons, and the players are dressed in uniforms of US infantry soldiers. The most successful players get an invitation letter from the recruitment office of the army. Actually, as early as in the 1960s, the

US military maintained an agency called "Joint War Games Agency" dedicated to the development of games for military purposes (Djaouti et al. 2011).

The earliest electronic game console for use in private homes, the Magnavox Odyssey, was shipped with both entertainment games and serious games. Its creator, Ralph Baer, had worked on it since 1966; he believed in serious applications of gaming (Baer 2005). The console came out in the US market in 1972. Since microprocessors were still in an early stage in those days, the console had specialized transistor circuits, and its display was an array of white lamps. Ever since, progress in digital electronics was reflected in both entertainment games and serious games.

In the 1980s, entertainment games were often played in arcades but those were not the right places for serious games. In contrast, in the home markets with PC games and video consoles, they slowly established their share. For example, exercise games were available in the 80s for the Atari 2600 and the Nintendo NES. They became really popular in 2006 with the arrival of the Wii (Nintendo 2008) which had a specialized interaction device, the Wii Remote Controller. It is a handheld pointing device, also containing a 3D acceleration sensor. A balance board is also available. They communicate with the main console via Bluetooth.

The next step in innovation came with Microsoft's Kinect in 2010 where the human body is used as the main interaction device. The console comes with a camera and infrared depth sensor detecting the joints of the human body in real-time. This kind of interaction is great for exercising; the Kinect is even used by US schools for dance training.

Whereas between two and 40 new serious games appeared per year from 1980–1990, that number increased to between 60 and 80 between 1990 and 2002. In the following years, between 70 and 240 serious games came out per year, with a significant increase after 2007 (Djaouti et al. 2011).

The main markets for serious games are North America, Japan, South Korea, and Europe. Whereas children were seen as the main players in the US, Japan, and Europe also had adults in mind. For example, *Dr. Kawashima's Brain Training* was a popular Nintendo health game in Japan. A European specialty is serious games for art and culture, with a goal to increase knowledge about cultural heritage in European countries. Examples include *Versailles 1685* and *Vikings* (Djaouti et al. 2011).

For a fairly complete overview of the current list of Serious Games, refer to http://serious.gameclassification.com/, where more than 3000 serious games are listed (Ludoscience 2014).

1.7 How to Use This Book

We conclude this introductory chapter with concrete advice on how to use this book in different contexts. Everybody is advised to read the introduction (Chap. 1) first; all other chapters assume that you have read the introduction beforehand. In particular, it is assumed that you are familiar with the terminology introduced in

Sect. 1.3 and have an overview of the concepts presented in the introduction. Otherwise, there are no more dependencies between the chapters. Thus, this book is highly modular, as you can select chapters in the order that is suitable for you. It is not required to read the book from start to finish. Each chapter is self-contained. To ease orientation, each chapter (except Chap. 12) adheres to the same basic structure. It starts with an abstract and an overview. At the end of each chapter, there is a summary and questions section to allow one to assess understanding of the material. The questions can also help to prepare for exams. This is followed by recommendations for further reading. It includes an overview of scientific journals and conferences that are relevant for the topics discussed in the chapter. Literature references conclude each chapter.

1.7.1 Organization of the Book

The basic chapter of the book is the introduction. All other chapters are clustered into four parts. The first part is concerned with the creation of serious games. This comprises the design of serious games (Chap. 3), authoring processes and tools (Chap. 4), and the content of serious games and its production (Chap. 5). The whole authoring process is an interdisciplinary effort requiring skills in areas such as computer science, art and design, psychology, didactics, and storytelling. The basics that are fundamental for interdisciplinary collaboration are laid in Chap. 2.

The second part focuses on the phase when the finished serious game is played. Important aspects are game engines (Chap. 6) that are the backbone during runtime. Peculiar for serious games is the need for personalization and adaptation; Chap. 7 deals with adaptation mechanisms, game balancing, and dramaturgy. Game mastering in serious games is often application-dependent. In game-based learning, for instance, the game master may have the role of a tutor or instructor at the same time; Chap. 8 discusses game mastering together with social aspects of serious games, especially in multi-player games.

The third part takes a look at the effects of serious games and their evaluation. Chapter 9 discusses the goal to entertain and shows how the game experience can be measured. It also introduces the term *player experience*. In addition, evaluation techniques that are vital for games in general (such as the evaluation of the game's usability) are addressed. Chapter 10 focuses on the assessment of how far the characterizing goals are met that are unique for serious games. In this chapter, evaluation techniques are presented, and indicators for the performance of a serious game are identified.

Finally, the topic of the fourth part is serious games in practice. First, Chap. 11 addresses economic aspects such as budgeting, cost benefit analyses, and serious game distribution. A collection of many examples of serious games is contained in Chap. 12 where each set of examples highlights a different characterizing goal.

1.7.2   Readership

Primarily, this book is a textbook that can serve as an accompanying text for a course, an introductory text for a seminar paper on a specific topic in serious gaming, a book of reference, or a basis for self-study. Serious games are always the result of interdisciplinary work. Appropriately, students of various disciplines (such as computer science, communication design, game design, pedagogics, psychology, or the humanities) are the main target group of this book. Chapter 2 provides brief introductions to these different disciplines.

Prospective users of serious game technology may find this book helpful as it provides them with a solid basis for judging the advantages, limitations and application areas of serious games. This target group will find part IV of the book with its application examples and the discussion of resources and other economic aspects particularly useful. Readers will be able to develop an understanding for the production process and to assess its complexity. Moreover, they will be provided with a methodology to evaluate if a serious game meets its goals.

Prospective developers of serious games are another target group of this book. Specifically, if developers are already familiar with games for entertainment, they can learn more about the specific issues regarding serious game design and development.

1.7.3   Teaching Suggestions

The modular design of this book allows it to cater to different learning goals and needs. Readers and instructors are able to choose what learning content they find appropriate. In the following, you can find five suggestions for courses (assuming one semester, two hours per week, 150 h workload) which can also serve as recommendations for self-studies of particular topics. Those suggestions should be adapted by instructors to individual student knowledge and interests.

Example 1: *Introduction to Serious Games*
Chapter 1, first four examples of Chapter 12, Chapter 3, Chapter 5, Chapter 7, Chapter 8, Chapter 10

Example 2: *Entertainment Technology*
Chapter 1, Chapter 4, Chapter 6, Chapter 5, Chapter 7, Chapter 2, Chapter 3, Chapter 9

Example 3: *Serious Game Design*
Chapter 1, Chapter 2, Chapter 3, Chapter 7, Chapter 8, Chapter 4, Chapter 9, Chapter 10, Chapter 12

Example 4: *Game-based Learning*
Chapter 1, Chapter 2, Chapter 3, Chapter 9, Chapter 10, Chapter 4, Chapter 5, Chapter 12

Example 5: *Applications of Serious Gaming (e.g., Serious Games for Health)*
Chapter 1, Chapter 12 (selection of application examples), Chapter 7, Chapter 8, Chapter 9, Chapter 10, Chapter 2, Chapter 3, Chapter 4, Chapter 11

Moreover, the book can serve as additional literature in a course (e.g., about game development or e-Learning) that touches on the subject of serious games. Here, reading Chap. 1 is recommended, followed by application examples for illustration (Chap. 12) and based on a selection of the specific chapter of interest.

1.8   Summary and Questions

Serious games are digital games where developers desire more than a singular goal to entertain, and pursue one or more characterizing goals. A typical characterizing goal is that the player learns something (e.g., facts about a subject, or specific skills). However, serious games are broader than just educational games. For instance, exergames pursue characterizing goals to both promote a healthy lifestyle and increase players' physical fitness. An additional characterizing goal besides entertainment affects the development process of a serious game, where subject-matter experts are included as part of the development team.

As a characterizing goal has a severe impact on game design, there will be a new tradeoff with existing entertainment goals. Experience shows that this tradeoff is solvable; many games exist that are both fun to play and serve a more serious purpose. Although the history of serious games shows that the idea of games having a serious purpose is not new—with serious games existing right after the invention of digital games—their development and usage is still a challenge today.

Check your understanding of this chapter by answering the following questions:

- Why is it necessary for a serious game to have an identifiable outcome?
- *Foldit* is an online game by the University of Washington where players solve puzzles concerning the 3D structure of proteins. Observing the players, researchers try to find algorithms for how a 3D protein structure can be predicted. Is *foldit* a serious game? If so, what is its characterizing goal? Can *foldit* be considered the result of a gamification process? Can *foldit* be classified as a game with a purpose?
- What are the differences between developing an entertainment game and a serious game? How does the characterizing goal of a particular game affect the differences?
- What are the additional costs for the development of serious games compared to entertainment games?

- Why are adaptation and personalization especially important for serious games? Which steps are necessary to establish personalized, adaptive serious games that match the needs and characteristics of individual users and user groups?
- Assume you need to create a serious game that raises awareness about sexually transmitted diseases (STDs). Budget limitations dictate that you could afford to hire at most five persons for the development team. What roles would you assign to the team members? Which skill set would you look for in each team member? How would you start the project in order to come up with a game idea? What could a suitable project plan look like?
- Do some research on input and output devices that are used for games. Assemble a list of 20 devices. Make a list of 10 characterizing goals for 10 potential serious games you can think of. Are there any specific input and output devices that would be particularly suited to reach the characterizing goal in each of the ten games?

Recommended Literature[1]

Ma M, Oikonomou A, Jain L (2011) Serious Games and Edutainment Applications. Springer, London, UK—*provides a pragmatic approach to the research and application area of serious games and edutainment applications. Case studies and underlying research and development aspects are covered, as well as business aspects and guidelines on how to use a serious game, e.g., in a classroom setting*

---

[1]Original work in game research and serious games research is introduced and published by a number of well-established scientific conferences in the field of artificial intelligence (e.g., AAAI Conference on Artificial Intelligence and Interactive Digital Entertainment, short: AIIDE), human-computer-interaction (ACM CHI Conference on Human Factors in Computing Systems), multimedia (ACM International Conference on Multimedia) or computer graphics (International Conference and Exhibition on Computer Graphics and Interactive Techniques, ACM SIGGRAPH) as well as business-oriented conferences and events (e.g., the Game Developers Conference or gamescom). Games-related scientific conferences include: Foundations of Digital Games, Advances in Computer Entertainment, International Conference of Interactive Digital Storytelling, and the International Conference on Entertainment Computing. Specialized international conferences include: eLearning and Games (Edutainment), European Conference on Game-based Learning, European Conference on Technology-enhanced Learning, and Games for Health in the fields of education and health. The few conferences that are specifically dedicated to serious games are: International Conference on Serious Games Development and Applications, International Conference on Games and Virtual Worlds for Serious Applications, and International Conference on Serious Games (originated by GameDays). Similarly, a number of scientific journals have been set up in the area of games, serious games and entertainment computing: International Journal on Artificial Intelligence in Education, International Journal of Game-based Learning, International Journal of Serious Games, Games for Health Journal, International Journal on Technology-enhanced Learning, IEEE Journal of Educational Technology and Society, IEEE Transaction on Learning Technology, Journal of Learning Science, Journal of Technology and Teacher Education, Journal of Usability Studies, Journal of Virtual Worlds Research, Journal of Virtual Worlds and Education, and Simulation and Gaming.

Ritterfeld U, Cody M, Vorderer P (2009) Serious Games—Mechanisms and Effects. Routledge, New York and London—*tackles the nature of serious games from a social science perspective, in the context of various best practice examples in the field of serious games for learning, serious games for development, and serious games for social change*

Bredl K, Bösche W (2013) Serious Games and Virtual Worlds in Education, Professional Development, and Healthcare. Information Science Reference (an imprint of IGI Global), Hershey PA—*primarily addresses educators indicating the potential of digital games for its use in multi-user instructional (learning) environments. Technically, methods and concepts for the creation (authoring), control and evaluation (measurement of effects) are described in the context of digital educational games and games for health*

Rabin S (2009) Introduction to Game Development. Second Edition. Charles River Media, Boston—*a standard textbook on the topic of entertainment games*

Salen K, Zimmermann E (2003) Rules of Play: Game Design Fundamentals. MIT Press, Cambridge, MA—*provides a benchmark in the field of game design. This includes a model for analyzing and understanding games as well as fundamental concepts such as "play," "design," and "interactivity" towards the creation of games and (playful) interactive systems in general*

References

Abt C (1970) Serious games. Viking Press, New York

Baer RH (2005) Videogames: in the beginning. Rolenta Press, Springfield

Bharambe A, Douceur JR, Lorch JR, Moscibroda T, Pang J, Seshan S, Zhuang X (2008) Donnybrook: enabling large-scale, high-speed, peer-to-peer games. In: Proceedings of the ACM SIGCOMM. ACM, New York, pp 389–400

Bredl K, Bösche W (2013). Serious games and virtual worlds in education, professional development, and healthcare. Information Science Reference (an imprint of IGI Global), Hershey, PA, USA

Card OS (1985) Ender's game. Tor Books, New York

Chen J (2007) Flow in games (and everything else). Commun ACM 50(4):31–34

Cooper S, Treuille A, Barbero J, Leaver-Fay A, Tuite K, Khatib F, Snyder AC, Beenen M, Salesin D, Baker D, Popović Z (2010) The challenge of designing scientific discovery games. In: Proceedings of the 5th international conference on the foundations of digital games. ACM, New York, pp 40–47

Csikszentmihalyi M (1990) Flow: the psychology of optimal experience. Harper & Row Publishers, New York

Csikszentmihalyi M (2009) Flow and the psychology of discovery and invention. Harper & Collins, New York

Deterding S, Dixon D, Khaled R, Nacke L (2011) From game design elements to gamefulness: defining "gamification." In: Proceedings of the 15th international academic MindTrek conference. ACM, New York, pp 9–15

Djaouti D, Alvarez J, Jessel JP, Rampnoux O (2011) Origins of serious games. In: Ma M, Oikonomou A, Jain LC (eds) Serious games and edutainment applications. Springer, Heidelberg, pp 25–43

Enercities consortium (2014) Enercities http://www.enercities.eu/. Accessed 09 Feb 2016

Freeman D (2003) Creating emotions in games. New Riders Publishing, Thousand Oaks

Fullerton T (2008) Game design workshop—a playcentric approach to creating innovative games. Morgan Kaufmann Publishers, Burlington

Gartner Inc. (2013) Forecast: video game ecosystem, worldwide, 4Q13 http://www.gartner.com/newsroom/id/2614915. Accessed 09 Feb 2016

Graesser AC, Ottati V (1996) Why stories? Some evidence, questions, and challenges. In: Weyer RS (ed) Knowledge and memory: the real story. Erlbaum, Hillsdale

Gregory J (2009) Game engine architecture. A K Peters Ltd., Natick

Hand E (2010) People power. Nature 466(7307):685–687

Hoffman HG, Doctor JN, Patterson DR, Carrougher GJ, Furness TA (2000) Virtual reality as an adjunctive pain control during burn wound care in adolescent patients. Pain 85:305–309

HopeLab (2014) Re-Mission game homepage. http://www.re-mission.net/. Accessed 09 Feb 2016

Hu SY, Liao GM (2006) VON: a scalable peer-to-peer network for virtual environments. IEEE Netw 20(4):22–31

IBM Corp. (2014) INNOV8. http://www-01.ibm.com/software/solutions/soa/innov8/index.html. Accessed 09 Feb 2016

Ipsos Media CT (2013) 2014 essential facts about the computer and video game industry. ESA-Entertainment Software Association

John OP, Srivastava S (1999) The big five trait taxonomy. In: Pervin LA, John OP (eds) Handbook of personality: theory and research, 2nd edn. Guildford Press, New York

Johnson P (2014) Security awareness games. http://mindfulsecurity.com/2010/09/14/security-awareness-games/. Accessed 09 Feb 2016

Kawrykow A, Roumanis G, Kam A, Kwak D, Leung C, Wu C, Zarour E, Foldit players, Samentha L, Blanchette M, Waldispühl J (2012) Phylo: a citizen science approach for improving multiple sequence alignment. PloS One 7(3):e31362

Khatib F, Cooper S, Tyka MD, Xu K, Makedon I, Popović Z, Baker D, Players Foldit (2011) Algorithm discovery by protein folding game players. Proc Natl Acad Sci USA 108 (47):18949–18953

Kickmeier-Rust MD, Mattheiss E, Steiner CM, Albert D (2011) A psycho-pedagogical framework for multi-adaptive educational games. Internat J Game-Based Learning 1(1):45–58

Knight M (2002) America's Army. Crown Publishing Group, New York

Lehn M, Leng C, Rehner R, Triebel T, Buchmann A (2011) An online gaming testbed for peer-to-peer architectures. In: Proceedings of the ACM SIGCOMM. ACM, New York

Ludoscience (2014) Game classification. http://serious.gameclassification.com/. Accessed 09 Feb 2014

Ma M, Oikonomou A, Jain L (2011) Serious games and edutainment applications. Springer, London

Mead GH (2009) Mind, self, and society: from the standpoint of a social behaviorist, vol 1. University of Chicago press, Chicago

Michael D, Chen S (2006) Serious games: games that educate, train and inform. Thompson, Tampa

Nintendo (2008) Nintendo Wii—Hardware Information. Nintendo. Archived from the original on February 12, 2008. Accessed 27 Nov 2014

OGRE (2014). http://www.ogre3d.org. Accessed 09 Feb 2016

Orbanes PE (2006) Monopoly: the world's most famous game and how it got that way. Da Capo Press, Boston

Persuasive Games LLC (2014) Homepage. http://persuasivegames.com/. Accessed 09 Feb 2016

Quinn AJ, Bederson BB (2011) Human computation: a survey and taxonomy of a growing field. In: Proceedings of the ACM SIGCHI conference on human factors in computing systems. ACM, New York, pp 1403–1412

Rabin S (2009) Introduction to game development, 2nd edn. Charles River Media, Boston

Raddick MJ, Bracey G, Gay PL, Lintott CJ, Murray P, Schawinski K, Szalay AS, Vandenberg J (2010) Galaxy zoo: exploring the motivations of citizen science volunteers. Astron Educ Rev 9 (1):010103

Raddick MJ, Bracey G, Gay PL, Lintott CJ, Cardamone C, Murray P, Vandenberg J (2013) Galaxy Zoo: motivations of citizen scientists. Astron Educ Rev 12(1):010106

Ritterfeld U, Cody M, Vorderer P (2009) Serious games—mechanisms and effects. Routledge, New York

Salen K, Zimmerman E (2003) Rules of play: game design fundamentals. MIT Press, Cambridge

Sawyer B, Rejeski D (2002) Serious games: improving public policy through game-based learning and simulation. Woodrow Wilson International Center for Scholars, Washington, DC

Serious Brothers GbR (2014) Imagine Earth. http://www.imagineearth.info/. Accessed 09 Feb 2014

Serious Games Association (2014) Serious games directory. http://www.grandmetropolitan.com/. Accessed 09 Feb 2016

Serious Games Interactive (2014) Global conflicts. http://globalconflicts.eu/. Accessed 09 Feb 2016

Sicart M (2008) Defining game mechanics. Game Stud 8(2):1–14

Sinclair J (2011) Feedback control for exergames. Dissertation, Edith Cowan University, Mount Lawley, USA

STEAM (2014) Homepage. http://store.steampowered.com. Accessed 09 Feb 2016

Sweetser P, Wyeth P (2005) Game flow: A model for evaluating player enjoyment in games. ACM Comput Entertain 3(3):Article 3A

The Walt Disney Company Ltd. (2014) Online games. http://disneyjunior.disney.co.uk/mickey-mouse-clubhouse/play/minnie-explores-the-land-of-dizz. Accessed 09 Feb 2016

Unity3d (2014) http://unity3d.com. Accessed 09 Feb 2016

von Ahn L (2006) Games with a purpose. Computer 39(6):92–94

Wiemeyer J (2014) Serious games in neurorehabilitation: a systematic review of recent evidence. In: Proceedings of the ACM international workshop on serious games. ACM, New York, pp 33–38

Wiemeyer J, Hardy S (2013) Serious games and motor learning—concepts, evidence, technology. In: Bredl K, Bösche W (eds) Serious games and virtual worlds in education, professional development, and healthcare. IGI Global, Heshey, pp 197–220

Wiemeyer J, Kliem A (2012) Serious games and ageing—a new panacea? Eur Rev Aging Phys Act 9(1):41–50

Wong WL, Shen C, Nocera L, Carriazo E, Tang F, Bugga S, Narayanan H, Wang H, Ritterfeld U (2007) Serious video game effectiveness. In: Proceedings of the ACE'07, pp 49–55

Contributing Disciplines

Ralf Dörner, Anna Lisa Martin-Niedecken, Mela Kocher,
Tom Baranowski, Michael Kickmeier-Rust, Stefan Göbel,
Josef Wiemeyer and Paul Gebelein

Abstract

Creating entertainment games is always an interdisciplinary effort, and becomes even more pronounced when serious game creation involves experts from a specific subject area or supporting disciplines, such as pedagogy. As these experts can come from almost any discipline, it is beneficial for interdisciplinary work to appreciate differences in approach. Understanding diverse technical terms is important; for example, a computer scientist and an artist will associate quite different aspects with the term "communication". But being in a specific discipline does not only affect vocabulary. Disciplines may have fundamentally different ways of thinking, or different methodologies how to approach a problem. People, who have worked in a discipline for a longer time, might be surprised when they reflect on how much this has shaped them as a person. As it is advantageous in the context of serious games to not only understand one's

R. Dörner (✉)
RheinMain University of Applied Sciences, Wiesbaden, Germany
e-mail: ralf.doerner@hs-rm.de

A.L. Martin-Niedecken · M. Kocher
Zurich University of the Arts, Zurich, Switzerland

T. Baranowski
Baylor College of Medicine, Houston, USA

M. Kickmeier-Rust
Graz University of Technology, Graz, Austria

S. Göbel · J. Wiemeyer · P. Gebelein
Technische Universität Darmstadt, Darmstadt, Germany

own discipline, this chapter contains brief introductions to the major disciplines involved in the field of serious games, with pointers for where to start when one wishes to obtain a deeper understanding of the field. The specific disciplines covered are computer science, art and design, psychology, didactics and pedagogy, and stories and storytelling. Finally, this chapter contains a section on best practices and typical pitfalls when working in an interdisciplinary team.

2.1 Computer Science

One major question in computer science is how to represent *data* in computing machinery; for instance, how to store the high score of a digital game in computer memory. The representation of the data will need a certain storage space that is measured in *bit* (8 bit = 1 byte, 1000 byte = 1 kB, 1000 kB = 1 MB). This measures also the *information* that is contained in the data. For example, in an 8 bit storage space, 256 different data values can be stored. Data is usually represented in a structured way. In computer science, many *data structures* such as *tables, lists, trees,* or *graphs* have been developed. The selected data structure determines the effort to process the data, e.g., the time required for finding a certain value in a data set. A discussion of data representations and data structures can be found in (Brass 2008).

Another fundamental question is how something can be computed. Thus, computer scientists are interested in finding an *algorithm*, i.e., a complete and detailed description of how to proceed to perform a calculation. For instance, there are many algorithms regarding how to find the shortest path a character can take from one position to another. Computer scientists analyze algorithms to assess their *efficiency* and their *correctness*. Ideally, the proof of correctness is made not by trials (as there might be so many possibilities that not all can be checked in a reasonable amount of time), but by using methodologies from mathematics. A collection of standard algorithms can be found in (Sedgewick and Wayne 2011).

In order to actually solve a problem, the computer has somehow to learn about the concept how to solve it—the algorithms, the data, and the data structures needed. One possibility is to build a dedicated hardware chip that *implements* the concept. More often, however, multipurpose hardware that can be *programmed* serves as basis for implementation. Unfortunately, natural language cannot be used to tell the computer what to do as it is ambiguous, and the meaning (the *semantics*) cannot be inferred by a machine. Therefore, artificial *programming languages* were designed that follow a formal *syntax* specified by a *grammar*. Machine language is closer to a way the computer works, but cumbersome to use. Therefore, *higher level programming languages* (e.g., C, C++, C#, Java) have been developed on a higher level of abstraction. *Abstraction* is a key method in computer science. *Higher level programming languages* abstract from the hardware used, making it feasible to write a single program for many hardware setups, e.g., different CPUs (central processing units). This program needs to be translated to programs in the machine language of different processors. The translation is not done by hand, but by specific software called a *compiler* that is often embedded in an *IDE* (*integrated development environment*), e.g., Microsoft Visual Studio or Eclipse. The compiling time can be significant. Instead of creating a new program by translation, an existing multipurpose program (an *interpreter*) can be used to reduce the wait time. The interpreter directly *parses* and *executes* commands written in an *interpreted language* (e.g., Python, Lua, Perl). Existing program code can be collected in *software libraries* and thus can be reused when writing a new program. Existing programs may also offer an *application programming interface* (*API*) that allows it to be extended by additional code. Madhav (2013) gives an introduction to programming in the context of games.

There are several subdisciplines in computer science. *Computer graphics* (Angel and Shreiner 2014), for instance, is concerned with creating imagery with a computer. For this, a *model* needs to be described; for example, creating an abstraction of a scene's objects or light sources to be shown that is complex enough to provide all relevant details, but still simple enough that it can be grasped by a computer). The model is rendered into an image by a program called *renderer*. The model can be described and the rendering can be programmed using dedicated libraries for graphics (e.g., OpenGL or DirectX). One can also use a *descriptive language* such as HTML5 just to describe the model. The rendering is then performed by an existing program, e.g., a Web browser.

Modeling is a fundamental task in computer science. One approach is to use *classes*, i.e., abstracted descriptions of models of real world objects or concepts. This approach is called *object-oriented programming* (Meyer 1997) and is a standard way to organize programs and make them manageable. *Software engineering* (Pressman and Maxim 2014) is the name of a subdiscipline that is concerned with such approaches and procedures how to best build software or organize program code. This also includes methods for testing and *debugging*, i.e., correcting software errors. Section 4.4 discusses examples of software engineering methods that are used in serious game development. The aim is to create software that is *correct*, easy to *maintain,* and *efficient*. In the area of computer games, software is often required to run in *real time*, i.e., to be quick enough to keep up with the user. For example, the game software should be able to create more than 60 images per second, or react within 100 ms to a user action. As it cannot be foreseen when writing a computer program how and when a user will act, the concept of *events* is used. The action of the user creates an event and according program code can be executed to *handle* this event.

Other subdisciplines of computer science are *databases* (Connolly and Begg 2014), *computer networks* (Tanenbaum and Wetherall 2010), *parallel and distributed systems* (Rauber and Rünger 2013), and *artificial intelligence* (*AI*). AI has developed methodologies such as neural networks or rule-based systems to enable a computer system to perceive its environment, represent knowledge, plan, learn, reason, and solve problems (Russell and Norvig 2009). An introduction to AI used specifically in games can be found in (Rabin 2013).

2.2 Art and Design

When thinking about *design*, what might first come to mind could be fashion, graphics, or furniture. But design has a more universal meaning than these commercial applications. A dictionary definition uses the synonym "plan": To design means indeed *to plan* and *to organize*. All *artifact developments* (building a physical prototype, architecting a software interface, constructing an argument or implementing a series of controlled experiments) are created within some *design methodology*, which guide the creative thought process and help ensure quality work (Hunicke et al. 2004).

Design is inherent in the full range of *art disciplines,* from painting and drawing to sculpture, photography, and time-based media such as film, video, computer graphics, and animation (Lauer and Pentak 2011). Design can be divided into specific disciplines, including *communication design, industrial design, system design, product design, sound design, interaction design, event design,* and *game design.* Most art and design disciplines are "mixed disciplines" since they hold aspects of, and are integral to, one another. Designing a game requires many art and design competencies. Every successful game needs to be easy to use and positively influence the user's (gameplay) experience by providing artistic visuals and animations, immersive game mechanics, sound and narration as well as a user-engaging game mechanic. Additionally, serious games include input from relevant subject-matter experts.

What art and design always have in common is that they plan arrangements of elements to form specific patterns, taking into account the variation of these elements depending on the field (e.g., painted symbols to scenic flats, or state of the art games). The result is visual, sonic, haptic, or interactive organization. However, when it comes to the relationship between art and design, it can be hard to distinguish where one ends and the other begins. In the arts, infinite variations in individual interpretations and applications are possible, "problems to solve" are mostly not given by a third person beside the artist herself and the contemplator, nor do predetermined solutions exist. In contrast, design is creative and "interdisciplinary problem solving" for other parties and can also be applied in more serious contexts. Innovative product development user examples include Third World countries (Brown and Wyatt 2010) or rehabilitation patients (He et al. 2005).

Since many interdisciplinary fields are affected by design, various design approaches and (research/evaluation) methods are established and guidelines are provided. Current design practice is experiencing a shift from product-oriented to purpose-driven; from employing *user-centered design* (*UCD*) to *co-designing* (*CD*)—respectively *participatory design* (*PD*) for collective creativity (Sanders and Stappers 2008). A forerunning participatory approach in the field of architecture is *invisible design thinking,* which aims to gain critical system and decision-oriented knowledge that extends to the design object itself (Burckhardt 2012). Today, *design research* has become an integral part of all art and design activities, since iterative, qualitative, and quantitative analyses support the designer in two important ways:

(1) they help the designer analyze the end result to refine implementation, and (2) they analyze the implementation to refine the result (Hunicke et al. 2004).

In the UCD process, the focus is on the thing being designed (e.g., object, communication, space, interface, system, service), looking for ways that this can meet user needs. The roles of the researcher, collecting user data, and the designer, interpreting these data/design criteria and developing the product based on these results are distinct, yet independent (Sanders 2002). The user and the designer may then come into the process of user tests with the product. Thus, the user is not really a part of the "team." In contrast to the UCD approach, the users become a critical component in the PD approach, since they are actively participating in the design process. The range of the typical roles of the researcher and the participant then can be described as participatory, observational, and self-reporting; the researcher and the participant also act as reviewers based on expert knowledge (Martin and Hanington 2012).

User-experience design (*UXD*) is the process of enhancing user satisfaction by improving the usability, accessibility, and pleasure provided in the interaction between the user and the product (Kujala et al. 2011). UXD encompasses traditional *human-computer interaction* (*HCI*) design, and extends it by addressing all aspects of a product or service as perceived by users. UC- and UX-based design approaches always imply *user tests* in order to evaluate *user experience*, which involves human perceptions and responses that result from the use (or the anticipation of use) of a product, system or service (Beccari and Oliveira 2011).

For all design approaches such as UCD and UXD that prioritize the skills, needs, and context of persons actually using the product or experience, the general term *human-centered design* (*HCD*) is used. The ISO-standard 9241, for instance, names Part 210 "human-centered design for interactive systems."

All of the aforementioned design approaches can be used in a variety of fields and design disciplines. On a more concrete level of methods and tools, there are many practices which originate in other, more traditional scientific disciplines and/or have been *adapted*, ranging from *quantitative to qualitative methods* and having a more exploratory, generative or evaluative purpose (Martin and Hanington 2012). *Traditional methods* employed for design processes are for example questionnaires, role-playing, secondary research, and interviews such as *triading*.

Examples for *genuine design methods*, which are user-oriented and participatory, are mind mapping, cultural probes, personas, generative research or crowdsourcing (Martin and Hanington 2012).

Eye tracking is an example for a technique that can serve as basis for a *quantitative method*, which has been adapted for design purposes from the field of cognitive psychology (Bojko 2012). The technology tracks what the user is looking at—and not looking at—when browsing, e.g., through a website or a video game; the data then can be visualized as a heat map. Since this method does not provide insights into user motivation or comprehension, it must be triangulated with complementary research methods.

Prototyping—the tangible creation of product or interface concepts—is used as a qualitative and iterative tool at different levels of development in various design fields (Martin and Hanington 2012). Especially the form of (rapid) paper prototyping is essential in game design; it represents on an abstract level the core game mechanics and the rule system without the narrative, audio and visual overlays and digitized interfaces. As an epistemological and simulative tool this method functions as "philosophical carpentry" (Bogost 2012).

On a meta-scientific level, Frayling's categorization into *research about, for, and through design* (Frayling 1993) provides a much quoted discursive model to discern various approaches and to reassess the dialectics between the traditional (self-)concept of research and the generally more applied and participatory practices of design and design research processes (Friedman 2008). As the object of design research, the *artifact*, continuously changes its shape, design can be understood as generative, illustrative, integrative, context-sensitive, and anticipative. With the *researcher* being involved in the design process to some extent, it has been proposed that science-related design shall rely on data-based or interpretational theoretical concepts such as grounded theory, action research, and hermeneutics (Reason and Bradbury 2001). The negotiation of theoretical framework in the field of *game studies*, e.g., (Mäyrä 2008), the academic discipline formed since 2001, and in the field of *gameplay experience research*, e.g., IJsselsteijn et al. (2007) illustrate perfectly how a scientific approach draws closely from (and feeds back into, e.g., Nacke et al. 2011) the practice-based design discipline of game design, as well as from traditional theories and approaches, while generating its own methodological approaches.

Summarizing the multifaceted theoretical, practical, and methodological characteristics of art and design gives an idea of how versatile game design as prime example of a "mixed discipline" can be.

2.3 Psychology

Psychology is the science of behavior, and is interpreted to include actual observable behavior and the mental processes underlying behavior. Many different approaches have been used by psychologists to study the many different aspects of behavior. Cognitive psychologists are interested in attention, perception, memory, recall, and motor control (Kellogg 2003). Operant conditioners understand behavior as the product of stimuli, responses, and reinforcement (Skinner 1953). Social psychologists investigate attitudes, norms, self-efficacy or perceived behavioral control, and behavioral intentions (Glanz et al. 2008). Neuropsychologists study the brain's structures and processes that underlie what the other psychologists study at a self-reported level (Andrews 2001).

Psychology's relevance to games tends to center around a small number of issues including human-computer interface (MacKenzie 2013), learning (Tenant 1997), and motivation (Ryan 2012). Human-computer interaction concerns how people interact with computers (interpreted inclusively) and in turn how to design interfaces and software to maximize players' acceptance or satisfaction and effects or outcomes. Learning concerns behavior change (Tenant 1997). Behavior change may include using the computer more effectively, better performance on math, reading, or history tests, or eating healthier, being more physically active, or stopping smoking (among many other health or behavior change outcomes). Some aspect of psychology is likely of interest to anyone who is designing interfaces or software for human use.

Human computer interface concerns issues of human multitasking, communication patterns, cognitive, social and emotional needs, differences between talking, teaching and wearing, differences between laboratory and real world research, and qualitative and quantitative methods, prototyping, data analysis presentation, and ethics—among many other issues, including learning and motivation (Rogers et al. 2011). So let's go directly to learning.

The way in which one thinks about learning determines what one might do to encourage it. We will consider three different ways of thinking about learning. *Cognitive approaches to learning* concern what constitutes information, factors which influence to what information someone pays attention, what they perceive when they attend to it, what they remember once perceived, how they can retrieve information from memory when needed, how they process information to address issues or solve problems, and how they mobilize the body to respond to thoughts processed (Kellogg 2003). From this perspective, learning is a very complex set of cognitive processes. Games could be designed to capitalize on this knowledge and influence each step in the process resulting in more effective learning. Eye tracking technology can inform game designers to what aspects of their game players are attending. What constitutes attractiveness to influence attention will depend on biological influences and one's learning history as well as media characteristics.

Operant approaches to learning were a response to introspective methods, and thereby take a more external approach to understanding behavior, minimizing the role of thought. Operant theory proposes that organisms are presented with many and diverse stimuli to which they perform responses (i.e., behaviors). Some responses are reinforced or rewarded more frequently than others, and thereby become more likely in response to these stimuli. Reinforcements can be provided regularly or intermittently, and the different patterns of reinforcement cement different response patterns. From the operant perspective, games can be designed to influence learning or behaviors by controlling the stimuli and/or the reinforcers. For example, earning points are commonly used in games and the extent to which they guide or otherwise influence behavior would be considered reinforcers.

Finally, social psychologists work on the assumption that intentions (sometimes called plans or goals) are the closest ("most proximal") influences on behavior. Intentions, in turn, are influenced by attitudes (i.e., calculations of benefits minus costs for doing behaviors), norms (i.e., what people believe others are doing or believe they should be doing), self-efficacy (i.e., the confidence a person has in being able to perform a behavior under different kinds of circumstances), habit (i.e., the extent to which one regularly does a behavior without even thinking about it), and a diverse variety of other personal, social, and environmental influences (Glanz et al. 2008). A game designer might try to influence a player's behavior by programming the game to show that everyone of concern is doing the desired behavior (manipulating the perceived norm).

A social psychologist won a Nobel Prize for showing that the way in which people process this information is biased, or nonlinear (Kahneman 2003), which led to the development of behavioral economics. Behavioral economics has become popular for proposing "nudges", small ways to influence behavior in large ways. For example, since game players often use the default choice, when presenting choices to players make the default choice the desired behavior (Thaler and Sunstein 2008).

Theories of *motivation* also have cognitive, operant, and social psychological versions. Operant versions tend to explain behavior as meeting some biological need, e.g., eating to satisfy hunger. Abraham Maslow created a hierarchy of needs where people first need to satisfy basic needs, e.g., hunger. However, as these lower-level needs are satisfied, they want to satisfy higher level needs, with self-actualization at the top of the hierarchy (Maslow 1972). The motivation theory most commonly used currently by game designers is *Self Determination Theory* (*SDT*) (Deci and Ryan 2002). SDT proposes that motivation varies along a continuum. At one end of the continuum, people are completely externally responsive, i.e., they perform behaviors to obtain external rewards (similar to the operant idea of someone else applying a reward). At the other end, people are completely intrinsically motivated: They perform behavior to meet their own internal notions of what is good or desirable (similar to Maslow's self-actualization). Between extrinsically and intrinsically motivated are steps along the continuum, each reflecting different combinations and forms of other- and self-control. SDT proposed that intrinsically-motivated behavior is most desirable, and likely to be the most stable. To encourage intrinsically-motivated behavior, a game should enable the player to meet three basic needs: autonomy (i.e., behavior as personal choice), competence (i.e., being able to do the behavior well, similar to self-efficacy), and relatedness (i.e., fulfilling social relationships).

An example of competence motivation in games is the idea of *flow* (Csikszentmihályi 1990). A game needs to present challenges to a player that are commensurate with their abilities, and as a player learns more about playing a game, their abilities increase, and they want more challenge. If a game is too easy, the player gets bored and stops playing. If too hard, the player gets frustrated and also stops playing. If the challenges increase commensurate with the player's ability, she enters a state of flow, which has several distinguishable characteristics, including they will continue playing your game.

A number of game designers have addressed the importance of a game being engaging, enjoyable, or fun (Koster 2005). Fun would be an important indication or component of intrinsic motivation. Research has used cognitive, psychological, and embodiment approaches to understanding fun (Mellecker et al. 2013), but this is not yet clearly understood. Flow may contribute to fun.

Psychology has much to offer game designers in terms of anticipating the experience of players, and designing the game to maximize the intended experience.

2.4   Didactics and Pedagogy

Conceptually, many researchers argue that playing computer games provides learners with a mental workout (Robertson and Howells 2008), i.e., that the *structure* of activities within computer games can develop cognitive skills due to the fact that end users are faced with decision making. Consequently they must plan problem solving strategies in advance, which involve the monitoring of a series of tasks and subtasks—also known as *Judgement-Behaviour-Feedback* loops (Garris et al. 2002). Therefore, the type of learning and cognitive development can be intended and/or unintended. Serious games have characterizing goals that can be considered *primary goals*, the intended effects of the game, *secondary outcomes*, e.g., facilitating meta-skills such as problem solving or logical thinking, and *tertiary effects*, which are effects that are not intended, not foreseeable, and perhaps unknown. An example would be the effects through the competition by playing games (e.g., by comparing scores in peer groups). Some of the main educational strengths of games are seen in the intrinsic motivation to play and to proceed in the game, a given set of clear goals and rules which offers a *scaffolding* for learning, a rich and appealing and above all meaningful learning context, and an engaging storyline with random elements of surprise (Prensky 2001). Further key aspects for learning are immediate feedback and the high level of interactivity, challenge, and competition (Kickmeier-Rust and Albert 2010).

All these characteristics of games are in line with almost all pedagogical theories or instructional design approaches. A prominent model of pedagogical and didactic strategies is Merrill's *model for successful learning* (Merrill 2002). Foundations of this model include motivation and incidental learning (Cordova and Lepper 1996). In literature, it is pointed out that memorable educational experiences not only have to be enriching but also enjoyable (Shneiderman 1998; van Reekum et al. 2004). David Merrill identified the first principles of instruction on the basis of previous research and existing models (Merrill 2002). The term *"first principles"* equals Reigeluth's (1999) term *"basic methods."* These principles are primarily based on the idea of *problem-based learning*, which is considered to be a very effective approach to learning. The principles are: (a) Relying on real-world problems, (b) activation of prior knowledge, (c) new knowledge must be demonstrated to the learner, (d) learners shall apply the new knowledge, and (e) the new knowledge must be integrated into the "the learner's world." Fundamental concepts are also the application or transfer, referring to the fact that new knowledge must be applied to relevant problems. Practice therefore must be consistent with the learning goal (Gagne 1985). During the application phase, errors are a natural outcome. Learning is facilitated when learners are provided with possibilities to recognize errors and how to correct them. Also, integrating new knowledge into existing knowledge is a fundamental premise of successful and durable learning. *"Knowledge is soon forgotten if it is not made a part of the learner's life beyond instruction"* (Merrill 2002). These first principles are a good summary of the general view of learning, no matter if we are talking about cognitive, constructivist, or behavioral learning theories.

An excellent pedagogical framework specifically for planning and designing serious games mechanics is the *Eight Learning Events Model* (8LEM). This approach emphasizes that learning events are based on eight basic components. According to Leclerqce and Poumay (2005), any number of training strategies can be deduced from—or any didactic strategy can be traced to—these basic components. An advantage of the 8LEM approach is that unlike methods and strategies, learning events can refer to intentional learning as well as incidental learning. The eight learning events are[1]:

- *Imitation* ↔ *Modeling*: Describes incidental or intentional learning through observation and subsequent imitation. The role of a tutor or teacher is to serve as a (role) model.
- *Reception* ↔ *Transmission*: Describes learning as receiving information or advice. The tutor's role is transmitting information or advice.
- *Exercising* ↔ *Guidance*: Describes "proceduralizing" and automating skills. The tutor's role is to give learners guidance and corrective feedback.
- *Exploration* ↔ *Documentation*: Describes learning by a free investigation of information with a certain degree of freedom. The tutor's role is to provide guidance, sources, or access.
- *Experimentation* ↔ *Reactivity*: Describes learning through manipulating environments and observing effects. The tutor's role is to provide an "experimentable" and manipulable environment, i.e., providing reactivity.
- *Creation* ↔ *Confrontation*: Describes learning by creating new content or objects (e.g., texts, music, objects). Creation also includes a reincorporation of known content. The tutor's role is to foster the creation process and/or confront learners with tasks of creation.
- *Self-reflection* ↔ *Co-reflection*: Describes learning by reflecting on one's own knowledge and skills, and even the learning processes itself. The tutor's role is to give guidance to a learner and help in reflection processes.
- *Debate* ↔ *Animation*: Describes learning by social interactions such as debates, arguments, and idea exchanges. The tutor's role is to "animate" and incite debates and discussions.

The advantages of this model are that it is observable; its components can be identified quantitatively and qualitatively. Moreover, the model is not deterministic; in specific situations, more than one learning event can be present. For example, watching TV might include imitation of viewed activities combined with perceiving information, or from the tutor's perspective modeling and transmission. The 8LEM allows describing existing learning or teaching strategies or programs. Moreover, from a prescriptive perspective, the model allows one to plan and track learning

---

[1]The term before the "↔" indicates the activity or action of the learner, while the term after the "↔" refers to the role of the teacher or the mechanism in the game.

and/or teaching activities. On this basis, 8LEM allows to assure a diversification of learning or teaching methods. Diversification of methods is a well-established pedagogical principle, and provides learners with a broader range of learning and teaching methods during the learning progress—instead of continuously use the same strategy (e.g., transmission). This approach is desirable from both individual skill development and motivation. It is in the learner's intrinsic interest to gain exposure to a broad range of learning modes. The learners' "learning polyvalence" can be answered by the teacher's *pedagogical polyvalence* as they orchestrate diverse experiences. The framework of 8LEM allows to plan learning and teaching on a very detailed basis. Furthermore, from a descriptive perspective, it allows designers to ensure a diversification of methods in order to empower learning and retain motivation.

When contrasting digital computer games and pedagogical principles, one can find a great and convincing match between the two worlds. However, computer games have clear weaknesses such as difficulties in providing an appropriate balance between playing and learning activities or between challenge and ability, in aligning the game with national curricula and in affording extensive costs of developing high quality games. Also, the lack of sound instructional models—based on pedagogical standards and didactical methods—is seen as common weaknesses of most educational games, and leads to a separation of learning from playing. When designing serious games, it is also important to consider gender differences and gender fairness, aspects of unwanted competition, social isolation, and perhaps the addictive potential of games.

In projects such as ELEKTRA and 80Days, approaches and frameworks have been developed to maximize the pedagogical utility and to minimize potential harmful effects. *ELEKTRA (Enhanced Learning Experience and Knowledge TRAnsfer)* made significant contributions to advancing the state-of-the-art of immersive serious games in terms of educational game design, integration of pedagogical models and taxonomies, and the possibility of personalization by the use of adaptive technology. The successor project 80Days is grounded in the framework of *Self-Regulated Personalized Learning* SRPL (Wouters et al. 2007), which propagates the importance of *Self Regulated Learning* (SRL) through meaningful choice and exploration, reflection, and self-personalization in the learning process. Self-regulation can include an interactive *process* involving both cognitive self-regulation and motivational self-regulation (Caprara et al. 2008; Entwistle and McCune 2004); where cognitive self-regulation can be taught, and students who use these self-regulatory skills obtain better grades in the content domain to which these skills apply (Boekaerts 1997). However, it is argued that self-regulated learning can be domain-specific or domain-transcending, and that competent performers in a specific domain rely on different types of previous knowledge related to that domain. Consequently, addressing the previous knowledge is always an important issue (Holzinger et al. 2008). This contributes towards the creation and *sustainability* of intrinsic motivation, which is a key factor of effective game-based learning.

From the psycho-pedagogical perspective, a framework for a computational handling of learning and competence development is the *Competence-based Knowledge Space Theory* (CbKST). This approach comes from the research field of intelligent tutorial systems and allows equipping serious computer games with some kind of "educational intelligence." CbKST was originally established by Doignon and Falmagne (1999). It is a well elaborated set-theoretic framework for addressing the relations among problems (e.g., test items). It provides a basis for structuring a domain of knowledge and for representing the knowledge based on prerequisite relations. While the original idea considered performance (e.g., solving a test item) only, extensions of the approach introduced a separation of observable performance and latent, unobservable competencies which determine the performance (Albert and Lukas 1999).

CbKST assumes a finite set of more or less *atomic competencies* (in the sense of some well-defined, small scale descriptions of some sort of aptitude, ability, knowledge, or skill) and a prerequisite relation between those competencies. A prerequisite relation states that competency *a* (e.g., to multiply two positive integers) is a prerequisite to acquire another competency *b* (e.g., to divide two positive integers). If a person has competency *b*, we can assume that the person also has competency *a*. To account for the fact that more than one set of competencies can be a prerequisite for another competency (e.g., competency *a* or *b* are a prerequisite for acquiring competency *c*), prerequisite functions have been introduced, relying on and/or-type relations. A person's competence state is described by a subset of competencies. Due to the prerequisite relations between the competencies, not all subsets are admissible competence states. By utilizing interpretation and representation functions, the latent competencies are mapped to a set of tasks (or test items) covering a given domain. By this means, mastering a task correctly is linked to a set of necessary competencies, and not mastering a task is linked to a set of lacking competencies. This assignment induces a performance structure, which is the collection of all possible performance states. Recent versions of the conceptual framework are based on a probabilistic mapping of competencies and performance indicators, accounting for making lucky guesses or careless errors. This means that mastering a task correctly provides the evidence for certain competencies and competence states with a certain probability. For in-game assessment and smart adaptions, the concept of *micro adaptivity* has been developed on this foundation (Kickmeier-Rust and Albert 2010).

It is important to highlight that not only a psycho-pedagogical concept underlying the game design is a prerequisite for the success of a serious games, but also that evaluation of pedagogical effects is equally important. It is a dual challenge to evaluate both the fun and serious aspects of games. Measuring the success of educational technology, and particularly of games, is a complex issue. Much of the literature in the field of educational technology revealed that inconsistent and, at best, non-significant differences were found between technology-based and traditional delivery media, e.g., (Russell 1999). Based on the results of previous research and guidelines for measuring the "success" of technology-based learning materials and environments, two key aspects can be summarized: *Criterion-based designs* and, for specific cases, *comparison-based designs*. Criterion-based designs utilize a-priori specified criteria to measure educational effectiveness, e.g., whether students learn what they were supposed to learn. Comparison-based designs can potentially be applied to evaluating and validating adaptive sequencing of learning material: Adaptive story generation and non-invasive assessment and interventions.

Psycho-pedagogical frameworks offer *scaffolding* for serious game design. However, up to date, didactic aspects have sparsely influenced the broad field of serious games. As described, when matching didactic guidelines with game mechanics a game-pedagogy can and must be established as a basis for effective and successful applied games. Insofar, psycho-pedagogical and didactic frameworks are the starting point for making games more than just another educational medium.

2.5 Stories and Storytelling

A *story* is a narration of events that are somehow connected. Stories can be presented in written words. Thus, stories are part of literature and have been analyzed in literature research. But stories can also be presented as *drama*, e.g., performed by actors on a stage. The word *drama* stems from a Greek work meaning action. In a sense, a digital game can also present stories where the virtual world is the stage and virtual characters function as actors. In addition, the player is part of the action.

Stories can play a vital role in the success of digital games. One famous example is the ego-shooter Doom that served as a basis for the computer game Half-Life. While Half-Life used the same game mechanics, in contrast to Doom it narrated a story. Some people attribute the higher success of Half-Life to this fact. In principle, game designers are often interested in experiences or even scientific findings in the area of stories. *Narratology* is the name of a research area that analyses stories with scientific methods. For instance, in narratology researchers have identified a three act pattern that structures many stories: *setup*, *conflict* and *resolution*. Even in the twentieth century, it was assumed that all human narratives have some universal structural elements in common. The new field of post structuralism has argued a different view.

Stories are also interesting for digital games because they are means for evoking emotion and facilitating immersion in a game. Stories are often structured in a suspenseful way and foster emotional engagement. Experiencing a good story can cause immersion in the imaginary world for the recipient. The research results in the area of affective computing show the considerable effects of emotional user interfaces (Picard 1997). Studies in neuronal sciences point out the importance of emotional engagement for learning efforts and motivation. For serious games, emotion and immersion can not only help to achieve the goal to entertain but also to motivate the user to continue playing and to achieve certain characterizing goals.

Besides the written form and the form as a play, stories can also be presented orally. *Storytelling* has a long cultural tradition. Stories are fundamental to culture and human understanding. They have familiar structures, which are recognizable and can easily be understood. In human tradition, stories were a means for information transmission and knowledge acquisition, e.g., within families and cultural communities. Children grew up with fairy tales that were not only interesting and entertaining, but also aimed at pedagogical objectives such as communicating values. This is similar to serious games that pursue both the goal to entertain but also at least one characterizing goal. Springer et al. (2004) identified pedagogical dimensions of storytelling. According to them, the telling of stories is humanistic (culturally rich, global in relevance), cross-disciplinary (stories apply to many subjects, including language arts, history, social studies, and humanities), cross-cultural (stories cut across cultural and geographic spaces and unite oral, written, and technological literacies), multi-sensory and multi-modal (the narration of stories can have not only auditory properties, but also gestures or visuals can be used), and constructivist (as storytelling is user-centered and tales are created out of an individual's knowledge and experience).

One peculiarity of storytelling is that it is more than just reading a text aloud. Ideally, the listeners are engaged, become part of the story—and may even influence it. Stories are then no longer *linear* (i.e., the connected events are presented always in the same pre-determined sequence) but *non-linear*. Digital games as an interactive, non-linear media are particularly suited to realize *interactive storytelling*. Since the 1990s, research in *digital storytelling* and interactive storytelling examines how a computer can support a storyteller or act as a storyteller. Methodologies from artificial intelligence have been applied to formalize stories and generate them automatically. The generation of stories can take the players' interaction into account and can generate an adapted story in real-time. *Story engines* are software systems that support this process. *Interactive drama* is the name of a genre for digital games that heavily use artificial intelligence methodologies in order to provide an experience that the player feels like an actor in an interactive stage-play. The game *Façade* is a prominent example, where the player can interact with two virtual characters using natural language and according to the interaction with the characters a story unfolds (see also Chap. 7). Crawford (2004) gives a good introduction to the field of interactive storytelling from a game designer's point of view.

For some researchers, stories have not only a cultural dimension but play also a very fundamental role in the human mind. According to Shank and Cleary (1995), stories constitute nothing less than the main building block of intelligence, memory, creativity, learning, and cognition in general. Shank and Cleary (1995) argues that we adapt to new situations and solve problems by recurring to already available stories, rearranging and recombining them in an attempt to cope with new challenges (known as *case-based reasoning*). Hence, using storytelling in a serious game that aims to educate would be an appropriate approach as it respects the way the mind truly works.

2.6 Interdisciplinary Collaboration

In the previous sections, a variety of disciplines contributing to a successful development and implementation of serious games have been introduced. In order to establish a high-quality serious game, these disciplines have to collaborate in a fruitful way. In this regard, it is not sufficient to just split up responsibilities and have every discipline deal with their tasks separately. Experience shows that this additive multi-disciplinary cooperation will lead to partial results that may not fit together. For example, computer scientists may develop an adaptation algorithm for an exergame using the heart rate (HR) as control variable. What they are not aware of is that the HR shows an individual (and also delayed) reaction to exercises and that a variety of specific training methods exist for aerobic training. Furthermore, to ensure sustainable use of the developed game, a variety of social, pedagogical, and psychological factors have to be considered that contribute to exercise adherence. A much more appropriate way is to closely cooperate with a sport scientist, a pedagogical expert and a social psychologist to integrate the knowledge of these disciplines from the beginning, i.e., starting with an interdisciplinary formulation of the problem to solve. In this sense, interdisciplinary cooperation means that two or more scientific disciplines work together to reach a common goal or establish a common product by integrating (rather than merely adding) disciplinary perspectives, knowledge and methods (e.g., Aboelela et al. 2007; Siedlok and Hibbert 2014). Integration can take different grades of intensity, ranging from the transfer of existing disciplinary knowledge or methods to the creation of new knowledge or methods. Transdisciplinary cooperation comes into play when various scientific disciplines cooperate with other (non-scientific) fields like business and government.

> *Interdisciplinary cooperation* as an umbrella term denotes the mode of cooperation between two or more disciplines. This cooperation can be characterized by (additive) division of work (i.e., *multidisciplinary* cooperation) or integration of work (i.e., *interdisciplinary* cooperation in a strict sense). *Transdisciplinary cooperation* means that scientific disciplines and non-academic partners cooperate.

Interdisciplinary cooperation is an inevitable sine qua non for high-quality serious games. However, the theory and practice of interdisciplinary cooperation raises several issues:

- Developing an interdisciplinary conceptual framework based on the heterogeneous disciplinary terminology
- Integrating different disciplinary cultures, traditions, and ways of thinking
- Integrating different theoretical frameworks
- Integrating different disciplinary methods for research and development

Due to the fact that highly-ranked journals show a bias for mono-disciplinary research, e.g., (Rafols et al. 2012), interdisciplinary projects may not be of equal importance compared to disciplinary projects. Therefore, the engagement of established scientific disciplines in interdisciplinary projects may not be as high as in disciplinary projects. At least, there may be the tendency to overemphasize the significance of one's own discipline that may affect cooperation on an equal footing.

Even if all disciplines share the common goals in a project, the communication between disciplines may suffer from different meanings of key terms. For example, in pedagogy, the term *experiment* has a substantially different meaning than in psychology or in computer science. The meaning of *adaptation* in computer science differs from sport science, and so forth. Therefore, it is important to develop an interdisciplinary conceptual framework or at least a glossary uncovering the different terminology. Communication is key.

Another major issue is the disciplinary culture and its way of thinking. For example, an engineer has been socialized into a specific way of problem solving—which differs substantially from the procedures in the humanities and art, where describing and analyzing a problem is much more important. Engineers may prefer methods from natural sciences, whereas art and design may apply aesthetic methods to evaluate a serious game.

Beyond these rather ambitious theoretical considerations, serious games are usually developed in projects with certain constraints. To create a successful collaboration and subsequent game, a realistic and pragmatic approach is crucial. To implement such an approach, the following is a *list of practical recommendations* which have been reported in relevant literature (Bronstein 2003; Derry et al. 2014; Siedlok et al. 2015):

- Provide an explicit commitment to realistic common goals and objectives
- Develop mutual respect and understanding
- Build an atmosphere of goodwill, respect, and trust
- Explicitly recognize and accept differences concerning ways of thinking, concepts, methods, and culture
- Develop a common conceptual basis ("interdisciplinary translation from disciplinary languages")
- Assign responsibilities in a clear and consensual manner
- Offer organizational support for interdisciplinary work, e.g., thematic workshops and seminars, discussion groups, sandpits and common publications
- Commit to consistent, ongoing communication (including informal "socializing" events).

Finally, it is important to point out that interdisciplinary cooperation is established between individuals rather than scientific disciplines. These individuals need to be aware of the potential problems of interdisciplinary teamwork, and be committed to actively work on their interdisciplinary collaboration skills.

2.7   Summary and Questions

Interdisciplinary, or even transdisciplinary, work is one characteristic for serious game development. The required interdependent collaboration is not easy to achieve—a lack of understanding and appreciation of disciplines outside of one's field, along with different terminology, diverse ways of thinking, and cultural differences can give rise to a variety of communication problems. A basis for common ground in an interdisciplinary team is both a shared vision and a clear sense of goals that the team is working toward. An atmosphere of openness and a cooperative framework for dealing with disagreement are contributing factors in finding common ground. Team members must also assume shared leadership responsibilities. Last but not least, empathy, awareness of differences, and a basic intellectual and emotional understanding of what it is like for team members from other disciplines to do their job is a necessity for successful cooperation. Therefore, serious game developers should know some basics of computer science (i.e., for realizing a digital game), art and design (i.e., for the user experience and gameplay), psychology (i.e., to increase player motivation and attention), didactics (i.e., for fostering learning processes that are often implied in achieving the characterizing goal), and storytelling and drama (i.e., for gameplay and players' emotional involvement). In addition, knowledge from other disciplines (such as health care, marketing, or sports) may be required depending of the application area of the serious game to be built.

Check your understanding of this chapter by answering the following questions:

- Characterize the subjects, objectives, basic concepts, methods, subdisciplines and relevant approaches of (a) computer science, (b) art and design, (c) psychology, (d) didactics and pedagogy, (e) digital storytelling.
- Find terms that are used with different meanings in different disciplines. Provide definitions for these terms that are understandable for persons with no background in the according discipline.
- Persons working on 3D models and 3D characters for digital games are often called artists. Would it be more precise to call them designers?
- What are cultural differences between computer science and psychology? What conflicts and problems could result from these differences in a serious game project?
- Imagine you start to work on a serious game in the field of oceanography. What sources could you use to acquire basic knowledge to collaborate with oceanographers (provided you are not an oceanographer yourself)? To what extent is it necessary to learn about oceanography?
- Imagine you have a serious game project about astronomy, and hire an astronomer who has never worked on a game before. To what extent would you consider it necessary for the astronomer to know about serious game development? How can you support the astronomer in acquiring this knowledge?

- Imagine you have the task of assembling and coordinating an interdisciplinary team for a serious game project. The team members do not know each other and have not worked in interdisciplinary projects before. What concrete measures would you take with regard to interdisciplinarity and transdisciplinarity?

Recommended Literature[2]

Scannell EE, Scanell M (2009) The big book of team-motivating games: spirit-building, problem-solving and communication games for every group. McGraw-Hill Education, New York—*this is a typical example of a book that provides some practical guidance in team building which extends also to interdisciplinary teams. A game-based approach to initiate team communication might be particularly beneficial for a project concerned with games*

Senge PM (2010) The fifth discipline: the art and practice of the learning organization. Random House Books—*this book gives an introduction to shared vision, team learning and learning organizations in general*

Schell J (2014) The art of game design: a book of lenses (2nd Ed), Morgan Kaufmann, Burlington MA—*this book is interesting from an interdisciplinary point of view as it promotes to view the game design process from different perspectives and as such trains game designers to adopt different views*

References

Aboelela SW, Larson E, Bakken S, Carrasquillo O, Formicola A, Glied, SA, Hass J, Gebbie KM (2007) Defining interdisciplinary research: Conclusions from a critical review of the literature. Health services research. 42(1p1):329–346

Albert D, Lukas J (eds) (1999) Knowledge spaces: theories, empirical research, and applications. Lawrence Erlbaum Associates, Mahwah, NJ

Andrews D (2001) Neuropsychology: From theory to practice. Taylor & Francis Inc, New York

Angel E, Shreiner D (2014) Interactive computer graphics: a top-down approach with WebGL, 7th edn. Addison-Wesley, Boston

---

[2]Literature concerning individual disciplines has already been named in the according sections of this chapter. Besides introductory texts and text books, there is a huge body of original literature available. It is worth checking associations of the according discipline whether they offer a digital library. For instance, the Association of Computing Machinery (ACM) and the Institute of Electrical and Electronic Engineers (IEEE) are well known societies that address all sub-disciplines of computer science. Both provide digital libraries (http://dl.acm.org/, www.ieeexplore.org). Moreover, publishers of scientific journals and books offer also digital libraries (e.g., www.link.springer.com, www.sciencedirect.com). Dedicated search engines (e.g., www.scholar.google.com) might also serve as a starting point for specific literature research. In the field of psycho-pedagogical frameworks, best practise surveys have been compiled by network projects such as GALA (the Game and Learning Alliance), which makes the reports available to the public (GALA 2015). The web-sites of some initiatives to bring multiple disciplines related to serious gaming together can also serve as an entry point for literature search, e.g., the European Serious Games Society or the Serious Games Association in the United States.

Beccari MN, Oliveira TL (2011) A philosophical approach about user experience methodology. Design, user experience, and usability. Theory, methods, tools and practice, Springer, Berlin, Heidelberg, 13–22

Boekaerts M (1997) Self-regulated learning: a new concept embraced by researchers, policy makers, educators, teachers, and students. Learn Instruct 7(2):161–186

Bogost I (2012) Alien phenomenology, or what it's like to be a thing. University of Minnesota Press, Minneapolis

Bojko A (2012) Eye tracking the user experience. Rosenfeld Media, New York

Brass P (2008) Advanced data structures. Cambridge University Press, Cambridge

Bronstein LR (2003) A model for interdisciplinary collaboration. Soc Work 48(3):297–306

Brown T, Wyatt J (2010) Design thinking for social innovation. Development Outreach 12(1):29–43

Burckhardt L (2012) Design ist unsichtbar: Entwurf, Gesellschaft und Pädagogik. In: Blumenthal S, Schmitz M (eds) Martin Schmitz, Berlin. English version: Burckhardt L. Design is invisible (1980). http://www.lucius-burckhardt.org/English/Text/Lucius_Burckhardt.html. Accessed 09 Feb 2016

Caprara GV, Fida R, Vecchione M, Del Bove G, Vecchio GM, Barbaranelli C, Bandura A (2008) Longitudinal analysis of the role of perceived self-efficacy for self-regulated learning in academic continuance and achievement. J Educ Psychol 100(3):525–534

Connolly T, Begg C (2014) Database systems: a practical approach to design, implementation and management, 6th edn. Addison-Wesley, Boston

Cordova DI, Lepper MR (1996) Intrinsic motivation and the process of learning: beneficial effects of contextualization, personalization, and choice. J Educ Psychol 88(4):715–730

Crawford C (2004) Chris crawford on interactive storytelling. New Riders, San Francisco

Csikszentmihályi M (1990) Flow: the psychology of optimal experience. Harper Collins, New York

Deci EL, Ryan RM (eds) (2002) The handbook of self-determination research. University of Rochester Press, Rochester NY

Derry SJ, Schunn CD, Gernsbacher MA (eds) (2014) Interdisciplinary collaboration: an emerging cognitive science. Psychology Press, Mahwah NJ

Doignon J, Falmagne J (1999) Knowledge spaces. Springer, Berlin

Entwistle N, McCune V (2004) The conceptual bases of study strategy inventories. Educ Psychol Rev 16(4):325–345

Frayling C (1993) Research in art and design. 1(1):1–5. Royal Collage of Art, London

Friedman K (2008) Research into, by and for design. J Visual Arts Practice 7(2):153–160

Gagne RM (1985) The conditions of learning and theory of instruction, 4th edn. Wadsworth Pub. Co., Andover

GALA—the Game and Learning Alliance (2015) Homepage. http://cordis.europa.eu/project/rcn/96789_en.html. Accessed 31 Jul 2016

Garris R, Ahlers R, Driskell JE (2002) Games, motivation, and learning: a research and practice model. Simul Gaming 33(4):441–467

Glanz K, Rimer BK, Viswanath K (eds) (2008) Health behavior and health education: theory, research, and practice, 4th edn. Jossey-Bass, San Francisco

He J, Koeneman EJ, Schultz RS, Huang H, Wanberg J, Herring DE, Herman R, Koeneman JB (2005) Design of a robotic upper extremity repetitive therapy device. Rehabil Robot IEEE ICORR 2005:95–98

Holzinger A, Kickmeier-Rust M, Albert D (2008) Dynamic media in computer science education; content complexity and learning performance: is less more? Educ Technol Soc 11(1):279–290

Hunicke R, LeBlanc M, Zubek R (2004) MDA: a formal approach to game design and game research. In: Proceedings of the AAAI workshop on challenges in game AI, San Jose CA

IJsselsteijn, W, De Kort, Y, Poels, K, Jurgelionis, A, Bellotti, F (2007) Characterising and measuring user experiences in digital games. In: International conference on advances in computer entertainment technology

Kahneman D (2003) Maps of bounded rationality: psychology for behavioral economics. Am Econ Rev 93(5):1449–1475

Kellogg RT (2003) Cognitive psychology, 2nd edn. Sage Publications, Thousand Oaks, CA

Kickmeier-Rust MD, Albert D (2010) Micro adaptivity: protecting immersion in didactically adaptive digital educational games. J Comput Assist Learn 26(2):95–105

Koster R (2005) A theory of fun for game design. Paragraph Press, Scottsdale, AZ

Kujala S, Roto V, Väänänen-Vainio-Mattila K, Karapanos E, Sinnelää A (2011) UX curve: a method for evaluating long-term user experience. Interact Comput 23(5):473–483

Lauer D, Pentak S (2011) Design basics. Cengage Learning, Boston MA

Leclerqce D, Poumay M (2005) The 8 learning events model and its principles. www.labset.net/media/prod/8LEM.pdf. Accessed 09 Feb 2016

MacKenzie IS (2013) Human-computer interaction: an empirical research perspective. Elsevier Inc, Waltham MA

Madhav S (2013) Game programming algorithms and techniques: a platform agnostic approach. Addison-Wesley, Boston MA

Martin B, Hanington B (2012) Universal methods of design. Rockport Publishers, Beverly MA

Maslow AH (1972) The farther reaches of human nature. The Viking Press, New York

Mäyrä F (2008) An introduction to game studies. Sage Publications, London, UK

Mellecker R, Lyons EJ, Baranowski T (2013) Disentangling fun and enjoyment in exergames using a expanded design, play, experience framework: a narrative review. Games Health J 2 (3):142–149

Merrill MD (2002) First principles of instruction. Educ Tech Res Dev 50(3):43–59

Meyer B (1997) Object-oriented software construction, 2nd edn. Prentice Hall, Upper Saddle River

Nacke LE, Kalyn M, Lough C, Mandryk, RL (2011) Biofeedback game design: using direct and indirect physiological control to enhance game interaction. In: Proceedings ACM SIGCHI conference on human factors in computing systems, pp 103–112

Prensky M (2001) Digital game-based learning. McGraw Hill, New York

Pressman R, Maxim B (2014) Software engineering: a practioner's approach. McGraw-Hill, New York

Picard RW (1997) Affective computing. MIT Press, Cambridge

Rabin S (2013) Game AI pro: collected wisdom of game AI professionals. AK Peters, Wellesley

Rafols I, Leydesdorff L, O'Hare A, Nightingale P, Stirling A (2012) How journal rankings can suppress interdisciplinary research: a comparison between innovation studies and business & management. Res Policy 41(7):1262–1282

Rauber T, Rünger G (2013) Parallel programming: for multicore and cluster systems. Springer, Heidelberg

Reason P, Bradbury H (eds) (2001) Handbook of action research: participative inquiry and practice. Sage Publications, London, UK

Reigeluth CM (1999) Instructional-design theories and models: a new paradigm of instructional theory, vol II. Lawrence Erlbaum Associates, Mahwah, NJ

Robertson J, Howells C (2008) Computer game design: opportunities for successful learning. Comput Educ 50(2):559–578

Rogers Y, Sharp H, Preece J (2011) Interaction design: beyond human—computer interaction, 3rd edn. John Wiley & Sons Ltd., West Sussex, UK

Ryan RM (ed) (2012) The Oxford handbook of human motivation. Oxford University Press Inc, New York

Russell S, Norvig P (2009) Artificial intelligence: a modern approach, 3rd edn. Prentice Hall, Upper Saddle River

Russell TL (1999) The no significant difference phenomenon: a comparative research annotated bibliography on technology for distance education: as reported in 355 research reports, summaries and papers. North Carolina State University, NC

Sanders EBN (2002) From user-centered to participatory design approaches. Design and the social sciences: Making connections, pp 1–8

Sanders E, Stappers P (2008) Co-creation and the new landscapes of design. CoDesign: Intl J of CoCreation in Design and the Arts 4(1):5–18

Sedgewick R, Wayne K (2011) Algorithms, 4th edn. Addison Wesley, Boston MA

Shank R, Cleary C (1995) Engines for education. Lawrence Erlbaum Assoc

Shneiderman B (1998) Relate-create-donate: a teaching/learning philosophy for the cyber-generation. Comput Educ 31(1):25–39

Siedlok F, Hibbert P (2014) The organization of interdisciplinary research: modes, drivers and barriers. Intl J Manag Rev 16(2):194–210

Siedlok F, Hibbert P, Sillince J (2015) From practice to collaborative community in interdisciplinary research contexts. Res Policy 44(1):96–107

Skinner BF (1953) Science and human behavior. Simon and Schuster, New York

Springer J, Kajder K, Borst Brazas J (2004) Digital storytelling at the national gallery of art. In: Bearman D, Trant J (eds) Museums and the web 2004: proceedings, archives & museum informatics, Toronto

Tanenbaum AS, Wetherall JW (2010) Computer networks, 5th edn. Prentice Hall, Upper Saddle River

Tenant M (1997) Psychology and adult learning. Routledge, New York

Thaler RH, Sunstein CR (2008) Nudge: improving decisions about health, wealth, and happiness. Yale University Press, New Haven CT

van Reekum CM, Johnstone T, Banse R, Etter A, Wehrle T, Scherer KR (2004) Psychophysiological responses to appraisal dimensions in a computer game. Cogn Emot 18(5):663–688

Wouters P, Tabbers HK, Paas F (2007) Interactivity in video-based models. Educ Psychol Rev 19 (3):327–342

Design of Serious Games

3

Philip Mildner and Florian 'Floyd' Mueller

Abstract

This chapter covers the topic of creating the design of a serious game. It first presents background information on games in general, and how they create engagement in particular—essential for serious games. The actual design process is similar to designing entertainment games; however, it differs when it comes to integrating the serious content itself. This chapter emphasizes these differences. It also presents solution strategies for how to create serious games. Beginning with an initial game idea, the steps of defining constraints for the game and adding suitable game mechanics are described. Finally, ideas are presented for how to organize the development process in a holistic approach, with a tight coupling of both the gaming and serious aspects.

3.1 How to Design a Serious Game

There are two main reasons to create a serious game for an application area. First, games in general create motivation, e.g., to get in-game awards, to beat the high score, or to be the best player in a multiplayer online game. Millions of players prove this fact every day. Serious game developers use these motivational aspects for other purposes than mere fun and entertainment. This does not mean that serious games should not be fun: on the contrary. Game designers, programmers, artists,

P. Mildner (✉)
University of Mannheim, Mannheim, Germany
e-mail: mildner@informatik.uni-mannheim.de

F. 'Floyd' Mueller
RMIT University, Melbourne, Australia

© Springer International Publishing Switzerland 2016
R. Dörner et al. (eds.), *Serious Games*, DOI 10.1007/978-3-319-40612-1_3

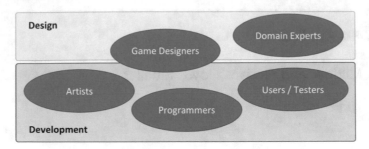

Fig. 3.1 Involved parties in the development of serious games. Domain experts and users can be included into the process to different degrees, as described in Sect. 3.7

and domain experts have to work together throughout the entire development process to create an enticing game.

Moreover, in many cases, developers of serious games have to cope with limited budgets; the details are discussed in Chap. 11. This may result in a sub-optimal balance of the fun parts and the serious parts of the game, e.g., when there are no resources for hiring professional game designers or artists. Figure 3.1 gives an overview of all the involved parties that should work together in the development of serious games. This is very similar to entertainment games, the only difference being that in serious games domain experts are included for the serious part. In addition to these domain experts, game designers play a central role in the creation process. They are the ones who combine characterizing goals and entertainment parts. While details can still be changed during the development process, the big decisions—e.g., game genre, main story and game world—have to be set in the first phase. It is often the game designer's task to both create the design and to ensure the entire team works on it throughout the development phase.

When comparing the game design process of pure entertainment games with serious games, there are two main differences. First, as mentioned above, there is an additional party involved in the process, namely the domain expert(s). They are the ones that bring knowledge about the serious content into the design process. For example, when developing a learning game for schools, teachers take the role of the domain experts since they know what content should be included in the game, and how it should be didactically delivered to the students. Game designers have to cooperate with domain experts to create a meaningful game. Second, a serious game always has some goal or message in addition to the fun part. In the example above, it would be the goal of delivering the learning content to the students. It is the task of serious game designers to carefully connect both parts, so the resulting game is both enjoyable and meaningful.

In the remainder of this chapter, we will discuss the design process of serious games. The chapter provides a general overview, raises questions, and points out possible strategies by referring the reader to in-depth articles and books.

3.2   Game Characteristics

Playing a good game is fun. Prensky (2007) even calls digital games "potentially the most engaging pastime in the history of mankind." However, what exactly is it that generates fun in a game? Prensky separates fun into two components: *enjoyment* and *amusement*. Enjoyment means being engaged into something, while amusement denotes pure leisure. These two components are both used by opponents and proponents of serious games: Opponents only see the latter, thinking that such applications only pose a distraction without using the motivational aspects that result from the enjoyment felt. As games are closely related to pure amusement, there is also the belief that they cannot be used for something meaningful at all. If considering the enjoyment part, however, games go very well together with a serious purpose, e.g., learning. After all, children learn many things by just playing. Bisson and Luckner (1996) also note that fun is an important part when learning because it provides a relaxed atmosphere where learners are willing to learn. Salen and Zimmerman (2004) describe pleasure as "the experience most intrinsic to games." So while there are strong indicators that fun can indeed help promote the characterizing goal of a serious game, as discussed in Sect. 3.1, what exactly makes a game engaging and fun to play?

All games build on a common set of basic characteristics that distinguish them from play (Charsky 2010). As already mentioned in the introduction, *play* is a free activity that does not follow specific rules, and it is isolated from the real world by a *Magic Circle* (Huizinga 1955; Caillois and Barash 1961). Players do not have to follow rules and can use their imagination to freely play. A *game*, on the other hand, is a structured activity that follows certain *rules* and has a beginning and an end. Players have to use these rules to work towards a *goal*.

This basic model does not say anything about how a goal and rules could look to create engagement and enjoyment. Many models have been presented in the literature that examine game elements on a more detailed level regarding the fun they create:

- Caillois and Barash (1961) created a list of four elements: Agôn (competition), Alea (chance), Mimicry (role play), and Ilinx (vertigo).
- Apter (1991) created the following list: exposure to arousing stimulation, fiction and narrative, challenge, exploration, negativism (i.e., working against rules), cognitive synergy (i.e., inventive thinking), and facing danger.
- Hunicke et al. (2004) list eight elements of how games create fun: sensation, fantasy, narrative, challenge, fellowship, discovery, expression, and submission.
- Prensky (2007) lists twelve elements: fun, play, rules, goals, interactivity, outcome and feedback, adaptivity, win states, conflict/competition/challenge/opposition, problem solving, interaction, and representation and story.

- Adams (2010) lists the following elements: gameplay, aesthetics, harmony, storytelling, risks and rewards, novelty, learning, creative and expressive play, immersion, and socializing.
- Fullerton (2014) defines the dramatic elements of a game as follows: play, challenge, premise, character, and story.

From this multitude of characteristics, a set of common denominators can be derived which will be presented in the following.

Play itself can be fun within a game. While games are a subset of the concept of play restricted by rules, playing without rules can or should also be a part of a game. Csikszentmihalyi (1991) therefore defined the term *autotelic*, a combination of auto (self) and telos (goal). Thus, players should be allowed to freely explore the game world and to experiment without fearing consequences. It does not matter if these actions arise out of pure curiosity and are just done because they can be done. To implement this characteristic, many games provide a *sandbox mode* where goals and some rules from the main game mode are disabled.

Although *rules* seem to limit players in their actions, at the same time they promise bigger satisfaction once the game has ended (Salen and Zimmerman 2004). By using stricter rules, the level of *challenge* is increased. In order to keep the players engaged, this level should not be too low to bore players and not too high to frustrate players, so that they stay in the *Flow* channel, introduced in Sect. 3.1 (Csikszentmihalyi 1991). If players are able to solve a challenge that is slightly too difficult for the perceived skill, they will feel rewarded and continue with the next challenge—maybe the next level or the next fight—in the game.

Everyone who has read a good book knows that *storytelling* is a strong engagement factor, and this is true for games as well. When drawn into a story, players want to know how it continues. The advantage of games is that players can influence the story by their actions. Closely linked to the story are its *aesthetics*. This includes the artistic style of the game, and especially how it presents itself to the players. An impressive graphical presentation alone can attract players to play a game.

Social factors are another characteristic that contributes to create a fun experience. By socializing, players build a team spirit if they successfully solve a task together with other players, e.g., a fight in an MMORPG where multiple players have to defeat a powerful enemy. In a team, players are able to do things that cannot be done alone. The interaction does not need to be performed with other players, though. Game characters can also be used when players can identify with them.

Even in pure entertainment games, the characteristic of *learning* is another engaging factor. Players feel satisfaction if they discover how to use a new game element or if they master the game by completing the last level. Some players invest a large amount of time to understand each and every rule, and they practice to become faster and better. It seems like a natural connection for serious games to use this intrinsic motivation to learn something new to achieve their goals.

Games, serious or just entertaining, are played because they are fun. This can be explained with different models that share common elements such as *play*, *rules*, *storytelling*, *social factors* and *learning*.

As mentioned above, games motivate players by including a variety of these elements. If this motivation does not come from an external source, but just from the game itself, it is called *intrinsic motivation*. Otherwise, it would be *extrinsic motivation*. So, when serious games are used as motivational tools, are they creating intrinsic or extrinsic motivation? The answer is not straightforward. When used mainly as a motivational tool, a serious game provides extrinsic motivation to its players. For example, a learner might not have a high intrinsic motivation to study for the next exam just by reading books. She might, however, be interested in playing a game where she competes against other students while learning for the exam. As soon as the exam is passed, the need for learning is over, and the player thus might end playing the game. This is extrinsic motivation, because the game is just regarded as a tool that helps to accomplish a certain goal.

But not all serious games have to follow this approach of "just being a tool." Games like *Civilization* or *Age of Empires* are good examples. These games deal with historic events in a playful manner and were successfully used in the classroom for teaching history (Squire and Barab 2004). In fact, there are people who state that the most they learned about history was by playing these games. The primary motivation to play these games, however, was most likely not to learn for the next history lesson, but just to have fun. Thus, the game can help to foster intrinsic motivation for the knowledge content because players then want to know more about a certain topic that was presented in the game.

Serious games can provide an extrinsic motivation to players who do not have an intrinsic motivation to engage with a topic otherwise.

Even though games can act as motivational tools, they do not appeal to every player in the same way. Some players like action games, others prefer real-time strategy games. Some like to play simple, casual games on their mobile devices while others invest a lot of money to have the fastest computer to play the most demanding and modern 3D games. There are as many different opinions about what the best game should look like as there are players. The age and gender of a player plays a large role in how highly they rate a game. For example, men prefer to have competition and spatial puzzles in games, whereas women prefer nurturing and verbal puzzles (Schell 2008). Also, children play different games than teenagers, adults, or the elderly.

In addition to such demographic factors, there are different psychological models that differentiate between player types. Bartle (1996) published a model consisting of four types, primarily targeting virtual multiplayer worlds: *killer, achiever, socializer,* and *explorer*. A finer-grained categorization—again tailored towards MMORPGs—was presented by Yee (2006), working with the main categories *achievement, social,* and *immersion*. Even though both models were created for players in virtual online worlds/MMORPGs, they are applicable to other games as well. Fullerton (2014) lists ten player types for games in general. Thus, when designing a game, it is best to examine what type of players is most likely to be attracted by it, and whether these players match the intended target audience of the game.

> Different players are attracted to different games based on various factors, including demographic – such as age and gender – and psychological factors.

Another aspect to keep in mind is that there are not only different types of players, but also different ways of how players work with the characterizing goal of a serious game. When looking at the educational sector, there is a multitude of different teaching and learning techniques. Some learners like to learn in a group, and others prefer to study on their own in the quiet atmosphere of libraries. While some learners value the additional possibilities offered by serious games, others might be satisfied by studying a textbook. This does not imply that either of these types is worse or better. By increasing the set of different learning tools, however, a greater number of learners can be reached, and serious games can provide a way to open up a certain topic for a new group of learners.

3.3 Defining a Game Scenario

The creation of a serious game most likely starts with defining the characterizing goals. For example, a therapist might have the idea to create a new training application for elderly patients and to increase their motivation to exercise; she/he decides to implement it as a game. Another scenario could be a publishing house deciding to create a new learning game for a foreign language to accompany its existing learning materials. In principle, each game—serious or not—starts with this initial idea.

In entertainment games, it is the game designer who comes up with the first idea for a new game, defining its core idea (Schell 2008). In serious games, there is at least one predefined constraint: the characterizing goal. Further constraints include the determination of a specific target group or the setting in which the game will be played. Looking at our training game, the constraints are that the game should be used in therapy, and that it should be tailored towards elderly patients. The resulting problem statement thus might be the following: "How can the training outcome for elderly patients be improved by including game elements into the training process?" Even technical elements can be included here. For example, when it is clear that the game might be used in an environment where only outdated hardware is available, it does not make sense to design a game with extensive hardware requirements. Defining such a question is important because at any time during the design process it can be checked if the project still follows this initial question.

Defining a clear *problem statement* helps to keep the design process and the project focused. In serious games, there is at least one *constraint* given by the characterizing goal.

Let us now look at another example, the learning game *Word Domination* (Mildner et al. 2014). This game was created in an academic setting without an external stakeholder. The main idea of the game arose out of two research questions:

- When creating a learning game, how close can it be to well-known entertainment games without sacrificing the explicit learning characteristic?
- How can the reusability of learning games be increased by offering an authoring interface that does not require any knowledge about programming or game design?

From these questions, several constraints emerge: The game should be based on a game principle often found in pure entertainment games, the characterizing goal should be *learning*, the game should allow for teacher-defined content, and entering this content should not require any changes to the core game logic. During the design process, the following decisions where based on these questions: One of the most popular game genres was used as the underlying game mode, namely a multiplayer first-person shooter. It was combined with a quiz game because this form of learning content can be used in a generic way and does not require any changes in the game, once implemented. Players have the goal of conquering platforms on a virtual map by stepping on them with their avatars. To hinder players of the opposing team from conquering a platform, a player can hit them by throwing balls at them. If they are hit, players are frozen in a glass bubble and have to answer a quiz question before they can continue conquering platforms. New quiz questions can easily be entered by the teacher on a web page, so no programming skills are required. In the end, all constraints were met with this game design, and the game is now available for anybody to use (Mildner 2014).

Most serious games are designed with a specific target group in mind. Whenever possible, the game should be crafted for the special needs and preferences of these users in order to be effective. Looking at the examples above, it would be the elderly patients for the training game. For the learning game there was no primary target audience defined, the game can be played by anyone. As discussed in Sect. 3.2, there are many different types of players and learners. Creating a game that fits all types of players is near to impossible because interests may not only be manifold but even conflicting. Instead, it makes sense to clearly decide on the intended target audience. If the designer has several audiences in mind it is important to concentrate on common denominators or non-conflicting features (Adams 2010). For example, when designing a game for children and their parents, it is a bad idea to include violence in the game because parents will reject this feature (and thus the entire game). Another trap independent game designers might face is to create a game for themselves instead of the target audience. When male game designers create a game, they might include only the features that they like best, making the game appeal only to males, even though the target audience might have included women as well. Thus, it is a crucial part of the design process to get in touch with the target audience, perform interviews, and regularly test the game ideas with representatives of the group (Christel et al. 2015).

> When determining the target audience and investigating game elements attractive for this audience, game designers should keep in mind that they do not design the game for themselves – but for the players.

From the very beginning of the game design process, the different parties should work together. Especially, game designers and experts for the characterizing goal should cooperate closely when defining the problem statement and the target audience. This is a crucial step towards a successful game. It helps to interview experts and, in return, present and discuss early design drafts.

Once the key game aspects are set, the development team should be assembled. Obviously the team will not only play an important role during the entire development phase, but it can also influence the game design. For example, when there is a visual artist with a specific art style, the game could be designed around it. On the other hand, if the budget is small, and there are no dedicated artists available—a situation academic projects often face—this fact should be considered as well. As a consequence, the game might only use a simple graphics style, or reuse existing materials.

> Constant collaboration with the stakeholders (experts, developers, target audience) from the beginning of the design phase helps to keep design efforts on track.

An aspect of the game scenario can also be the intended play environment, i.e., the settings in which a game is played. Different aspects should be considered here:

- Supervision: Should the game be accompanied by an instructor (e.g., in a school environment or in therapy)?
- Environment: Should the game be played during leisure time or in a controlled environment?
- Re-playability: Is the game intended to be played just once, or should the game be repeatable (as a training application)?
- Timeframe: How much time should be available for playing the game?

Looking again at our training game, the following statement could thus be added to the design document: "The game is intended to be played by elderly patients at home for 30 min each day over a period of several weeks." If the game was designed with a story that only lasted for a couple of hours, players would have to play the story again and again, so they would probably get bored soon. A session-based game with an ongoing story where parameters are changed for every new session (level, difficulty) would a better alternative for this scenario.

As some serious games are created with a specific research question in mind, for example in gamification, as explained in Sect. 3.1, the evaluation of the game is another important factor. For example, when evaluating long-term effects, the game should feature mechanics that keep players motivated over a long period of time. A question game designers also have to keep in mind is whether adapting a game to the players is desirable and feasible.

3.4 Experimental Game Design

As designing serious games is a creative process, it can be valuable to draw from the processes used by other creative practitioners. For example, designers can not only tap into practices used in the design of "regular" games (both digital and non-digital), but also from the design of interactive systems, industrial designs, or even architecture.

As it is a creative process, there is no fixed formal structure that guarantees success. However, over the years, techniques and strategies have emerged that support the creative process. Some of the strategies designers can employ are:

- *Examine (and play) other serious games for inspiration and guidance.* The serious games under investigation do not need to have the same characterizing goals. Being familiar with a broad spectrum of games can provide inspiration. For example, when designing a serious game for mental health, designers could be inspired by serious games for physical health.
- *Examine (and play) other games, including digital and traditional games*, such as board games and outdoor games. Investigating these games can lead to a rekindling of game enjoyment that could inspire new game ideas.
- *Examine traditional interventions in the corresponding "serious" field*, for example, games for mental health might look into mental health interventions such as regular meditation classes for inspiration. Although these interventions do not draw on "play" as a motivating factor, they often employ established theories that are deeply embedded in the structure of the intervention. As these theories have been used by other designers when they created the intervention, it could be useful for designers of serious games to learn from them: the creative process of turning an abstract theory into a practical intervention or into a game shares many similarities.

In addition to learning from previous approaches, there are also other ways to support the creative game design process. A popular approach is the use of Game Jams. Game Jams are fast-paced group activities in which small teams, typically three to five people, develop a game from concept to realization in a very short time, such as 48 h (Goddard et al. 2014; Preston 2014). The teams are usually given a broad theme to start off with and then compete for a price of the best game at the end of the event. The time constraint, and consequently lack of sleep, often creates an intense atmosphere that celebrates the creative process with all its ups and downs. Serious game designers have adopted this format of game creation for their purposes. For example, the SwimGames initiative uses game jams to create physical games to address the sedentary lifestyle of young people in the Netherlands (Deen et al. 2014). The advantage of Game Jams is that many games will be created in a very short time frame, usually one per team. These games are at least at a prototype stage, so they could be deployed to the target group and played by them to get feedback. However, game jams are not a sustainable model to produce high-quality serious games.

Using game jams for creating serious games comes with the challenge of how to introduce the "serious" component to the participating teams. Research workshops on this topic (Deen and Tieben 2012; Chatham et al. 2013) have begun examining this issue, as the requirements of a "serious" component can conflict with the traditional format of a game jam. The aforementioned introduction of a topic can inspire the participating teams, however, it might not provide enough guidance to fulfill the demands of the "serious" requirements.

Furthermore, academics have begun reporting on the design process of serious games (Isbister et al. 2010; Malone 1980; Rabin 2009). For example, Khaled and Ingram (2012) have reported that critical factors in serious game projects are project organization, technology, domain knowledge, user research, and game design.

Our recommendation to support the creative serious game design process is to make sure that the holistic approach to serious games is taken into account. This includes the full range of the process, including the ideation phase. It is advised not to fall into the trap of coming up with an idea for an entertainment game, and then sit back and think one can fit in the "serious" component in hindsight. The same applies to the opposite direction: a holistic approach also rejects the idea that designers can take a traditional intervention and fit a game on top. The design of a serious game needs to be an integrated approach, and the best way to achieve this is by taking a holistic approach from the start.

> The design process for serious games has to be treated in a holistic way from the beginning: Neither should the game be a mere add-on to the serious content, nor should the serious content be added to an unaltered entertainment game.

3.4.1 Practical Advice

We now present practical tips from our design practice that we believe have supported the creative game design process, hoping that this might also help others in their practice.

- During the first stages of the ideation process, have tangible ideation tools ready at hand to inspire you. This can include not only pen and paper and other stationery, but also game figurines, play objects, etc. To complement these traditional design tools, we find it useful for serious game design sessions to also introduce underlying theories that might be considered in some tangible form or another. For example, a theory could be printed on a large sheet of paper, or its building blocks could be represented through Lego bricks that have labels attached to them. Such tangible objects support the participants to "play" with the building blocks that later form the serious game.
- Consider using technology inspiration. As most serious games utilize technology to make content more engaging, it could be useful to use the technology itself as inspiration. In order to facilitate this, engagement with the technology itself is needed as part of the creative process. This can involve introducing participants to novel technology, such as a new interface, explaining them how it works, and letting them playfully experience its capability and limitations.
- Ensure that domain experts take part in all stages of the design process to ensure that entertainment and serious content gets equal consideration. This can be challenging, as domain experts often have a different availability, schedules, and experiences with such processes—and possibly divergent expectations about how the process should work. However, even though this can require extra effort, the win in terms of a better game is worth it. Furthermore, working with domain experts throughout the process also advances a sense of connectedness and appreciation for each other, which contributes to the sense of having achieved the goal together. And if people believe in having achieved a goal together, they are more likely to invest in future activities, such as distributing the game among their contact circles, or even igniting further serious game developments.
- Consider strategies to gather a large number of ideas. We found that having more ideas to choose from is advantageous, and therefore recommend considering ways to facilitate the creation of many ideas, even though they might not be feasible, on-topic, relevant, etc. This follows the original brainstorming idea that more ideas are better, even if they are outlandish and will not be used. We agree with this idea that more ideas are better; after all, you can always throw ideas away. Similar to the brainstorming rule that no idea should be initially criticized, we suggest to develop an environment where a breadth of ideas is encouraged. Research on the value of multiple ideas shares our sentiment: it has been shown that having multiple ideas results in better outcomes than refining a single one during the same timespan (Dow et al. 2010).

3.5 Bringing Together Serious Content and Gaming

One of the key aspects when creating a serious game—maybe even the most important one—is the integration of the characterizing goal with the game content. Prensky (2007) calls this the "art" in the creation process. Without a successful integration, the game will either be just an entertainment game or a (technology-enhanced) learning application. If done wrong, the resulting application will either not be fun to play, or will not help to promote the actual serious goal. For every new game, designers have to decide which path to follow.

A fundamental decision is whether the characterizing goal and game should be linked *statically* or *dynamically*. The former is the more common approach: Serious content and the game are designed and developed together from the beginning to the end of the product lifecycle.

A game to learn the Italian language can be used as an example. The game could tell a story about going to Rome and experiencing a series of events where players get to know Italian. The game would be accompanied by a matching story, artwork, soundtrack, and of course learning content. What, however, if the publisher suddenly decided to create a similar game that teaches Japanese? The entire process would have to start again from the beginning by creating a new story, different artwork, and so on. The changes do not have to be that big to run into problems, though. There might also be a situation where a teacher decides to use the learning game in an Italian class, but the learning content does not match her requirements well. If the learning content is statically linked, there is no way to easily change it.

The alternative is the dynamic integration of the serious content. The idea here is to provide a game where the serious content can be changed after the game has been created. The game then just consists of a set of predefined building blocks that can be filled with content later. Coming back to our example, the teacher might have to provide a set of pictures, a song and a list of vocabulary items and grammar exercises out of which the framework then creates a custom game. With statically linked games, there is a higher degree of freedom during the design process, and the game can have a deeper integration of serious content and game content. Dynamically linked games, on the other hand, allow for reusable game elements.

> When integrating serious content into the game, designers have to decide if the content should be linked *statically* or *dynamically* and how deeply both components should be integrated (intrinsic vs. extrinsic).

The decision to use a static or dynamic integration should not be confused with the integration of the serious content into the actual gameplay. Malone (1981) differentiates between *intrinsic* and *extrinsic* learning games (see Fig. 3.2). Intrinsic games

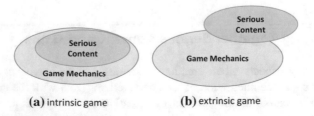

(a) intrinsic game (b) extrinsic game

Fig. 3.2 Different integration strategies

provide a tight integration in a way that the gameplay is the characterizing goal itself. A popular example here is a flight simulator that is used for training pilots. Another intrinsic game is a multiplayer role-playing game that is used to train teamwork. In extrinsic games, there is only a loose connection or none at all. If, in the flight simulator, players had to answer questions about biology every 30 s, this would be a completely extrinsic game for teaching biology. It would not be a good game after all because the serious content is just used as a "blocker" for the main game to proceed, and players might see it as a punishment. A better alternative could be to use a "jump'n'run" game that takes place in a specific biological setting (e.g., the human body), where players have to answer related questions to defeat an enemy. The serious content and the game scenario get connected with this setting, but the actual handling of the serious content is still not the main component of the gameplay.

As described in Sect. 3.2, games are mainly played because they are fun. For many players it is just a leisure activity, not connected to studying or being confronted with serious content. Still, there are entertainment games that can be seen as serious games. *Angry Birds*, for example, teaches basic principles about physics and ballistics. *Dance Dance Revolution* promotes exercising, and it is actually used successfully as an *exergame* (Blumberg et al. 2013). Yet if asked, most players will probably not say that they just played a serious game. Although these games may not have been designed to be a serious game in the first place, they show how well serious content can be "hidden" within a fun game. In educational or learning games, this concept is sometimes called "*stealth learning*" (Breuer and Bente 2010). It can be used on purpose by designers of serious games. As with the decisions above, there is no right or wrong here, but the decision mainly depends on the intended usage scenario of the game. If a game is developed for classroom use, it might not be necessary to hide the fact that it is a serious game. On the other hand, if a game is supposed to incorporate stealth learning, but the integration is not done subtle enough, or the designers overshoot somehow, the following can happen: As soon as the players notice that they are supposed to learn something, they instantly boycott the game because they wanted to play a fun game, not a serious game. A better way to achieve the desired effect might be just to primarily design the game to be fun to play. If players really enjoy a game they will not mind if some serious content is contained in it. The best indication of this effect is if players notice only after playing the game that they have actually learned something useful. In other situations, users actively look for a serious game, e.g., to use it as a motivational tool. Then it is not negative if the game reveals its nature as a serious game. *Dr. Kawashima's Brain Training* published by Nintendo is an example for a specific learning game that is mostly played in leisure time. Thus, when deciding which of these paths to follow, it should be clear in what context the game is supposed to be used.

A serious game can either reveal itself as such, or hide the serious characteristic. The latter is called *stealth learning*. Both forms appeal to different user groups, and they are applicable in different situations.

Gameplay in digital games can be separated into *slow-paced* (e.g., in a turn-based strategy game) and *fast-paced* (e.g., in a racing game). Ideally, the way how the player interacts with the serious content should be reflected in the gameplay. Prensky (2007) differentiates between action games and reflective games. In action games, players have to react quickly, whereas in reflective games, players are allowed to think about the next move. This should be taken into account in the type of serious content. For example, when learning to type on a keyboard, users should be able to train typing actions without too much active thinking. Consequently, the game *The Typing of the Dead* combines this issue with an action game where players have to defeat approaching zombies by correctly typing words as fast as possible. In a setting where more thinking is required, such a game would be highly ineffective because of the built-in conflict: If players think too much they will lose the game, and if they do not think the game will not fulfill its purpose. To avoid such a mismatch, it should be clear which pace the serious content requires.

> The serious content and the game mechanics should follow a similar pace. For serious content requiring reflective thinking, a slow-paced game mode should be used. Fast-paces games should be chosen if fast reaction matters.

3.6 Game Mechanics

Chapter 1 already gave an overview of game mechanics. The combination of all game mechanics and game rules results in the gameplay that the players experience. They define what players can do in the game, how they perceive the game world, and what story they experience. This section gives an overview of common game mechanics.

Each game takes place in a *space*. There can be very different forms of such a space. In the case of a game with a physical equivalent it can just be a soccer playground or a chess game board. When it comes to virtual games, game designers have a high degree of freedom of how to create the game space. It can be as simple as a game board for playing TicTacToe, or it can be a complex 3D game world with a landscape, characters and objects in it.

A game space can be represented in different forms. Common techniques are to use a 2D or 3D environment that is rendered to the screen of the player through a virtual camera. Different perspectives are possible here: Top-down, first-person, flying camera, and so on. Yet other representations are possible as well: The game *Blindscape* (Blindscape 2015) does not use a graphical representation at all, but just provides acoustic feedback that is triggered by touching the black display of the player's mobile device. Apart from simple board-based games, the player is normally allowed to move in the game space. This can be done by controlling a virtual avatar or by using a birdseye view with a flying camera. Some games allow the

Fig. 3.3 Different representation forms of a quiz game: a 2D representation with a *three-in-a-row* game board (*left*) and 3D representation in a virtual world with a first-person perspective (*right*)

player to see and explore the entire space, while others limit the visibility by employing techniques such as *fog of war* (Adams 2010).

The decision for a characterizing goal does not imply the type of the game space. Figure 3.3 shows two completely different games that share the same basic principle, namely a quiz game. The first game uses a simple 2D space with no option for the player to move in it. In contrast, the second game takes place in a virtual 3D world where players experience the first-person perspective of a moveable avatar to perform actions in the world. The decision for one or the other game space can depend on the preference of the target audience (casual or hardcore gamers) or the intended hardware (mobile devices or desktop PCs).

If not working with an abstract game principle, there are normally *characters* in a game, as in the example shown in Fig. 3.3 (right). This includes the player character (or avatar), non-player-characters (NPCs) controlled by the game, or other human-controlled characters in a multiplayer setup. There are few limitations on how these characters can be modeled. An early and simple example of "characters" in games can be seen in *Pac-Man*. The game includes an avatar that is controlled by the player (Pac-Man) and four NPCs (the ghosts). Even though the NPCs follow very simple rules, players seemingly observe complex behavioral patterns with them (Millington and Funge 2009). Modern games normally include much more complex character types that can speak, express feelings or perform complicated actions, making them comparable to characters from novels or movies. Players may control one hero or even a group of them that become more powerful as the game proceeds. If players do not control an avatar directly, they often take the role of a director that can influence parts of the game (e.g., giving commands to NPCs, building structures, etc.).

Both the game world and the characters contribute to the *story* of the game. The element of story includes two aspects: narrative, and progression in the game. The narrative uses common storytelling techniques also found in novels or movies. During the game, players can experience an exciting story with dramatic elements. The *Hero's Journey* is a common template for creating an appealing story (Campbell 1968). It includes several stages where players experience ups and downs and grow more powerful until they face the final battle. Compared to

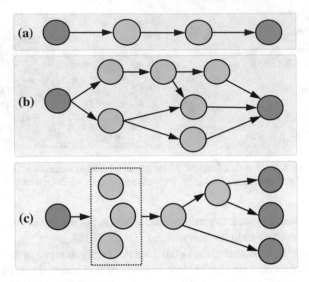

Fig. 3.4 Games with different forms of *progression*, reaching from simple linear layouts (**a**) to more complex layouts with branches (**b**) or level groups and alternative endings (**c**)

traditional media such as theater plays or movies, there is a fundamental difference: Games do not have to follow a linear way. This is a great opportunity for game designers because the story can change according to the players' actions.

This is where the element of *progression* comes into play. A game consists of at least one level or scene the players have to complete in order to win the game. Figure 3.4 gives an overview of possible progression types. The traditional way is a linear layout. Several levels are just connected consecutively, and players have to win all levels to win the game. More complex setups include branches where players can decide which path to follow. When applied to a role-playing game, for example, players could have to possibility join different factions. As a consequence, players will not be able to see the entire game content during one play-through. While this increases the re-playability of the game, it also increases the complexity and the design and development effort. Other progression types include level groups and alternative endings. In a level group, players have to solve a subset or all of the levels in an arbitrary order before they can proceed to the next stage. Alternative endings provide another way to increase the complexity and non-linearity of the story.

Independent of the extent at which characters and story are included in a game, players always perform *actions*. According to Schell (2008), the actions are based on a set of *rules* that determine what players are allowed to do in certain situations. As a result of an action, *objects* in the game alter their *states* and *attributes*. For example, in a soccer game, an action would be to kick the object "ball" because a rule prohibits throwing the ball. If done so, the ball changes its attribute "position" and enters the state "moving." Actions can be performed either based on *skill* or based on *chance*. The soccer game is mostly influenced by skill. However, factors such as the wind can influence the game in an unforeseen way and thus incorporate chance-based actions. Actions and rules are elements that give a game structure and thus are an integral part of the game design. By changing the set of rules, very different games can be created while leaving the other game mechanics untouched. For example, a multitude of game modes can be created with the same deck of cards. Therefore, the core rules of the game should be designed carefully to reflect the original intention of the game, including transporting the characterizing goal.

> Common game setups include a *game space* and *characters*. Players can experience a *story* and perform *actions* in the space.

There are also different forms how players can interact in a game. If there is just one human player, the game mode is called *single-player*. Computer-controlled opponents can take the role of other players (NPCs). Examples for this mode are single-player racing games or strategy games. In both cases, the human player has to compete against an artificial-intelligence-based (AI) opponent. However, other games exist that do not require an AI component, like a simple card game or a puzzle game. Here, players just have to follow the game rules in order to win.

If the characterizing goal of a serious game depends on communication between players, a *multi-player* mode should be designed and implemented. We distinguish three different multi-player modes: In a *competitive* setting, players compete against each other, only one party can win the game. If a *cooperative* mode is used, players have to work together in order to win. This is similar to single-player games, only that there is more than one player who tries to be successful. A third form is the *collaborative* mode, which is slightly different from the previous mode: Although cooperative games have one common goal, all players have their own tasks which contribute to this goal. Such a game could look as follows: Players have to solve a set of puzzles to win, but solving each puzzle requires only one player. Thus, the game can be won faster when more players are in the game, but specific game actions are still smaller tasks in single-player mode. If, however, an action requires more than one player to collaborate, the game becomes *collaborative*. Wendel et al. (2013) used this approach to build a serious game to train team-building skills. Of course, combinations of the different modes are possible as well. For example, players might have to collaborate in a team while competing against another team. The design decision for what mode(s) could be used in a game should be based on the underlying serious content, so that the interaction modes of serious content and gameplay match.

Every game interacts with its players through an *interface*. It connects the virtual game space to the players' minds. For example, if a player has the thought "my avatar should go from one room to another," the game should provide a way to translate this thought into an action in the game. This includes both *input* and *output* interfaces. Common inputs are keyboard, mouse or game controllers. More recent techniques include touchscreens, Microsoft's *Kinect*, Nintendo's *Wii Remote*, accelerometers found in mobile devices, and virtual reality controllers such as the *Rift* by Oculus VR (2015) or the Steam VR (2015).

The output component is responsible for showing the current game state to the player. As discussed in the section about game spaces above, the output can take different forms in terms of design, e.g., as a 2D or 3D world with different forms of cameras. The physical output normally is a screen. Still, it is important to consider its properties such as size (e.g., desktop monitor, mobile device or TV screen) and rendering capabilities (2D, 3D or virtual reality headset).

The decision to choose a specific input and output technology can be directly influenced by the characterizing goal of a serious game. For example, if it is a training game that involves whole body movements, the Kinect might be the best option. The technologies should also be matched with the target audience. When creating a game for users that are inexperienced with a PC, choosing a first-person controller with mouse and keyboard will result in a very steep learning curve; an alternative approach that just uses the mouse only might work better. Then again, game-experienced users might get frustrated by the missing degree of freedom. Available hardware can also be a limiting factor. For example, when a serious game is intended to be used in school environments with outdated hardware, this circumstance should be taken into account when designing the game.

Due to their interactive nature, games should always provide *feedback* to their players. Whenever players perform actions in a game, there should be some indication about them. This can be as small as highlighting an object after clicking on it, or as big as displaying the "game over" screen when the game ends. A good interface design also includes preparing players before important decisions. For example, if a game includes a story with branches, it is good practice to notify the players before they choose a path from which they cannot return so that they can think twice about their decision.

The level of immersion a user experiences depends on the implementation of the *user interfaces* (UIs), which comprises all menus and elements that are not directly part of the game world. Designing those in an intuitive way helps players getting along in the game. Players should know how to interact with objects in the world, or just where to find the settings menu to save or quit the game. There is a difference between UI elements that are part of the game world and those that are not. If players have to open a menu to perform a game action or change a setting, they will be drawn out of the game world and will lose the immersive feeling. The action of saving a game state can act as an example here: The common way to implement it is to provide a menu where the player can choose a "save" slot before returning to the game. This action breaks the immersion. If the game is an avatar-based game, saving can also be implemented without that break: A player could collect gems that can be used at certain locations to buy save-games. The same is true for including the serious content into a game. The interface to the serious part can either be plugged into an existing game as a menu, or integrated into the game world and its mechanics. When creating an educational game that includes a quiz component, there are different ways how to include the quiz into the game. If the game features a world in which players can move and interact, an easy way would be to display a UI window that contains a question as soon as the player triggers an according action. The game would pause and continue as soon as the player answered the question. This approach draws players out of the immersion each time they have to answer a question. A better alternative would be the following: When players have to answer a question, they have to do that in the game world by jumping on a platform that represents the correct answer, or by destroying objects that do not contain the correct answer. In this way, game designers can create immersive serious game interfaces that create a seamless gaming experience for their players.

In an ideal world, game designers would create the perfect game by picking all of the best game mechanics. Unfortunately, a limited budget often does not allow one to do that. This is especially true for serious games that are often developed with a small amount of resources. As a consequence, it can make sense to concentrate on the most promising game characteristics. The presentation mode of a game is an area that allows for a variety of designs, e.g., when creating a game with a strong connection to the real world, such as a training simulation. The game design could look as follows: The player should be able to explore a city in which several points of interest are located. In each of these locations, the player should handle a situation connected to the serious content of the game. With the recent advances on 3D environments and virtual reality, it may be desirable to use these technologies for that game. Players could then freely explore a realistic virtual environment and feel almost as if they were really there. Creating such a complex environment, however, takes up a lot of resources. Furthermore, it bears the danger of *falling into the uncanny valley* (Tinwell 2015). This concept describes that the more realistic a computer-generated scene/object is, the more skeptical users are in accepting it. Thus, creating a realistic and believable virtual environment is a very complex task that requires considerable work from both programmers and visual artists. A more practical alternative could be the following: Instead of a complete virtual environment, players just see a map of the city where they can click on the different locations. Each location is then modelled by a set of panoramic images in which players can look around and interact with objects. The images can be shot at those locations with very little resources, and the result will probably be better accepted by the players than a not fully realistic virtual environment.

3.7 The Development Cycle

Most entertainment game design follows an iterative cycle in which the game is iteratively improved over time. This includes user testing, where players from the target audience play prototypal versions of the game, which provides feedback to help refine the game. Most serious game development processes follow a similar cycle; however, the challenge with serious games is that there is an additional stakeholder, the domain expert.

Moreover, many serious games target specific demographic groups that are different from the target group of traditional games. This can be challenging, as many game designers are used to designing games for players like themselves (and game companies often hire designers that design games they like themselves). This is usually not the case with serious games, where the game designers are often very different from the target group. So the question in the design process of serious games is: how does one design for the values and expectations of the different shareholders, in particular the players and the domain experts?

Participatory Design (PD) (Spinuzzi 2005) can help with this, as it is an approach to design for the values and expectations of specific audiences. Participatory design is a common approach for interactive systems in general, however, it is not as popular in the game design community (Khaled et al. 2014), probably for the reason outlined above: if the designers are similar to the players of their games, there is not much need to bring in additional players, especially when considering the resource constraints of many small game studios.

However, the consideration of participatory design in serious games is increasing (Khaled et al. 2014). Key themes here are that disempowered user groups should be empowered, and that diverse knowledge should be integrated. Furthermore, non-designer stakeholders should participate in design decisions that affect them. Khaled et al. (2014) also mention typical participatory design methods used in serious games: design games (Brandt 2006) and future workshops (Kensing and Madsen 1992). Moreover, it has been acknowledged that participatory design in serious games is not without its challenges, and the process rarely runs smoothly (Khaled and Ingram 2012).

In order to aid the use of participatory design in serious games, Abeele et al. (2012) developed a framework for the design of serious games. This framework proposes to build the serious game design on four conceptual pillars: player-centered, iterative, interdisciplinary and integrated.

- *Player-Centered Design*: The involvement of players should go beyond employing them to resolve usability issues, offering players the opportunity to participate also in the creative part of the game design process. This is important especially with serious games, as the target audience differs from the game designers probably more than in traditional entertainment games. The authors propose several methods to involve the players throughout the design process, including ethnographically inspired inquiries at the start of the project and participatory design sessions during the design phase, as well as user testing throughout the development.
- *Iterative Development*: The framework proposes an iterative and incremental approach to game design and development, consisting of three main phases: concept design, game design, and game development. The concept design phase is used to acquire an understanding of the player group and the problem domain. After the concept design phase has been verified, the game design phase transforms the concept into a detailed game to serve as input for the game developers. In the final game development phase, milestones and user tests are

defined, and the biggest risks the project faces in regard to serious goals, fun, and/or technological challenges are described. Concept design and game development typically last 3–6 months, and game development between 6–12 months.

- *Interdisciplinary Teamwork*: The framework suggests an interdisciplinary approach in which "all team members, not just the designers, participate in every aspect of the development process and learn from each other's field of expertise" (Abeele et al. 2012).
- *Integration of Play and Learning*: The framework proposes that play and learning needs to be integrated as closely as possible (Garris 2002). As the authors' background is in learning, it is not surprising that learning is featured here. However, we believe that the importance of integration equally applies to other "serious" content. This integration is facilitated by what they call "intense" collaboration between all the parties involved (Abeele et al. 2012).

This framework highlights the importance of bringing both players and domain experts into the game design process of serious games. To facilitate this, we now articulate four common ways how these can be brought into the design process, borrowing the categorization from prior work on co-designing with children by Hourcade (2008) and Druin (2002).

- *Stakeholders as users*: When players and domain experts are treated as users, they are often brought in at the beginning or end, utilizing them through ethnographies to understand how they currently engage with the "serious" aspect (beginning) and to assess its effectiveness (end). Both can be very useful for serious games, however, there are additional ways how stakeholders can be involved, which we describe next.
- *Stakeholders as testers*: When stakeholders are testers, they are invited to test prototypes and possible alternatives. This works well in the iterative process as the team gets feedback early, which reduces the overall cost and improves the quality of the final game. While this approach engages the stakeholders more, it does not provide them with a voice in the design process.
- *Stakeholders as informants*: When stakeholders become informants, they act as consultants to the team, sharing ideas at specific times. Common techniques are interviews, questionnaires, and focus groups. The Personas technique described by Antle (2004) can also be used to keep the different stakeholders in mind when they are not available.
- *Stakeholders as design partners*: When stakeholders join as design partners, they enter the highest level of involvement. As mentioned previously, the teams need to consider the different backgrounds and perspectives of the stakeholders in order to integrate them successfully in the design process; simply inviting them will not necessarily do. However, the outcome will be worth it, as all participants of the team will be able to fully buy into the process and thus in the outcome, facilitating the success of the game. Common techniques used here are contextual inquiry and participatory design. In contextual inquiry, players and

the entire team observe each other while playing the game to facilitate discussions on competing approaches. In participatory design sessions, prototypes are developed collaboratively to ensure that the stakeholders' diverse opinions are considered when it comes to feature selection.

In sum, the design of serious games can benefit from a player-centered, iterative, interdisciplinary, and integrated approach. Designers are advised to collaboratively engage not only the players, but also the domain experts, as they are both stakeholders in the process. This is a very different scenario from entertainment game design.

3.8 Conclusion

Game designers face a large responsibility: They lead the way for the entire development process of a game, from the initial idea to the final game. Therefore, they first should understand what makes a game a game, how it differs from play, and how it creates fun. This is especially important when designing serious games because they are frequently used as motivational tools to promote their characterizing goals.

The approaches differ slightly from game design for entertainment games. First, an initial game scenario is identified based on a set of problem statements. This scenario is then filled with ideas and game elements that are iteratively refined. With serious games, however, a very important part is the integration of the characterizing goal into the game. It begins with the definition of the game scenario, where the characterizing goal and the intended usage of the game act as additional constraints.

Keeping these constraints in mind, game designers create an initial game idea. Here, inspiration can come from looking at existing gaming and non-gaming applications. Furthermore, events like game jams can provide a series of prototype games in a short amount of time. Game designers also have to decide how to combine serious content and fun game elements. Both components can be linked statically to create a tight connection between them, or they can be linked dynamically to support interchangeable serious content and to enable the reusability of the game for different purposes.

When designing a game from scratch, a set of game mechanics have to be added to it. This includes basic elements such as a game space, actions and rules. More elements like a story, characters, or a multiplayer mode can be added to create more complex games. Interfaces provide functionalities for the players to interact with the game and give them feedback on their actions.

Once the first game design is finished, the development team can start to implement a first prototype of the game. The prototype is then iteratively improved until it becomes the finished game. Throughout the entire development phase game designers should constantly review the progress by talking to domain experts and developers. Testing the game regularly with representatives of the target audience is another important step towards a successful serious game.

It is important to treat serious game design as a holistic approach from the beginning, integrating both the characterizing goal and the fun part. Consequently, the entire design process should also be holistic. Designers should bring together knowledge, props, and constraints from all involved stakeholders—including the stakeholders themselves.

Check your understanding of this chapter by answering the following questions:

- Why do games engage players? What components of the game attract players to invest such a large amount of time into them?
- Look at existing games (serious or not) and examine which game characteristics they employ.
- Formulate at least three game scenarios by exactly defining problem statements and constraints.
- Design the same game idea for different target audiences (e.g., tech-savvy teen-agers vs. elderly players) and different environments (e.g., classroom vs. leisure time). Do only parts of the design have to be changed, or do different audiences require completely different game types?
- Design a game prototype just by using pen, paper, and physical objects. Can you cover the entire game idea with that?
- Can any characterizing goal be turned into an intrinsic serious game, or are there limits regarding the set of available game mechanics?
- Match the pace of serious content and game. For example, choose from racing game, turn-based strategy game, platformer, first-person shooter, training vocabulary, physical exercises, learning how to do medical operations, learning how to drive a car, and acquiring a new language. Which elements can be connected naturally, and which are a poor fit?
- Look at existing serious games: Did they start as just the serious content, as an entertainment game, or were they created with a holistic design approach from the beginning?

Recommended Literature

Salen K, Zimmerman E (2004) Rules of play: Game design fundamentals. MIT Press—*Covers game design with a lot of background and theoretical information; a good introduction for readers interested in the core mechanics of games*

Fullerton T (2014) Game design workshop: A play-centric approach to creating innovative games, 3rd edition. CRC Press, Boca Raton, FL—*Presents the topic of game design with exercises, examples, and interviews from actual game designers. With this practical scope, it is especially suited for learning the basics of the creative aspects of game design*

Schell J (2008) The art of game design: A book of lenses. Morgan Kaufmann Publishers Inc., San Francisco, CA, USA—*Builds up the game design process by working along so-called lenses, or small units of the process, and gives the reader many possibilities to reflect on the covered topics to get started with game development*

Adams E (2010) Fundamentals of game design, second edition. Pearson Education, Berkeley, CA, USA—*Covers the topic of game design from a very technical perspective; suited for readers that want to start designing a specific game*

Prensky M (2007) Digital game-based learning. Paragon House—*A book specifically for learning games, describing theoretical foundations and different application fields. It is a useful resource when creating educational games*

Rabin S (2009) Introduction to game development, 2nd edition. Course Technology PTR, Boston, MA, USA—*Covers the entire game development process and thus provides a good overview beyond the scope of game design itself; helps to keep the big picture in mind*

Michael DR, Chen S (2006) Serious games: Games that educate, train and inform. Thomson Course Technology—*Gives a broad overview of the field of serious games and is a good introductory lecture for readers new to the field*

References

Abeele VV, De Schutter B, Geurts L, Desmet S, Wauters J, Husson J, Van den Audenaeren L, Van Broeckhoven F, Annema, JH, Geerts DP (2012) A player-centered, iterative, interdisciplinary and integrated framework for serious game design and development. In: Serious games: the challenge, Springer, pp 82–86

Adams E (2010) Fundamentals of game design, 2nd edn. Pearson Education, Berkeley, CA, USA

Antle A (2004) Supporting children's emotional expression and exploration in online environments. In: Proceedings conference on interaction design and children: building a community, ACM, pp 97–104

Apter MJ (1991) A structural phenomenology of play. In: Kerr JH, Apter MJ (eds) Adult play: a reversal theory approach. Swets and Zeitlinger, Amsterdam, pp 18–20

Bartle R (1996) Hearts, clubs, diamonds, spades: players who suit MUDs. J MUD Res 1(1):19

Bisson C, Luckner J (1996) Fun in learning: the pedagogical role of fun in adventure education. J Exp Educ 19(2):108–112

Blindscape (2015) http://www.blindscapegame.com/. Accessed 17 Feb 2016

Blumberg FC, Almonte DE, Anthony JS, Hashimoto N (2013) Serious games: what are they? What do they do? Why should we play them? In: Dill KE (ed) The Oxford handbook of media psychology. Oxford University Press, pp 334–351

Brandt E (2006) Designing exploratory design games: a framework for participation in participatory design? Proceedings ninth conference on participatory design: expanding boundaries in design, vol 1. ACM, pp 57–66

Breuer JS, Bente G (2010) Why so serious? On the relation of serious games and learning. Eludamos J Comput Game Cult 4(1):7–24

Caillois R, Barash M (1961) Man, play and games. University of Illinois Press

Campbell J (1968) The hero with a thousand faces. University Press, Princeton, NJ, USA

Charsky D (2010) From edutainment to serious games: a change in the use of game characteristics. Games Culture 5(2):177–198

Chatham A, Schouten BA, Toprak C, Mueller F, Deen M, Bernhaupt R, Khot R, Pijnappel S (2013) Game Jam. In: CHI'13 extended abstracts on human factors in computing systems. ACM, pp 3175–3178

Christel M, Trybus J, Shah SD, Chang BH, Dave R, Pavani A, Sawant, OD, Song J, Inglis J, Kairamkonda SS, Karrs C, Ke X, Kron E, Lu X (2015) Bringing biome exploration into the classroom through interactive tablet experiences. serious games. In: Huddersfield, UK, Göbel S, Ma M, Hauge J B, Oliveira M F, Wiemeyer J and Wendel V (eds) 1st joint internat conf on serious games JCSG (2015) Springer LNCS, vol 9090. Springer, Heidelberg/New York

Csikszentmihalyi M (1991) Flow: the psychology of optimal experience. Harper & Row, New York, USA

Deen M, Tieben R (2012). Swimitate Swimgames. http://www.swimgames.nl/. Accessed 17 Feb 2016

Deen M, Cercos R, Chatman A, Naseem A, Bernhaupt R, Fowler A, Schouten B, Mueller F (2014) Game jam: [4 research]. CHI '14 Extended Abstracts on Human Factors in Computing Systems (CHI EA '14). ACM, New York, NY, USA, 25–28

Dow SP, Glassco A, Kass J, Schwarz M, Schwartz DL, Klemmer SR (2010) Parallel prototyping leads to better design results, more divergence, and increased self-efficacy. ACM Trans Comput Human Interac 17(4):18

Druin A (2002) The role of children in the design of new technology. Behav Inf Technol 21(1): 1–25

Fullerton T (2014) Game design workshop: a playcentric approach to creating innovative games, 3rd edn. CRC Press, Boca Raton, FL, USA

Garris R, Ahlers R, Driskell JE (2002) Games, motivation, and learning: a research and practice model. Simulation and gaming 33(4):441–467

Goddard W, Byrne R, Mueller F (2014) Playful game jams: guidelines for designed outcomes. In: Proceedinigs 2014 conference on interactive entertainment, ACM, Newcastle, NSW, Australia, pp 1–10

Hourcade JP (2008) Interaction design and children. Found Trends Human-Comput Interac 1 (4):277–392

Huizinga J (1955) Homo ludens: a study of the play element in culture. Beacon paperbacks, Beacon Press, Boston, MA, USA

Hunicke R, LeBlanc M, Zubek R (2004) MDA: a formal approach to game design and game research. In: Workshop on challenges in game AI, association for the advancement of artificial intelligence. Miami, FL, USA

Isbister K, Flanagan M, Hash C (2010) Designing games for learning: insights from conversations with designers. In: Proceedings SIGCHI conference on human factors in computing systems. ACM, pp 2041–2044

Khaled R, Ingram G (2012) Tales from the front of a large-scale serious games project. Proc ACM SIGCHI, ACM, New York, USA, pp 69–78

Khaled R, Vanden Abeele V, Van Mechelen M, Vasalou A (2014) Participatory design for serious game design: truth and lies. In: Proceedings first ACM SIGCHI annual symposium on computer-human interaction in play. ACM, pp 457–460

Kensing F, Madsen KH (1992) Generating visions: future workshops and metaphorical design. L. Erlbaum Associates Inc

Malone TW (1980) What makes things fun to learn? Heuristics for designing instructional computer games. In: Proceedings 3rd ACM SIGSMALL symposium and the first SIGPC symposium on small systems. ACM, pp 162–169

Malone TW (1981) Toward a theory of intrinsically motivating instruction. Cog Sci 5(4):333–369

Mildner P (2014) Word domination. https://www.knowledge-gaming.de/. Accessed 17 Feb 2016

Mildner P, Campbell C, Effelsberg W (2014) Word domination: bringing together fun and education in an authoring-based 3D shooter game. In: Göbel S, Wiemeyer J (eds) Games for training, education, health and sports, lecture notes in computer science, vol 8395. Springer, Heidelberg/NewYork, pp 59–70

Millington I, Funge JD (2009) Artificial intelligence for games, 2nd edn morgan kaufmann series in interactive 3D technology. Morgan Kaufmann Publishers/Elsevier, Burlington, MA, USA

Oculus (2015) The oculus rift. www.oculus.com/en-us/rift. Accessed 17 Feb 2016

Prensky M (2007) Digital game-based learning. Paragon House, St Paul, MN, USA

Preston J (2014) Serious game development: Case study of the 2013 CDC games for health game jam. In: Proceedings 1st internat workshop on serious games. ACM Internat Conf on Multimedia, Orlando, FL, USA

Rabin S (2009) Introduction to game development, 2nd edn. Course Technology PTR, Boston, MA, USA

Salen K, Zimmerman E (2004) Rules of play: game design fundamentals. MIT Press, Boston, MA, USA

Schell J (2008) The art of game design: a book of lenses. Morgan Kaufmann Publishers Inc, San Francisco, CA, USA

Spinuzzi C (2005) The methodology of participatory design. Tech Commun 52(2):163–174

Squire KD, Barab SA (2004) Replaying history: learning world history through playing civilization III. Indiana University, Bloomington, IN, USA

SteamVR (2015) Steam VR. www.steampowered.com. Accessed 17 Feb 2016

Tinwell A (2015) The uncanny valley in games and animation. CRC Press, Boca Raton, FL, USA

Wendel V, Gutjahr M, Göbel S, Steinmetz R (2013) Designing collaborative multi-player serious games. Educ Inf Technol 18(2):287–308

Yee N (2006) Motivations for play in online games. Cyber Psychol Behav 6(9):772–775

Authoring Processes and Tools

4

Florian Mehm, Ralf Dörner and Maic Masuch

Abstract

The creation of a serious game comprises a multitude of tasks ranging from idea finding to playtesting. A crucial step is the implementation of the game design as a computer system. The quality—and to a lesser extent, cost and future adaptability—of a serious game depends heavily on the processes chosen to coordinate and to support all authors involved. This chapter aims at presenting a foundation for specifying authoring processes and selecting authoring tools for an individual serious game project. It starts with looking at the challenges authors face when trying to accomplish their tasks, and discussing approaches that support the authors. On a more general level, basic concepts are introduced with user-centered design and agile development techniques that are often reflected in successful authoring processes for serious games. Finally, software tools for supporting authors are addressed. Here, two examples are examined in more detail: a general-purpose tool for authoring digital games, and an authoring tool that specializes in creating a certain subset of serious games.

F. Mehm (✉)
Technische Universität Darmstadt, Darmstadt, Germany
e-mail: florian@mehm.net

R. Dörner
RheinMain University of Applied Sciences, Wiesbaden, Germany

M. Masuch
University of Duisburg-Essen, Duisburg, Germany

© Springer International Publishing Switzerland 2016
R. Dörner et al. (eds.), *Serious Games*, DOI 10.1007/978-3-319-40612-1_4

4.1 Authoring Challenges

In this chapter, we focus on the task of assembling, aggregating, and integrating all parts of a game to build the final product. Several challenges have to be faced by the development team regarding this authoring task, especially during the production of a serious game.

One of the main differences between an entertainment game and a serious game production is the composition of the game production team. A serious game requires domain experts to contribute their knowledge of the game's domain (Marfisi-Schottmann et al. 2010). The better integrated into the team and its workflow the experts are, the better the game will be in the end. Therefore, the amount to which the authoring tool supports not only the game developers, but also the domain experts, is crucial. Since domain experts are usually not skilled in game programming or other typical game production tasks, the first challenge lies here in providing adequate workflows and interfaces for them.

Apart from consulting the game developers during the design, domain experts usually provide data for a game—such as target vital parameters for exergames or pools of tasks combined with learning content for educational games. First of all, the game and the authoring tool must be compatible with these data. In practice, this often means that the authoring tool must be extensible to allow the data to be handled. Then, the data input/integration must be carried out efficiently and effectively, with appropriate user interfaces. Since this data can be extremely varied, this is a challenge for providers of authoring tools.

Another challenging characteristic of serious games is *adapativity*. Many types of serious games require the game to be adaptive to the choices and characteristics of the players, in order to reach the game's characterizing goals as best as possible. This requires a specialized authoring tool in several regards. First of all, adaptivity often requires more content than a non-adaptive game to cater for all possible adaptive paths through the game. Therefore, content must be authored as efficiently as possible. Since adaptivity leads to non-linear, highly interactive games, it can be hard for an author to foresee how changes to the game will play out for different players. Therefore, an authoring tool should also support authors in handling game adaptivity as best as possible. Adaptivity and personalization aspects are discussed in more details in Chap. 7.

One more challenge is introduced by the size of game teams and the amount of authors who collaborate using an authoring tool. As noted above, serious game developers have to cooperate with domain experts. Apart from basic necessities of collaborative work—such as methods for merging changes made to the same game and allowing simultaneous work—the authoring tool should further support multi-user authoring, i.e., by adding task management, game designers can add tasks for domain experts to provide their specific data for game parts where needed.

In the following, we use the terms *authoring tool/system* in the same sense as Bulterman and Hardman (2005) defined it in the context of interactive multimedia presentations:

In order to achieve the characterizing goal of a serious game, the author is required to specify the individual parts of the according software system (in particular the game assets) and the relationships that exist among these assets. An *authoring system* allows the author to develop a narrative structure based on a collection of game assets and a creative intent that manages the serious game's visual and temporal flow.

We highlight the aspect of inter-relatedness that Bulterman and Hardman include in their description: instead of content creation tools and processes which aim at creating individual assets, authoring tools connect all the individual assets into a larger game.

Authoring tools for games have evolved in the same way as game production in general has evolved. The first digital games were created in hardware and had their rules and content "hard-wired" in a literal sense. However, as games grew in size and complexity, integrating content and building a final game needed to become data-driven. In this approach, a game engine is built in such a way that it is controlled by data; for example, a XML file encodes the logic and the required assets of the game. This very flexible data-driven approach has given rise to game editors and more advanced authoring tools. In practice, several approaches can be found in game projects: from minimal editors that only handle some tasks, to authoring tools that are intended for the whole production.

The positive aspects of using an authoring tool are especially important in the context of serious games. Among the main advantages are:

- *Cost efficiency*: Especially if an off-the-shelf authoring tool is used, costs can be reduced in several ways. For example, since these tools foster collaboration between different user groups, overhead due to collaboration is reduced.
- *Automation*: As will be seen in the examples below, authoring tools can leverage their use of abstraction and structured workflows to automate tasks found in game development.
- *Specific author support*: Authors can be supported in several ways, increasing their productivity as well as the quality of the overall product.

4.2   Authoring Approaches

4.2.1   Basic Approaches

In this section, we examine approaches that are shared by many authoring tools. In many cases, these approaches determine how the workflow of creating a game is presented to authors and how they can manipulate the game they are authoring.

The first basic principle lies in the connected aspects of *abstraction* and *structured authoring processes*. Since authors are not intended to work directly on game code in order to build the game, abstraction is a necessity for game authoring tools. In this regard, authoring tools have internal models of the game that abstract from the actual game code in different ways. For example, the game models of game editors—such as Unity (http://www.unity3d.com) or Unreal Engine (http://www.unrealengine.com)—are very closely related to the technical nature of the game engine (cf. Chap. 6), featuring scenes in which authors manipulate game objects realized as 3D meshes or 2D sprites directly. Concordantly, in such tools, authors often work directly with code in the form of scripting languages or visual programming languages.

Other authoring tools abstract more from the technological basis and are oriented more towards the structure of the game. Often, such tools are more aligned with certain genres than others. For instance, the StoryTec system (cf. Sect. 4.5.4 and Chap. 7) is built on an abstraction that borrows from theater or storytelling, with the basic building blocks being scenes which are manipulated by authors.

Closely linked to abstraction is structured authoring. The game model that is chosen is directly linked to a structure for the game. For example, a "scene" in a game could be composed of a background image and one or more actors in the scene. The authoring tool would then offer an interface to choose the background image and add the actors. This structured authoring then gives rise to a set of workflows that are useful to follow when working with the authoring tool. We will give examples of such workflows below.

A third important basic mechanism of authoring tools can be summarized as *providing different views to authors*, based on their specialization. Instead of providing the same interface to each user, authoring tools can adapt to their users and their specific background by providing views that only display those data that they are interested in. For example, a physio therapist providing parameters for a workout in an exergame is not interested in changing the positioning of 3D models or the game mechanics; instead, he or she is interested in providing parameters such as the target heart rate or the duration of the workout. Therefore, the authoring tool could hide the former data and provide an interface for which the latter content can be efficiently authored.

4.2.2 Author Support Mechanisms

Based on the basic mechanisms shown in the previous section, which often underlie authoring tools, more specific support mechanisms can be added to authoring tools.

Completeness checks can be added to various degrees. They draw upon the game models and structured authoring paradigms. By declaring syntactic and semantic rules for games, an authoring tool can check the game that is being authored and give suggestions how to continue or where more work is needed. The E-Adventure authoring tool has been extended with such as system (Moreno-Ger et al. 2009), as has the StoryTec tool described in Sect. 4.5.4. From a broader perspective, the

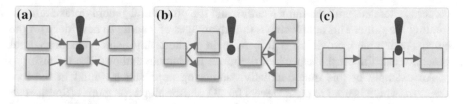

Fig. 4.1 Examples of completeness checks. **a** a dead end, since the game scene has no exits, **b** dead ends due to no connections to the rest of the game, **c** dead end due to a mistake in logic that never triggers an exit

practice of checking the game model against certain criteria is an example of model checking (Clarke et al. 1999).

A very basic check is for fields that need to be filled out in order for the game to work. If the game model requires a starting point for the game to be defined (such as a level in which the game starts), the authoring system can alert the author if no starting point has been defined. A more semantic check is that for a *dead end*. A dead end is a situation in which the game cannot be completed by a player. A simple case of this situation would be a scene or level which can never be left since an exit is missing. A more challenging example for a dead end is a situation where game logic prevents the player from completing the game. For example, a key might be required to unlock a door. However, the key requires a flag to be set in the game which can only be set by an action performed on the other side of the door. Especially if game parts can be quickly moved during authoring, e.g., by dragging and dropping them, this kind of error can be introduced.

Non-trivial cases of dead end detection require more advanced solutions. Several such approaches have been proposed. These include agent-based simulations, where a game is tested by artificial intelligences that randomly or semi-randomly test each option in the game. However, if the search space becomes too large due to too many options and possible game states, these approaches become unable to test all possible paths. Figure 4.1 shows an overview of types of dead end detection.

For the context of multiplayer games, Reuter et al. (2015) proposed a solution based on Petri nets, i.e., a graphical notation to describe transitions and flow relations in concurrent processes (Murata 1989). In this approach, the state of each player is represented by a token in a Petri net. Each possible game state is represented by a node in the net. This representation is derived automatically from the game model. The Petri net can then be analyzed by standardized tools, resulting in an analysis that shows dead ands. Since the case of a single player can be modelled by a Petri net with only one token, this approach is also valid for checking single-player games.

Using techniques of *procedural content generation* (described in Chap. 5 in more detail), some authoring tools provide a *mixed-initiative authoring approach*. In this approach, parts of the game are generated automatically by a procedural content generation algorithm. Then, the author can change the generated content or provide further rules which govern the generation process of the generator. This process is iterated, with the human author and the procedural generator take turns in creating the game. This approach has the advantages of leading to new ideas for the human author and providing a full game in a short time, since the procedural generator can fill out the aspects of the game the human author did not finish.

An example of this mixed-initiative authoring approach is found in the tool *Tanagra,* which is used to create levels for 2D platforming type games (Smith et al. 2010). The tool can make a first draft, creating a randomized level that is guaranteed to be playable. The author can then change the level, adding gaps or platforms. In the next iteration, the procedural generator will respect these manual changes and make sure that the level remains playable (note that this aspect is another example of the "completeness check" approach).

Similarly to mixed-initiative authoring tools, *iterative authoring* is concerned with testing the current state of the game early and often. This is closely related to the paradigm of rapid prototyping and the agile family of software development processes (see Sects. 4.3 and 4.4). In game development in general, rapid prototyping is used to assess early whether a game is fun or if central components are working correctly. A necessary requirement of rapid prototyping is taking care of keeping the current version of the game playable at all times so that it can be tested. This is also often a prerequisite for experts involved in the creation of a serious game to provide meaningful input.

Authoring tools can help here in the sense that they can support rapid prototyping, both from the creation and from the testing side. For creation with rapid prototyping in mind, the authoring tool can be created in such a way that it supports games that are only partially finished. For example, if the game works with placeholder content or when the game logic is not completely entered, this can allow testing the game at an early stage. Furthermore, since authoring tools usually feature a finished game engine, the game should usually be playable immediately since no more programming is required ideally.

For testing and receiving feedback, the authoring tool and especially the runtime environment can be augmented with support. The game engine can feature visualizations to allow authors to see the current state of the game engine and find faults in the game logic, for example. It can also include substantial logging facilities, saving a log of all the events in the game. Figure 4.2 shows how such a combination of authoring tool and rapid prototyping tool can be understood.

Ideally, the data can be analyzed, either with a special tool or in the authoring tool itself. As an example, the analysis tool can aggregate data from several playtests and present this data in the context of the authoring tool. One example is in a branching game, where the analysis can show the distribution of probabilities for players to choose one of the branches. This could indicate that most players only choose one branch, and the game author could think about whether the choice is obvious or not and whether the design should be changed at this point. Such a tool is further described by Mehm et al. (2010).

Another important area of support is *collaborative authoring* (Johnson and Valente 2008). This means that several game authors can work together on one game at the same time. A basic necessity is that the game can be safely edited at the

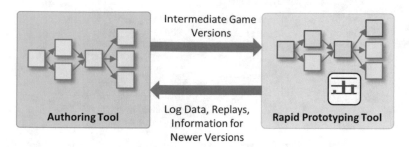

Fig. 4.2 The exchange of data between an authoring tool and a dedicated rapid prototyping tool. For example, the prototyping tool can log the paths players took in a branching game, along with logging all information that can be gathered from a playtest

same time by several authors; for example, using a mechanism where authors can lock a part of the game, so that only they can change this part of the game for a certain duration of time. Building upon this basic functionality, the authoring tool can cater for multiple author collaboration in several ways. For example, authors could be allowed to add notes and annotations to parts of the game, e.g., to indicate to a domain specialist or artist what has to be done. Furthermore, the authoring tool can provide different interfaces for each authoring role, such as a simplified interface that does not include game logic for domain specialists.

Even if an authoring tool has a simplified way of specifying game logic—such as a visual programming language—a non-programming author will still not be able to create more complex game logic that requires programming. One way of still allowing more complex game logic is by the use of *templates*. Templates in this sense are configurable parts of a game that encapsulate certain functionality. An example is given in the section on StoryTec (cf. Sect. 4.5.4). For an author, the added complexity is transparent, and the template can be instantiated and configured similarly to other authoring tool objects.

4.3   User-Centered Design

When engineers build a bridge, they can use the laws of physics and mathematical simulations to predict whether this new bridge will meet its goals (e.g., withstand certain wind forces or carry a certain weight). When game developers create a digital game, they have no way of simulating complex human behavior and calculating to which extent the goal to entertain the players will be achieved by the software they are designing. The developers can rely on previous experience. However, predictions based on experience are not as dependable as predictions founded on mathematical models. In serious games, the uncertainty whether the game will meet its goals is even higher compared to entertainment games. In addition to the goal to entertain, characterizing goals also need to be fulfilled. Moreover, even experienced entertainment game developers find it difficult to

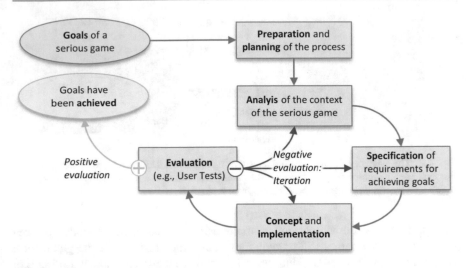

Fig. 4.3 Iterations in a user-centered design process (adapted from ISO 9241-210)

predict results when trying to achieve multiple, interdependent goals in a serious game.

Given the substantial level of uncertainty as to whether a game will be successful, a typical engineering approach of planning the game software at the beginning and then building it is too risky. Instead, *iterative* approaches have established themselves as best practice where designs are revised several times and the game is developed step by step. The basic principle is depicted in Fig. 4.3. Here, a crucial element is the evaluation phase. The evaluation results decide whether the development is finished or a new iteration needs to be started. Instead of calculating the degree of goal achievement, the current version of the game is simply tried out and assessed by either experts or, more usually, playtesters from the game's target group. There are several techniques available for conducting an evaluation, e.g., test sessions followed by *questionnaires* and *interviews,* or observing players during the game—where they might be asked to vocalize their thoughts, to make emotions or cognitive processes better observable ("*thinking aloud test*").

If the evaluation is not successful, developers might need to refine the concept (e.g., the game design) and change the implementation accordingly. The implementation does not need to be a fully functional and robust software system. To increase the number of iterations in the project duration, the first implementations might also be *prototypes* or *mockups* (Buxton 2007). Even *storyboards*, i.e., a serious of drawings that illustrate the gaming experience, or *paper prototypes*, i.e., a simple board game version of the digital game, can be used. If the evaluation reveals more fundamental issues, developers might need even to go back to analyzing and understanding the context of the serious game. For this, *scenario-based design* (Carroll 2000) can be used, where short stories are written that describe how a user will interact with the game. These stories are then discussed with users. The scenarios can be refined to use cases and described more formally, e.g., as *UML use case diagrams*. Thus, users of the game are not only regularly involved in the evaluation phase, but also during analysis or requirement specification. Hence, these iterative process models for developing software are called *user-centered*. In the literature, several approaches to *user-centered design* are described (Vredenburg et al. 2002). Some of them even have the status of ISO standards (e.g., EN ISO 9241-210, ISO/PAS 18152).

4.4 Agile Software Development

In technical terms, a serious game can be seen as a typical software product. Its development is characterized by the manufacturing of code and assets in a software development process. The umbrella term *software engineering* embraces all methods for design, development, and maintenance of applications. Roles, artifacts, a specific sequence of actions, and intermediate deliverables are meant both to control the project and to secure a successful outcome. Software engineering differs from project management, as it embraces all aspects of the production of software and not only the management of the production process. A profound overview can be found in (Sommerville 2015). Recently, developers shifted software engineering away from sequential construction process approaches (e.g., the waterfall model) towards more iterative and flexible models. Nowadays more and more software is developed using *agile software development* methods. "Agile" means that the development process does not follow a previously laid out, rigid plan; instead, it is flexible to adjust to changing requirements and software specifications. These changes are caused, for example, by insights gained during the development process. Agile development can be seen as a lightweight, lean, and self-organized approach, and there are many variations. By far the most popular methodology is *scrum*. A fundamental principle of scrum is the empirical insight that most software projects are far too complex to rely on the perfect plan. Scrum is empirical, incremental, and iterative, and accepts the unpredictability of the software development process as a whole, neglecting the traditional sequential approach. The methodology can be described as a framework consisting of values, roles, events, and artifacts (see Fig. 4.4).

There are essentially three different roles: (1) The *product owner* can be seen as the customer and should be represented by one person. He or she describes the functionality and scope of the planned software with items (also called *user stories*) and prioritizes them (e.g., as critical/must-have/nice-to-have) in a *product backlog*. A product owner stays on a certain meta-level of the project and may discuss scope and timeline, but is not concerned with technical aspects. (2) The *scrum team* consists of small groups (5–10) of developers or other project members that are self-organized, sometimes of cross-disciplinary profession. (3) The *scrum master* is responsible for a smooth production flow and acts as an interface between the team and the product owner. Hence, the scrum master can be seen as a facilitator whose

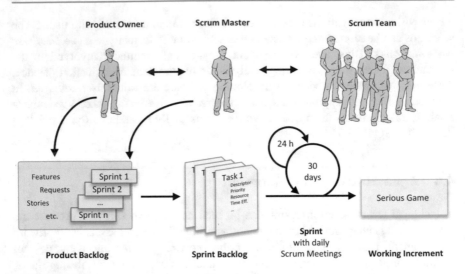

Fig. 4.4 Scrum framework overview

primary goal is to help others: Either the product owner (e.g., to transform the product vision into a product backlog) or the team (e.g., to eliminate impediments). This role is quite different from that of a project manager as it explicitly excludes resource management or the power of decision. As scrum puts emphasis on self-organization, the team has not only the responsibility for the work but also the right to make decisions, i.e., team members decide together which task they will work on.

A software development phase in scrum is called a *sprint*. It consists typically of a fixed, not extendable period of time—usually between one to four weeks. It starts with the sprint planning event, where the team assesses the effort, duration, and responsibility of tasks derived from items in the product backlog. The selected tasks necessary to bring the prototype closer to completion are listed in the sprint backlog. They form a prioritized to-do list, and the estimated time for their completion is depicted in a *burn down chart* (see Fig. 4.5). During the sprint, the team may not be disturbed by external stakeholders (who, for instance, request changes of requirements).

Priorities and items can be changed during a sprint while being processed, as team members constantly review and evaluate these items during the daily scrum meeting. This concise stand-up meeting informs team members about goals met yesterday, goals planned for today, and any obstacle that might prevent today's completion of items. Issues have to be solved by the scrum master and responsible team members outside the meeting. This constant reflection and evaluation is called *backlog refinement*. To a very large extent, it is responsible for the flexibility of scrum as an agile method.

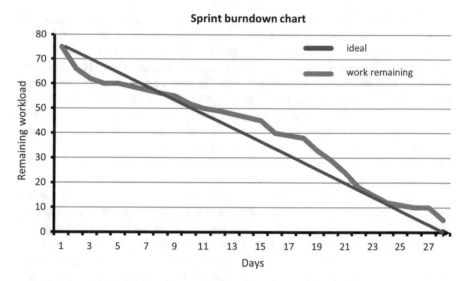

Fig. 4.5 A sprint burndown chart is a visual representation of the remaining work for a current sprint. It may differ from the ideal completion rate to the worse (tasks have to be dropped) or to the better (tasks can be added) and it is a constant reminder for the team to hold the desired deadline. Thus, as a side effect, it enforces a strong priority management

After each sprint, completed (and uncompleted) tasks are reviewed, as well as working conditions of the office. This retrospective aims at improving the production process and workflow itself. At the end of each sprint, the game is expected to be in a working state and able to be demonstrated to both the product owner and external stakeholders (e.g., customers or potential users). Specifically for serious games, the demonstration can be used to allow experts (such as domain experts) to better grasp the concepts, potentials, constraints, and usage scenarios of the game being developed and in turn to provide higher quality feedback. A *scrum of scrums* can be used to build up a hierarchical structure of large teams (200+ members), with team members or scrum masters as ambassadors informing other teams about what their team achieved, what they are now doing, and any impediments.

There are many more details about scrum; a recommended follow-up reference can be found in (Rubin 2012) or the original description in (Beedle and Schwaber 2002). There are a number of other agile software engineering frameworks, but scrum remains the most prominent among them all. What makes it so successful? Many empirical experiences, as well as research studies, show that scrum actually works. It is a non-trivial, but easy to understand concept that ideally results in increased productivity, better quality, higher customer satisfaction, and increased well-being of developers. It tackles one of the biggest issues in software engineering: The flexible response to requirements changes during the development process. It forces developers to focus on the most important tasks in a strict time frame while also iterating short feedback loops with the user. However, scrum is not a silver bullet per se. There are projects with unresolvable issues where even the most talented developers and the most advanced software engineering methods fail. Also, it is often necessary to adapt the agile method used to the individual project and individual development team (e.g., sprint length or team size).

In general, game development projects are good candidates for critical projects. They are complex multimedia projects, running with cutting edge technology and often alpha-status drivers and hardware. They consist of cross-disciplinary teams with many junior and few senior developers. The vast majority of game projects are underfunded, beside many other issues. Serious games, due to their peculiar financing (cf. Chap. 11) and their inherent claim to achieve more goals than entertainment, even aggravate that situation. In such a situation, scrum is particularly helpful.

As an agile methodology, scrum is very well suited to follow a user-centered design approach in a serious game project. Often, designers of a serious game project need to follow an explorative process model, as the characterizing goal of such an application cannot be specified complete at the beginning of the project. User testing needs to be conducted with early prototypes to adapt to evaluation results found during the development process. Here, incremental refinement comes in handy. As each iteration after a sprint can be demonstrated to the product owner, testing can be accomplished in a very early product stage. This results in a systematic risk management, where severe risks can be recognized and anticipated early. Here, the product owner plays an important role in a serious game development process. Scrum even adapts quite well to the different roles and skills of a customer, who is represented by the product owner or the customers themselves. In certain special cases, it is also possible to combine product owner and scrum master in one person, e.g., when a team decides to produce their own serious game (Schild et al. 2010) or to have more than one product owner, each representing one characterizing goal of the serious game. Scrum can be so flexible, it also adapts to situations like these.

4.5 Authoring Tools

4.5.1 Categorization of Tools

We start our overview of authoring tools with a categorization. The first scale that we analyze is the dependence on additional tools. One extreme is an authoring tool that tries to facilitate as many game production tasks in them as possible. At the other end of the spectrum is an authoring tool that focuses on the task to aggregate data from a multitude of other tools. This scale of *task universality* is also reflected in the discussion of tool chains in this chapter. Note that game authoring tools can change their position on this scale based on their extensibility by adding functionality using plugins. For example, Unity 3D (see Sect. 4.5.3) has very few content creation facilities in the standard version, but can be extended vastly to include simple 3D modeling, painting, and other tools.

Next, authoring tools can be specialized for a certain genre of games, or can be more versatile with regard to genres. This characteristic of *genre universality* is usually reflected in the complexity of the authoring tool: If only one or few genres are supported, authoring tool providers can make many assumptions and therefore provide many functions that are specialized for a genre. For example, several authoring tools are specialized for the genre of point-and-click adventure games, and therefore can make assumptions, such as: No multiplayer system will be required. The game will have a certain structure consisting of screens, characters, inventory items, dialogues, etc. The disadvantage of such a specialized authoring tool is that creating games that do not conform completely to the genre is harder than with a general-purpose authoring tool. For example, if an author wants to add a racing sub-game to a point-and-click adventure game to spice up the gameplay, this can be almost impossible in a dedicated point-and-click authoring tool.

A further characteristic of authoring tools is the *abstraction level*. A low level of abstraction would mean that authors work with objects and constructs that are very close to the game programming side. For example, for moving a character across the screen in an authoring tool with low abstraction, the author could handle the object as an image drawn at a certain location that is animated by changing a position vector variable. This would be very close to how a game programmer might implement this directly in a game engine. This low level of abstraction, however, allows the creation of many types of games.

On the other end of the spectrum are highly abstract authoring tools. In such an authoring tool, high-level constructs such as "character," "dialog," or "goal" could be implemented. Instead of controlling the character directly using code, the author would only specify parameters—such as the look of the character and the initial position—and the game engine would handle the rest. Instead of a programming language, the authoring tool would feature a domain-specific language, for example, one in which the possible goals and actions of a character could be specified. As can be seen in the difference of semantics, the latter type of authoring tools is more restrictive for authors, as they build on certain structures for games. Instead of handling only low-level objects such as textures moving across the screen—which could have varying semantics—the abstract authoring tool would know only about characters, dialog, etc. For a discussion of the semantics in authoring tools, see (Spierling et al. 2006).

4.5.2 Toolchains and Ecosystems

In practice, it is rare to use only one tool to create a complete game. Rather, several tools are used to assemble a game, e.g., for creating and editing different types of assets. This is due to the need to provide specialized tools for content producers that would be hard or impossible to integrate into one tool.

Some game creation tools integrate other tools for content production into their features. This can be due to either the intent to provide all necessary tools in one package, or to the evolution of an authoring tool from a content production tool.

The former case is true for the *Game Maker* (Overmars 2004) game creation toolkit; for example, it adds a sprite editor that can be used both to create sprites for a game, and use them immediately in the game. The latter case is exemplified by the 3D content creation toolkit *Blender* (http://www.blender.org), which started out as a 3D digital content creation (DCC) tool and later was augmented with a game engine. Today, 3D and 2D assets created and configured in Blender can be immediately used in the Blender Game Engine.

However, in practice, integrated content production tools are often lacking in comparison to dedicated DCC tools, and therefore are mostly used by novice game creators or those untrained with dedicated tools. For example, a dedicated image editing tool such as *Gimp* or *Adobe Photoshop* features many more filters, brushes, and tools than an integrated content creation tool in an authoring tool can provide.

When several tools are added to the game production process, they are usually arranged into a *toolchain*: Tools are arranged in a chain, where the content created in one tool is used in the next. However, in game production, a toolchain usually refers not only to the tools used, but also to the associated processes. This includes practical and necessary conventions, such as naming rules for files and management of files, i.e., in a content management tool. Furthermore, it usually includes review processes and a distribution of responsibilities in the team. Figure 4.6 gives an overview of a possible ecosystem of tools used in game production.

Finished assets are then integrated into the game using an authoring tool. Ideally, the assets can be directly integrated. This can include necessary metadata (such as annotations for learning content) that has already been added as part of moving through the toolchain.

Depending on the toolchain chosen, the output of the authoring tool (i.e., the completely assembled game) could be further processed and finalized by other tools in the chain. For example, if content is produced in high quality (high resolution,

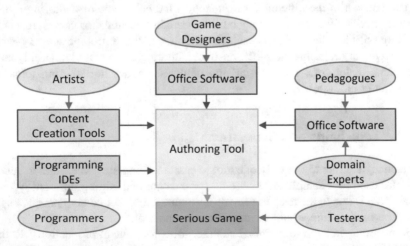

Fig. 4.6 An example ecosystem of users with different roles and different programs, working to create the necessary assets and game design to be combined in the authoring tool

detailed 3D models, etc.), this content could be compressed down to different sizes based on the target platform (e.g., low resolution to older mobile devices, and high quality for PC platforms). Other tools can be used to package the game for different platforms (such as packaging and signing a mobile application) and then finally to upload the game so it can be distributed.

4.5.3 Example: Unity

Unity is a game engine with a prominent game editor associated closely with it. It started out as a Mac-only application in 2005, and was later also released in 2009 for Microsoft Windows. It is able to target all major PC, mobile, and console platforms. Since Unity makes very few assumptions about the games created, it is very compatible to many game genres. Despite the name, it supports both 2D and 3D games (including virtual reality applications).

The tool is a clear example of the "game editor" side of authoring tools. However, the use of the editor is not only restricted to building a level—it also features code editing. The unmodified workflow of Unity is mainly oriented towards programmers to get a full game working.

When a new project is started in Unity, the user sees an empty scene. This scene can be filled with content either by adding 3D primitive objects such as planes or cubes, or by importing 3D assets created in a dedicated 3D modeling tool. A hierarchical view of all objects in the scene allows an author to see all the objects and to quickly navigate to them. When an object is selected, the properties of the object can be edited quickly in the *inspector* tab.

When only content is added, the game will not be interactive in any way when started. Unity is based on a *component-based architecture* for games, indicating that each game object is composed of several components—each of which handles a specific subset of the object's behavior. The basic component all objects in Unity share is a *transform* behavior, which indicates where in the 3D/2D world the object is placed and oriented.

A behavior created by a programmer can update the state of the game object each frame, reacting to the input of the player, to other objects or the overall game state. Some simple and often-used behaviors are supplied along with Unity, such as the *FirstPersonController*, which realizes a first-person camera control using a mouse and keyboard.

Unity has been used for several serious games. Due to the close cooperation with Serious Games Interactive (http://www.seriousgames.net), the engine has been used for several games of the company, prominently the "Global Conflicts" series (Buch and Egenfeldt-Nielsen 2007, see also Chap. 12). The games "Escape from Wilson Island" and "Woodment" have been created in Unity as well (Wendel et al. 2013).

Unity by itself has no specific support for the creation of serious games, especially when it comes to integration of serious game content. This is mainly due to Unity being designed to be very flexible and not specialized for a specific gameplay or genre. However, Unity lends itself very well to extensions, which includes the editor as well as the engine. This extensibility starts with the scripting facilities described above: When a component is created by a programmer, it is treated in the same fashion as the built-in components of Unity. This means that it can be attached to any object, and will be shown in the editor in the same way as a regular component, including the possibility to change the properties of the component in the editor. In the case of a serious game for the treatment of phobias, for example, a dedicated component can be written that turns the general-purpose Unity authoring tool into a software tool where a psychiatrist can change certain parameters of a serious game in order to adapt the game to the patient's progress.

The next level of extensibility can be reached with *custom inspectors*. In this case, the look of the inspector of Unity can be changed for a custom component. For example, imagine that the target intensity of a training session in a game for health should be defined with a continuous value over time indicating the target intensity at that time. Without a custom inspector, we might realize this with a set of integer values that the user has to enter, e.g., one value at each minute. With a custom inspector, the same input can be realized as a curve that can be manipulated instantly. This would give much better and immediate feedback to the user and be much easier to understand due to the improved visualization.

Editor scripts are a tool for improving Unity even further. These scripts are not intended for the runtime of the engine, but instead focus on the editor. Using such scripts, the user interface of the editor can be thoroughly adapted to one's needs, including adding new menu items, panels and drawing additional information in the 3D viewport. Using editor scripts, the interface can be adapted to be well suited for entering the data required for serious games.

Apart from scripts for extending Unity's functionality, *plugins* in the form of pre-compiled code can be used to extend Unity. One common scheme is to handle the integration of the plugin as an editor script and to have the plugin functionality in a dynamically linked library, which can offer more performance and protect the source code of the plugin. Furthermore, Unity can be connected to Web services, which allows content to be loaded from sources on the Web, or to move costly computations to a Web service.

Unity 3D Use Case

This use case utilizes Unity in the production of a serious game for training new employees in an international company, and is analyzed based on the previously described functionality of Unity 3D.

The goal of the game is to inform new employees of the company's vision and specific company policies and procedures (e.g., how to book a trip via a travel agency). For this purpose, players are placed in a 3D version of the company headquarters, which is populated by *content markers* with which the players can unlock new information.

The graphical content of the game is built in 3D modeling software and imported into Unity as a set of assets. The serious purpose of the game is being taken care of, since the virtual world is modelled to represent the real world location as closely as possible.

In this case, serious game content is primarily content markers with the associated learning content. For these markers, a new *component* is created, which has custom properties for specifying the associated content, e.g., from which area the content comes from (i.e., corporate vision, management processes) and which URLs in the company intranet can be visited to find more information. This information can be easily added using the *inspector tab* in Unity.

To generate a map for players to help them find all content markers, an *editor script* can be created that will export an image of the game surroundings from above, highlighting content marker positions.

For maintenance purposes, the content of the game should be changeable after the game has been released (e.g., by changing the URLs when they change or become invalid). Since Unity has a relatively complex user interface even when using custom components and inspectors, we can opt to instead build an alternative interface as a stand-alone application. This is an example where maintenance of a game is simpler using a specialized tool instead of the authoring tool. The configuration of the game is written to an . xml file that is placed on the server the game runs on. A good pattern for implementation is to have the Unity game ask the embedding web page via JavaScript where the .xml file can be loaded from. Then the game loads this data and fills the components with the loaded data. In this way, the game can be moved to any other web server, and is not closely tied to a hard-coded URL of the .xml file.

4.5.4 Example: StoryTec

StoryTec (Mehm et al. 2013) is an authoring tool developed explicitly for the creation of serious games. As the name implies, StoryTec is geared towards projects that feature some kind of narration—but it can also be used for other purposes. This authoring tool is composed of an editor and a runtime engine. A game is created in the editor by aggregating all assets that have been created for the game and by combining them to form an interactive game. The finished game can be exported for a multitude of platforms. Figure 4.7 shows a screenshot of the user interface of StoryTec.

A game in StoryTec is built up in a similar way as a movie or a theater play. The basic unit is a *scene*. This metaphor has been chosen since in other narrative contexts, a scene is a smaller part of a larger experience, which is coherent when concerning actors, props, and stage setup. In terms of a game, this means that important properties define the scene—mainly the assets that are used in the scene.

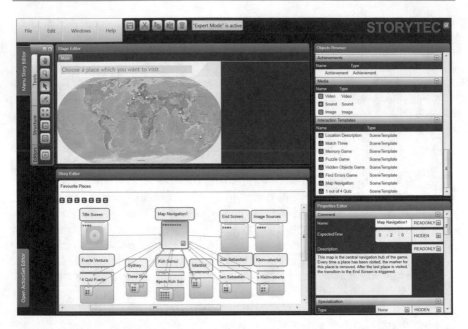

Fig. 4.7 The user interface of StoryTec. The Story Editor in the *lower left part* visualizes the overall game model, while the Stage Editor in the *upper left part* allows authors to change parameters of one scene interactively

Scenes can be nested inside each other. This is similar to an act in a play: For example, all the scenes in the act (common parent scene) share the same background. In game terms, this is comparable to a level. Objects in the scene such as images, buttons, characters, or non-visualized objects such as timers are placed in each scene. Nested scenes all share the common objects of a common parent scene. This is useful for establishing a common background in all scenes or for adding user interface elements that should be visible everywhere. Figure 4.8 gives an example how the game model of StoryTec can be visualized.

Scenes can be connected by *transitions*. In the editor, transitions are visualized as arrows that connect a start and end scene. These arrows can be easily drawn, changed, and removed. While a transition indicates that the two scenes are connected, it does not mean that the transition will actually be used in the game. For example, if the game is branching, several transitions leave one start scene, and the players might see only one of the branches during a play session. Furthermore, opposed to common forms of theater and movies, games are interactive and usually progress only when the player interacts with them. Therefore, transitions have to be triggered by the game.

The mechanism for triggering actions such as a transition between scenes is handled in StoryTec using a visual programming language. In such a language, instead of writing programming code, users manipulate a visual diagram which shows how the program works. In StoryTec's game model, such a program can be

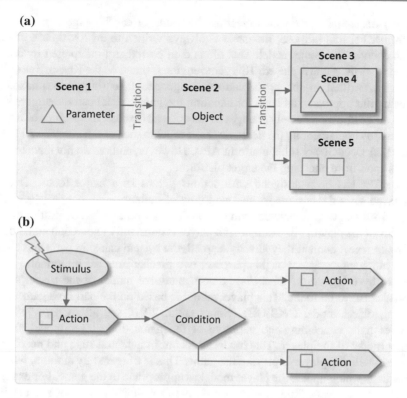

Fig. 4.8 The game model of StoryTec. **a** Scenes connected via transitions. **b** An ActionSet, indicating what actions should be carried out by the game in response to a user input (stimulus)

attached to many important events (*stimuli*), such as when the player makes an input or when a timer runs out. The simplest *action* would be to change the current scene. With only this functionality, one could already create interactive comics by adding clickable hotspots to images and handling the clicks on the hotspots with transitions to other scenes with appropriate comic strips. However, StoryTec offers many more actions, including: Playing audiovisual content, starting and stopping timers, changing properties of objects (e.g., showing or hiding user interface elements), and more.

In order to handle different states of the game, users can select between different branches of action sequences in a tree-like structure. In this way, one visual script can react to different user inputs or adapt itself to the current state of the game. For example, if the player already failed several times at a task, the author can add a condition that chooses a sequence of actions that includes hints for the player to help him or her with the current problem. *Conditions* are formulated using Boolean logic, again in a visual fashion by visualizing the individual slots where something can be changed (which variable to use, which operator to use) and how the individual terms are bracketed. The lower part of Fig. 4.8 illustrates such a program.

After an author has finished creating the game, it can be exported to various platforms. For this purpose, the game is always written to an XML-based format which encodes the game model. This file is then parsed and interpreted by a game engine when the game is played. This game engine is based on the Kha engine (http://kha.tech/), written in the cross-platform language Haxe (http://www.haxe.org). By using this approach, all code for handling the game model can remain the same across all platforms. The only changes to the code are to cater to specifics of a target platform, by implementing the necessary calls to APIs such as the graphics API (e.g., DirectX or OpenGL) or other platform APIs. However, authors do not have to work on this apart from choosing the target platform.

StoryTec has been designed with serious games as a major focus. This has influenced several decisions for the workflow of authors.

Adaptation. Games created using StoryTec can be adapted at runtime to the specifics of the player. For example, if a player is constantly underchallenged due to having to repeat content they already learned, the system can skip parts and choose other, more appropriate. For this purpose, two mechanisms are important:

First, by using *player modelling*, a computational model of the player's characteristics has to be found. This player model is based on the narrative game-based learning object model (NGLOB) (Göbel et al. 2010, see also Chap. 7) which includes traits concerning the narrative of the game, the player model and the learner model of the player. This model starts out in a neutral state and needs to be updated while the player is playing the game. This is triggered by authors, who can add actions which update the player model as appropriate to the game. For example, if a player takes very little time on a task, the probability that he or she has fully understood the underlying principle is very high, which means that the game can be adapted to become more challenging.

Second, this adaptation is done in the following step, in which the appropriate content for a player is chosen. In this step, StoryTec introduces *free transitions*, which are an extension of the transitions described above. If an author places several free transitions between scenes, this indicates that the scenes are connected. However, it also marks the target scenes as equivalent in the sense that they all make sense as a next scene, and different in the sense that they are differently suited to various player models. When a player input indicates that the scenes should be left, the author triggers an action that chooses one of the connected scenes, based on maximizing the fit between the current player model and the target scene's model.

In practice, this system can be used in various ways. A common pattern is that the tasks in the beginning of the game are used to assess the player model—since in the beginning, nothing is known about the player. As the game progresses, the systems understands the player better and better, and therefore can make more adaptive choices. However, each decision can still influence the player model even in the later stages of the game.

Domain-Specific Modes. In situations where several authors are involved in the creation of a serious game, it is important to provide each author with an appropriate interface to use. For example, in a larger production, one author might be primarily concerned with entering the gameplay using the authoring tool, while another author might be a domain specialist who cares primarily about domain-specific properties. These might be vital parameters for a game for health, or learning content for an educational game.

In StoryTec, this need for appropriate interfaces is based on the game model. All attributes of an object or a scene can be tagged as being appropriate or inappropriate for different author groups. When an author chooses their role after starting the authoring tool, all the properties that are not relevant for this role are hidden and the interface therefore made simpler.

Interaction Templates. It is not an easy task to provide authors with the possibility of creating non-trivial games while simultaneously not requiring programming using a conventional programming language. One method to provide gameplay possibilities to non-programmer authors that are too complex to be programmed using a visual programming language is to provide *interaction templates*. These templates provide a certain kind of gameplay when they are used. They are encapsulated, and only provide a small set of configuration parameters for authors. In practice, they are used in the same way as an object in StoryTec is used. One simple example is the "puzzle" interaction template of StoryTec. This interaction template realizes a puzzle created from an image that the author provided. The image is cut automatically into parts; during runtime, pieces can be dragged and dropped into position using either a mouse or a touch device, as appropriate. The whole game logic is contained in the interaction template; the author only has to provide the image that is used as the basis for the puzzle, and specify the reactions of the game to the events that the player solved or failed the puzzle after a certain time.

4.6   Summary and Questions

Using authoring tools in a serious game project offers advantages—especially in the areas of cost efficiency, automation, and author support. Tools are able to provide different views on the game project for different author roles and enable these authors to become more productive. Moreover, they can provide feedback (e.g., via completeness checks or *dead end testing*) to the authors. As serious game projects are inherently interdisciplinary, there is no single author. Thus, tools are particularly helpful as they can support the collaboration of multiple authors and the integration of their contributions in one game system. Often, not a single tool is used; toolchains have to be conceived. As a result, the tools reflect the authoring process and structure for the creation of serious game software. When creating the authoring process of an individual serious game, it is worth considering fundamental methodologies generally used in interactive software. Here, user-centered design highlights the necessity for iterative process models that strive for continuous testing and evaluation of the serious game while it is produced. The insights gathered during evaluation are fed back to the revision of the game in the next cycle. Second, agile software development techniques are suited to serious game development, as they provide flexibility to react extensively on evaluation and playtesting results. They also offer mechanisms to cope with the uncertainty inherent in serious game development due to lack of experience.

Check your understanding of this chapter by answering the following questions:

- What are the categories that can be used to describe authoring tools?
- What are the basic authoring tool mechanisms that most authoring tools share?
- What are advanced author support mechanisms that are included in some authoring tools?
- How can user-centered design be reflected in an authoring tool?
- Search for other authoring tools for game development. GameMaker:Studio is an example of an authoring tool (it can be found at http://www.yoyogames.com/studio). Compare Unity and the authoring tool you found. Name criteria for the comparison that are of special importance in the case of serious game development.
- How does a method from software engineering such as scrum shape the authoring process of a serious game?
- What other software engineering concepts might be suitable for serious game development?
- Which features could an authoring tool for serious games offer in order to support agile software development techniques?
- Examine an authoring tool that has not been described in detail in this chapter (such as Blender, Unreal Engine, Game Maker, Storytelling Alice, or E-Adventure) and analyze it in terms of the categories described in Sect. 4.2. Describe the game model that the authoring tool uses, and how it is presented to the authors. Is the authoring tool especially suited for serious game authoring? If so, what features are well suited for serious games?

Recommended Literature[1]

Gibson J (2014) Introduction to game design, prototyping, and development: From concept to playable game with Unity and C#. Addison Wesley—*this book is an example of books that explain game development by sticking closely to a general-purpose game development tool. In this case, Unity is used but there are also similar books available that use other game development software (e.g., the unreal engine)*

---

[1]For game development tools, online materials are also of interest. For instance, Unity is widely used in professional and amateur projects, and therefore a multitude of free online resources for learning and getting help exists. The tutorials provided on Unity's homepage (http://unity3d.com) are a good starting point.
No single conference or journal dedicated primarily to authoring tools for games exists. Research on serious games' authoring tools is often published in outlets for serious games, such as the *International Journal of Game-Based Learning*, *Game Days*, or the *European Conference on Game-Based Learning*

Keith C (2010) Agile Game Development with SCRUM. Addison Wesley—*an introductory text in agile software development techniques and how they can be applied to game development in general*

Lightbown D (2015) Designing the user experience of game development tools. Apple Academic Press Inc.—*an interesting read for persons who want to provide authors with custom-tailored tools*

References

Beedle M, Schwaber K (2002) Agile development with scrum. Prentice Hall

Buch T, Egenfeldt-Nielsen S (2007) The learning effect of "Global conflicts: palestine. In: Paper presented at the Media@Terra conference, Athens

Bulterman D, Hardman L (2005) Structured multimedia authoring. ACM Trans Multimedia Comput Commun Appl 1(1):89–109

Buxton B (2007) Sketching user experiences: getting the design right and the right design. Morgan Kaufmann, San Francisco

Carroll JM (2000) Making use: scenario-based design of human-computer interactions. MIT Press, Cambridge

Clarke E, Grumberg O, Peled D (1999) Model checking. MIT Press, Cambridge

Göbel S, Wendel V, Ritter C, Steinmetz R (2010). Personalized, adaptive digital educational games using narrative game-based learning objects. In: Entertainment for education. digital techniques and systems, lecture notes in computer science, vol 6249. Springer, Berlin/Heidelberg, 438

Johnson W, Valente A (2008) Collaborative authoring of serious games for language and culture. Proc SimTecT 2008

Marfisi-Schottman I, George S, Tarpin-Bernard F (2010) Tools and methods for efficiently designing serious games. In: Proceedings of 4th European conference on games-based learning. Academic Publishing International, Reading, 226

Mehm F, Wendel V, Göbel S, Steinmetz R (2010) Bat cave: a testing and evaluation platform for digital educational games. In: Proceedings of 3rd European conference on games based learning. Academic Conferences International, Reading, 251

Mehm F, Göbel S, Steinmetz R (2013) An authoring tool for educational adventure games: concept, game models and authoring processes. Int J Game-Based Learn 3(1):63–79

Moreno-Ger P, Fuentes-Fernández R, Sierra-Rodríguez J, Fernández-Manjón B (2009) Model-checking for adventure videogames. Inf Softw Technol 51(3):564–580

Murata T (1989) Petri nets: properties, analysis and applications. Proc IEEE 77(4):541–558

Overmars M (2004) Teaching computer science through game design. Computer 37(4):81–83

Reuter C, Göbel S, Steinmetz R (2015) Detecting structural errors in scene-based multiplayer games using automatically. In: Proceedings of found digital games 2015

Rubin K (2012) Essential scrum: a practical guide to the most popular agile process. Addison-Wesley

Schild J, Walter R, Masuch M (2010) ABC-Sprints: adapting scrum to academic game development courses. In: FDG'10—Proceedings of 5th international conference on the foundations of digital games

Smith G, Whitehead J, Mateas M (2010) Tanagra: a mixed-initiative level design tool. In: Proceedings of foundations of digital games. ACM, New York, p 209

Sommerville I (2015) Software engineering, 10th edn. Pearson

Spierling U, Weiß A, Müller W (2006) Towards accessible authoring tools for interactive storytelling. In: Proceedings of 3rd international conference on technologies for interactive digital storytelling and entertainment. Springer, Berlin/Heidelberg, p 169

Vredenburg K, Mao JY, Smith PW, Carey T (2002) A survey of user-centered design practice. In: Proceedings of ACM SIGCHI, pp 471–478

Wendel V, Gutjahr M, Göbel S, Steinmetz R (2013) Designing collaborative multiplayer serious games. Educ Inform Technol 2(18):287–308

Content and Content Production

5

Florian Mehm and Benjamin Guthier

Abstract

Once a game design has been created and production begins, a game development team's two main activities are programming and content production. While a relatively small, experienced programming team can provide the necessary support for a state-of-the-art game, an art department and other departments have to produce the game *content*. In this chapter, we examine the production of content, including an analysis of what kinds of content exist in serious games, technical implications of the different kinds, and content production management. We also provide an introduction into procedural content generation, i.e., techniques to produce content algorithmically. Finally, we provide considerations for integrating serious content, and how the integration should be reflected in the organization of the overall game production.

5.1 Overview

In this chapter, we examine the content of serious games and the production processes behind it. We look at content not from the perspective of game design (that was done in Chap. 3), but rather from the perspective of all the content produced based on the game design. This includes all elements of the game that can be seen or heard: 3D models, images, sounds and user interface elements, as well as content

F. Mehm (✉)
Technische Universität Darmstadt, Darmstadt, Germany
e-mail: florian@mehm.net

B. Guthier
University of Mannheim, Mannheim, Germany

© Springer International Publishing Switzerland 2016
R. Dörner et al. (eds.), *Serious Games*, DOI 10.1007/978-3-319-40612-1_5

in other forms, such as task pools for educational games, or dialogue structures for games with character dialogues.

Looking closely at the content of serious games is warranted by the large influence the content has on the effect of a game on the player. Even if the game design has a certain intended effect, this effect can be changed considerably by the content. For example, the way in which content is produced influences the realism of the game, varying from abstract, to cartoon-like, to photorealistic. If content is produced without a clear art direction that pulls everything together, the game can appear cheap, as if it were pulled together from different sources.

Closely connected to this aspect is the associated cost of producing game content. In general, photorealistic content is the most expensive one, requiring state-of-the-art content generation tools and specially trained artists. For example, current physics-based game engines reach their level of photorealism by using 3D models and textures captured from reality using photogrammetry, thus requiring artists to capture the materials from reality. In contrast, a flat-shaded cartoon look can be achieved much more easily and less costly.

Similarly connected is the associated need for a state-of-the-art game engine and hardware. Especially for serious games that are not only played by well-versed gamers or company employees who have high-performance hardware at their fingertips, it is necessary to include older or mobile hardware that is not capable of running the latest game engines with all their features. The level of content quality and realism also has an effect on how broadly the game can be distributed and used.

Not only the content itself, but also the way in which it is produced, has an influence on the game's quality and cost. If production is not well managed, required content might be completed too late, priorities might be given to the wrong content, and content might need to be recreated as it does not fit with the rest of the game. Especially if this is found out in the later stages of game production, it can result in costly additional work. Therefore, managing the content production is an important topic that will also be considered in this chapter.

In game development, an individual piece of content is often referred to as an *asset*. For example, game engines such as Unity 3D use this term for any piece of content that is imported and then managed by the game engine. An asset can also refer to several pieces of content that belong together and are interrelated, such as the 3D mesh, textures, and animation data that are connected to build an avatar.

In the following, we will first give an overview of all the types of content that are usually found in a serious game. This is followed by a look at the game production pipeline from a technical viewpoint, highlighting how different kinds of assets are created, and what steps are required before they are ready to be loaded into the game. Procedural (algorithmic) content generation as an alternative to manual content generation will also be explained. We conclude our look at content in serious games with an overview of content management and content integration in serious games.

5.2   Definition of Content

We begin by a definition of content. This definition is the same for serious games and entertainment games. In both cases, it is common practice to separate the game engine from the content of the game. The game engine consists of code written by a programmer in a language like C++ that is compiled to run on the intended hardware platform. It contains the core functionality of the game and encompasses aspects like rendering, sound, player interface, and event processing. Details about game engines will be presented in Chap. 6. While the game engine specifies *how* the game data is processed, the content assets are *what* needs to be processed.

The *content* of a game consists of assets, often designed by artists. Examples include avatars, houses, trees, other related objects, and sounds. At runtime, the content is brought to life by the game engine.

Separating the game engine code from the asset data has many advantages. Creating an entire game engine from scratch takes a lot of effort, and a team of experienced software developers is required. If, on the other hand, the game engine code is separated from the game content, a new serious game can be created by reusing a suitable existing game engine and by only developing the content of the game. Game designers and artists can thus focus on the creation of game assets, while only a small number of programmers is necessary to adapt the existing engine code.

In the following, we give an overview of the different types of content that can be found in a serious game.

5.2.1   Triangle Meshes

Triangle meshes are the main method how the shapes of objects in a 3D game are described. Every character, vehicle, or prop that we see in a game is modeled by a large number of triangles that approximate its surface. If the triangles are small enough, even round shapes can be approximated well. The reason why triangles are so popular is because they are the simplest possible planar 2D shape. They also remain triangles under most geometric transformations. The triangles themselves consist of exactly three vertices: that is, three points in a three-dimensional space. A vertex, on the other hand, is generally part of multiple triangles which all meet in this particular point in space. A subset of the triangles in a mesh may be grouped into a submesh according to common visual properties. Figure 5.1 shows an example of a graphical object with its mesh representation and its submeshes.

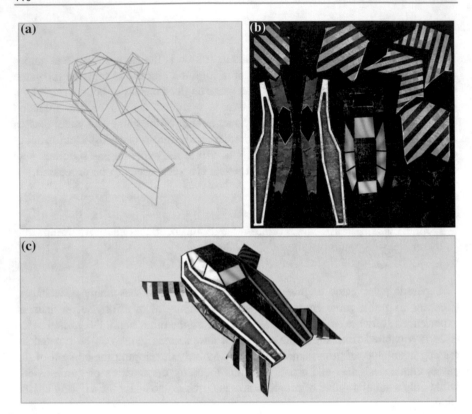

Fig. 5.1 A graphical object as an asset: **a** mesh, **b** textured submeshes, **c** final object (from Mildner et al. 2014)

5.2.2 Materials

A triangle mesh only describes the *shape* of a three-dimensional object, but not the visual appearance of its surface. All the necessary information on how to render a mesh is stored as a *material*. Each submesh of a mesh can be assigned a different material. For example, a character's arms are rendered using a skin material, the clothes use a cloth texture, and the tool the character is using has a wood material assigned to it.

Closely related to the material is a shader program that runs on the graphics card when the material is rendered. It calculates how light interacts with the material to produce a color value for each point on the surface of the object. To achieve this goal, materials come with a number of texture maps for various purposes.

5.2.3 Textures

A *texture* is a raster image that is mapped to a mesh to add a more detailed structure without increasing the number of triangles used for its representation. The elements of a texture are referred to as *texels* to distinguish them from the pixels on the screen. In its simplest form, each texel specifies the diffuse color value at the corresponding position of the mesh.

However, textures do not always need to specify a color. They can also define other surface attributes such as glossiness, transparency, bumps on the surface, or the amount of ambient light that reaches the surface ("ambient occlusion"). In order to map a texture onto a triangle, a two-dimensional (u,v) coordinate is assigned to each of its vertices to define the triangle's location in the texture. This process is called UV mapping; the letters "U" and "V" denote the two axes of the 2D texture. An example of textures is shown in Fig. 5.1. As an optimization step, a texture may contain the same raster image in multiple resolutions, so that the appropriate texture resolution can be chosen at runtime. This depends on the distance of the mesh from the camera.

5.2.4 Animation

The process of animating characters or other objects differs greatly depending on the number of dimensions. Animating 2D artwork is very similar to how traditional cartoons are made, where each frame of an animation is drawn individually. In 3D, *skeleton-based animation* is currently the prevalent technique. When the mesh of a character is first created, it is built in a default pose, the so-called bind pose, usually with outstretched limbs. *Rigging* is the name of the process both to create a skeleton composed of virtual joints and limbs (vertices) inside the mesh and to bind the mesh's vertices to one or more joints. When the animator brings the mesh to life by moving the joints into a new pose, the positions of the mesh vertices are automatically updated to follow the motion. Moving only the skeleton into a new pose and automatically updating the mesh is much easier than forming the mesh manually for each pose. Virtual joints can even be rigged to a character's face to model facial expressions. The animator only needs to create the key poses for an animation sequence. A smooth motion can then be created automatically by interpolation.

5.2.5 Audio

Serious games may contain a wide array of audio elements, from simple sound effects to spoken dialog text and a full musical score. Ideally, audio clips have been recorded without reverberation in a studio with sound-absorbing walls. In the game, sounds are then rendered in a way that is somewhat similar to the rendering of graphics: Echo effects can be added to reflect the size and the acoustic properties of the current game environment, and stereo effects to simulate sound coming from a particular direction can be produced by adjusting the relative volume and delays between the left and right channel. Multiple audio clips and metadata are usually combined into a sound cue to achieve the desired sound effect. For example, the sound of a chair that is pushed across a room starts with a short audio clip for the onset of the sound, followed by another clip that is looped while the chair is in motion, and finally a stopping sound with reverberation.

5.2.6   User Interface Elements

Graphical user interfaces are an important part of any game. The graphical elements of a user interface, e.g., the buttons, checkboxes, and window frames are provided as 2D assets to the game engine. If they are designed as vector-based graphic elements, they can be scaled to arbitrary sizes; they thus work for many different screen resolutions. Figure 5.2 shows an example of a graphical user inter-face element.

This is also true for the fonts that are used throughout the serious game. All of the user interface labels, tool tip texts, help texts, and all of the in-game dialogs are textual assets. Usually, textual assets are stored in separate resource files that can be exchanged to provide the content of the game in another language.

5.2.7   Miscellaneous Assets

There are many more types of content in serious games that cannot be covered in detail here. Among them are the assets that are required for creating in-game cut scenes like the parameters of virtual cameras, the motion paths for game objects

Fig. 5.2 An example for a graphical user interface element (from Mildner et al. 2014)

(e.g., cars), and behavior scripts. Interruptions of the normal game flow help to add more depth to the game.

In a similar fashion, different types of light sources spread out over the game world, or particle effects for weather, fire, or various special effects can enhance gameplay and increase motivation to keep playing the game. All of these assets are provided as data to the game engine, and are thus considered content as well.

5.2.8   Combination of Assets

The majority of objects in a serious game are a mixture of multiple assets of different types. A car, for example, may be composed of a triangle mesh with sub-meshes, materials and textures that are attached to them, audio sources, and possibly particle systems. Another example could be a character that consists of a triangle mesh with materials, a skeleton with associated animations, voice samples, and corresponding dialog text. Whenever an object is a composition of other assets, this composition is stored as a reference with the game object for efficient reuse. Instead of maintaining many copies of common materials, a single metal material may be used for multiple metallic objects. Likewise, the same set of animations may be used for multiple characters (e.g., avatars and NPCs) that share a common skeleton structure.

5.2.9   Serious Content

As noted earlier, it is important that serious content and fun content are integrated for a good serious game. By "serious content," we refer to content that is both specifically related to a serious game's characterizing goal and essential to its success. Very little content is exclusively found only in serious games and not in entertainment games. Examples of such SG-exclusive content are task pools in educational games and health or training parameters in exergames.

Since a serious game should integrate the serious purpose of the game in as many aspects as possible, all created content should be examined for its suitability for the purpose. For example, in an educational game where players learn about history, the way the world looks (e.g., the architecture of houses and cities) as well as how it feels (e.g., the way characters act) should be in line with historical facts. For this reason, at all points during a game production, the inclusion of domain experts in the content production process is important. Depending on the relevance of each kind of content for the serious purpose, this could range from an initial briefing of the involved artists and content creators by a domain expert to the detailed involvement of domain experts during the content production process itself. For example, for important assets, the production process could include a review by a domain expert which an asset has to pass before it is included into the game.

5.3 Content Production Pipeline

When content is produced for a serious game the assets undergo a transformation process, from their initial creation in a design tool until they are ready to be loaded into the final game. This process is referred to as the *content production pipeline*. An abstract view of such a pipeline is shown in Fig. 5.3. Artists first create game assets using specific software tools (i.e., Photoshop or 3DS Max). Data is then either exported into an intermediate format by a custom-made plugin for the tool, or saved in a file format that is specific to the tool and then converted into the intermediate format in a separate process. In the last step, the assets are optimized and repackaged into platform-specific archives, where they are ready to be loaded into the serious game. The software to export, convert, and optimize assets is often implemented by the game developers in parallel to the actual game. It is important to make sure that as many steps of the pipeline as possible are automated. Long delays between asset modification and preview may discourage artists from quickly and easily testing developed content, and may thus decrease the overall asset quality. The following sections describe the steps of content creation, conversion, and optimization in more detail.

5.3.1 Content Creation

The content is either created in commercially available software, such as Photoshop or 3DS Max, or by using game-engine-specific tools such as a game world editor. Whereas most commercial tools are specialized in the creation of a specific type of asset (e.g., 3D meshes, textures or audio), the game world editor is the place where all the different assets are brought together and integrated into the game environment. Game designers use the game world editor to shape the terrain with water, hills, and walls, and they place props like trees, buildings and furniture into it. Some game world editors use the same rendering engine as the game itself, thus allowing artists to preview the appearance of their work. In addition to placing assets into the

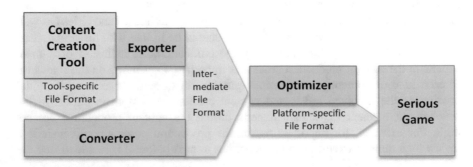

Fig. 5.3 Overview of the content production pipeline

game, world editors can also be used to both create new game objects as a combination of assets and adjust their properties.

The game world can be further enhanced by adding conditions to it that trigger scripted events, with the goal to create interesting and playable surroundings that guide the player during gameplay and control their pace.

Early in the development process, the game designer needs to decide whether to create a 2D or a 3D game. This decision affects the majority of game assets and determines the required tools and skills. Examples for graphical assets in a 2D game are animated sprites, layered background images, and sets of 2D tiles. They must be designed and then drawn for every frame of an animation. When creating an animated character sprite, it only needs to look good from exactly one viewing angle in exactly one pose at a time. In contrast, a 3D character is created by first modeling the 3D mesh, drawing and mapping a texture onto it, creating and binding the skeleton, and finally animating it. A 3D character needs to look good from all viewing angles, under differing lighting conditions, and in a multitude of different poses. It can be said that asset creation generally takes much less effort and is much less costly in 2D than in 3D.

5.3.2 Exporting

Once the assets are created, they need to be transferred into the serious game. Most content creation software comes with its own dedicated file format that supports the rich features of the tool. They store many pieces of additional information, such as a history of applied effects, specific settings or layer information that is helpful for later editing. A lot of this data is not required for using the asset in the game. In order to reduce the file size and to simplify further processing, the assets are brought into a specific intermediate file format. This format helps to reduce the complexity of the content production pipeline and serves as a common ground between the diverse formats in which content can be created and the target format that is optimized for the game engine. The conversion can be done either by implementing a customized plugin to export the asset directly from the tool, or by building a converter between the tool-specific file and the intermediate format (see Fig. 5.3). It is possible to implement correctness and consistency checks into the conversion tools that test for proper texture resolutions, vertex counts, etc. The conversion is driven by metadata that controls aspects like the type of compression, the range of an audio file or the tessellation parameters for meshes. For instance, a game that is played on a mobile device with a four-inch display will use other tessellation parameters than a game that is played on a game console connected to a 46″ television set with full HD resolution. Different asset types like meshes, materials and animations that have been created together may be broken up by the converter into individual files, while references between the files and information about their interdependencies are maintained.

5.3.3 Optimization

From the intermediate file format, assets undergo further processing before they are ready to be loaded into the serious game. The goal is to bring them into a format that is memory-efficient both on disk and in computer memory, fast to load into the game, and efficient to process at runtime. During the development process, runtime and memory efficiency can be traded off for faster processing of the pipeline to ease debugging.

In the final version, runtime efficiency is improved by optimizing the assets. For example, costly lighting effects like global illumination, static shadow maps, or ambient occlusion can be pre-rendered into textures inside the asset pipeline to increase the frame rate during gameplay. Other good candidates for such a pre-calculation are different levels of detail for meshes and textures, or pathfinding information for a map. If assets are large and meant to be streamed from disk at runtime, they are brought into a format that supports streaming. Examples for such large assets are background music or a narrator's voice recording.

Another observation is that if the file structure already closely resembles the memory layout, less processing is required when loading assets into the game. As an example, the order in which vertices of a mesh are stored in memory may be arranged in a way that maximizes cache hits, or textures may be converted into the compression scheme used by the graphics card. Such optimization strategies are, of course, platform-dependent, so different techniques may be used for different target platforms.

The last step of asset optimization is packaging. A serious game is composed of a sizeable number of individual assets. Storing them as individual files would drastically increase seek times when loading them from disk. Therefore, multiple assets are combined into a single archive that may optionally be compressed or encrypted to prevent reverse engineering. Archive files are created in a way ensuring that assets that appear at similar instances in the game, e.g., all props in a level, are packaged together. It is also desirable to separate all language-specific assets (e.g., text and spoken dialogs) to simplify availability of the game in different languages.

5.4 Procedural Content Generation

Procedural content generation (PCG) refers to a set of techniques for creating game content using algorithms with different levels of automation and randomness (see for example Togelius et al. 2011 and Green 2016). In Shaker et al. (2015) the term is defined as follows:

Procedural content generation means the algorithmic creation of game content with limited user input. In other words, PCG refers to computer software that can create game content on its own, or together with one or many human players or designers.

As an initial example from the domain of serious games, we examine an exercise pool of mathematical tasks, such as a series of addition tasks like

$$5 + x = 7 \rightarrow x = ?$$

The concrete task can be seen as an instance of a class of mathematical exercises that could be described as "compute the second operand in an addition with integers in the range of 0–10."

If we want to create a game that features such exercises, we would like to have a large pool of them to increase re-playability and to keep the challenge high—all of that aiming to keep the player in the flow. One way of achieving this would be to ask a human author to create a set of such problems. However, this would be a very repetitive task for the author, and it would increase the effort for producing the game since authors are bound building exercise pools. Instead, we could formulate a general rule which can generate all the exercises in this pool when applied systematically, such as

$$\text{find } x, y \in \mathbb{N} \text{ with } x + y < 10$$

This expression could then be evaluated by the game at runtime, and each time, a new exercise is generated.

This little example shows several properties of procedural content generators. First, in order to generate content procedurally, we need to be able to describe the *class of objects* we want to generate, for example mathematical formulae or suburbs of a big city. When we have found a good way to describe this class (i.e., mathematically, as in the example above), our generator will be able to generate all instances of this class of objects. We find this aspect in Fig. 5.4 in the form of parameters that influence the procedural content generator.

The second factor is *randomness*. Instead of enumerating all instances in a sorted order, the generator can create instances using choices. In the example above, the values of z and one of x or y could be drawn randomly, resulting in a new set of numbers each time. This property can help in many ways; for example, it increases the interest for a human player since the next instance cannot be predicted. As human players are very apt at spotting repeating structures, the result of a randomizing procedural generator often looks more natural than one that always generates the same pattern.

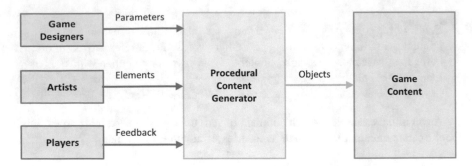

Fig. 5.4 An overview of PCG input and output in the content production process

Note that randomness is not a defining characteristic of procedural content generation. In many contexts, full randomness is not a desired property. For example, if the result of procedural generation could be offensive or not suitable for the target audience (such as a random name generator generating offensive names), developers might want to manually check the result or define constraints for the content generation.

Finally, the amount of *human interaction* can be as little or as much as required. In games such as *Minecraft* (Duncan 2011), the procedural generation is done before the game starts, allowing players to only interact with the result of the generation. On the other hand, generators used in content production tools will usually expose ways of interacting with them, i.e., by allowing an artist to change the automatically generated 3D model of a terrain and then letting the procedural generator make another refinement pass over it.

5.4.1 Basic Methods of Content Generation

Even the most intricate procedural generators can be broken down into basic algorithms that are combined to produce new content. In this regard, the procedural content generation community has brought forth a classification of procedural generators: *teleological versus ontogenetic*. The former refers to approaches that create an accurate model of a natural phenomenon and model it in a realistic fashion. For example, terrain generated using this approach might use a model of tectonics or volcanic activity to generate mountains, and then erode them using simulated water flow. On the contrary, ontogenetic generators are built with the final outcome of the process in mind; they try to find ways how to generate this result in an efficient way. An ontogenetic terrain generator might use a noise function such as Perlin noise (Ebert et al. 2002) to generate terrain point heights semi-randomly, which results in a natural-looking terrain.

The basic algorithms for content generation are often concerned with creating patterns or classes of objects that have some degree of randomness and structure at the same time. For graphical content, this can mean visual patterns. Simple patterns could be grids of simple objects such as polka dots, rectangles, or similar shapes. To bring more randomness into such patterns, individual copies of elements can be varied, i.e., by randomly offsetting their position and orientation.

In a broader sense, a formal grammar can be used to generate objects of various kinds in such a fashion. For example, a grammar has been successfully used to create 3D models of houses based on steps that lead to realistic blueprints, walls, roofs, etc. In the field of virtual botany, *L-systems* (Prusinkiewicz and Lindenmayer 1990) have successfully created 3D models of trees, plants, or bushes by specifying the plant growth processes in the form of grammatical rules.

While graphical objects are among the most researched PCG areas, other areas of games have been created as well. For example, music can be generated from a set of different musical samples, combining them with a grammar specifying which samples can follow each other (Collins 2008).

5.4.2 Best Practice for Procedural Content Generation

While PCG can speed up game production (and make it feasible in the first place for a small team and budget), it needs to be handled with care. In order to create an object procedurally (be it logical such as a game rule, or a multimedia object such as an image), the content needs to be understood well. Furthermore, team members working on the procedural content—including programmers, designers, and artists—need to be aware of the needs and the complexity inherent in PCG.

For example, artists might not create individual assets by themselves, but generate parts that can be recombined procedurally to create assets. This requires them to understand the procedural generator's workings to the point where they know how the input components should be built.

The more content generation is done automatically, the less predictable the end result can be—especially if several PCG systems interact. For example, if one system generates a terrain and another system generates vegetation based on the terrain, a small change in the terrain system can lead to very different vegetation. This could also lead to bugs that are not easily found since no tester is continually testing the PCG systems. In such a case, it is best practice to add as many visualization and debugging options to the game as possible. For example, the PCG-driven game "No Man's Sky" (Duncan 2015) features a procedurally generated galaxy populated with a very large number of planets that can all be visited. Game developers created AI-driven drones that visit planets randomly and try to find errors in the PCG algorithms. They also take snapshots so that the developers can get a feeling for the effects of changes without having to play the game.

5.4.3 Examples of Procedural Content Generation in Serious Games

So far, a major field of research for PCG in serious games has been that of scenario generation. Scenarios of any kind, from triage situations for first response rescue teams to classroom situations for teachers, have been created procedurally. The focus on this field is understandable, as serious games can benefit from scenarios that are not repeated (in order to raise the re-playability of the game). Also, scenarios can be made adaptive to the players, i.e., they can be created to best suit the player's knowledge and skill. Lopes and Bidarra (2012) provide an overview of challenges and current solutions in adaptive serious game scenarios.

Few serious games have explicitly been created exploring the interplay between PCG and the characterizing goal. One example is the game GRACE (Smith and Harteveld 2013) which is intended to teach players the usefulness of computer science. To this end, it features the 2D version of a house with an individual blueprint for each player. The intended learning goal is about minimal spanning trees, a structure in computer science that optimally connects all points in a plane with a tree.

5.5 Content Management

Since content is a major part in the production of a game, it is important to carefully plan and manage content production. If the production process involves several team members, or parts of the production are outsourced to external studios, it is especially important to always keep an overview of the current state.

During the course of a game project, the development team often defines intermediate game versions as *production stages*. A typical example is found in Fig. 5.5.

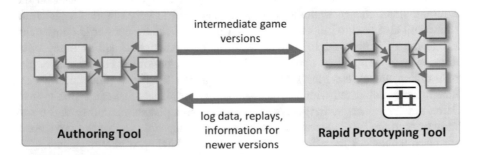

Fig. 5.5 The phases of a game production. Based on Cohen and Bustamante II (2009)

Another example of such intermediate game versions is from Bates (2004). He distinguishes the following nine phases:

- Concept Development
- Preproduction (Proof of Concept)
- Development
- Alpha
- Beta
- Code Freeze
- RTM (Release to Manufacture)
- Patches
- Upgrades

During *preproduction*, the produced content is not used directly in the game. Rather, concept artists work on generating main ideas for the game and establishing its artistic style.

In the *production/development phase*, the actual content of the game is created. In order to be agile and to test content early, some studios establish early phases in which temporary placeholder content is created in order to establish the overall size and composition of the game, and to test other subsystems such as movement or physics, which can already work on this placeholder content. In some cases, this phase is referred to as a *"white" or "gray box" phase*, since the placeholder assets are not textured and thus only feature a white or gray material.

During the production phase, the workload of creating the content of the game is often distributed to many content producers, including external studios or free-lancers. Especially in the latter case, the organization of the content production process is essential. This includes

- **Naming conventions**: Naming assets should allow one to identify the type and intention of each asset. For example, it could include the type of asset, e.g., texture or mesh, as well as information about its usage and context.
- **Versioning**: To be able to return to earlier stages and to have a backup system, it is useful to employ a versioning content management system. Often, this versioning system is separate from systems used for code management such as GIT or Subversion. These systems often do not perform well for binary data, which is the type most game content is stored in. Instead, versioning tools designed for binary files are often used, such as Perforce (2015).
- **Review process**: To enforce parameters such as consistency with the art direction, performance values such as the polygon budget for a specific asset or the consistency of the asset with the serious purpose of a game, a review process is often in place during content production. This process includes information about the person responsible for the review and what the possible results of the review are (rejection of the asset, what changes have to be made, etc.).

In larger teams, the work is often organized hierarchically, with a lead artist at the top of the hierarchy and department heads at intermediate levels. In practice, an asset (e.g., a 3D mesh) will be given to an artist as a task. This artist works on this asset and provides a version to the supervising artist. This is ideally done using a content management tool, automatically backing up files and managing the revision and comment process. If everything about the asset is in compliance with the art/content direction of the game, it is approved and finally integrated into the game.

5.6 Serious Content Integration

An asset in its final version will be integrated into the game. In addition to the technical background of this step, we will examine the design implications and how they relate to authoring tools and game editors.

For serious game content, i.e., content that is connected to the characterizing goal of the game, special care has to be taken of this content's integration. The major challenge is to integrate content in a manner coherent with the game's purpose, its setting, and other elements. For example, many educational games are plagued with a dichotomy between learning elements and gaming elements. Often, the two elements hardly overlap. Instead, players are "rewarded" by the fun game content when they have learned enough in the learning part of the game.

Furthermore, even if the two areas overlap, care has to be taken that the coherence of the game is not destroyed by the serious content. For example, teaching sailing techniques using a pirate setting with sailboats as a natural part of the narrative would be quite fitting; however, answering questions about mathematical geometry or calculus related to such a setting might not be a good fit. While these topics are primarily solved at the design stage, they have to also be reconsidered during the content production workflow. For example, if a 3D asset has an educational value for the game (e.g., a sail for a boat), the artist working on this asset has to be briefed on this value and be given guidelines—i.e., the sail does not have to look good, but it needs to have the right shape and size to be usable for real-world sailing.

For many serious game topics, game editors and authoring tools can assist the authors in integrating the serious content (see Chap. 4). Usually, the serious aspect of the game requires integrating the gameplay mechanics so that the characterizing goal can be met, and it often requires content that has to be in a special format. Consider, for example, an exergame in which the movement of a player is tracked using a Microsoft Kinect, capturing the movement of the player's joints. The content to be integrated into the game is

- information about the target movement, to be given to the players,
- information for the game to assess whether the movement has been carried out correctly by the player.

Information about the target movement could be provided in different ways. A video could be produced, where an actor demonstrates the correct movement. This would entail costs for using an actor—but the result might be of high quality, and the actor could be specially trained to do the correct movements only. On the other hand, this reduces the versatility of the game, since each time a new exercise is added, a new video would have to be produced. Another option would be to create a 3D animation of a virtual character showing the correct movement.

Data about the correct movement could also be provided in different formats. If the correct movement is the change between two poses, e.g., from standing to squatting and back, each pose (stand, squat) could be provided as a configuration of a virtual skeleton (similar to the way virtual characters are animated). The game could then measure the difference between the target motion and the captured motion of the player. Another option could be to let a domain expert (a trainer or physician) determine the correct range of certain joints in the body (e.g., "the elbow should be bent between 70 and 80 degrees").

Molnar and Kostkova (2013) have investigated the basic question of whether educational content presented via text or via content embedded in the game mechanics was more effective. Unfortunately, they could not show a clear result for the games they studied.

Ryan and Charsky (2013) draw upon a study conducted with game designers for serious games. Their first finding is the idea of using "boss levels" to reinforce or consolidate the learning goals. Traditionally, boss levels have been challenges placed intermittently in games where players are challenged beyond their current level. The boss level embodies all the challenges players have already encountered until this point and more. Apart from solidifying the challenge in such a way, participants also underlined the need for repetition of important serious concepts of the game.

Wendel et al. (2011) outline the following points for successful serious games:

- Define the serious game purpose and the target group.
- Based on the serious game purpose, the target group, the target group's age, and the desired gameplay, decide which game genre to use.
- Decide on the desired degree of realism.
- Decide which parts of the serious game content may be integrated in active elements and which ones in passive elements.
- Define how the evaluation of the game will be performed (e.g., by logging).
- Define the methods of feedback and if a game master is reasonable/helpful.
- Decide how the degree of difficulty can be adapted to the players' capabilities.
- Decide what other adaptation and personalization algorithms fit best for the game.

5.7 Summary and Questions

In this chapter, we have examined game content and its production, with special attention on serious game content. As we have seen, game content and its production is a wide field—requiring artistic talent and craftsmanship, as well as coordination and management. Only if all those elements come together, a successful serious game can be created. We want to point out that people, especially those from an engineering or computer science field, often underestimate the importance of this area. As current successful game productions show, the content production departments are those that have grown the most, while programming teams have only grown moderately. Without a well-defined production process and a thorough understanding of the specific needs of the serious game, the content will not optimally support the purpose of the game.

In order to check your understanding of this chapter, choose a (freely available) serious game and analyze what kind of content this game features. Specific questions to ask include the following:

- Is the content coherent? Does it look and feel like it has been created in a holistic process, or does it appear to be cobbled from different individual sources?
- What is the content's naturalism? Is it photo-realistic, cartoon-like, or is there a mixture of the two?
- What content is influenced by the serious purpose? In which way?
- Are the assets visible in the folder structure of the game, or are they packaged into archives? Can they be opened and viewed with external software?
- Why do asset files need to be converted before importing them into the game?
- What are the typical phases in a game production process?
- What are the basic principles of procedural content generation?

Recommended Literature[1]

Chandler H (2008) The game production handbook. Jones & Bartlett Learning. *For readers interested in the practical side of game production, we recommend this book, which covers the entire process of game production. Furthermore, the books by Bates (2004) and Cohen and Bustamante II (2009) are suggested*
Shaker N, Togelius J, Nelson M (2015) Procedural content generation in games: A textbook and an overview of current research. Springer, Berlin/Heidelberg *The "PCG book" is a compilation of research topics on procedural content generation. This thorough summary of the topic is available for free on the website of the book,* http://pcgbook.com/, *and is highly recommended reading in this field*

---

[1]The PCG community has as one of its main meeting points the Workshop of Procedural Content Generation, usually co-located with the Foundations of Digital Games conference. Other conferences with a strong PCG influence are the IEEE Conference on Computational Intelligence and Games (CIG) as well as the AAAI Conference on Artificial Intelligence and Interactive Digital Entertainment (AAIDE).

Harteveld D (2011) Triadic game design—Balancing reality, meaning and play. Springer, Berlin/Heidelberg. *Concerning the requirements of serious game content, we refer the reader to Chapter 3, "Reality" of Harteveld's (2011) Triadic Game Design, in which the author examines the properties of serious game content in more detail*

References

Bates B (2004) Game design. Thomson Course Technology, Boston, MA, USA

Cohen D, Bustamante S II (2009) Producing games: from business and budgets to creativity and design. Focal Press, Oxford/Burlington

Collins K (2008) Game sound: an introduction to the history, theory and practice of video game music and sound design. MIT Press, Cambridge

Duncan G (2015) How I learned to love procedural art. Talk given at the Game Developer's Conference 2015. http://www.gdcvault.com/play/1021805/Art-Direction-Bootcamp-How-I. Accessed 24 Feb 2016

Duncan S (2011) Minecraft, beyond construction and survival. Well Played 1(1):1–22. ETC Press, Pittsburgh, PA, USA

Green D (2016) Procedural content generation for C++ game development. Packt Publishing

Ebert D, Musgrave F, Peachey D, Perlin K, Worley S (2002) Texturing and modeling—a procedural approach, 3rd edn. Morgan Kaufmann, Burlington

Lopes R, Bidarra R (2012) Adaptivity challenges in games and simulations: a survey. IEEE Trans Comput Intell AI Games 3(2):85–99. IEEE, New York

Mildner P, John B, Moch A, Effelsberg W (2014) Creation of custom-made serious games with user-generated learning content. In: Proceedings of the ACM network and system support for games (NetGames), pp 1–6

Molnar A, Kostkova P (2013) On effective integration of educational content in Serious Games: text vs. game mechanics. In: Proceedings of the IEEE 13th international conference advanced learning technologies (ICALT). IEEE, New York, pp 299–303

Perforce (2015). http://www.perforce.com. Accessed 24 Feb 2016

Prusinkiewicz P, Lindenmayer A (1990) The algorithmic beauty of plants. Springer, Berlin

Ryan W, Charsky D (2013) Integrating serious content into Serious Games. In: Proceedings of the Foundations of Digital Games 2013. Society for the Advancement of the Science of Digital Games, Santa Cruz, CA, USA

Shaker N, Togelius J, Nelson M (2015b) Procedural content generation in games: a textbook and an overview of current research. Springer, Berlin

Smith G, Harteveld C (2013) Procedural content generation as an opportunity to foster collaborative mindful learning. In: Proceedings of the Foundations of Digital Games 2013. Society for the Advancement of the Science of Digital Games, Santa Cruz, CA, USA

Togelius J, Yannakakis G, Stanley K, Browne C (2011) Search-based procedural content generation: a taxonomy and survey. IEEE Trans Comput Intell AI Games, 3(3):172–186. IEEE, New York

Wendel V, Göbel S, Steinmetz R (2011) Seamless learning in Serious Games—how to improve seamless learning content integration in Serious Games. In: Proceedings CSEDU Conference, Noordwijkerhout, Netherlands, 2011. SciTePress—Science and Technology Publications, Setúbal, pp 219–224

Game Engines

6

Jonas Freiknecht, Christian Geiger, Daniel Drochtert,
Wolfgang Effelsberg and Ralf Dörner

Abstract

From a technical perspective, a game engine represents the basis of a game, providing the functionality for optimized and efficient graphic rendering, file system access, player input via devices such as keyboard and mouse, sound playback, and networking—as well saving and loading the game state. Game development studios realized that reusing software is not only the way to make the development process more efficient, but that it is also important to free developers from the tedious tasks of merging graphics, sounds, and storytelling "manually." As a result, many software tools were written, adapted, and packaged with the runtime game engine, providing easy-to-use editing facilities and allowing collaboration in large teams in the development process. In this chapter, we give an overview of modern game engine architecture and its integrated modules. We also address the challenges game engine designers face with respect to multi-platform development, extensibility to new hardware devices, and a better integration of content designers in the overall development

J. Freiknecht (✉) · W. Effelsberg
University of Mannheim, Mannheim, Germany
e-mail: j.freiknecht@googlemail.com

C. Geiger · D. Drochtert
Düsseldorf University of Applied Sciences, Düsseldorf, Germany

R. Dörner
RheinMain University of Applied Sciences, Wiesbaden, Germany

© Springer International Publishing Switzerland 2016
R. Dörner et al. (eds.), *Serious Games*, DOI 10.1007/978-3-319-40612-1_6

process. Usually serious games use game engines designed for digital games in general; there are no specific game engines for serious games. Yet, it is important to understand the general architecture of a game engine to find solutions for how to best integrate serious aspects into a game.

6.1 The Architecture of Game Engines

Game engine architecture is a wide field, since there is not only one concrete path of designing an appropriate base for arbitrary kinds of games. One of the most significant differences is to either choose a *static* engine, which is written for a specific game genre (e.g., a point and click adventure game or a strategy game), or to choose a *dynamic* engine, which is independent of the game genre and the platform. The latter type is frequently designed to be reused in other projects or to be publicly offered to other teams to save them the development effort needed to write their own engine (Tracy and Reindell 2012).

The analogy of a game engine and the engine of a car is frequently used in the literature. Both take care of an uninterrupted, comfortable journey, and both do not need to be seen or manipulated by the driver/the player at any time.

In the majority of today's game engines, there is a reoccurring schema of modules interacting with each other. Figure 6.1 provides an overview over those components. It should be seen as a general reference, since there is neither a definition for a set of standard components of a game engine nor an official specification what functionality a game engine should provide. As Fig. 6.1 shows, modularization has been established as a valuable concept for game engine design and programming (Lange and Hammer 2014). Instead of hard-coding functionality—such as multi-platform support of gameplay elements—into the core layer, those modules are designed to be easily replaced by new ones without touching other modules. The exchange of the two most commonly used graphics APIs, *DirectX* and *OpenGL*, are a good example for this modularization concept: A well-written rendering pipeline will allow to replace *DirectX* by *OpenGL*—or conversely, to allow porting a game from a *Windows* platform to *Linux*, *Android,* or *iOS*.

In the following subchapters we discuss the thirteen module groups of Fig. 6.1.

6.1.1 Hardware

The hardware layer at the bottom of Fig. 6.1 describes the physical machine the game is running on. The hardware can be classified into four main subgroups:

- *Handheld Devices*: Pandora, PlayStation Portable, Nintendo 3DS, etc.
- *Smartphones*: Various Android and iOS smartphones and tablets
- *Game Consoles*: XBox One, Playstation 4, Wii U, etc.
- *PCs*: Various desktop and laptop PCs.

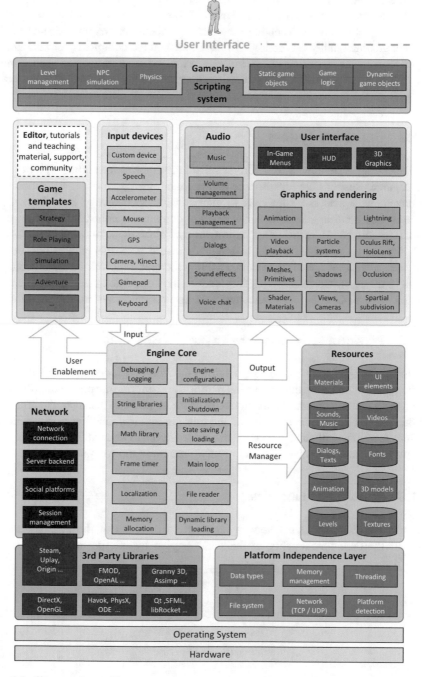

Fig. 6.1 Game engine architecture

Consoles and handhelds follow a strict hardware specification, which is helpful for development teams since the hardware differs only in minimal aspects (resolution of a connected TV, version of the installed operating system, etc.) so that the game's graphic quality can be highly optimized, and the complexity of testing and quality assurance is manageable. However, PCs and smartphones exist in a large variety of configurations. They need extensive testing and quality assurance throughout the entire development process.

6.1.2 Operating System

The operating system, with basic driver software, serves as the software platform to run a game. Responsible for resource management, provision of services, and task management, it acts as a core layer to interact with the hardware layer below.

In former console generations, operating systems were embedded into the game itself (Gregory 2014), so that when starting the console without inserting a cartridge or CD, the screen remained blank. In today's console game generation, the device provides a "visible" operating system, enabling the user to download digital content, listen to music, or watch a movie. This leads to the conclusion that a console can be compared to a PC with a very strict hardware and operating system specification.

6.1.3 Platform Independence Layer

On top of the *Operating System Layer* resides the *Platform Independence Layer*. It is responsible for detecting the underlying platform and offering the proper interfaces for file system access, communication via the network, or memory management. The goal of this layer is to provide a consistent and transparent view onto the main operating system functions without the need for the game engine to know it. Figure 6.2 shows the platform independence layer and its environment in more detail.

6.1.4 Third Party Libraries

Next to the *Platform Independence Layer,* a variable set of third-party libraries support the core functionality of the game engine by offering sets of functions,

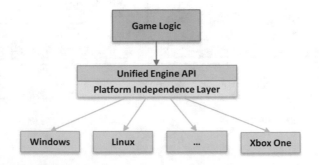

Fig. 6.2 Platform independence layer

algorithms, and frameworks. As an example, *Havok, PhysX,* or *ODE* act as physics engines. They provide functions to simulate fluids, joints, and rigid or soft body mechanics. Since a physics simulation is supposed to behave similarly in any game, it makes sense to package those capabilities in a separate library. Of course, the physics behavior can be parameterized for changes, e.g., the world's gravity, or the angle of rotation of a joint. So, parameterization and adaptability are a core requirement for third party libraries.

In addition to the physics engine, numerous other library types exist. Figure 6.1 names only a few:

- Audio middleware and multimedia libraries (e.g., FMOD, OpenAL)
- User interface frameworks (e.g., Qt, libRocket, SFML)
- Animation and modeling libraries (e.g., Granny 3D, Assimp)
- Graphics APIs (e.g., DirectX, OpenGL)
- Digital distribution platform APIs (e.g., Steam, Uplay, Origin).

Licensing plays an important role when using third-party libraries. Even though a library might be freely available, credits or the license text have to be added in many cases to the shipped product. License costs or license interferences (e.g., the usage of a *GNU Lesser General Public License* library which is required to be editable but the engine code itself is not published as open source) made some major game engine developers rethink their strategy and implement components by themselves. Examples include the animation system of Epic's *Unreal Engine Persona,* or Unity's UI system.

6.1.5 The Engine Core

The central element of a game engine is the *Engine Core,* which is based on the *Platform Independence Layer* and diverse *Third Party Libraries.* Also frequently referred to as the core runtime, this layer maintains the engine's state, handles the scheduling via the frame timer, keeps the engine's thread(s) alive, and manages all interactions with other module groups like the graphics or input handling components. All modules in the engine core are somehow game-related even if they seem, at first glance, to be classic application programing interfaces. We now briefly explain four of them as examples.

The *debugging and logging module* is frequently enhanced with functions to print system states, or with other features that are not required in a common windowed or command line application. Since the engine's main loop is repeated at a very high frequency,[1] those logging functions would be called far too often so that an engine logging framework needs a specific adaptation.

---

[1]An interactive game should run at a minimum frame rate of 30 frames per second (fps), ideally at least 60 fps: "60 Hz, 30 hurts". In a 3D game, even higher frame rates might be necessary since 3D displays require different frames for the right and left eyes.

The *math library* not only contains simple operators such as addition, subtraction, multiplication, and division of scalar values, but is also able to execute those operations on vectors (mostly 2D, 3D and 4D) and on matrices. Furthermore, advanced numeric functions such as splines are also supported.

The *file reader* is capable of parsing file formats for encrypted resource files, including protected assets, 3D models or other game-specific data, as well as stream data.

The *memory allocation module* is responsible for (pre)loading models, textures, and sounds into memory to avoid lags during gameplay. Similar to a garbage collector, modern implementations are able to determine if the diverse resources in main memory will be reused again or can be purged. This ability is frequently used in open world games, where levels are too huge to be loaded into main memory as a whole. In the best case, an engine provides a functionality to load levels partially from disk into memory and purge all the other parts that cannot be accessed by the player in the current game state. As a result, there are no loading times—even if the player moves quickly in an extremely large world—as the memory allocation module automatically takes care of loading and purging game objects during gameplay.

Next to those elementary modules, the following subchapters will provide a deeper insight into two modules in the *Engine Core* group that are based on a more complex concept. These modules play a fundamental role in game programming.

6.1.5.1 The Main Loop

A common practice in designing event-driven applications is to execute one single loop that runs as long as the process exists. In many common programming languages, this loop is shielded from the user (e.g., Java or C#), in others it is clearly visible (C++).

A game is event-driven—but not in the common sense. An event can be a mouse interaction with a user interface element, as known from classic applications, but it can also be a collision of two racing cars or an interaction with an NPC (Non-player Character). The difference between the first and the two latter examples is that only the first is initiated by the user. The two latter events are raised by the game itself. In fact, developers can freely create event types, depending on their needs and the type of game.

The reason for these events is that a game requires frequent checks to determine if something has happened that requires an immediate reaction. This is the reason why many game engines still rely on one main loop. The most common events that are processed by the main loop are user inputs via keyboard, mouse, or any other input device, updates of game states, and rendering of the state to be shown on the screen.

6.1.5.2 The Timer

Correct timing is at the heart of every game engine. All game motions must be represented correctly with respect to time.

We can distinguish *real time* (or wall clock time), *game time*, *frame rate*, and the *screen refresh rate* of a game. Whereas real time proceeds irreversibly at a fixed rate, the game time and the frame rate can vary. For example, the game time can be slowed down when a game is tested, and an animation can even be tested stepwise. The screen refresh rate depends on the display device: US television sets run at 30 Hz whereas European ones run at 25 Hz, and computer displays typically run at 60 Hz. For stereo vision, the screen refresh rate is often doubled: Two different frames have to be computed for every frame time.

In older games, the CPU timer was often the only device determining the speed at which motion was represented. The consequence was that a game developed for a specific CPU would not run properly on a faster CPU. For example, when a player representing a frog tried to cross a street with cars driving along, the cars would travel so fast on a faster CPU that it became impossible for a player to cross the street.

In modern games, the game engine is responsible for maintaining the correct timing, independent of the target CPU. A first step to do that is to define an internal frame rate. The frame rate is the rate at which the CPU computes new (complete) frames. The CPU has to perform a considerable amount of work for each new frame to be shown: Moving objects have to be placed into their new positions, animations have to be computed, and particle effects for waterfalls, fire, and fog have to be computed. The relationship between the work to be done by a slow and a fast CPU, resulting in different frame rates, is shown in Fig. 6.3.

The frame rate is variable because the amount of work to be done varies from frame to frame. For example, if an explosion occurs in the game, considerable additional computation is necessary: Yellow pixels spread quickly, many objects shake, and smoke spreads out. The resulting amount of additional work is illustrated in Fig. 6.4.

The game engine guarantees that a reasonable relationship between the game time and the frame rate is always maintained. For this purpose, it maintains a variable often called *frame time* or *delta time* (Δt). Δt is the inverse of the frame rate (or frame frequency). As shown in Fig. 6.4, the frame rate can vary depending on the amount of work the CPU currently has to do. Thus, a moving average of the frame computation time is often taken as Δt. When the game programmer specifies

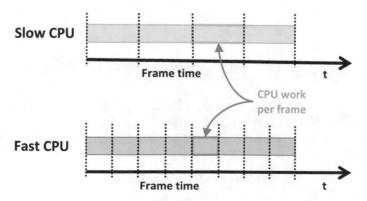

Fig. 6.3 CPU load and frame rate on a slow and a fast CPU

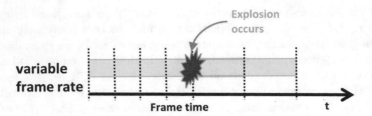

Fig. 6.4 Variable CPU load per frame

a moving object with speed v, and x_1 and x_2 are the positions of the object in frames 1 and 2 respectively, the object's speed has to be multiplied with Δt to reach x_2:

$$x_2 = x_1 + \Delta x = x_1 + v\Delta t$$

Δt is always available from the game engine as a global variable, and the game programmer must use it for all kinds of motions.

If the game engine had complete control over the display device, it would simply set the screen refresh rate to the internal frame rate, and the game would run smoothly at a slightly varying speed. However, since our game is supposed to run on various available devices, the game engine has to map the frame rate to the display device's screen refresh rate (e.g., 25 Hz). A feature of old CRT tubes is often used to perform this mapping: the vertical blanking interval. On a CRT, the screen was drawn line by line, beginning in the upper left corner. When the beam arrived in the lower right corner, it was turned off and moved back to the upper right corner; the time this took was the vertical blanking interval. Although modern display devices do not use cathode rays anymore, this *v-sync interval* still exists. The v-sync rate is the same as the screen refresh rate. Thus, to run properly on existing display devices, the game engine has to synchronize its internal frame rate with the v-sync rate of the current device: If a frame is computed in less time than the v-sync interval, the CPU is put to sleep; if it takes more time the last frame is repeated. This is illustrated in Fig. 6.5.

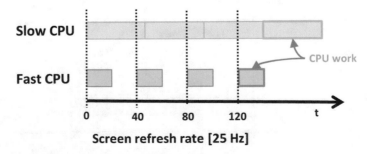

Fig. 6.5 Mapping the frame rate to the screen refresh rate

On modern multiprocessor CPUs, game timing gets much more complicated because each processor has its own clock. The details go beyond the scope of this book; the interested reader is referred to the excellent book by Gregory (2014).

6.1.6   The Network

Games can be classified into local, single-player games and networked games. A network layer only exists in networked games. It consists of procedures to establish, manage and monitor connections between the game client(s) and the game server. The responsibility for this task is mostly assigned to the *Network Connection* and *Session Management* modules. Those two determine which network protocol to use (e.g., TCP or UDP), whether there is an existing session the player is connected to, and to which server the player wants to connect next. The last task leads to the next module in the Network Layer, the *Server Backend*. This backend runs on the game server only. It often consists of many threads handling multiple player connections and game states. The reason for a dedicated server is to have a reliable and static infrastructure for the game, storing the global game state. Updates, i.e., player movements, are generated on the game client and communicated to the server. The server communicates the global state back to the clients periodically. The server is also responsible for resolving conflicts, i.e., when two players shoot at each other at nearly the same time.

In general, tasks done on the server backend are of a logical nature; they deal with the game's state and not its graphical representation. The reason is to transfer only the absolutely necessary information via the network to guarantee both a consistent state for all players and a fluent gameplay. The following list names operations that are computed on the server side:

- updating the position of objects in the virtual world
- checking for a collision of objects
- maintaining the global game state (current score, game paused, save player skills, etc.)
- verifying that all clients are still connected.

On the other hand, the following list names operations that are typically processed on the client side:

- model animation
- rendering objects
- particle effects
- sound generation.

The last module in the network layer refers to *social platforms* that might be used to share achievements, game statistics or even videos of the player's last session. Typical examples are Valve's *Steam*, Ubisoft's *Uplay* and Electronic Arts'

Origin. Instead, browser games focus more on a Facebook API or on proprietary platforms like *Bigpoint* or *Gamingo.*

6.1.7 Resource Management

Resources are as essential to a game as the game logic itself. Figure 6.1 shows a variety of resource types, namely materials, UI elements, sounds, music, videos, texts, models, skeletal animations, levels, and textures. Those resources are combined to create an environment to achieve the desired level of immersion. During the last decades the effort to produce high-quality resources, especially 3D models, levels, and music, has led to growing investment in the artistic branch of game design (Back and Madsen 2007). Imagine a game consisting of thousands of sounds, models, and graphics that are loaded from various resource packages before and while the game is running: An advanced resource management system is clearly needed.

In recent years, with the evolution of multiplatform game development, resources are not only separated by data type but also by platform. For example, mobile games use textures with a lower resolution than PCs. The responsibility for handling various platform-dependent resources also lies with the resource manager.

6.1.8 Input Devices

Approximately 90 % of traditional games are controlled by mice, keyboards, and gamepads. With the release of Nintendo's *Wii Remote* and Microsoft's *Kinect,* there was a cautious but encouraging shift to more exotic devices. They were well accepted and made other hardware designers come up with innovative ideas such as the *Leap Motion* finger sensor or the body movement sensor *Virtuix Omni.*

Serious games have rather different requirements since various simulations depend on custom controls. Examples are flight simulators, medical device trainings, or dialog trainings. Whereas the latter can use existing speech-to-text engines, the other two examples often rely on custom hardware.

Figure 6.6 shows an example: A device called *laparoscopic controller*, developed by Cutting Edge (CuttingEdge 2015) to train surgeons using the Nintendo *Wii* and the *Wii Remote.* It is plugged twice into a surgeon's training device and is operated by the player using both hands. The corresponding game is about a robot and a girl trying to escape an underground world, where the player has to clear the robot's way by removing obstacles.

6.1.9 Audio

At first sight, audio playback seems to be one of the less complex module groups in the game engine architecture. However, taking a detailed look at modern games shows that audio far exceeds the sole playback of sound effects and music. Playing

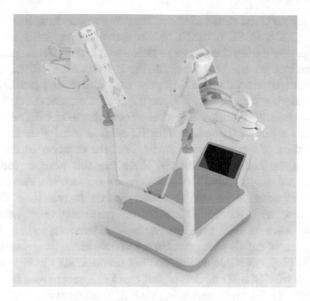

Fig. 6.6 The laparoscopic controller as a custom input device: two regular Wiimote game controllers are integrated in the device (*Source* CuttingEdge 2015)

dialogs (either via a text-to-speech framework or recorded voice samples), offering a voice chat in a multiplayer environment, and managing volume and playback are the core functions that are not visible at first glance.

Another challenge is to create a realistic sound in a 3D space so that a sample is played louder if the player approaches the sound-emitting object; the sound should also be adjusted if the player's avatar rotates its head. More recent sound frameworks for games have also introduced effects reflecting the environment surrounding the avatar. For example, a large hall might create an echo.

6.1.10   Graphics and Rendering

Calculating and rendering graphics are among the most challenging tasks in designing and implementing a game engine. Several rendering algorithms such as *raytracing* or *radiosity* are well known. The most popular algorithm today is called *pipeline rendering*, as the 3D model is processed in several steps (e.g., calculation of geometric transformations, calculation of the lighting, rasterization, texturing, shading, anti-aliasing, calculation of occlusions) that are arranged in a sequence. The advantage of this pipeline architecture is that it can process the data in parallel, e.g., by employing multiple rendering pipelines.

Usually, a rendering pipeline is typically realized in specific hardware called a *graphics processing unit* (GPU). While the game engine code is usually executed on the CPU, the rendering is accomplished by the GPU. Some of the processing steps of the rendering pipeline can be programmed. These programs that are executed by the GPU are called *shaders*. They are written in special programming languages, e.g., Cg, GLSL or HLSL. Many game engines offer an interface for game developers, allowing them to write their own shaders. Thus, game developers have a fine-grained control how the rendering is executed by supplying their own code for particularly crucial processing steps of the rendering pipeline.

Besides rendering, a game engine's graphics module carries out other tasks such as 3D model animation, collision detection, or complex 3D model simplification (in order to ensure a certain framerate). The 3D models usually contain information about the vertices of the geometric model, and the duration of the rendering is proportional to the number of vertices. Reducing this number can shorten the rendering process significantly. The game engine implements many sophisticated optimizations in order to be able to render frames in real time. Besides using multiple *levels of detail* for the 3D models, the game engine might use dedicated data structures such as BSP trees or quadtrees. Moreover, *culling* is often performed, i.e., parts of the 3D scene that are not visible in the image are removed. For instance, if the player is inside a room and has no possibility to view objects in the neighboring room, all the 3D models of that room can be removed from processing.

Another strategy for saving rendering time is to perform calculations before the games runs, not during. As calculation results need to be stored, time for a calculation during the game is traded for storage space. Examples are the pre-calculation of lighting conditions and their storage in a light map, or the processing of textures to be used in the rendering, e.g., by applying lighting results to the texture, a process called *texture baking*.

Another problem addressed by the rendering module is the fact that in pipeline rendering not the entire 3D scene is processed at once, but single vertices are processed in parallel. As a result, it is not possible to render shadows properly, as it is necessary to know the entire scene's information to determine whether another object exists that casts a shadow on the current object. Similarly, other effects such as reflections cannot be calculated with pipeline rendering. Therefore, game engines often contain algorithms that are workarounds to simulate such effects.

6.1.11   The User Interface

Quite often, the *User Interface* modules work on top of the *Graphics and Rendering* module group. They are responsible for displaying and managing UI controls such as buttons, slider panels, bitmaps, or text. In former days, most popular engines, e.g., Epic's *Unreal Engine 3* and Crytek's *CryENGINE*, made use of the UI middleware *Scaleform* which is capable of rendering assets based on *Adobe Flash*. The industry's movement from expensive engine licenses to a free-for-all culture forced some engine developers to remove the proprietary *Flash* format from their UI system and implement a new set of custom controls (e.g., in *Unreal Engine 4* and *Unity*). These controls are either used to provide information on the player's state and interactions during the game, or to render menus to start a new game, save the current game state, load, quit, or change settings.

6.1.12   Gameplay and Scripting

To handle the gameplay and the game logic, a game engine's scripting system is often based on a high-level language such as Lua, Python, or JavaScript—where Lua is most frequently used in game development (>50 %, DeLoura 2009). Those scripting languages share common characteristics:

- They can communicate with the engine core.
- They can be debugged during gameplay. They are interpreted, and therefore changes to the code can be made without compiling the program from scratch. Recompiling would not only introduce an annoying delay during development, but also all information about the game state would need to be reconstructed to continue playing seamlessly after the change.
- Variables can be monitored at runtime.
- The languages are extensible.

Such a scripting language is used to describe the player's quests and/or movements, or to program the behavior of a game object; it is not used for hardware-related tasks such as rendering or memory management. The modules it generally controls are shown on top of the scripting language module in Fig. 6.1. Many game engines offer a visual scripting editor like *Blueprints* in *Unreal Engine 4* or *Flow Graph* in *CryENGINE 3*. Figure 6.7 shows a script fragment to switch a light on and off in CryEngine's visual scripting tool *Flow Graph*.

There are various reoccurring gameplay modules that make heavy use of the scripting engine. They are thus provided in the form of script functions. For example, the behavior of non-player characters and static and dynamic game objects is often scripted—since they are required to react dynamically to specific game states, and their behavior needs to be fine-tuned during game balancing. As another example, physics engines tend to communicate with the game logic and the engine core via the scripting engine.

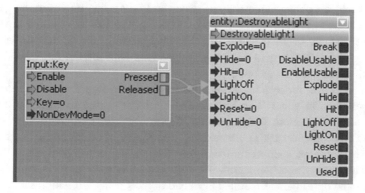

Fig. 6.7   A script fragment to switch a light on and off in CryENGINE's *Flow Graph*

Most modern games have an interface to such a scripting language to enable hobby developers to write and publish modifications (so called *mods*) for a game. A mod either edits game resources to change the appearance of a level or an object, and/or they partially change game behavior.

6.2 Event Processing

Similar to desktop applications, games are event-driven. Events are used extensively; for example, they are created when two game objects collide or when the player starts to communicate with an NPC. But what exactly are events? Events notify other game objects or parts of the game logic that something happened that could have an influence on their behavior. Sometimes, engines offer a fixed set of events like *OnClick*, *OnCollide*, or *OnConnect*, and hence cover the most common types of events. Some languages allow assigning code to an event that is executed when the event occurs; others provide a global *OnEvent* method, allowing the programmer to react to any event within this method.

To optimize a game's runtime performance, some engines require the programmer to add a box or a mesh around an avatar or an object to activate collision events when the game object's boxes or meshes overlap. It is much easier to detect colliding boxes than to detect a collision between the detailed structures of objects.

The advantage of an event-driven architecture is obvious: When an event occurs, the interested game objects are notified. For example, when a game without an event handling mechanism is paused the function *pause_game()* has to call *pause_player(), pause_npcs(), pause_weather(), pause_particles(),* etc. That would obviously lead to complex and confusing code.

6.3 Animation

Animation is defined as the art of bringing artificial objects to life. For example, non-rigid objects change their shape—water flows, or a flag moves in the wind. An animator's job is to take a static object and bring it to life by defining how object attributes (such as shape, position, or color) change over time. In the special case of animating characters, proper design of movements with respect to given situations results in a character's personality.

The production process for animations has been developed since the early days of film production when Walt Disney and his team started to work on animated feature films like *Snow White and the Seven Dwarfs*, *Pinocchio* and *Fantasia* (Thomas and Johnston 1981). Since then, the process has been refined and adapted to new technologies, such as computer-assisted animation and computer animation. In computer animation, animators use software tools to create 3D models, apply texturing and lighting, and animate the static objects using animation methods such as keyframing, inverse kinematics, or physics-based animation.

6.3.1   The Animation Production Process

We begin with a short introduction into the animation production process for *movies* where this was done successfully for decades. In professional movie production, the animation process is fairly sophisticated. A detailed description can be found in (Parent 2012; Milic and McConville 2006; Levy 2009). The animation process begins with an initial idea about the story to be told. This idea is briefly sketched in a small document called a *treatment,* and further refined in a *script* by a professional writer. From that, a director breaks down the story into sequences composed of scenes, each consisting of a series of shots. A shot consists of a single take, i.e., a recording of a static or continuously moving camera that is not interrupted.

The story is then presented graphically, and a *storyboard* is the most appropriate method for that. A storyboard is similar to a comic book, as it contains several panels of sequential drawings of the story. The storyboard is an important tool to provide a common understanding of the story and its visual look. For characters, a dedicated *character sheet* or *character study* defines the appearance, pose, and gestures. Character sheets are needed to standardize the appearance if many animators are involved in the production process. Figure 6.8 shows an example of a character sheet.

Once the storyboard and the character sheets are complete, individual panels are edited along with dialog, music, and sound effects to experience the motion as a series of moving images. These *animatics* act as templates and help to determine how much animation is really needed for each take. *Previsualization* ("previs") is a cost-effective technique widely used in 3D animation and special-effect filmmaking. Low-cost digital content is used to determine potential problems in each shot before

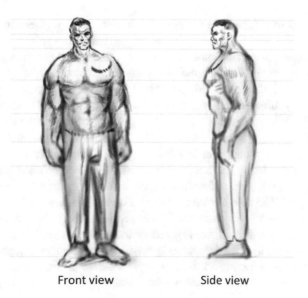

Front view   Side view

Fig. 6.8 A character sheet

substantial effort is put into the final production. Based on the previs, the design of the overall "look and feel" is then developed and documented. For characters, this description is sometimes called a *character bible*, containing all information about how a character should look, move, and behave.

The real production of the animated character starts with the *modeling phase*. In this phase, the character's appearance is created, e.g., head, face, body, arms, and legs. Many techniques exist to create a 3D character model, and commercial tools like 3DSMax and Maya include most of them. In *box* or *subdivision modeling*, the artist starts with simple 3D primitives of low resolution and further refines the shape where needed (e.g., shaping a hand with fingers from a 3D cube). Box modeling is the most common form of polygonal modeling; it is often used together with edge modeling, which allows one to create complex surfaces by a set of single polygonal faces. *Digital sculpting* is an innovative modeling technique that frees the artist from the tedious manipulation of polygons. It allows the user to work in a way similar to real sculpting with clay. With a real pen and a tablet, virtual brushes, scalpels, and other clay modeling tools are simulated, leading to very organic models. *Procedural modeling approaches* are appropriate if complex model structures can be described and created by algorithms. Prominent examples are large forests, landscapes like mountains, or complex cityscapes. Dedicated tools like SpeedTrees, Vue d'Esprit, or CityEngine help artists to apply these complex algorithms. Another semi-automated technique is *image-based modeling*. It allows creating 3D models based on a series of static 2D images. This cost-effective approach is often used in low-cost productions where an artist cannot create a full 3D asset from scratch. *3D scanning* is a suitable option to digitize real-world objects and human actors. It is often used when a digital representation of a real character is needed (e.g., faces of premier-league club players in the soccer game *FIFA2016*).

A digital 3D model needs a texture, which creates the impression of a material look on the model's surface. Textures can be anything from solid colors to realistic surface properties of metal, plastic or glass. To simulate the complex light behavior on materials like water, ice, or reflective surfaces dedicated shading programs can be created that simulate nearly all possible light-object interactions.

It can be very difficult—or even impossible—to animate a 3D character based on specifying single key frames and interpolating the in-between frames. 3D character models need bones, joints, or other rigging systems to allow realistic body part manipulation. Once a character has been rigged, an animator can simply create motions by manipulating the bones like a virtual puppet. With a properly rigged character, it is possible to define key positions of bones and interpolate between them, creating a believable motion sequence. Figure 6.9 shows a rigging with bones and joints for an animated character. It was produced with the 3DSMax editor.

Another approach to animate a rigged character is to simulate a physical environment with mass, forces, friction, and gravity and to animate a character based on this dedicated simulation model. Such a *physics-based animation* allows creating a complex physically inspired behavior without the need to define a large number of

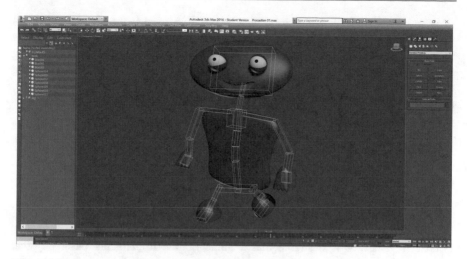

Fig. 6.9 Rigging with symbolic bones and joints (from Guthier and Sharmin 2016)

key frames. However, the physical simulation is often limited to a coarse approximation of the real physical behavior.

If lifelike behavior of 3D characters is needed, *motion capturing* is the method of choice. Motion capturing ("*MoCap*") is the process of first recording the movements of real persons, animals, or objects, and then processing and storing this information to animate the corresponding digital character model. Persons often wear special suits with markers for a more precise motion recording.

Similar to procedural modeling, *procedural animation techniques* allow animating complex models based on algorithmic approaches. It is also possible to simulate large numbers of animals (e.g., flocks of birds, herds of dinosaurs, and schools of fish) simply by a number of local behavior rules (e.g., "stay near other group members, but do not collide").

6.3.2   Animation for Games

Although the design of animations for games uses similar techniques as the animation for movies, it is a misconception to believe they are the same. Animated movie designers have complete control over the user's viewing experience. They only have to worry about one camera angle at a time, because the viewer cannot decide to look at another point in the scene. This allows one to "cheat" in many ways, as shots are designed to only look perfect from a predefined viewpoint. Games, on the other hand, are meant to be interactive, and the user wants full control of the digital character. This requires a scene to look good from many possible viewpoints. For example, in a first-person game, the player may turn the head at any time to look around, and the scene must still be presented correctly. While a character in a movie shot only moves with a single animation at any given time, in a game multiple animations must be possible because the player can control the character interactively. The character may walk, run, jump, fight, or manipulate objects. This requires a large set of possible animations. Also, a smooth blending between two animations has to be designed in a believable way, e.g., from running to walking to stopping. Because such a large number of animations is needed, animation techniques such as physics-based animation, motion capture, and procedural techniques are often used in games.

6.4 Physics and Collison Detection

6.4.1 Simulating Physics

For most games, it is desirable that a game engine implements basic physical concepts. For example, a physics simulation is needed for realistic character movement, or for vehicle or environmental dynamics.

The goal of physics calculations in game engines is not necessarily a physically perfect simulation—as it would be required in engineering simulations—but an *efficient* simulation that delivers a believable recreation of the real-world physical behavior in real-time. Approximations in the physical simulation are crucial for a well-performing game. Almost all game engines include a physics engine for this purpose. As a result, game developers are not required to program the physics behavior from scratch.

The most common form of physics simulation in games is rigid body dynamics (solids) following classical mechanics, e.g., Newton's laws of motion. The main variables of rigid body dynamics for a developer are velocity, acceleration, friction, mass, and forces. Forces can be user-defined; they are the main component that makes objects move around in the virtual environment. Game engines have a pre-defined global force to simulate gravity that moves objects down along the y-axis by 9.81 m/s^2. The developer can change the gravitational force to archive different effects such as moon physics or zero gravity environments. Furthermore, forces can be created to act in certain areas of the environment (for example, windy zones). During runtime, the physics engine will also create new forces dynamically—for example, to calculate repulsion not only when objects collide, but also spring forces, damping, or air drag. An object's mass and friction will determine its behavior both when forces act on it and when collisions with other objects occur. Forces also manipulate the velocity and acceleration of rigid body objects. Additionally, the developer can change the velocity and acceleration values in his/her program. For rotational movement, angular velocity and acceleration are also taken into account by the physics engine.

Beside rigid body dynamics, other more complex forms of physics simulations are also popular. Examples include elastic body dynamics for simulating soft bodies, and particle/fluid dynamics for waterfalls, smoke, fire, or clouds.

6.4.2 Collision Detection

One of the more complex tasks of a physics engine is handling collisions between objects. In addition to the actual geometry of an object, calculating collisions requires a second mesh, the so-called *collider*. It is used by the physics engine to calculate collisions and determine the repulsion force after a collision has happened. The choice of the collision mesh is crucial to the performance of the collision calculations. Most game developers choose a mesh as simple as possible to determine the *bounding volume* of the object. This bounding volume is often a simple sphere, capsule, or bounding box; but it can also have a complex geometry when more details are needed.

The high computational effort for the collision detection arises from the fact that dozens, if not hundreds of objects can be part of a scene and need to be checked for collisions, pairwise against each other. Many methods exist to speed up the collision detection process. The core idea is to split up the scene into sections in a spatial data structure, such as an octree. If two objects are in the same section, a very simple collision routine runs first to get a quick result. The simplest case of collision detection is conducted between two spheres; here it is enough to check if the distance between the centers is smaller than the sum of their radii. There is a wide variety of algorithms that are used to efficiently check collisions between various geometries. If a potential collision is detected in this first phase, the collision is investigated further.

To calculate the response to a collision, information about the exact point of the collision needs to be collected, as well as the velocity and the momentum of the colliding objects. The appropriate resulting forces will then be applied to the objects. The developer can also program custom functions to manipulate the behavior of colliding objects.

The collision detection is usually calculated at fixed time steps. A list of occurring or upcoming collisions is created in each step. The advantage of this method, called *discrete collision detection*, is that the physics simulation can be calculated at constant intervals, independent of frame rate fluctuations in the game. The problem with this method is that the actual moment of the impact is usually missed, and collisions of fast-moving objects can be missed entirely because they pass through other objects from one discrete time step to the next. The solution to this problem can be a continuous collision detection, where the trajectory of fast-moving objects is predicted based on various physical variables; in this way, collisions, including the actual moment of the impact, can be anticipated.

6.5 Lighting

The human eye sees objects in the world as a result of light reflecting off surfaces and subsequently striking receptors in the eye. To understand and model this process, it is necessary to understand both the nature of different light sources and the ways different materials reflect the light. Realistic lighting calculations are very complex, and thus lighting techniques used in computer graphics are usually heuristic. Believable results are often computed instead of realistic simulations. Instead of just specifying a single color for an object, game developers and artists often define material properties and the material's response to different kinds of light.

6.5.1 Light Sources

When no light sources are present in a scene, rendering leads to a black image. However, it is sometimes desirable to create scenes without light sources, where objects are displayed through *emissive lighting*. Such objects light themselves but do not give light out into the scene. Scenes with emissive lighting result in very fast rendering, but unrealistic results. Emissive lighting is thus often used to achieve certain effects in combination with other lighting techniques, for example to create very simple and fast representations of the headlights of a car or of neon signs.

In the real world, light is reflected off objects countless times. This results in the effect that light passing through a little slit under a door into a completely dark room will illuminate the entire room enough for us humans to see. In order to easily simulate light that appears to be equally distributed after being reflected many times, a constant color is used, called *ambient lighting*. It is simply added to the color of a surface.

In addition to ambient lighting, we can distinguish the following forms of light:

- **Directional lights** represent a light source at an infinite distance, shining light into the scene in parallel direction at a certain angle with equal intensity. Directional lights are most commonly used to approximate light that originates from outside the game scene, such as sunlight. Due to its nature, the position of a directional light is not important, and it can generally be placed anywhere in the scene. The developer must define the color, the overall intensity, and the direction of a directional light source.
- **Point lights** are simple light sources that can be imagined as a bulb hanging from a cord, giving off light in equal amounts in all directions. The light intensity gets weaker with the distance from the point light source. Thus, objects closer to the point light appear brighter than those further away. The developer can customize point lights by defining color, intensity, location, and the fall-off function.
- **Spot lights** radiate light in a cone with a certain radius along a directional axis— comparable to a constrained point light. Spotlights can be imagined as flashlights or car headlights. Simple spotlights distribute light equally over the area of the cone. A more complex light behavior can be achieved by defining a fall-off function that determines the light intensity in the center and the softening towards the edges of the cone.
- **Area lights** are defined by rectangles, placed in the game scene, from where light is emitted into the scene. For example, area light is useful to create a light-emitting object such as a TV screen. Area light calculations are more

complex due to light originating from the entire area instead of a single point. As a result, objects illuminated by an area light will have a softer and more realistic brightness distribution than those illuminated by a point light.

6.5.2   Material Reflection (the Phong Reflection Model)

In common cases, the appearance of a virtual object is made up of ambient light, *diffuse reflection*, and *specular reflection*. This is known as the *Phong reflection model*, which is an empirical model; it is not based on physical accuracy, but on the observation of the real-world behavior of light. As discussed above, ambient light reflection is trivial to compute. Diffuse reflection represents dull surfaces, and the brightness of a spot on an object depends on the angle between the normal on the surface and the direction of the light source. Note that diffuse reflection is independent of the viewer's position. The resulting light is multiplied with the material's diffuse reflection coefficient and the intensity of the light source.

Specular reflection creates shiny highlights on objects. Materials with strong specular reflection components are typically metals or plastics, while mirrors are fully specular. Wood, on the other hand, has a very low specular reflection. In order to determine the specular reflection, the angle between the direction to the viewer and the direction of the light's reflection off the surface must be calculated. Thus, the appearance of specular highlights depends on the viewpoint. Additionally, the size of the specular highlight in the real world depends on the shininess of the material. To control this effect, another term is introduced into the equation as an exponent (the Phong exponent) to the angle between the viewpoint and the reflection. A high value will result in a small, sharp reflection, whereas a smaller value leads to a larger, more spread-out specular highlight. A sphere illuminated with the three different types of reflection computed with the Phong model is shown in Fig. 6.10.

Fig. 6.10 A sphere rendered using the Phong reflection model: **a** ambient reflection, **b** diffuse reflection, **c** highlight added by a specular reflection

6.5.3 Shading Models

The simplest way to color an object based on the previously discussed lighting is to color each polygon in one color based on its material reflection and its surface normal (i.e., a vector that describes how the polygon is oriented in space—an important piece of information for calculating the lighting). This approach is called *flat shading*. A major drawback of flat shading is that objects with curved surfaces that are approximated with polygons (e.g., a sphere) do not appear smooth, but the straight edges of the polygons can be seen. A solution is to calculate not one color per polygon but to calculate colors at each vertex. In the case of a triangle, for example, three colors at each vertex would be calculated using the lighting equations. And the normal vectors that are used in the lighting equations are not necessarily the surface normal of the triangle. For instance, if one vertex is part of four triangles, the normal for calculating the lighting could be an average of all four surface normals.

If color that results from lighting is only calculated at the vertices, which color do points have that lie in the interior of the polygon? This is determined by a shading model. The most often used shading model is called *Gouraud Shading*. Here, the color values in the interior of the polygon are generated by linear interpolation between the edges. The polygon is filled one horizontal line ("a scan line") after the other by linear interpolation between the points on the edges. Gouraud shading suffers from artifacts when highlights lay within a polygon. In this case, a highlight disappears entirely because only the vertices of the polygon are considered; since the highlight does not touch the vertices, it is not taken into consideration.

Gouraud shading is not the only way to determine the color of the interior of a polygon based on the colors calculated at the vertices. In fact, there are many different shading algorithms that are used today that can make the 3D models look like a cartoon, an oil painting, or a pencil drawing.

6.5.4 Atmospheric and Post Processing Effects

Atmospheric effects can create a sense of depth by mimicking the real-world phenomenon that particles in the air make objects further away look less saturated than closer objects. For example, fog is implemented by blending the calculated color of a pixel with a predefined background color in a ratio that is proportional to the distance between the camera and the object. Objects that are farther away get a greater fraction of the background color relative to the object's color, and hence fade into the background. Fog begins at a starting distance, and all colors slowly transition to the fog color towards the ending distance. The blending can occur linearly or exponentially. Fog is added after the rasterized image is created from the 3D model data.

Other post-processing effects include image blur (e.g., motion blur or creating depth of field), lens flares, or blooming effects.

6.5.5 Global Illumination

Global illumination is an umbrella term for several methods to achieve a more realistic lighting distribution by taking into account global scene geometry beyond the conventional direct light-object-camera relations. The main problem from which the need for global illumination arises is that the usual pipeline rendering does not take into account the effect that scene elements have on each other (see Sect. 6.1.10). An example is light that is diffusely reflected from every surface and thereby distributed around the scene (indirect light). In order to cope with this issue, computer graphics traditionally used the ambient lighting constant described above. Modern game engines support different global illumination methods to create a much more realistic lighting.

Ray Tracing is a method that is used to create different light effects. Single rays are traced starting at the camera (or eye), passing through the image plane, reaching the object's surface and going from there to the light source. Beginning at the camera is much more efficient than beginning at the light source because only a small percentage of the rays from the light source ever reach the camera. Even though it is computationally expensive because it treats every ray separately, ray tracing is an essential technique to create soft shadows, mirror reflections, and refractions by tracing rays to and from the light sources to determine how objects affect the light. There are numerous variations of the basic ray tracing idea.

Radiosity is a method to model the energy transfer between surfaces. Originally developed to calculate heat transfer, the radiosity method is based on the assumption of energy conservation within a scene. In rendering, this implies that all light reaching a surface will be reflected (unless it is absorbed). To calculate radiosity, a view factor that describes the spatial relation—or more precisely, the amount of direct visible contact between every combination of surface pairs in the scene—must be determined. Following, through different methods, light is emitted from the sources and algorithmically distributed throughout the scene. Radiosity is independent of the viewpoint and can therefore be precomputed for use in real-time applications.

Photon Mapping is another computer graphics technique to create sophisticated light effects such as refractions, caustics, or subsurface scattering. The idea is to shoot small objects, abstracted as photons, from the light source into the scene. If a photon reaches a surface with material properties, it might get reflected, refracted, scattered, or absorbed. If the photon reaches a diffuse surface, it is saved in a photon map, which can later be used for various rendering effects.

Ambient Occlusion is used to enhance the quality of the ambient lighting assumption by taking the environment of a surface into account. It is based on the observation that the amount of light reaching each surface decreases with the amount of other surfaces in its proximity. Ambient occlusion can be pre-computed for static surfaces, as it is independent of the viewpoint.

6.6   Shaders

Before GPU hardware became commonplace on graphics cards, Pixar made the the first approaches for manipulating the rendering pipeline through *shader* programs. They introduced a shading language for RenderMan in 1989 (Upstill 1989). RenderMan is a rendering API between the models and the image generation, intended for high-quality offline rendering of Pixar's animation films. The shading language was developed to allow more customization in the rendering pipeline than the Phong reflection model could offer. Shaders were thus introduced to act as programmable parts in the image production pipeline. Originally not intended for dedicated hardware, the shader paradigm was later broadly adopted, and specific hardware was developed to run a shader on a GPU to boost performance for rendering in real-time.

Several programming languages for shaders have evolved since. OpenGL's GLSL (Graphics Library Shading Language) and DirectX' HLSL (High-Level Shading Language) are most common today, and at least one, often both are supported by major game engines. Additional languages exist, such as Cg, a shading language created by NVIDIA, and ShaderLab, an intermediate language for Unity. The code written in this intermediate language is translated to either GLSL or HLSL depending on the current runtime platform.

Shaders can be distinguished into different shader classes such as vertex, fragment, and geometry shaders, depending on which aspects of the rendering process they handle. A *vertex shader* is executed first during the rendering process. It operates on a per-vertex basis, and is executed for each object separately and in parallel within the geometry subsystem of the rendering pipeline. Let us take the example of a water simulation. A vertex shader would be utilized to calculate positions of vertices to create waves on the surface (for example, with a simple sine function), to determine the directions to the light, and the viewpoint for subsequent shading. A *fragment shader* (also known as a *pixel shader*) is executed after the rasterization step of the pipeline. It can work on the data that was previously calculated by the vertex shader. Fragment shaders operate on fragments, i.e., 2D surface pieces the size of a pixel that are created during rasterization and that might become pixels in the final image if they are not occluded by fragments from other objects. *Geometry shaders* are a newer form of shaders. They allow manipulation of the geometry on a per-point, per-line, or per-triangle basis. They are executed after the vertex shader and before the rasterization step (and thus the fragment shader) of the rendering pipeline. They allow for procedural geometry generation and manipulation during runtime.

6.7   Game Object Editors

Game engines also support the creation process of game objects (assets). They come with a number of editors to build avatars, landscapes, levels, etc. For example, creating an avatar is done by choosing a female or male person, making it

Fig. 6.11 A landscape from *Word Domination* created with the landscape editor of Unity3D (Mildner et al. 2014)

bigger or smaller, supplying clothing, and perhaps personal weapons. Some games even allow players to create their own avatars (e.g., *Diablo*).

Landscapes can be designed by first creating a mesh representation. The height of hills and mountains can be randomly generated. Then, a texture is laid over the mesh. Finally, trees, rivers, lakes, buildings, etc. are added. Figure 6.11 shows an example of a landscape created with the editor of Unity3D (Mildner et al. 2014).

Most game object editors allow importing objects from other software tools. For example, 3D buildings can be generated with 3DSMax and then imported into the game engine's editor. They are converted into the format used by the game engine for compatibility with the game world at runtime. This process was explained in detail in Sect. 5.3.1.

6.8   Game Engine Support for New Hardware

6.8.1   New Hardware Devices

Traditionally, games were mostly played with consoles, mice, joysticks, and game controllers. In recent years, a number of new hardware devices have been developed for more natural interaction in games and other interactive experiences. They are of special interest for serious games, as they allow simulating real-world situations more convincingly and with higher fidelity—which might benefit directly the extent to which characterizing goals can be met. These new hardware devices can be classified as follows:

- *Full body tracking*: With the release of the Kinect sensor for the XBox 360 and the PC in 2010, low-cost depth sensing became available for interactive experiences. The Kinect allows for voice recognition and 3D motion capture, including gesture and facial expression. Other depth-sensing devices like Asus Xtion and SoftKinetic provide a similar functionality. The Kinect 2 was released in 2014 with a wider field of view and a higher resolution of the depth cam. It can also detect hand shapes and the user's emotional states, and it can monitor the user's heart rate.

- *Mobile 3D scanning*: Scanning the environment with the Occipital Structure Sensor is now available (Occipital 2015). The sensor can be attached to a mobile device such as an iPad, and can be used to detect and track the environment. This is important for augmented reality applications that need to combine virtual content with the real environment.
- *Finger and hand tracking*: With an increasing number of virtual reality headsets and 3D displays, it is important for a natural user interface to detect hands and fingers and their motion. The Leap Motion controller is a small device that allows tracking both hands with individual fingers in front of the user. Attached to a VR head-mounted display, it provides a highly immersive virtual reality experience (Leapmotion 2015).
- *Eye tracking and face tracking*: The user's face may provide important information for a game. With current technology it is easy to detect, track and analyze a person's gaze in real time. Affordable sensors are available from Tobii (Tobii 2015), EyeTribe (EyeTribe 2015) or myGaze (MyGaze 2015). Pupil Labs provides an open source solution for mobile eye tracking (Kassner et al. 2014). Face tracking is easily possible with a 3D depth sensor, and software like FaceGen allows for a markerless facial motion capture.
- *Walking*: Until now, walking interfaces have only been presented as prototypes in larger VR labs or as part of military research projects. The Virtuix Omni is an omnidirectional treadmill peripheral for gaming and virtual reality (Virtuix 2015). It uses a platform to simulate walking if the user puts on special shoes to reduce friction. The Austrian startup company Cyberith has developed a similar product called "Virtualizer" that allows walking, running, jumping, crouching, and even sitting (Cyberith 2015).
- *Brain-computer interfaces*: The idea to control technology simply by thought is not new, and devices that allow a direct neural interface exist, with different levels of fidelity. The use of non-invasive brain computing interfaces for entertainment is sometimes called neurogaming. The Emotiv Epoc is a 14-channel EEG device that can read four mental states, thirteen conscious states, facial expressions, and head movements (Emotiv 2015).

Ideas for new devices are presented on a regular basis. Enthusiasts develop new ideas and build custom prototypes using available sensors and prototyping hardware platforms like Arduino, Gadgeteer, or Phidgets. With this trend, many new approaches for computer games will be possible in the near future.

6.8.2 Virtual and Augmented Reality

Well-designed games have the potential to provide a strong feeling of presence, the "feeling of being there." But technically, the audio-visual representation with consoles and high-resolution TV screens, PCs, and monitors or mobile devices provides only a windowed view into the game world.

Many experts consider virtual and augmented reality as an important interaction paradigm for games. *Virtual reality* extends a real-time 3D world by the concept of immersion. This means that as the users become part of the 3D scene, they are immersed in the virtual world. This is realized using viewpoint tracking—including head, eye, and body movements—and dedicated devices like head-mounted displays, or large immersive setups like L-Shapes or CAVEs (i.e., large projective displays where the user can even stand on a display and is surrounded by virtual imagery), together with full-body tracking systems.

For gaming, head-mounted displays seem to be more appropriate. Recently, a number of head-mounted displays have been proposed, and large companies like Google, Facebook, Sony, and Valve are working on virtual reality headsets. The Oculus Rift is the most prominent device currently under development (Oculus 2015). Started as a Kickstarter project in 2012, the company Oculus VR created two developer kits with a resolution of 1920×1080 pixels at a 75 Hz refresh rate. In 2014, Facebook announced that they acquired Oculus VR. The consumer product has a resolution of 2160×1200 at 90 Hz with a full six-degree-of-freedom positional and rotational tracking. Oculus has partnered with Microsoft; they will release a consumer version with a standard XBox game controller, and XBox One games will be playable with a VR headset. Oculus has also recently presented a more advanced input device, the Oculus touch (Oculus 2015). It is a pair of tracked controllers with a pistol-like grip that delivers the feeling of virtual hands in 3D. It provides an analog joystick and buttons for the thumb and index finger. Hand gestures are recognized quite well.

Augmented reality is often considered to be the successor of VR. According to Azuma (1997), augmented reality is defined by (i) the combination of real and virtual content, (ii) interactivity and real-time computation, and (iii) 3D registration of virtual elements in the real scene. This requires additional sensors for the environment. Cameras are often used to track the environment which is then combined with computer-generated content. Figure 6.12 shows a prototypical augmented reality board game.

6.8.3 Support for New Hardware in Game Engines

For many projects, it is essential to provide an interface to prominent game engines like Unity and Unreal. These game engines offer useful approaches to interface to new devices with their modular SDKs. For important new hardware, like the Oculus Rift, built-in support is quickly provided. Dedicated drivers are often developed by the inventors of these devices.

Fig. 6.12 A prototypical augmented reality board game

6.9 Selection of a Suitable Game Engine

The Internet is full of discussions about which engine is the best and should be chosen to start a new project. Programmers argue about the efficiency of different programming languages, designers about the tools allowing them to simultaneously work on the assets, and publishers about multi-platform support to reach the broadest customer group. So, which engine is the right one to choose?

There is no universally valid answer, since the recommendation depends on each individual use case. The following list provides requirements to help to identify the most appropriate engine.

- What platforms will the game run on?
- Should the game be 2D or a 3D?
- Is there a budget for licensing an engine?
- How many people will work simultaneously on the game?
- Should experts from a serious game application domain be able to perform authoring tasks with the game engine's tools? What is the background and skillset of these authors?
- What is the preferred programming language?
- Does the team require engine support by the engine vendor?
- Is there an active community using the engine?
- Should the engine be designed for a certain genre?
- How well should the content pipeline be covered? What editors are needed?
- Is the engine required to be extensible? Should the engine's source code be available?
- Is it necessary to integrate a specific third-party library into the game engine?
- Is there a concrete roadmap for the engine, and will its development be continued in the future?

When some questions of the above list remain unanswered, it is recommended to obtain a demo license to test and evaluate an engine and its tools. Nowadays many of the game engines provide an easy-to-use, one-click installer with a simple demo game to test visuals, functionality, and usage from both the author and player perspective. Comparing game engines is a difficult undertaking; while features and workflows differ a lot, they can still lead to similar results regarding gameplay and graphics. In order to illustrate how different game engines can be compared to each other, we include a brief review of three popular game engines.

6.9.1 Unreal Engine 4

The *Unreal Engine 4* was published in March 2014, and is the successor of the UDK (*Unreal Development Kit*). The engine's manufacturer Epic not only has many years of experience in engine design, but also an excellent knowledge of the game production process—since the company started to produce Unreal in 1998, a former milestone of first person shooters, and has continued to create many innovative games over the last few years. Working with *Unreal Engine 4,* users will recognize that Epic's game development experience found their way into the engine and the integrated toolset. The engine itself is accompanied by a strong resource management tool, animation, and visual scripting components, as well as an integration into Microsoft's *Visual Studio*. The most advertised features are the lighting engine and the blueprint scripting tools. The latter allows defining a behavior for diverse game objects via a drag-and-drop approach. Thus, Unreal Engine 4 explicitly encourages non-programmers to develop games with the engine.

6.9.2 Unity 5

Unity 5 is a highly visible game engine for independent game developers. It has a strong position in the educational sector, both because a strong user community supports it, and because it provides well-written or audio/video-recorded tutorials to support beginners. With the release of *Unity 5,* the manufacturer tries to address not only the casual or mobile game developers, but also those who develop desktop games with a focus on visuals. One of the remarkable strengths of *Unity 5* is the *Asset Store,* which provides free and commercially available extensions for the editor and the engine, learning materials, and other assets like music or 3D models. Being directly integrated into the engine, the *Asset Store* allows one to download a package of assets directly into the current game project. Supported programming languages are C#, UnityScript, and Boo.[2] *Unity* does not yet provide a visual scripting system,

---

[2]Unity has evaluated their editor statistics and found that 80 % of their customers use C#, 19 % use UnityScript, and <1 % use Boo.

but the integration of C# into the integrated development environment *MonoDevelop* works well and fits seamlessly into the object-based, hierarchical game architecture.

6.9.3   CryENGINE 3

Similar to Epic, Crytek is a well-known game developer (*FarCry*, *Crysis*) who put his experience with game design into the company's engine CryENGINE 3. The engine is either offered for download via the Internet or as a subscription on Steam. Crytek stresses the engine's impressive visuals as well as the sandbox editor in their advertisement. When using the editor for the first time, features like the road and river tools, procedural content placement, the vegetation system and the time-of-day system demonstrate that the company's focus was on creating realistically looking virtual worlds with a relatively low effort for the developer. Furthermore, the *CryENGINE 3* provides a visual scripting tool called *Flow Graph* (see Fig. 6.7) which serves not only as an interface to design the game object behavior but also to profile and debug the game before and while playing. Regarding visuals, *CryEN-GINE 3* offers cutting edge graphics.

6.9.4   Other Engines

There are many more engines on the market, including Valve's *Source Engine 2*, Havok's *Vision Engine*, GarageGame's *Torque*, Id Software's *idTech* engine, Blender's *Game Engine,* or Emergent Game Technologies' *Gamebryo*. They cannot all be discussed in detail here, but the named features and topics presented above will help to gather information on them, supporting the decision for the most appropriate engine for a serious game project (Table 6.1).

6.10   Summary and Questions

This chapter has shown that game engines provide a valuable basis for developers of serious games, as they make readily available knowledge and groundwork from various disciplines such as graphics design, platform programming, user interfaces, workflow optimization, mathematics—and of course, programming. After years of work and research, today's game engines have reached a maturity level that enables smaller independent development teams and entire studios with hundreds of employees to use one single product. They provide a general yet powerful way to create serious games for different genres, from adventures to racing to board games.

An advantage current game engines have is the variety of learning material provided online. Tutorial videos, free eBooks, or even meetings in larger cities offer the possibility to quickly dive into the newest features and feel comfortable with coding and design. Topics focus not only on fundamentals, such as the usage of the

Table 6.1 Game engine overview

	Unity 5	CryENGINE 3	Unreal Engine 4
Supported platforms	Windows PC, Mac OS X, Linux, SteamOS, iOS, Android, Windows Phone 8, Blackberry 10, Tizen, WebGL, WebPlayer (Plugin), PlayStation 3, PlayStation 4, PS Vita, Xbox One, Xbox 360, Wii U	Windows PC, iOS, Android, Xbox One, Playstation 4, Wii U	Windows PC, Mac OS X, Linux, SteamOS, iOS, Android, HTML5, PlayStation 4, Xbox One
Development environment	Windows XP SP2, Windows 7, Windows 8, Mac OS X >10.8	Windows Vista SP1, Windows 7, Windows 8	Windows 7 64 bit, Mac OS X > 10.9.2
Engine source code access	Yes (not free)	Yes (not free, full license required)	Yes
License costs	Free (personal edition), $75 per month (professional edition), no royalties	$9.90 USD per month, no royalties (standard subscription)	Free to use, 5 % royalty on gross product revenue after the first $3000 USD per game per calendar quarter
Limited to a specific genre	No	No	No
Programming languages	C#, UnityScript, Boo	C++	C++

level editor, but also on next-generation issues such as virtual reality and modern input devices.

The following questions should help to consolidate the reader's understanding of this chapter:

- What are the main advantages of a modular game engine design?
- Why is the platform independence layer useful when you port your game from a Windows PC to a Mac?
- Your game, written and tested on a slow computer, runs very fast on newer machines. Players claim your game is unplayable since they cannot control the player's movement. What might have been your mistake during the development process?
- Why do game engine editors convert input from external sources to their internal format?
- Describe the different steps in the animation process of a game character.
- How would you animate a game avatar? What method would you use?
- What forms of light do you know?
- Why is shading very compute-intensive?
- What is the difference between lighting and shading for a game and lighting shading for an engineering simulation?

- Which new hardware devices do you know, and what characterizing goal would each of them be especially useful for?
- You have the task to design a new outdoor mixed reality game that allows to familiarize new employees of a chemical company with the complex production facilities and to inform them about safety regulations. Describe the input and output devices you would select for this game.
- Imagine you want to build a game for health, running on a PC, with elderly people as players. Which of the three game engines presented briefly above would you pick?

Recommended Literature

McShaffry M, Graham DR (2012) Game coding complete, 4th ed, Course Technology—*This book covers the entire cycle of game development from setting up a development environment, code and asset management to engine programming, game editor development, quality assurance and final shipping of the game. The book has a strong technical focus and provides hundreds of lines of code written in C++ and even assembler but is yet well explained and follows an "explain by code" approach*

Gregory J (2014) Game engine architecture, 2nd ed, Taylor & Francis Ltd.—*This fairly thick book (more than 800 pages) contains a detailed description of all aspects of game engines. It is a very technical book. The author has many years of practical experience as a game designer and a game programmer, and his style of writing is geared towards those who want to really understand game engines and develop their own games*

References

Azuma RT (1997) A survey of augmented reality. In: Presence: teleoperators and virtual environments 6(4):355–385

Back E, Madsen A (2007) Procedural character generation—implementing reference fitting and principal components analysis. Aalborg University, Denmark

CuttingEdge (2015) http://www.undergroundthegame.com/. Accessed 16 Dec 2015

Cyberith (2015) http://cyberith.com/. Accessed 30 Nov 2015

DeLoura M (2009) http://www.gamasutra.com/blogs/MarkDeLoura/20090302/83321/The_Engine_Survey_General_results.php. Accessed 15 Nov 2015

Emotiv (2015) https://emotiv.com/. Accessed 30 Nov 2015

EyeTribe (2015) https://theeyetribe.com. Accessed 30 Nov 2015

Gregory J (2014) Game engine architecture, 2nd edn, Taylor & Francis Ltd., New York, USA

Guthier B, Sharmin F (2016) Survival of the Monnolinos. Lehrstuhl für Praktische Informatik IV. University of Mannheim, Germany

Kassner M, Patera W, Bulling A. (2014) Pupil: an open source platform for pervasive eye tracking and mobile gaze-based interaction. In: Proceedings ACM internat joint conf on pervasive and ubiquitous computing, ACM, New York, NY, USA, pp 1151–1160

Lange T, Hammer P (2014) Making games. IDG Entertainment Media GmbH, München, Germany

Leapmotion (2015) https://www.leapmotion.com/. Accessed 30 Nov 2015

Levy DB (2009) Animation development—from pitch to production. Allworth Press, New York, USA

Mildner P, Campbell C, Effelsberg W (2014) Word domination: bringing together fun and education in an authoring-based 3D shooter game. In: Göbel S, Wiemeyer J (eds) Games for training, education, health and sports, LNCS 8395. Springer, Heidelberg/New York, pp 59–70

Milic L, McConville Y (2006) The animation producer's handbook. Open University Press, Maidenhead, UK

MyGaze (2015) http://www.mygaze.com/. Accessed 30 Nov 2015

Occipital (2015) http://occipital.com. Accessed 30 Nov 2015

Oculus (2015) https://www.oculus.com. Accessed 30 Nov 2015

Parent R (2012) Computer animation—algorithms and techniques, 3rd edn. Morgan Kaufmann, San Francisco, CA, USA

Thomas F, Johnston O (1981) Disney animation: the illusion of life. Disney Editions, Life, Hyperion, New York, NY, USA

Tobii (2015) http://www.tobii.com/. Accessed 30 Nov 2015

Tracy S, Reindell T (2012) CryENGINE 3 game development. Packt Publishing, Birmingham, UK

Upstill S (1989) The RenderMan companion: a programmer's guide to realistic computer graphics. Addison-Wesley, Harlow, UK

Virtuix (2015) http://www.virtuix.com/. Accessed 30 Nov 2015

Personalization and Adaptation

7

Stefan Göbel and Viktor Wendel

Abstract

Computing machinery allows the creation of intelligent, personalized, adaptive systems and programs that consider the characteristics, interests, and needs of individual users and user groups. In the field of serious games, storytelling and gaming approaches are used as motivational instruments for suspenseful, engaging learning, or personalized training and healthcare. This chapter describes models and mechanisms for the development of personalized, adaptive serious games with a focus on digital educational games (DEG). First, the term adaptation is defined—both in general and in the context of games—and basic mechanisms such as the concept of flow are described. Then, player and learner models are analyzed for classification of player characteristics. For the control of serious games, adaptive storytelling and sequencing mechanisms are described. In particular, the concept of Narrative Game-based Learning Objects (NGLOBs) is presented, which considers the symbiosis of gaming, learning, and storytelling in the context of an adaptive DEG. Finally, the presented theoretical concepts, models, and mechanisms are discussed in the course of the 80Days project as a DEG best-practice example—which considers authoring, control, and evaluation aspects, and its practical implementation in 80Days using the authoring framework StoryTec.

S. Göbel (✉) · V. Wendel
Technische Universität Darmstadt, Darmstadt, Germany
e-mail: stefan.goebel@kom.tu-darmstadt.de

© Springer International Publishing Switzerland 2016
R. Dörner et al. (eds.), *Serious Games*, DOI 10.1007/978-3-319-40612-1_7

7.1 Adaptation—Definition

Adaptation is a major field of research in gaming, especially in serious games. It is desirable to adapt games in various dimensions, like those stated above. As stated by Charles et al. (2005), "learning and adaptation are viewed by some as a having a crucial part to play in next-generation games." Different adaptation principles, techniques, and methods that are especially relevant for serious games are (Kickmeier-Rust and Albert 2012a, b):

- Procedural and adaptive level and content generation
- Adaptive behavior of agents
- Adaptive and interactive storytelling
- Guidance, hinting
- Motivational interventions
- Adaptive presentation
- Adaptive curriculum sequencing
- Navigation support
- Intelligent solution analysis

What exactly is adaptation? A common definition is the "ability to make appropriate responses to changed or changing circumstances" (Kaukoranta et al. 2003). Moreover, various common explanations of the term define it as an adjustment to a changed circumstance or environment.

In computer science, adaptation refers to a system or process, in which a system changes its behavior for individual users based on information acquired about those users and its environment (https://en.wikipedia.org/wiki/Adaptation_%28computer_science%29). However, this definition indicates a static behavior, a one-time change based on information about a (set of) user(s). It does not state anything about how the system or process behaves when the environment, the users, or their behavior changes during use or play.

In the context of learning, Steinmetz and Nahrstedt (2004) define adaptive learning systems as "learning programs capable of adapting themselves to the individual abilities of the learner, e.g., previous knowledge, interests, weaknesses or preferences with regard to forms of representation." This, again, does not consider a reaction to a change, but rather an adaptation to the static personal properties of a learner.

Adaptability is commonly considered as the ability of a system to adapt itself or to be adapted according to a change of circumstances (http://www.thefreedictionary.com/adaptability).

Hence, in computer science, the term *adaptivity* refers to "a system that adapts automatically to its users according to changing conditions, i.e., an adaptive system" (https://ahdictionary.com/word/search.html?q=adaptation). This, in contrast, relates to an adaptation as a reaction to a change.

> **Adaptation**: The act or process of adapting, or the state of being adapted; something that is changed in order to become suitable to a new condition or situation.
> **Adaptability**: The ability to adapt or to be adapted; a system is considered adaptable, if it is designed to be able to adapt itself or be adapted.
> **Adaptivity**: Adapting automatically according to changing conditions; a system is considered adaptive, if it adapts automatically according to changing conditions.

In the context of games, often the term *personalization* is used for a (static) one-time adaptation of a gaming aspect to the needs of a user, whereas adaptation refers to the continuous adjustment of the game towards the actions and performance of a user and the current state of the game. In sum, adaptation in the context of games refers to a reaction to either a change of the (game) environment or a situation or the context of a player. Personalization refers to a change of information, services, adjustments, or other parameters to a player's personal preferences, abilities, needs, or requirements. Rule-based personalization is a technique which adapts content to the given user profile based on a given, relatively rigid rule set.

Adaptation can be applied at various points in a game: (1) at the start of the game (i.e., personalization—in the sense of configuration) or (2) repeatedly during the game. In the second case, the adaptation moment and the adaptation rate are distinguished. Adaptation can happen continuously (i.e., x times per y seconds) or at discrete points in the game (e.g., after a special event as a reaction to a player action, between levels, etc.).

> **Adaptation and personalization**: In the context of games, often the term *personalization* is used for a (static) one-time adaptation of a gaming aspect to the needs or preferences of a user, whereas *adaptation* refers to the continuous adjustment of the game based on the actions and performance of a user and the current state of the game towards a desired state.

In addition to point of adaptation, adaptation is characterized by what to adapt. Generally, everything which is relevant in a game can be adapted, from visual and optical appearances over sound to elements of a game relevant to gameplay. Those are highly dependent on the game itself. In a shooting game, those might be the number of enemies spawning and their hit accuracy; whereas in a simulation, this might be several parameters that describe the ability of an AI opponent, or random events which impact the game's difficulty.

Therefore, in the context of serious games, it appears reasonable to not only look at what elements of a game can be adapted specifically, but to look at a meta level on what to adapt, when to adapt it, how and to what degree to adapt it and why something should be adapted. Hence, serious games generally can be adapted in terms of gaming or gameplay, and in terms of the goal of the game. Concerning the latter, for various goals there are established models and concepts existing. For example, if the characterizing goal is learning in the broadest sense, learner models can be used to characterize the state of the game, identify deficits, problems, or learning difficulties, and based on those decide on how to adapt the game. Hence, in the following, established concepts and models in the areas of difficulty adaptation (*flow*), player modeling (adaptation in terms of gameplay), learner modeling (adaptation in terms of learning), and story models (adaptation in terms of narration) will be further investigated in the following sections.

7.2   Adaptation—Dimensions and Mechanisms

Various aspects of a serious game can be adapted. The following section addresses three main adaptation dimensions: *difficulty*, *player*, and *learner*. Further, an overview will be provided regarding existing adaptation concepts, algorithms, and mechanisms.

7.2.1   Difficulty Adaptation—The Flow Concept

A *challenge* is a major component of every game. Players want to test and master skills relevant for the game (Lazzaro 2004; Fu and Houlette 2002). A major element of many games is to overcome challenging opponents (Vorderer et al. 2003) in order to reach a desired goal (Fabricatore 2000). Gee (2005) states that it is necessary that all players, regardless of their current skill level, perceive the game as challenging, but feasible.

In 1990, Mihalyi Csikzentmihalyi proposed the concept of *flow*, for a state in which a person is totally immersed into an action, in a way such that he/she even forgets about time (Csikszentmihakyi 1990). He states that a person in flow experiences the following characteristics:

- Clear goals and immediate feedback
- Equilibrium between the level of challenge and personal skill
- Merging of action and awareness
- Focused concentration
- Sense of potential control
- Loss of self-consciousness
- Time distortion
- Autotelic or self-rewarding experience

Figure 7.1 illustrates the concept of flow using the *flow channel*. A person is considered to be within the flow channel, if the person's skill in a task matches the task's challenge for this person (e.g., A1). If the skill level becomes too high (e.g.,

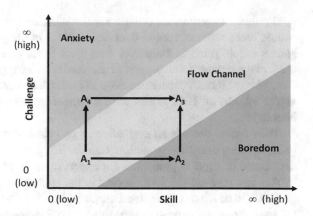

Fig. 7.1 Flow channel after Csikszentmihalyi (adapted Schell 2008)

by improving, or learning new skills) for the challenge, the person moves towards the boredom zone (A2). On the other hand, if the challenge rises, but the skill level does not improve, the player moves towards the anxiety zone (A4). Hence, flow is the small channel where challenge matches the given skill. Given that a person's skill improves either when exercising a task over a longer time, or repeating a task, it is assumed that the respective skill will improve over time (A1 → A2). In order for the person to stay in the flow channel, task difficulty needs to be adapted accordingly (A2 → A3). If, however, the challenge is too high for the person's current skill, the person might come back to the flow channel when she or he improves (A4 → A3). Otherwise, in order for the person to stay in the Flow Channel, task difficulty needs to be adapted again (A4 → A3).

Game Flow

Sweetser and Wyeth (2005) extended the flow concept specifically for games: GameFlow. They transfer the concept of flow to games with the goal of designing and evaluating enjoyment in games. Their model includes the eight dimensions *concentration, challenge, player skill, control, clear goal, feedback, immersion,* and *social interaction.*

For concentration, they argue among others that "players shouldn't be burdened with tasks that don't feel important," or that "games should have high workload, while still being appropriate for the players' perceptual, cognitive, and memory limits," and that "players should not be distracted from tasks that they want to need to concentrate on."

Regarding challenge, they state among others that "challenges in games must match the players' skill level" and that "games should provide new challenges at an appropriate pace."

In terms of player skill, they argue that "players should be able to start playing the game without reading the manual" or that "game interfaces and mechanics should be easy to learn and use."

Similarly, they provide criteria for the dimension of *control,* (i.e., that players should feel a sense of control over their actions in the game), *clear goals*, (i.e., that games should provide the player with clear goals at appropriate times), *feedback* (i.e., players must receive appropriate feedback at appropriate times), *immersion* (i.e., players should experience deep but effortless involvement in the game), and *social interaction* (i.e., games should support and create opportunities for social interaction).

They further provide an evaluation of two similar games, *Warcraft 3* and *Lords of EverQuest*, using the gameflow criteria. They conclude that the gameflow concept could be used as guidelines for expert reviews or other types of play-testing.

Another view on the flow concept in the context of games is proposed by Chen (2007). He concludes three fundamental conditions for flow to occur: The game (1) needs to be intrinsically rewarding, (2) offers the right amount of challenge to match player ability, and (3) provides the player a sense of personal control over the game.

Further, Chen explains that different players have different flow channels, respecting the fact that hardcore gamers tend to have a more steep flow channel than average gamers, or even novice gamers. Further, Chen explains that designers can adapt players' flow experience through the choices they build into the experience (cf Fig. 7.2). Chen argues that for an enjoyable interactive experience, games should offer adaptive choices which allow players to enjoy flow in their own personal way and to embed choices inside the core activities to ensure that flow is never interrupted.

Abrantes and Gouveia (2011) developed a survey to test for flow experience in game. Their survey (questionnaire) uses the five dimensions: control, attention focus, curiosity, intrinsic interest (Trevino and Webster 1992), and sense of time (McKenna and Lee 2003). Those are based on the characteristics described by Csikzentmihalyi.

Fig. 7.2 Flow experience based on designer choices

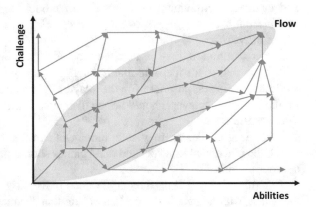

7.2.2 Player Modeling

The center of a game is its player(s). Hence, especially within the context of adaptation, a major focus is the question of how to adapt a game to a player's needs and preferences. In order to be able to suitably adapt a game to a (set of) player(s), player characteristics need to be known. Therefore, the concept of player modeling will be the focus in this section, which covers how players in games can be modeled.

> In order to have an impact, Serious Games must be more concerned than traditional games with creating an accurate model of the player. This is in order to better tailor the game experience to the player's needs and preferences, including potential Non-Player Characters (NPCs) to accurately communicate with and hopefully persuade the player.
> (Encarnação 2009)

Up to date, there is a multitude of player models available focusing on different aspects of players, their interaction with other players, or their interaction with the game. Smith et al. developed a taxonomy of player modeling (Smith et al. 2011a, b). In their taxonomy, a player model is defined by four dimensions: *scope of application, purpose of use, domain of modeled details,* and *source of model's derivation or motivation.*

An application's scope differentiates based on applicability, i.e., one player (individual), a class of players, all players (universal), or hypothetical. In terms of purpose, they differ between generative and descriptive. The domain specifies whether the model defines game actions or human reactions. The source facet has four characteristics: *Induced* (learned by algorithmic means), *interpreted* (concluded via reasoning from records), *analytic* (derived purely from the game's rules and related models), and *synthetic* (justified by reference to an internal belief or external theory).

Using this taxonomy, they classified 31 existing player model concepts. [Note: The Passage player model was classified as both class-based and individual (theoretical and empirical). Thus, it appears three times in the taxonomy.] Table 7.1 summarizes the taxonomy by Smith et al.

One of the best known player models is Bartle's player model (Bartle 1996). Bartle categorizes players along two axes: acting versus interacting and players versus world (see Fig. 7.3).

In the resulting four quadrants, four prototypical player types are placed.

Players who tend to act in connection with the world are called *achievers*. These players are assumed to have most fun when trying to accomplish everything they can within the game, i.e., solve every puzzle and overcome every obstacle in order to have beaten all aspects of the game (i.e., obtain all achievements).

Players who tend to act in connection with other players are called *killers*. In roleplay games, this is often associated with fighting, or otherwise comparing skills with other players. Hence, the term *killer* was chosen to reflect this often-aggressive style of play, where the supreme goal is to be the winner.

Players who tend to interact with the world are called *explorers*. Those players usually focus on experiencing the game (world). Hence, they like to explore it to

Table 7.1 Overview of player models according to Smith et al. (2011b)

Instance	Scope	Source	Purpose	Domain
"Speedrunner" and "Completionist"	Class	Interp.	Descr.	Active
Bartle's player types	Class	Interp.	Descr.	Both
WoW guild archetypes (Thurau)	Class	Induced	Descr.	Active
PaSSAGE (Thue)	Class	Synth.	Gen.	Reactive
Storyboards (Fullerton)	Hypo.	Synth.	Descr.	Active
Ludocore (Smith)	Hypo.	Analytic.	Gen.	Active
Houlette	Individ.	Induced	Descr.	Active
Playtracer (Andersen)	Individ.	Induced	Descr.	Active
PaSSAGE (Thue)	Individ.	Induced	Descr.	Active
Race track generation (Togelius)	Individ.	Induced	Gen.	Active
NonyBots	Individ.	Interpret.	Gen.	Active
Drivatars	Individ.	Induced	Gen.	Reactive
Polymorph (Jenning-Teats)	Individ.	Induced	Gen.	Reactive
Interactive fiction walkthroughs (Reed)	Individ.	Synth.	Both	Active
QuakeBot (Laird)	Individ.	Synth.	Gen.	Active
IBM's Deep Blue and Watson	Individ.	Synth.	Gen.	Active
Mario Bots (Togelius)	Individ.	Analytic.	Gen.	Reactive
PaSSAGE (Thue)	Individ.	Synth.	Gen.	Reactive
Heatmaps for Halo 3	Univ.	Induced	Descr.	Active
Preference modeling (Yannakakis)	Univ.	Induced	Descr.	Reactive
Polymorph (Jenning-Teats)	Univ.	Induced	Gen.	Reactive
Engames tablebases (Bellman)	Univ.	Analytic.	Gen.	Active
EMPath (Sullivan)	Univ.	Analytic.	Gen.	Active
IMPLANT (Tan)	Univ.	Analytic.	Gen.	Active
Ludocore (Smith)	Univ.	Analytic.	Gen.	Active
Market Bots	Univ.	Synth.	Gen.	Active
Launchpad (Smith)	Univ.	Synth.	Gen.	Active
EMPath (Sullican)	Univ.	Synth.	Gen.	Reactive
Racetrack generation (Togelius)	Univ.	Synth.	Gen.	Reactive
Flow inspired (Czikszentmihalyi)	Univ.	Synth.	Gen.	Reactive
Mario bots (Togelius)	Univ.	Analytic.	Gen.	Reactive

experience every piece of it, often trying to find hidden places or Easter eggs in games.

Lastly, players who tend to interact with other players are called *socializers*. Their favorite play style is talking, chatting, or otherwise interacting with other players. In roleplay games, these players are usually connected to the aspects where players play together, often with dialogue-intensive parts of the game.

Bartle's player model assigns a value in the range [0...1] for each of these types to a player, indicating to which extent the player is an achiever, explorer, etc. This

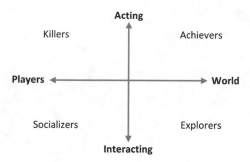

Fig. 7.3 Player model after Bartle (1996) showing the two axes Players versus World and Acting versus Interacting. The four player types are located between the axes

player model is also descriptive. According to Smith et al. (2011a), its scope is class-based, the source is empirically interpreted, and the domain defines both game actions and human reactions.

Laws (2002) describes a different approach that classifies role-players into the following classes: *power gamer, butt-kicker, tactician, specialist, method actor,* and *casual gamer.* The power gamer uses the rule system to maximize his/her power; usually tries to use weaknesses in the system for his/her advantage. The butt-kicker favors simple gameplay and action. The tactician wants rules to be realistic, consistent, and logic, and favors tactical decisions over roleplay. The specialist focuses on a special character type and its related class challenges. The method actor values roleplaying his/her character above everything else. In contrast, the casual gamer plays to be part of a social group, rather than for the game itself. This can be considered a rather descriptive player model.

A more generic model is proposed by Houlette (2004). The model allows using a set of player traits which can be freely defined according to the game domain. Each trait is assigned a value in the range [0...1], indicating to which extent it is fulfilled for a player. The least-mean-square heuristic is used to update player traits according to

$$traitValue = \alpha \cdot observeredValue + (1 - \alpha) \cdot traitValue$$

Here, traitValue is the value of the respective trait, which is updated using the current value and an observed value, and a weighting variable α, which defines to which extent the old value is weighted compared to the observed value. Depending on observed player behavior (i.e., player choices, actions, etc.), traits are updated. The entirety of traitValues for a player forms the player model.

Again, this is a descriptive player model. This player model's scope is on individual players, the source is empirically induced, and it defines game actions.

The process of player modeling in adaptive games consists of several steps: First, an initial model of the player is established using player preferences. This model is used throughout the game to adapt it. However, the model should be

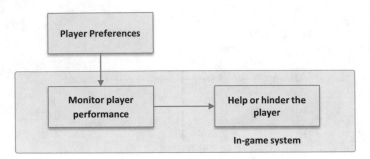

Fig. 7.4 Basic adaptive game system after Charles and Black (2004)

updated during the game according to the player's actions and behavior. This cycle of reevaluating the player model and adaptation of the game is shown in Fig. 7.4.

Charles and Black (2004) and Charles et al. (2005) propose a player model based on neural networks. Their system uses a feedback loop for measuring if an adaptation had a positive influence (according to its intention). They infer that if an adaptation was bad, either the wrong adaptation was chosen or the player model was incorrect. They use this data to then remodel player types and reevaluate the adaptation algorithm.

Finally, the four player types do not seem to be mutually exclusive or independent. Rather, preferences can take any value on the four aspects of modes and objects of interest (e.g., Yee 2006).

7.2.3   Learner Modeling

Similar to a player's role in a game in general, the learner is core to serious games with a learning focus (i.e., Digital Educational Games). Thus, it is necessary to capture learner performance in serious games. This incorporates not only a learner's knowledge state, but also learning styles, learning speed, and learning motivation.

Hence, *learner modeling* refers to capturing a learner's state of knowledge, learning style, and learning path, i.e., the order in which a learner acquires new knowledge. Especially in digital learning environments—or games where learning content might be presented in a predefined order—interdependencies between the learner's state of knowledge and the game progress are supposed to exist. Therefore, the learning path is expected to become especially meaningful in such a scenario. Learner modeling thus can be used to assess a learner's state of knowledge, learning preferences and learning style.

A well-established basic model for modeling knowledge of a specific problem is the Knowledge Space Theory by Doignon and Falmagne (1999). Their model focuses on observable solution behavior and does not consider learning objectives, skills, or competencies (see also Chap. 10). They state that "'knowledge' of an individual in a particular domain of knowledge can be operationalized as the solving behavior of that individual on a domain-specific set X of problems." A learner's knowledge state is defined as the subset of problems he/she is able to solve.

An extension of the Knowledge Space Theory is provided by Korossy (1999). Korossy introduced the Competency-based Knowledge Space Theory (CbKST). The goal of this extension is to be able to link observable behavioral aspects with the non-observable construct of skills or knowledge related to the behavior. Korossy defines performance as "...the observable solution behavior of a person on a set of domain-specific problems." Further, competence is defined as "a theoretical construct accounting for the performance." The term knowledge structure is further defined as the pair (X, K) where X is a set of problems and $(K$ is a family of subsets of X, the empirically expectable solution patterns. The elements of (X, K) are called knowledge states. Finally, the knowledge space is defined a knowledge structure *(X, K)* with $\emptyset, X \in K$ and 'K is stable under union'.

The concept of knowledge space theory is further extended by Heller et al. (2006). Their extension links learning objects and assessment problems with relevant skill. The Extended Knowledge Space Theory includes a set of assessment problems, a set of learning objectives, and a set of skills relevant for solving problems, and taught by the learning objects. Subsequently, the knowledge structure is defined K over a domain Q as the collection of possible knowledge states of Q, with $\emptyset, Q \in K$. In this model, the knowledge domain is modeled using Hasse diagrams.

Figure 7.5 shows a Hasse diagram of a knowledge domain with five elements and dependencies between them. A dependency between element x and y is considered to be an "x-requires-y"-relation. For example, element b requires element a.

Based on the structure of the knowledge domain, the knowledge structure can be deduced using the relationship between the elements of the knowledge domain. The knowledge structure contains the set of all possible knowledge states. It further includes knowledge about which knowledge needs to be acquired as a prerequisite for another piece of knowledge. In Fig. 7.6, the corresponding knowledge space for the knowledge domain in Fig. 7.5 is shown.

Valuable information can be gathered from the current knowledge state of a learner.

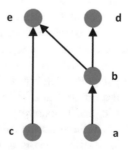

Fig. 7.5 Example of a knowledge domain $Q = a, b, c, d, e$ and dependencies in form of a Hasse diagram (from Heller et al. 2006)

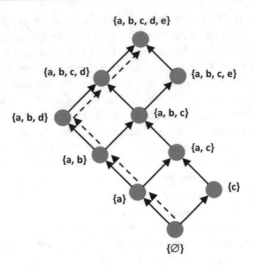

Fig. 7.6 Example of the knowledge space for the skill graph shown in Fig. 7.5 modeled as a Hasse diagram (from Heller et al. 2006)

The *outer fringe* of a knowledge state is the set of problems which can be tackled next based on the current knowledge state. It is defined via the successor states of that knowledge state. Using the example from Fig. 7.6, the two successor states of $\{a, b\}$ are $\{a, b, c\}$ and $\{a, b, d\}$. Those are the states which enhance the current knowledge state about either $\{c\}$ or $\{d\}$. Therefore, the *outer fringe* of the knowledge state $\{a, b\}$ is the set $\{c, d\}$.

The *inner fringe* indicates what a learner already knows and subsequently which problems the learner can solve at this state. It can also be interpreted as what a learner learned most recently. For the knowledge state $\{a, b\}$, this is the set $\{b\}$. For the knowledge state $\{a, b, c\}$, it is the set $\{b, c\}$.

The *Extended Knowledge Space Theory* (Heller et al. 2006) extends the model about the concept of learning objects and skills. The set of skills S contains relevant skills for solving the problems of set Q. They are taught through the learning objects of set L. This is meant to be a more fine-grained description of a learner's capabilities. A mapping r associates a subset of skills—the required skills—to each learning objective. A mapping t associates a subset of skills—the taught skills—to each learning objective. Thus, it is possible to define which skills need to be acquired in order for a learning objective to be taught and what a learning objective teaches the learner. Similar to the knowledge structure, the competence structure can be modeled via a Hasse diagram (Kickmeier-Rust and Albert 2013) (see Fig. 7.7). Thus, competencies are ordered in a semi-order using a directed graph which is reflexive, anti-symmetric, and transitive.

A crucial part of learner modeling is the assessment of a learner's state of knowledge, i.e., the assessment of the learner's state of skills or competencies. In this context, Kickmeier-Rust and Albert state that "assessment is the one thing in successful

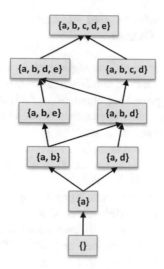

Fig. 7.7 Example of a competency graph modeled as a Hasse diagram (from Kickmeier-Rust and Albert 2013)

adaptation" (Kickmeier-Rust and Albert 2012a, b), and further propose a list of performance-related indicators considered relevant for serious games. Those are:

- Score
- Task completion rates
- Task completion times
- Task success rate
- Task success depth
- Progress in the game world
- Incongruent behavior

A *score* can be an in-game defined assessment of player performance (e.g., a high score). *Task completion* denotes which percentage of a task was completed; whereas the task completion time refers to how many times a task was completed. The *task success rate* denotes the percentage of successful, i.e., correct completion of a task, whereas *success depth* differentiates between different degrees of success. *Progress* in a game world refers to how far players were able to go within a game. This might be matched to player performance, which would be considered progress steps related to obstacles/tasks that need to be overcome and for which knowledge or special skills are required. Finally, it might be helpful to track *incongruent behavior* as an indicator for succeeding by chance.

In the context of games, Augustin et al. (2011) provide a theoretical model for assessment of knowledge and learning progress in digital learning games. Their approach is based on a mathematical framework that describes a learner's problem-solving behavior in an explorative, problem-oriented gaming situation. It is noteworthy that all concepts based on the CbKST have share a common theme that domain experts are required to establish the family of knowledge states (or competence states).

7.2.4   Adaptation Concepts and Algorithms
in Educational Games

Next, existing adaptation concepts and algorithms in the contexts of learning and games are reviewed, with some in combination with player and learner models.

A user model-based approach for adaptation of a learning game is proposed by Carron and Marty (2012). In their approach, a desired user model is defined, which reflects e.g., an improvement of a skill or something similar. The adaptation algorithm responds to recognized deficits or unwanted player behavior and updates the user model accordingly. The adaptation algorithm then chooses the appropriate adaptations to achieve the desired model.

Bellotti et al. (2009) propose an adaptation engine that selects tasks based on a player model. According to the definitions of player and learner models in their work, the player model can also be considered a learner model due to the fact that it models learning behavior, knowledge, and skill. Tasks are defined through parameters describing their entertainment value, skill relevance, covered learning styles, difficulty, difficulty adaptation range, and others. The adaptation algorithm then calculates costs for sequences of tasks and chooses the optimal one.

Mehm et al. (2013) proposed an approach to enable an author of a serious game via an authoring tool to define adaptivity within a scene-based game. This enables the author to define adaptive story paths on a macro level, or micro adaptivity on scene level. The latter means adapting scenes or scene properties to the characteristics of a player. The authoring tool *StoryTec* (Göbel et al. 2008; Mehm et al. 2009) allows an author to specify which scenes or scene shapes are a best fit for the right type of player and how a player model can be derived from player decisions within the game (see also Sect. 7.5).

In the context of the <e-Adventure> serious games authoring tool, Torrente et al. (2008) define an adaptive learning pattern that enables an in-game adaptation that is able to fit different learning styles by displaying different game behaviors. Their model operates on two layers: Choice of an individual game path to diversify the learning experience, and choice of game content for a more fine-grained adaptation. Those layers are comparable to the macro and micro adaptation of StoryTec.

Further, there are various approaches based on agents (Westra et al. 2009).

The approach by Vassileva and Bontchev (2009) uses a 3-dimensional model consisting of a learner model, a domain model, and an adaptation model. Predicate logic was used to define adaptation rules. Rules are composed of starting rules, pass-through graph rules, and rules updating the learner model. Based on the present model, the adaptation engine calculates an optimal course for a learner through the learning environment.

Spronck et al. (2006) use dynamic scripting to adapt opponent strategies in roleplay games to provide players with opponents who match their skill level. They assume that a player's skill level improves while playing a game over a longer time span. Thus, players should be held in the flow channel by using opponents which adapt their skill based on the player's skill level.

Yannakakis and Maragoudakis (2005) define an algorithm based on criteria which make a game interesting. Based on those criteria, they derive a metric using difficulty, diversity in opponents' behavior, and a preference to aggressive behavior of opponents. They show that the use of their algorithm can generate more interesting game instances for players using the game *Pacman*.

7.3 Adaptive Storytelling—Story Models, Interaction and Sequencing

Stories have been used for thousands of years in human history. In ancient days, people sat together around a fire and told stories—whether ficticious content or real facts and incidents put into a suspenseful, exciting form. Later on, storytelling concepts have built the basis for theatre and drama. Modern forms of storytelling include (electronic) books, films and games. For that, well-proven narrative approaches in the form of story models are used to "guarantee" a suspenseful story (environment) for the overall game based on a dramatic arc. The big difference between the different story forms is caused by the level of interactivity of the digital media: Whereas books or films are usually linear, with the audience as passive recipients "consuming" a story without interactions, computer games are characterized as highly interactive, non-linear media with constant interaction by players. Hence, players in a computer game have much more influence about the unfolding process and control of a (story-driven) game compared to spectators in a cinema.

In the following, fundamental storytelling concepts and story models are described, before mechanisms for interactive storytelling and the combination/use of storytelling and/in games are discussed.

7.3.1 Story Models

Among the earliest attempts at finding formal structures common to stories are the writings of Aristotle on drama. Finally, most story models are based on that simple dramaturgic arc model of Aristotle (330 B.C.) for telling linear stories with the three elements of *Exposition, Rising Action to Climax*, and *Denouement* (see Fig. 7.8).

Based on Aristotle's observations, Gustav Freytag specified the pyramidal model of contemporary drama (Freytag 1863; see Fig. 7.9). Here, after an exposition in which the story's protagonist is presented to the audience, the suspense of the plot increases until a climatic event in the middle of the story is reached. Freytag posits that the suspense should be released, leading to the end of the story in the form of a catastrophe.

In modern stories, especially in popular movies, the catastrophe is replaced by a *Happy End*, in which the story does not reach a tragic end. This is one of many changes the classical model of storytelling has undergone to become accepted by modern audiences. Another change concerns the shift of the climax from the strict

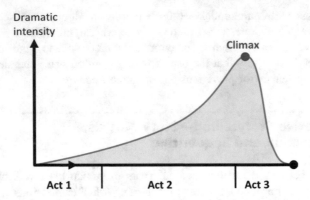

Fig. 7.8 Three-Act-Model based on Aristotle with the climax shifted to the end

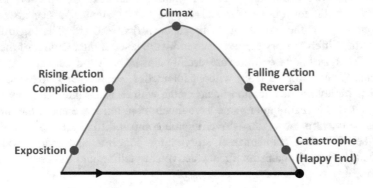

Fig. 7.9 Pyramidal Model based on Freytag (1863), extending the Three Act Model by Aristotle

middle towards the end, in order to capture audience (recipients) attention as long as possible (as shown in Fig. 7.8).

With regard to its usage for film scripts, Field (1988) extended the Aristotle model—whereby, script pages (=film minutes) are used for temporal structuring (see Fig. 7.10). That model is based on certain rules (especially in the commercial filmmaking business), which are the result of a detailed analysis of many successful films. They are mostly guidelines, which are flexible—and can even be dismissed if

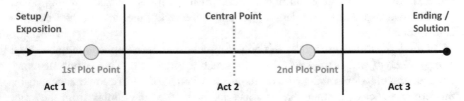

Fig. 7.10 Syd Field story paradigm with two plot points, adapted from Field (1988)

the story calls for an unusual structure. Most of the popular narrative films follow this dramatic approach, whereby dramatic scripts are linear and chronological.

A *plot point* represents a significant change in the story; for example, the hero is confronted with a new and unknown situation. The *central point* in the middle of the story is used to separate the second, longest act into two halves to keep up the suspense through this act (see Fig. 7.11). As for the timeline of the plot itself, there are some basic rules, which are only rules of thumb, but seem to be generally accepted in the film industry, e.g., the common film is ~ 120 min long, one page of script is equivalent to 1 min of film, the first act shouldn't be longer than 30 min, in the first 10 min the *hook* has to take place (audience attention has to be locked) and all the necessary information has to be conveyed (who is the hero, what is the story about, what is the hero's aim, what is the conflict, etc.), in a dialogue each character should have no more than 2 or 3 lines to say, monologues should be avoided, or a scene should not be much longer than 3–4 min.

Further story structures and dramaturgic models are provided by Tobias (1999), providing 20 master plots, or by the Russian formalist Vladimir Propp (2010), who analyzed hundreds of Russian fairy tales and extracted 15 morphological functions/components appearing in all these stories. Further, Propp defined characters (*Dramatis Personae*) representing rules within the stories, e.g., an enemy, a hero, a magic agent (helper) or a princess (prize/award). Hereby, Propp's Morphology of the Folktale provides a description of folktales according to their constituent parts, and the order in which they appear. The functions of characters serve as stable, constant elements in a tale, independent of how and by whom they are fulfilled. The number of functions known to the fairy tale is limited and the sequence of functions is always identical. There are only few variations of this rule.

Although Propp's work is mainly descriptive, its abstractions also allow for generative purposes, and have already been used as the base for storytelling systems. Fairclough and Cunningham (2003) describe a massively multiplayer online role playing game (MMORPG), where the story is controlled by a director module, using a case-based system combined with a rule system based on Propp's functions. Grasbon and Braun (2001) also describe a story director that provides high-level guidance of the story, by means of rules based on Propp's morphology. Machado et al. (2001) describe an architecture for guiding collaborative story creation that is also based in this morphology. These approaches demonstrate the applicability of Propp's morphology to interactive storytelling.

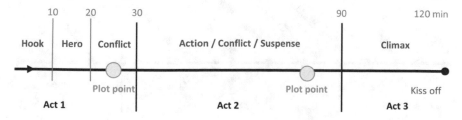

Fig. 7.11 Timeline sketch for the three acts model and with two plot points

Campbell (2008) analyzed the myth of the hero in different kinds of stories from various regions and times. In all his stories he found the same story model, which he later called the hero's journey, or *monomyth*. The latter conceals Campbell's true meaning: Not only are myths structured in the form of the monomyth, but also all existing stories, even every joke, can be traced back to these ancient rules of storytelling. Following this postulate, applications for digital storytelling should also fit into this model—after all, they are also stories. Campbell particularly analyzed myths with regard to their symbolic meaning and tried to extract their psychological meaning as well. He realized that every adventure can be interpreted as an inner journey of a hero. This way each myth contains insight and self-awareness.

> It is a journey in which the hero grows and changes. He begins his journey with a particular state of awareness. He then comes into an in-between-world, where his original state cannot be held. In this world he learns of his fears, his self-dillusions and his true qualities.

Vogler (1998) took Campbell's monomyth and adopted it into a manual for scriptwriters: "Modern heroes may not be going into caves and labyrinths to fight mythical beasts, but they do enter a Special World and an Inmost Cave by venturing into space, to the bottom of the sea, into the depths of a modern city, or into their own hearts."

The story of the hero's journey begins in the ordinary world of the hero (see Fig. 7.12). The hero is introduced in his everyday surroundings. An incident that leads to the action is depicted in all popular story models. Seger (1997) writes about a catalyst, while McKee (1997) quite simply calls it the *inciting incident*. Other terms are *point of attack*, *impetus*, or in the hero's journey, the *call to adventure*. In any case, the calling has to prevent the hero from living his life the way he used to. How this happened is left to the author.

Most heroes refuse the call to adventure at first. In this case a mentor helps the hero to overcome his fears or reluctance and start his journey. The character of the mentor is well known from fairytales and myths; it is often an old man or old woman who gives magical gifts to the hero. If there is not an actual mentor, many scripts include an element which takes over the functions of a regular old man or woman. An item could give the hero courage, information or anything else that might help him to overcome the first threshold.

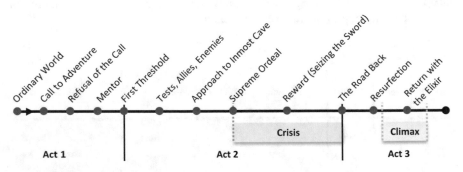

Fig. 7.12 The structure of the Hero's Journey, adapted from Vogler (1998)

When the first threshold is overcome the adventure—and the actual story—begins. There might be riddles to solve or obstacles to fight at the threshold, but the phase of testing usually starts after the first threshold has been successfully overcome.

The hero now has entered a special world—according to Campbell the place of initiation. This phase is also well known from fairytales, for instance Russian fairytales analyzed by Propp (2010): The hero learns about the special world and has to pass tests in preparation for the supreme ordeal (crisis). At first, the tests are easy—but they become more and more difficult in time, and seemingly unmanageable close to the end, when finally the last test takes place: The supreme ordeal. The supreme ordeal is connected to a heightened suspense: The hero goes through a crucifying time. He has to stand up to his own deepest fears and has to fight for his life. This crisis has to be so stirring and thrilling that the hero is changed forever.

After the hero has surpassed his supreme ordeal, he/she will be rewarded for bravery. Joseph Campbell writes about the hero's new self-awareness as the reward, but Vogler tells scriptwriters to include a more worldly reward—primarily that the hero is accepted as a hero now.

After the supreme ordeal, the hero travels back to the ordinary world. Before the hero reaches home, one further event has to occur, so the hero can prove him/herself. He/she is tested one last time, and once again applies the newly received knowledge and experience to escape death. With this resurrection, the hero is reborn and comes home as a new (wo)man.

7.3.2 Interaction—Interactive Storytelling

The story models described so far are primarily settled and well proven in the fields of literature, theatre, or film/cinema. These domains are characterized by linear story representation and non-interactivity (of course in the case of theatre, the actors have the chance to receive some kind of generic feedback by the audience and can consider it during the ongoing play/their performance). In sum, the audience (users/recipients of a story) is passive and has no chance to interact or to influence the story. In contrast, interactive media such as computer games are characterized and dominated by interactive setups and (continuous) user interaction. This leads to the field of Interactive Storytelling—the relationship between storytelling and games.

The international game developers association (http://www.igda.org/) describes that transformation process of linear storytelling to interactive storytelling (i.e., interactive media such as videogames) as follows:

Interactive Storytelling: Stories have most likely been part of the human experience from the earliest days of language, but until recently the storytelling medium has been largely static. Barring different versions of the same story, any given tale unfolds the same way every time a person reads it. Computer games promise the potential to move beyond this strictly linear form by offering stories that interact with the player, allowing them to participate in the decisions or actions that shape the narrative.

Both approaches—storytelling (dramaturgy, suspenseful stories) and games (play, interaction)—are used to improve the user experience and to increase the motivation of users and user engagement in general. However, these approaches fundamentally differ from each other, with a conflict between narration (linear approach, dramaturgy, plot) and interactivity (interaction, user participation, game approach). As indicated above, Chris Crawford and others suggest that this never will work together. In the Interactive Storytelling research community, this phenomena is summarized as a *narrative paradox* (Louchart and Aylett 2003) (Fig. 7.13).

Lindley (2004) also tackled the narrative paradox by elaborating the ludic space with the three-dimension *simulation, ludology,* and *narratology*—with the latter two directly addressing the contradictory poles of the narrative paradox. Different media types, game genres, and dedicated games are sorted within the ludic space according to their characteristics in terms of interactivity (ludology) and narratology (story-based approach).

Adaptive Storytelling Systems

Corresponding to the narrative paradox and the gap (continuum) between predefined stories (structures, following a story model) and emergent narrative (stories evolve depending on user input/interaction), storytelling systems might be categorized in plot-based systems (with a focus on narration), emergent narratives (with

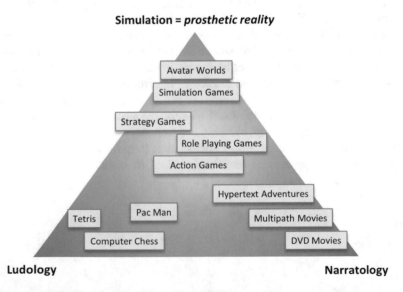

Fig. 7.13 Ludic Space—derived from Lindley (2004)

a focus on interactivity, e.g., Aylett (1999), Figueiredo et al. (2008), Kriegel and Aylett (2008) or Louchart et al. (2008) and guided character-based systems (as mixture, cf. Hoffmann et al. 2005).

Much research effort has been investigated so far in order to overcome that obstacle of the narrative paradox; up to now, there has been no well-proven system combining both approaches, i.e., providing a suspenseful, exciting story/plot AND enabling the user/audience to interact and influence the story (story unfolding process). Mateas and Stern (2003, 2007) created Façade, which often is referenced as most promising system for Interactive Storytelling, and directly addresses the narrative paradox (see Fig. 7.14).

In fact, Façade also might be categorized as guided character-based system, since the underlying methods and concepts (a) include a drama manager as a story engine to provide a red thread of the story and (b) enable the user to interact with the two protagonists Grace and Trip to influence the story (an unfolding process) via a chat system (see Fig. 7.15).

Within that context, the strong relation to computer games (in particular the game genre of Role Playing Games, RPG) also becomes obvious: The role of the human *Game Master* in pen-and-paper RPG's (cf. Sect. 8.2) might be compared with a drama manager in an Interactive Storytelling system.

Besides, Façade indicates the trend to use more and more AI (Artificial Intelligence) and (path/story) planning technology within Interactive Storytelling (systems), as basis for both sequencing scenes and the unfolding process of dialog parts within a scene. Most prominent examples underlining that trend provide Riedl and Sugandh (2008) as well as Stern (2008), Ryan (2008), and Cavazza et al. (2008).

Further information about these research and technical development (RTD) trends and future perspectives of interactive storytelling have been elaborated in the Network of Excellence's *IRIS—Integrated Research in Interactive Storytelling* (Cavazza et al. 2008, 2009), see also http://iris.interactive-storytelling.de/).

Fig. 7.14 Façade screenshot, accessed from http://www.interactivestory.net/#facade

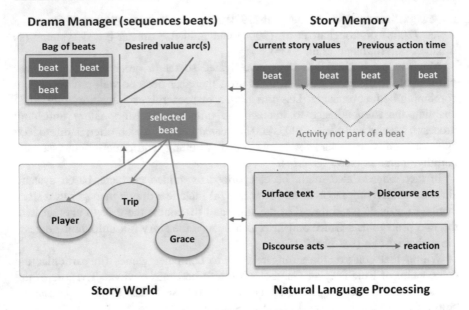

Fig. 7.15 Façade—Architecture: Drama Manager as Story Engine

7.3.3 Sequencing—Linear and Non-linear Story Forms

With respect to the question of how a story or game continues at a specific moment during play, Fig. 7.16 presents the main classes of story forms, and the pros and cons of their usage for sequencing in (storytelling based) systems and applications such as serious games.

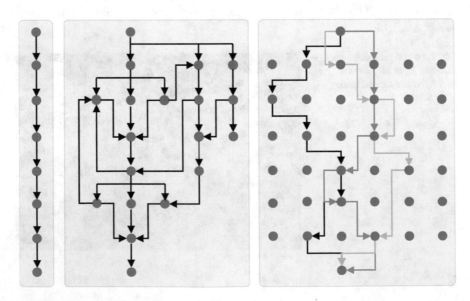

Fig. 7.16 Story Forms: Linear (*left*), branching, non-linear (*center*), modular, re-use (*right*)

The simplest form represents the linear approach. The advantages are obvious: The author has full control of the story and it is quite easy to implement that approach (exactly one possible sequence of game levels, game situations) from a game developers' perspective. In contrast, the major drawback is the lack of flexibility and possibilities for personalization and adaptation. Branching is a little more complex than the pure linear approach and more expensive in terms of content production; however, there is still full authorial control and a lack of flexibility for sequencing and adaptation.

In this context, Nandi (2004) provides an interesting approach, discussing the question: "*Who has control about what is presented at which time of the story?*" He compares films, graphic novels (comics etc.) and interactive media, and summarizes the first two under the term *sequential art*. Nandi points out that time control is an essential difference in consuming the narrative: The reader has control over the flow in graphic novels, while the author and director impose the rhythm of the telling to the viewer. Crawford (2004) supports this view, when he says that continuous play of a complete story is not possible: "(…) a story world is composed of closely balanced decisions that could reasonably go either way. These decisions require thought from players; they cannot be made in split second." Thus, unless the decisions are very simple, an *unbroken time flow* is not possible.

This problem of missing authorial control grows worse in the case of story worlds including chats or direct dialogues between users and/or with virtual actors—as in Façade, which Szilas (2004) describes as "*key feature of interactive drama, (which) allows the user a wide range of dialog choices during the inter-action.*" Such unstructured parts of interaction, in which we can include games as well, may entirely blow any concept of time control, but empirical knowledge helps to deal with some of them. Practically, traditional and recent board games such as *Monopoly* or *Siedler* are excellent examples for this, because all of them provide average game times that astonishingly seem to match reality in many cases (even when taking into account the difference between playing a game at a first run or several times).

The non-linear approach is more flexible and provides much more freedom for adaptation and sequencing of story units (in game levels/game situations) due to the variety of transitions per story unit. Nevertheless, there is a limited possibility to combine and reuse story units in different scenarios, story lines, and contexts, i.e., different user groups, game lengths, or game modes.

Within the modular approach, the set of story units might be understood as a sea of story modules, which might be (in principle) freely connected and combined with each other. This approach builds the basis for emergent narrative Storytelling systems—(Figueiredo et al. 2008; Louchart and Aylett 2004)—and offers best opportunities for adaptation—with an almost endless set of possible storylines/paths or sequences of story modules. On the other hand authorial control is very limited and the player gets more or less full control over the scenario—and it becomes quite difficult to "guarantee" a suspenseful story. Besides, from a developer's perspective, it is practically neither possible to produce fully elaborated content for any

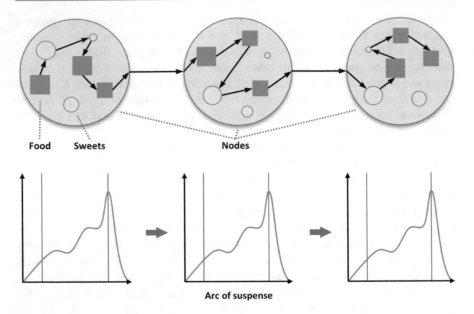

Fig. 7.17 String of pearls model

(theoretically possible) evolving story, nor to provide adequate AI mechanisms for (appropriate) automatic content production "on the fly" during play.

A mixture of sequential, linear and non-linear, modular elements is often used within role(play) games using the so-called *String of Pearls* technique for sub-linear narration (see Fig. 7.17). A serious of explorative worlds is hereby interconnected in a nonlinear form. Examples of this include the *Final Fantasy Series* (Final Fantasy 2004) or *Tomb Raider* (Tomb Raider 2004).

Hoffman et al. (2005) provides further information about the use of storytelling mechanisms and the use of different linear and non-linear approaches within edutainment applications. In that context, Göbel et al. (2006) also provides a rough algorithm implementing interactive storytelling applications in museums, which consider story pacing (timing) mechanisms for sequencing linear and interactive story units.

7.4 Narrative Game-Based Learning Objects

For integrating adaptive storytelling and gaming mechanisms within personalized digital educational games, Göbel et al. (2010) elaborated the concept of narrative game-based learning objects (NGLOBs). This section represents an excerpt of the original work and describes the conceptualization and the resulting formalized definition of NGLOBs. The concrete implementation is presented in the course of the best practice example 80Days in the next section. Hereby, the understanding of the terms macro adaptation and micro adaptation is as follows:

In contrast to the original definition by Cronbach (1967), the interpretation of the authors for micro and macro adaptation is that *micro adaptation* is an adaptation inside a scene/situation of the game, i.e., shaping it. *Macro adaptation,* on the other hand, concerns the question of how to proceed with the game, i.e., which scene/situation (or a game level) to choose next (cf. sequencing).

7.4.1 Conceptualization of Narrative Game-Based Learning Objects

In a first step, formalization of narrative, gaming, and learning objects is briefly discussed in the respective contexts of learning, gaming, and storytelling. Hereby, a major aspect during the conceptualization of NGLOB has been set on the integration of measurable, quantitative, and qualitative elements and annotations of narrative, gaming, and learning contexts.

Personalization and Adaptation in the Learning Context

Adapting DEGs while incorporating learning issues mainly consists of adapting the game's story structure (macro adaptation, sequencing), or to trigger appropriate pedagogical interventions (micro adaptation, personalized presentation of a scene) (Conlan et al. 2006).

Therefore, it is necessary to track and to evaluate the learner's knowledge state to obtain a sound basis for decisions to be made. Based on the gathered information, the next scene presented to the player should be determined in a way such that the learner is neither unchallenged nor overwhelmed by the complexity of the contained tasks. Rather, it should be ensured that learner knowledge is steadily increased up to full knowledge mastery.

Based on the CbKST (see Sect. 7.2.3), a set of skills S, and a prerequisite relation R among these skills, is defined by the author. The given relation is stored in the DEG's learning context. R provides a way to derive a competence structure C from the skills of S. Let a knowledge state KS be a set of skills $\in S$ satisfying the condition

$$If(s, s' \in S) \wedge sRs' \wedge (s' \in KS), then(s \in KS)$$

$C \leftarrow$ then is the sum of all knowledge states KS. Using C the player's knowledge state can be determined and meaningful learning paths can be provided.

Skills are presumed to be not observable atomic competences, or pieces of knowledge obtained by the learner. These are uncovered by associated tasks, which each require a certain subset of skills to solve them. Additionally, an availability probability ap_i for each skill $skill_i$ in the set of all skills describes how far the skill can be assumed to be already gained by the learner. Using a probability instead of a binary solution like "the learner has achieved skill x" or "the learner does not have skill x" prevents wrong assumptions, as lucky guesses and careless errors made by the player can introduce noise on the measurement of certainty. The subset of skills that are gained up to a certain time are defined the actual Knowledge State KS_j of the player; refer to Figs. 7.5 and 7.7 in Sect. 7.2.3.

To support such a concept within a story-based DEG such as 80Days, each scene must be assigned with a subset $P \leftarrow$ of all skills, which are assumed necessary to solve tasks associated to the scenario. $P \leftarrow$ is called the scene's Prerequisite Skills. Further, each scene is associated with a subset of skills that is meant to be improved by the covered learning objects. This set, the Associated Skills A, describes the knowledge gain that can be expected if the scene's challenges are successfully mastered. After finishing a scene, the availability probability value ap of all skills in set $A \leftarrow$ must be updated. To realize this, actions triggered by the user (e.g., right or wrong answers, clicking at the right position of an image) can be used to increase or decrease ap_i of a particular skill $skill_i$ or a set of skills. The amount of update is defined by the author and depends on the learner's performance (e.g., increase $skill_i$ much for a correct answer, increase it lower for a partially correct answer or decrease it for a wrong answer).

To determine the next meaningful scene for the player's learning progress, the parameters stated above are used to assign an appropriateness value av to each available scene. Scenes where the prerequisites $P \leftarrow$ are not fully contained in the player's knowledge state KS_j receive a value of zero, because the scenes are not suitable for the learner up to that time. A skill $skill_i$ is assumed to be element of KS_j if its availability ap_i exceeds a certain threshold p_{min}. Among the remaining scenes, those are rated with higher values for av that deliver a reasonable set of additional skills in $A \leftarrow$ when accomplished. Having assigned av to each scene, all scenes can now be ordered according to their quality to fit as the next scene in the learning context.

Personalization and Adaptation in the Gaming Context

Adaptation according to the gaming context means changing the game in a way fitting better to a determined player model. For that we use an approach based on the player model proposed by Bartle (1996), which distinguishes four categories of players: Killers, achievers, socializers, and explorers. However, in our model, we do not sort a player into one of these categories. Instead, for a player P we assign a model $M_P = (p_k, p_a, p_s, p_e)$, which is a quadruple of normalized values ranging from $[0...1]$, indicating how much the player fits into each category.

The player model can be assigned by applying a questionnaire at the beginning of the game to find out the player's preferred style of play. However, as player interests and preferences depend on various factors such as mood, excitement, etc., this player model can change during play. The game needs to keep track of these changes by evaluating the player's decisions and putting them into a gaming context. Whenever a situation can be handled in more than one way by the player, the different options have to be put into a context by the author in advance. When the player chooses an option in the game, the player model gets adapted/updated. A simple example clarifies this: The player must retrieve an item from an NPC.

He/she can either talk to it and try to persuade the NPC to give the item to the player or he/she can simply attack the NPC. Obviously, the first option is strongly related to the socializer type while the second one is a typical killer approach.

To decide which scene to choose next from the current scene according to the player model, a gaming context C_N is assigned to each NGLOB to indicate how good the scene fits for each player type. This can easily be done by assigning an appropriateness vector A (*playerFeature, appropriatenessFactor*) as a list of tuples to each scene *Si*. The length of this vector depends on the number of modeled features. Of course, we use the same model as for player modeling. Scenes are then ordered according to an evaluation metric, which calculates an appropriateness value *av* for each scene, making use of the player model and the appropriateness vector A. The one with the highest value is the best candidate for the next scene according to the current player model. One such metric could be as follows: Let n be the number of features of the player model. Appropriateness value av_i of scene S_i for player model M_p is:

$$av_i = \frac{1}{n} \sum_{j \in \{features\}} \left(1 - \left|a_{i,j} - m_j\right|\right)$$

Here, the factor $\frac{1}{n}$ is a normalization to the interval [0,1]. Inside the sum, for each of the player types the difference between the model value m_j and the appropriateness value of scene i $a_{i,j}$ is calculated as $\left(\left|a_{i,j} - m_j\right|\right)$ and subtracted from 1. By this, the matching of model value and scene value is normalized between 0 (no match) and 1 (total match). Table 7.1 provides an example of a player model and four scenes. In the last row the appropriateness of each scene is shown. Note that of all scenes, Scene 2 is closest to the example player model. Consequently, the calculated appropriateness value of Scene 2 is the highest one (Table 7.2).

Personalization and Adaptation in the Storytelling Context

From a storytelling perspective, the major challenge is to overcome the Narrative Paradox (see also Sect. 7.3.2) providing both (a) a motivating, thrilling and suspenseful narrative environment based on well-proven story structures and patterns such as the Hero's Journey (Campbell 2008; Vogler 1998) and (b) an adaptive, interactive environment, enabling the user to interact and (at least in parts) take control of the story structure during play. Therefore, the system needs to take into

Table 7.2 Appropriateness of four example scenes to the player model

	Player model	Scene 1	Scene 2	Scene 3	Scene 4
Killer	0.80	0.00	0.90	0.20	0.40
Achiever	0.00	0.60	0.10	0.00	0.40
Socializer	0.00	0.80	0.00	0.00	0.60
Explorer	0.40	0.00	0.40	0.80	0.60
Appropriateness value av		0.40	0.95	0.75	0.60

account player/user/learner characteristics as well as overall (learning/knowledge transfer vs. gaming) strategies defined by an author (pedagogue vs. game designer), which implicitly decreases the level of influence by the user/player/learner.

As a result of extensive research tackling the Narrative Paradox and the use of appropriate and flexible storytelling methodologies (Louchart and Aylett 2003; Göbel 2009; Champagnat 2008). Göbel et al. (2009) suggest the use of a combined approach based on the Hero's Journey as underlying, well-proven (mostly linear) story model and emergent, non-linear parts: The middle part of the Hero's Journey, with the dramatic step of *The Road of Trials*, is very flexible, and provides the possibility to integrate as many story units as needed and to combine those units in any order. Because of that, this story part is especially suitable for adaptation and personalization. As the scenes can be ordered in various ways, it is possible to provide an individual learning and gaming to the players. Furthermore, the possibility for replay is increased if a new game can run in completely different manner.

7.4.2 Definition of NGLOB

Starting with the storytelling perspective, Narrative Objects (NOBs) represent the smallest, atomic units of story-based DEG. For the formalization of NOBs and narrative contexts, the idea is to map and annotate NOB as far as applicable, corresponding to the steps and dramaturgic functions of underlying story models—such as the Hero's Journey.

> **Narrative Object**: A basic unit of a story-driven application that has a specific function in a story model (e.g., introduce the protagonist or serve as climax of the story).

With respect to learning issues, the idea is both to formalize learning and learner context and to provide machine-readable information about associated and prerequisite skills of a learning object (LOB) respectively learning situation based on the CbKST. Thus, for sequencing purposes—presumed that an open, modular, emergent (narrative) environment is available without hardcoded transitions as in pure linear approaches—it is possible to decide whether a learning situation is appropriate for a specific learner (learner has prerequisite skills) or not (learner would be overstrained).

> **Learning Object**: An atomic-level, reusable unit of learning content. By combining learning objects on similar topics, a learning application can be composed.

Concerning the gaming context, the interaction concept in form of interaction templates (e.g., drag-and-drop, multiple-choice and puzzle templates in classic courseware or an explorative 3D environment) provides useful attributive information. Second, similar to the learning context, the idea is to build a correlation between gaming situations/GOB and the users (i.e., players in the gaming context) and underlying player models. Hence, all gaming situations are set into context with player types and annotated with appropriateness factors.

> **Gaming Object**: A basic unit of a game or game-like application.

In sum, the model for a NGLOB is built by a composition of context information resulting in a triple vector $C_N x C_G x C_L$. The narrative context C_N provides a list of tuples (*storymodelStep, appropriatenessFactor*), whereby *storymodelStep* is encoded by the initials of a story model (for instance "SM HJ" for Hero's Journey) plus a number for the step/part of that model. The parameter *appropriatenessFactor* indicates how much the scene fits to the according *storymodelStep* and is normalized in the range [0,1]. The gaming context C_G primarily tackles the appropriateness of individual GOB and gaming situations for different players and player types. Analogously to the narrative context C_N, the gaming context C_G also provides a list of tuples (*playerFeature, appropriatenessFactor*). Here, "PM BA x" describes the player type based on the classification of Bartle. For example, "PM BA E, 0.9" indicates that the GOB is very appropriate for the Bartle player type "Explorer". The model for the learning context C_L provides a vector composed of two parts listing all Associated (A_{xyz}) and Prerequisite (P_{xyz}) Skills for a specific learning situation/LOB, whereas 'xyz' is a unique identifier. In Fig. 7.18, an example for such a NGLOB is provided:

Apart from that quantifiable part described above, the model for NGLOB contains further descriptive elements such as short texts/abstracts summarizing the synopsis of narrative, gaming, and learning functions of a specific NGLOB. Examples are provided in the next section in the course of 80Days as a best-practice example for adaptive digital educational games.

$$
\left(
\begin{array}{c} C_N \\ \begin{vmatrix} (SM\_HJ\_1, 0.1), \\ (SM\_HJ\_4, 0.2), \\ (SM\_HJ\_8, 0.1) \end{vmatrix} \end{array},
\begin{array}{c} C_G \\ \begin{vmatrix} (PM\_BA\_K, 0.2), \\ (PM\_BA\_S, 0.4), \\ (PM\_BA\_E, 0.9) \end{vmatrix} \end{array},
\begin{array}{c} C_L \\ \begin{vmatrix} \langle A101, A102 \rangle \\ \langle P210, P217 \rangle \end{vmatrix} \end{array}
\right)
$$

Fig. 7.18 Quantifiable part of the model for Narrative, Game-based Learning Objects

7.5   Adaptive Digital Educational Games—Best Practice 80Days

Inspired by the Jules Verne novel *Around the World in Eighty Days*, the idea for project 80Days was born. *80Days—Around an Inspiring Virtual Learning World in Eighty Days* (http://www.eightydays.eu) was initiated as an EU-funded project in FP7, situated in the ICT field of *Technology-enhanced Learning* (contract number 215918). The project ran from April 2008 to September 2010. The overall aim of 80Days was to combine adaptive learning, storytelling, and gaming technology in order to build intelligent, adaptive, and exciting learning environments in the form of story-based digital educational games (see Fig. 7.19, left).

Key research and development aspects tackled the (cost-)effective (yet high-quality) creation of personalized (playful) learning content matching the preferences (learner and player model) of individuals as well as the question "*How does a story continue at a specific moment during play?*"

Concerning content production and authoring, ETH Zurich elaborated automatic content creation mechanisms to build a 3D virtual environment based on satellite images, and TU Darmstadt developed an authoring tool supporting authors (e.g., teachers) to create playful, adaptive learning content. Hereby, special emphasis was set on the support of authors with little to no programming skills.

Referring to personalization and adaptation, TU Graz and Trinity College Dublin worked on micro and macro adaptation mechanisms for intelligent, adaptive knowledge transfer. Based on those mechanismsm the NGLOB concept was elaborated by TU Darmstadt. Industrial partners Takomat and Testaluna focused on the practical aspects, including implementing educational game(s) into a 3D environment—using a game engine enhanced by a character engine to control Feon,

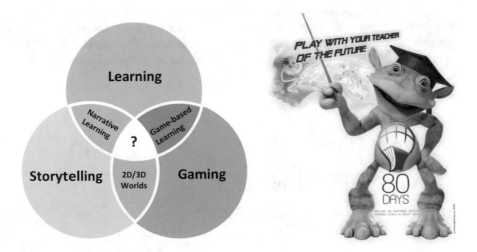

Fig. 7.19 Technology-enhanced Learning with Storytelling and Gaming (*left*), and Feon as the main Character of the 80Days game (*right*)

the main character of the 80Days stories (see Fig. 7.19, right). Finally, the University of Leicester was responsible for the evaluation portion of the project, and contributed valuable results and insights about effects of digital educational games (primarily user experience).

During the course of the project, the interdisciplinary consortium prototypically implemented two games:

- A fully elaborated demonstrator game titled *Save the Earth* for teaching geography—with a target audience of 12–14 year-old students in European countries.
- *Bat Cave* as a technical demonstrator to validate authoring theoretical concepts and mechanisms (using the authoring environment StoryTec), and for macro adaptation (sequencing) and micro adaptation (shaping individual story/game/learning situations according to the players/learners preferences).

In the following these games/game environments are analysed in detail.

Further comprehensive information about the 80Days project, its tangible outcomes, and underlying research concepts is provided at the project website http://www.eightydays.eu and the 80Days Methodology Guide Book (Kickmeier-Rust 2012a, b, see also http://www.eightydays.eu/mgb.html).

7.5.1 Save the Earth

The demonstrator game *Save the Earth* is intended to teach geography for a target audience of 12–14 year-old students, and follows European curricula on the subject. The consortium identified the type of an adventure game as promising genre for this area. Then, the major task (and effort) was to transform existing learning content for the topics covered in the curriculum to playful learning game elements.

Story

Within the adventure game, the learner takes the role of an Earth kid. The game starts when a UFO lands in a backyard, and an alien named Feon contacts the player. Feon is an alien scout who has to collect information about Earth. The player assists the alien in exploring the planet and creating a report about the Earth and its geographical features. This is accomplished by having the player fly to different destinations on Earth, and explore them, while collecting and acquiring geographical knowledge (Fig. 7.20).

Gameplay

During play, the player navigates a UFO and explores the world (Europe in particular). As soon as the UFO reaches a certain city, it is beamed to earth and the player (i.e., learner) gets information about geographical topic that is associated with individual cities, their corresponding countries, and geographic locations (Fig. 7.21).

Fig. 7.20 80Days geography game *Save the Earth*—underlying story design, derived from *The 80Days Game* (Schwarz et al. 2012) published in Kichmeier-Rust and Albert (2012a, b)

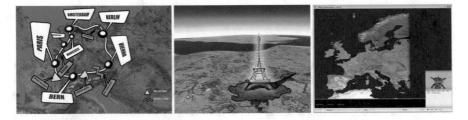

Fig. 7.21 GamePlay—Air Race over Europe (*left*), Landmark in Paris (*middle*), Map Task (*right*)

Story structure

For the overall narrative structure, the story model of the Hero's/Writer's Journey (Campbell 2008; Vogler 1998) has been identified as most appropriate referring to the needs and aims of 80Days: On the one hand, it provides a clear overall story structure—based on a well-proven dramaturgic model—being used as red thread of the 80Days story *Save the Earth*. On the other hand it is flexible enough to realize adaptation (by means of adaptive Storytelling, Learning and Gaming): Micro Adaptation can take place in all story units/game situations. The Road of Trials part of the Hero's Journey is predestined for non-linear macro adaptation (sequencing) (Fig. 7.22).

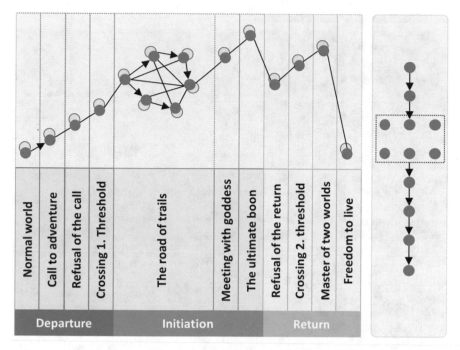

Fig. 7.22 Story Model of the Hero's Journey (*left*); Linear and Modular Story Units (*right*)

In 80Days, learning content and game design is structured in two levels: On a higher level, so-called *micro missions*—similar to game levels—are used. This level also corresponds to the steps/units of the Hero's Journey. On a narrower level, the micro-missions are composed by a number of *situations*. All situations have three dimensions: Storytelling dimension (dramaturgic function), Gaming dimension (gaming function), and Learning dimension (learning function, which subject should be taught). The multi-axes situations represent the smallest, atomic units of the story/game, corresponding to NGLOBs.

The overall story structure of Save the Earth follows the story model of the Hero's Journey described above (see Fig. 7.23): An *Intro Screen* with a pre-assessment to categorize player/users, a *Cinematic Intro* to initiate the story—corresponding to the first departure of the Hero's Journey, an *Interactive Tutorial* introducing the topic and providing information about the gameplay—might be understood as *Crossing 1. Threshold*; the micro missions *MM1* to *MM4* represent different game levels or quests—referring to *The Road of Trials* in the middle part of the Hero's Journey. Further story/game units would be necessary to cover the remaining steps of the Hero's journey (i.e., the later steps of the initiation phase and the return phase, see Fig. 7.22).

Objectives   Game Chapters

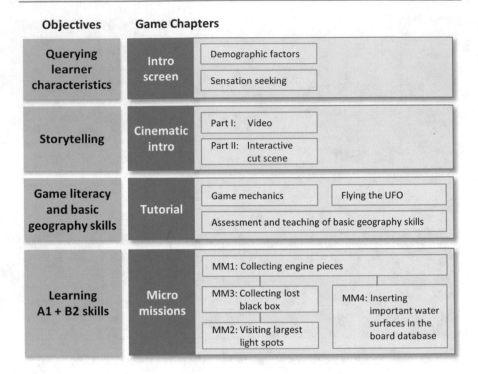

Fig. 7.23 First part of the story structure of the 80Days game *Save the Earth*

Adaptation

Concerning intelligent personalization, adaptation and the re-use of (learning) content for different user scenarios and contexts, the 80Days consortium has elaborated different concepts:

- On a game level, different game modes have been introduced, which represent different (speed/sensation seeking) versions of the game. For instance, within the relaxed version, the game provides explorative flying without any time pressure; within the driven version, there is some time pressure and Feon motivates the player to hurry up at certain moments; the fast version provides a distinct time limit, exciting background music, etc. These game modes are set into relation with the player types.
- For macro adaptation and sequencing of micro missions or story/game situations, all missions and situations are annotated referring to its dramaturgic (storytelling), gaming and learning function and additional appropriateness factors for individual learner and player types or a dramaturgic function of a story model (cf. NGLOB concept). During play, based on the NGLOB concept, the most appropriate next situation/micro mission is selected, which considers both the current gaming context and the player/learner type and knowledge space.

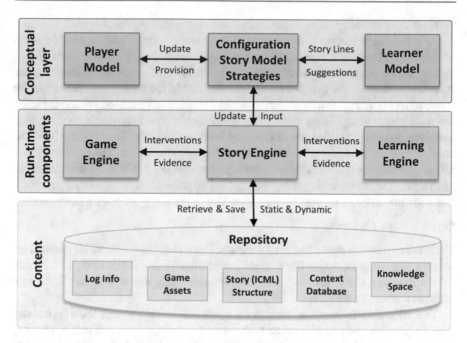

Fig. 7.24 Architectural framework with a three-layered structure: conceptual layer (models, top of image), run-time components (engines, middle of image) and content layer (repository with game and story assets, etc.)

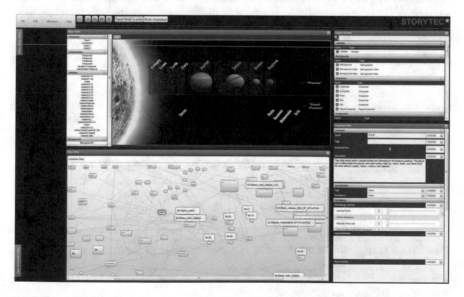

Fig. 7.25 Authoring Tool StoryTec—Main GUI with the Story Editor (*lower left part*), Stage Editor (*upper left part*) and the Objects Browser and Property Editor (*right side*)

How does the adaptation and personalization work in practical terms? Within a login screen at game start, the players (i.e., learners) are asked to provide some information about their age, gender, game experience and sensation seeking tendency. Based on these assessed criteria, the users' preference for different game modes is estimated; the user is then assigned to one of the user groups related to the game modes (*relaxed, driven,* or *fast version*) as basic configurations/versions for the different player types. Then, during play the player/learner behavior is continuously observed and the player/learner model is updated accordingly. Based on the NGLOB concept, a next "best-fitting" micro mission/situation is selected. The basis for this is all micro missions and situations are annotated according to the three dimensions of storytelling, learning, and gaming—including appropriateness factors of the situations for the different player/learner types, and dramaturgy steps of a story model.

Game Design Document

Each micro mission as well as the Cinematic Intro provide a unique ID and a short description/synopsis, optionally a visual representation (e.g., a sketch) and it is split into storytelling (StS), learning (LeS) and gaming/gameplay situations (GpS) on a narrower level (Table 7.3).

The situations themselves vary in its emphasis on either one specific context (e.g., a pure story-driven situation without any gameplay and minor/nor learning effects, see situation *CI_scene1* in Table 7.1) or a combination of contexts (e.g., *LeS 1.3* as game-based learning situation, see Table 7.4).

So far, that kind of style for a Game Design Document might be useful for authors, serving as compact storyboard; however, from a technical point of view the problem is the lack of metrics—quantifiable information necessary to be interpreted and processed by computing machinery systems—e.g., in order to determine whether a situation is appropriate to fulfill a specific dramaturgic step within the story model of the Hero's Journey or not.

Table 7.3 Extract from the game design document for the cinematic intro

Characteristics	Description
Situation	CI_scene 1
Short description	We see the original NASA film footage of the Apollo 8 mission
Picture	
Function for story	Create the beginning of a mystery story; set the mood and frame of the story..
Function for learning	This is a visual metaphor for our philosophy for teaching Geography..
Function for gameplay	–

Table 7.4 Extract out of the game design document for the learning unit 1: B2 skills european capitals and countries

Characteristics	Description
Situation	LeS 1.1 Pre-test of existing knowledge
Short description	Alien asks boy: "You know what cities are these?" The boy now can link illuminated spots and city names on a desk…
Function for story	Now, Mr. Jackanapes has to struggle a first time to keep up his blarney of being an all-knowing earthling
Function for learning	Reflection on and pre-test of existing knowledge without immediate feedback…
Function for gameplay	Introduction: Game play mode "Global view/Map desk" in simplified 2D view
Situation	LeS 1.3 Position of cities without known names
Short description	The gamer can fly above Europe in the UFO and the 2D night map in the HUD gives him his precise position and supports him in deciding to which city (light spot) he wants to fly next
Function for story	
Function for learning	The player can freely explore Europe while having the learning goals on a map in front of him (cities shown as light spots)
Function for gameplay	To verify the cities' names the player has to fly there and to stay paused above them (logging)

For that, the concept of Narrative Game-based Learning Objects with measurable, quantitative and qualitative elements and annotations for the narrative, gaming and learning contexts has been elaborated, see Sect. 7.4.

Technical Implementation

The elaborated methods and concepts for the 80Days approach have been integrated within a technical framework with three layers:

- The upper layer contains the theoretical basis including methods, concepts and models corresponding to the three dimensions of (adaptive) storytelling, learning, and gaming. More concrete, this theoretical player provides the player model, learner model, and story model. These models and concepts (i.e., rules for updating a player profile according to distinct player behavior during play) serve as input for the runtime components in the middle layer.
- Similar to the conceptual layer, the execution layer also contains three main units: The story engine as the overall control unit, the (adaptive) learning engine, and the game engine. Both the game engine and the learning engine observe the player/learner behaviour during play, analyse it and send adaptive interventions how to continue during play. The story engine is responsible for keeping the overall story structure. Further, the story engine receives the adaptive interventions and is responsible for solving problems, i.e., deciding how the game continues in the case of contradicting suggestions (for interventions) by the learning and gaming engine (cf. the phenomenon of the Narrative Paradox, see Sect. 7.3.2).

A specific point about the runtime components is that the story engine offers an abstraction module as interface to the game engine facilitating the integration of different game engines: Whereas for the geography game *Save the Earth*, the game engine nebula 2 has been used, the Bat Cave scenario (see Sect. 7.5.2) has been implemented with the StoryTec player *StoryPlay*—previously referred to as *Bat Cave* (Mehm et al. 2010).

Authoring

For the creation of the story structure and its population with micro missions and story/gaming/learning situations, the authoring tool StoryTec (http://www.storytec.de) provided by TU Darmstadt has been used and further developed within the course of the 80Days approach (Mehm et al. 2009; Göbel et al. 2010, 2012).

Figure 7.26 shows the four main components in the GUI of the authoring tool: The Story Editor is the place to structure a new story—using the terminology of *scenes*, which are equivalent to micro missions or game/story situations in 80Days. Within the Stage Editor, the situations are populated with story/game objects (game assets) such as images or texts. Further, similar to Microsoft's Powerpoint™, a set of interaction templates is offered. The Objects Browser is the place to store the actual data/content, and is categorized into object types such as virtual characters, background images, or sound objects. The Property Editor is closely connected to the Objects Browser: Here, attributes for the game/story objects are entered, e.g., for the attribution of objects according to the NGLOB principle. Further, editors not visualized in Fig. 7.25 include the Action Set Editor, a place to enter speech acts and other activities within micro missions and situations, and the Condition Editor, where conditions are entered (by visual programming) for sequencing and branching between micro missions or situations. Finally, a Skill Tree Editor is provided, enabling authors to enter skill trees in the form of competence spaces as described in Sect. 7.2.3 (see Fig. 7.26) (Fig. 7.24).

The technical result of the authoring process within the StoryTec authoring environment are XML-encoded stories in the ICML format. ICML stands for

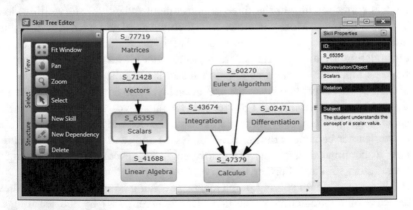

Fig. 7.26 StoryTec—Skill Tree Editor with a subset of learning topics covered in 80Days

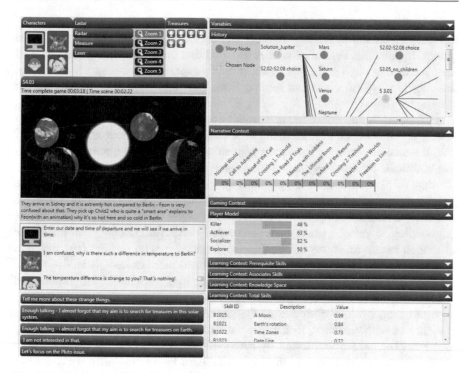

Fig. 7.27 Bat Cave player with gameplay part (*left*), and real-time visualization of the unfolding story, story context, gaming context and player model, and learning context (*right*)

Inscape Communication Markup Language and has been elaborated within the EU project INSCAPE (Interactive Storytelling for Creative Peoples, see Balet 2007). These ICML files are loaded into the runtime environment of the 80Days framework in the form of an executable story graph in the Story Engine. Then, the story starts and unfolds according to user/player/learner interactions, behavior, author-supplied rules and application logic, and context information. The context information of NGLOB is hold within the content layer (repository, see lower part of Fig. 7.24).

Evaluation

The demonstrator game *Save the Earth* was a subject of in-depth evaluation activities. The evaluation work has been focused on the objectives of defining an evaluation framework and of implementing an array of evaluative activities. In close collaboration with different disciplines, game design concepts were validated in schools in England and Austria. Multi-method approaches were applied to analyze the empirical data thus collected (Law et al. 2010). Empirical findings yielded beneficial effects of playing the game, as evident with an overall satisfying usability and user experience. Implications for the future development of the game prototypes and the design of evaluative activities were drawn. In particular, the theoretical knowledge and practical experience gained will contribute to advancing the research area of evaluating usability and user experience in digital educational games. In principle, evaluation studies revealed that the educational game was well received among pupil and gender independent—especially in contrast to traditional learning in a typical classroom setting. Both girls and boys enjoyed playing the geography game.

Unfortunately, no concrete statements have been possible concerning learning effects in terms of the characterizing goal (teaching and learning geography). For that, it would be necessary to conduct comparative studies with a control group who use traditional teaching methods for the same subjects.

Also, no clear statements are possible when referring to success or failure of the psycho-physiological founded principles on micro and macro adaptation: On the one side, a technical implementation and integration of the adaption dimensions (storytelling, learning, gaming) was successfully achieved. On the other hand, due to limited resources, it was not possible to produce enough content (i.e., different varieties of micro missions and gameplay situations more or less distinctive to one of the storytelling, learning, and gaming dimension) in order to fully apply and validate the elaborated adaptation mechanisms.

Apart from evaluation studies of the geography game with the primary target audience of schoolchildren, further evaluation has taken place about the authoring tool StoryTec, which was tested by authors/teachers and game developers. Both validation studies have been promising with regard both to usability issues (use of StoryTec by authors without programming skills) and the technical integration of the authoring tool into professional game development processes.

7.5.2   Bat Cave

This demonstrator has been established in order to test and validate the authoring and adaptation mechanism (NGLOB concept) within 80Days. Contrary to the educational game Save the Earth, with Bat Cave (Mehm et al. 2010) it was not the aim to create a fully elaborated game, but to focus on the underlying technical concepts and game mechanics.

The Bat Cave platform is built upon the Story Engine as shown in Fig. 7.25. In Fig. 7.28, a screenshot of the Bat Cave player can be seen. The GUI is divided into a left part for simulating the gameplay, and a right part (which can be hidden by users who are not interested in that kind of real-time analysis) for visualizing various useful sets of data that are accumulated during play. This includes the state of the user models, the history of previous choices by the adaptation algorithms, as well as the state of variable. This tool can therefore aid authors in evaluating games they created concerning the adaptation effects, by allowing them to check the results of annotations and user models early during development. A slider allows quick tuning of the weights associated with the adaptive choices along the narrative, educational and gaming axes/dimensions.

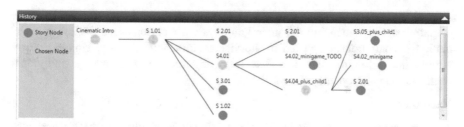

Fig. 7.28 The history visualization component. *Yellow* nodes indicate the path taken

Both parts act as observers of the Story Engine, with the visualization parts passively visualizing the incoming information and the gameplay part also converting user input into Story Engine commands afterwards. Hence, the player allows authors to quickly export a game from StoryTec even when unfinished, and test it using the current state of the game (Fig. 7.27).

Gameplay

In order to generate user input and to visualize results of computations inside the Story Engine, the left part of the Bat Cave application is dedicated to a prototypical gameplay implementation. Among the output mechanisms used in Bat Cave are background images, characters and their speech acts, "treasures" that can be collected, and descriptive text. For the Bat Cave scenario, the following elements are used as input mechanisms for the Story Engine:

- Hotspots: Rectangular hotspots can be overlayed onto the background image for a range of different effects. They can be directly linked to stimuli which are injected into the Story Engine when they are clicked.
- Multiple-Choice dialogues: In the lower part of the player, dialog choices for the player's avatar are offered, which again result in stimuli being injected.
- Adaptive Interventions: Adaptive Interventions as issued by the Learning Engine are internally transformed into stimuli and injected into the Story Engine.
- Specialized prototyping modules: Software modules which, when loaded, take control of the player and the communication with the Story Engine. They are used to provide more specialized prototype gameplay than is possible with the regular Bat Cave system.

Internally, all output mechanisms are either directly associated with Story Engine objects (which are linked to an output game element, e.g., an image) or an action (such as the speech act of a character).

Scientifc Analysis

Whereas the left part of the Bat Cave user interface is dedicated to gameplay representation and is linked to a certain degree to the used game objects, the right side of the user interface is composed of several general-purpose and reusable components for visualizing the underlying system's current state. Relevant information is continuously updated in the visualization interface and simultaneously written into a log for later use. The following sections describe the individual visualization components in more detail.

Variables

The first visualization found in Bat Cave is used to display the active variables found inside the current game session. Variables can either be defined locally for a certain scene or globally for the whole game. They can be used in several traditional ways such as flags (e.g., to indicate that a certain, important point in the game's story has been passed or that a certain event has happened) or as counters (e.g., for counting the number of times a player visited a certain location or the number of failed tries for a given challenge).

History

This component, shown in Fig. 7.28, fulfills a multitude of visualization and assistance functions during a test session. It displays game units (situations) as dots, similar in abstraction to the way they are displayed in the Story Editor of StoryTec. Situations are distinguished by colors, with yellow indicating the situations that have been visited previously as well as the currently active scene. Whenever branches are possible (as inferred by inspecting the transitions defined from a certain scene), they are visualized inside a new column to the right of the currently active scene.

Additionally, when the mechanism of NGLOBs is used in the form of *free transitions*, i.e., transitions between game situations that are influenced by the adaptive algorithms in the system, a context menu offers detailed information about the algorithmic parameters that lead to a certain choice (Fig. 7.29).

Narrative Context

The visualization for the Narrative Context displays the individual steps of the story model that is used as the basis for the game's story. For each step, a percentage shows the appropriateness values as entered by the author. For easy visual

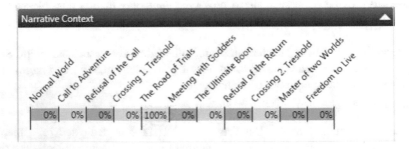

Fig. 7.29 The Narrative Context visualization component

Fig. 7.30 The player model and gaming context visualizations

reference, all steps for which the current appropriateness value exceeds a certain threshold are marked in yellow. Furthermore, the cell background color for story model steps previously visited in the game session are marked in a brighter color. This allows the tester to see how far along in the narrative he/she currently is, and what steps have already been visited.

Player Model and Gaming Context

Two different visualizations are provided in Bat Cave, which are associated with the current state of the player model and the gaming context of the current scene. Each player attribute is represented by a bar that shows the percentage to which this attribute is set, as well as the exact value as a percentage (Fig. 7.30).

Skills, Knowledge Space

The visualizations described here are all related to the learning context of NGLOBs. The associated and prerequisite skills as specified for the currently active scene are each listed together with their current values as determined by the Learning Engine. The Total Skills visualization similarly lists all skills defined in the skill structure for the active game together with their current values.

As an alternative to the Total Skills visualization, the structure defined by the skills and the dependency relations between them is visualized in the Skill Tree visualization component (see Fig. 7.31). This component features a graphical representation of the skill structure, with skills being shown as rectangles and the dependencies between them as arrows. For each skill, its current probability value is used to determine the color of the node representing it, interpolated from red for 0 to green for 1. This allows one to quickly see areas of the skill structure that have been covered well in a certain play-through and others that have been less covered during play, especially when skill structures get larger.

7.6 Summary and Questions

In general, personalized, intelligent, adaptive systems are highly desirable in order to meet the characteristics, needs, and interests of individual users and user groups. The same is true in the context of serious games, such as digital educational games

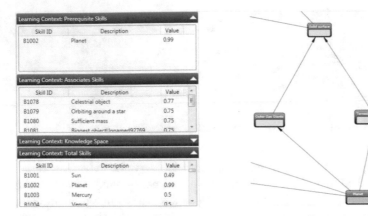

Fig. 7.31 Visualization of associated, prerequisite and total skills (*left*) and an extract of the visualization of the player's skill state (*right*)

(DEG): The better a game meets the learning background and learning and playing style of a user, the better the expected fun factor and learning outcome.

Thus, it is desirable to adapt such a game to player preferences. While some prefer action games, others prefer story-based adventures or roleplaying games. It is certainly not possible to create a custom game for each player type, but it would be a great advance if an educational game were flexible and customizable enough to be able to adapt to the heterogeneous needs of different players preferences by using adaptive technologies. Therefore, adaptation and adaptivity should consider the selection of appropriate content and presentation forms to teach subjects and skills of a curriculum as well as the speed and order of learning units in order neither to bore nor overstrain pupils and students.

For adaptation to player preferences, a player model is indispensible. Much research in the field of player modeling has been done up to now. One of the first player models was designed by Bartle (1996). Houlette (2004) introduced a player model that keeps track of several player traits to create a model, which can be used to adapt the behavior of Non-Player Characters.

Concerning motivational aspects, a game should also contain an interesting, suspenseful, and entertaining story, and should be challenging without stressing too much. Providing a good and suspenseful story however, is often a restricting factor to the variability of a game: Underlying story models—well-proven in literature and film as linear, non-interactive media—promise to "guarantee" an exciting story, but this approach is contradicting to highly interactive and non-linear media such as computer games—leading to the narrative paradox in systems using both story-telling and gaming mechanisms.

For the integration of adaptive storytelling and gaming mechanisms within digital educational games, the concept of Narrative Game-based Learning Object (NGLOB) has been elaborated by Göbel et al. (2010) in the context of the 80Days approach. In the authoring phase of digital educational games, game units are annotated with appropriate factors to serve as learning/gaming/storytelling situations regarding dedicated story and player models—as well as learning contexts (skills). During play, the most appropriate NGLOB is selected based on the computation (matching) between the current context (story, player, and learner model/behavior) and the annotated NGLOBs in order to decide how a story-based DEG continues.

Future research towards intelligent, adaptive systems will integrate the investigations into mechanisms for automatically created content such as the generation of virtual environments or automatic and dynamic difficulty adaptation according to player background. Referring to procedural content generation for games, Hendrix et al. (2013) summarize game content types that can be automatically generated: Game Bits (textures, sound, vegetation, buildings, behavior, fire/water/stone and clouds), game space (indoor maps, outdoor maps, bodies of water), game systems (ecosystems, road networks, urban environments, entity behavior), game scenarios (puzzles, storyboards, story, levels), game design (system design, world design) and derived content (news and broadcasts, leaderboards). Mechanisms for automatic difficulty adaptation are widespread—not only in the educational sector, but also in health games (cf. adaptive balance training with *Balance Fit*, see Chap. 12).

Check your understanding of this chapter by answering the following questions:

- What is the difference between configuration, personalization, and adaptation in serious games?
- What is the difference between adaptation, adaptivity, and personalization in the context of (serious) games?
- Why can the flow concept be used to model challenge and challenge adaptation in games?
- Which dimensions for adaptation are there, and what models can be used for adaptation in each dimension?
- Compare the role of book author with a film scriptwriter and a game designer for a digital educational game—what are the differences? What are common tasks?
- Why is it difficult to realize Interactive Storytelling systems?
- What are the costs (effort) for the development steps of adaptive educational games? Please consider the complexity compared to the development of web-based training courses in traditional eLearning?
- How many different stories can evolve in an adventure game based on the Hero's Journey story model?
- What is the challenge to implement story-based educational games using the NGLOB concept? Which tasks are necessary within the game development phase, how to control a game during run-time?
- Think about (and conceptualize) your own educational game/game design, providing both a suspenseful story within the overall course of the game and enabling users to interact in all game situations and to influence the evolving story.

Recommended Literature

Doignon JP, Falmagne JC (1999) Knowledge Spaces, Springer Verlag, ISBN 978-3540645016. *This book covers the concept of knowledge spaces and offers a mathematical foundation for knowledge assessment.*
Falmagne JC, Albert D, Doble C, Eppstein D, Hu X (2013) Knowledge Spaces—Applications in Education, Springer Verlag, ISBN 978-3642353284. *This book covers applications and relevant theoretical results in the field of knowledge space theory, with a focus on the ALEKS system. It further provides cognitive interpretations to the combinatoric structures obtained.*
Russel S and Norvig P (2010) Artificial Intelligence—A Modern Approach. *This book offers a comprehensive, up-to-date introduction to the theory and practice of artificial intelligence. Further, it explains the concept of simulation in form of agent-based modeling—from simple reflex agents, model-based agents, and goal-based agents, to the more complex utility-based agents.*
Kickmeier-Rust MD, Albert D (2012) An Alien's Guide to Multi-Adaptive Educational Computer Games. Santa Rosa, USA: Informing Science Press. Retrieved from http://books.google. i.e.,/books?id=OKZJnHKdchQC. *This provides a summary of achieved results within the 80Days project. This includes tangible results as the authoring tool StoryTec, as well as mechanisms for the creation and control of adaptive digital educational games, combining the three dimensions of (adaptive) storytelling, learning, and gaming.*

Referring to adaptive, interactive storytelling, the International Conference on Interactive Digital Storytelling (http://icids.org/) provides a good entry point for further research. Based on the former international conferences on Virtual Storytelling (ICVS) and Technologies on Interactive Digital Storytelling and Entertainment (TIDSE), the Joint Conference on Interactive Digital Storytelling was established in 2008. Since that time, an annual conference takes place, with conference proceedings in Springer LNCS. Further, the website provides links to the *Wiki on Interactive Storytelling and Narrative Theories*, a publication database on Interactive Storytelling and a repository on interactive story creation (i.e., authoring tools and creation methods). This originated within the IRIS Network of Excellence on Integrated Research in Interactive Storytelling.

References

Abrantes SL, Gouveia LB (2011) Evaluating adoption of innovations of mobile devices and desktops within collaborative environments in a higher education context. Communications of the IBIMA, vol 2011. doi:10.5171/ 2011.341897
Aristotle 330 BC (1987) The Poetics of Aristotle, translation and commentary by Stephen Halliwell. Duckworth
Augustin T, Hockemeyer C, Kickmeier-Rust MD, Albert D (2011) Individualized skill assessment in digital learning games: basic definitions and mathematical formalism. IEEE Trans Learning Technol 4(2):138–148
Aylett, R (1999) Narrative in virtual environments—towards emergent narrative. In: AAAI symposium on narrative intelligence
Balet O (2007) INSCAPE: an authoring platform for interactive storytelling. In: Cavazza M, Donikian S (eds) Proceedings of the virtual storytelling. Using virtual reality technologies for storytelling. Springer, Berlin, pp 176–177

Bartle RA (1996) Hearts, clubs, diamonds, spades: players who suit MUDs. J MUD Research 1 (1):19

Bellotti F, Berta R, De Gloria A, Primavera L (2009) Adaptive experience engine for serious games. IEEE Trans Comput Intell AI Games 1(4):264–280

Campbell J (2008) The hero with a thousand faces, 3 edn. New World Library

Carron T, Marty JC (2012) Enhancement of adaptation and monitoring in game-based learning environments. student usability in educational software and games: improving experiences, p 201

Cavazza M, Donikian S, Christie M, Spierling U, Szilas N, Vorderer P, Hartmann T, Klimmt C, André A, Champagnat R, Petta P, Olivier P (2008) The IRIS network of excellence: integrating research in interactive storytelling. Proceedings of interactive storytelling. Springer, Berlin, pp 14–19

Cavazza M, Champagnat R, Leonardi R (2009) The IRIS network of excellence: future directions in interactive storytelling. Proceedings of the interactive storytelling. Springer, Berlin, pp p8–13

Champagnat R, Delmas G, Augeraud M (2008) A storytelling model for educational games. In: Proceedings of the first international workshop on story-telling and educational games

Charles D, Black M (2004) Dynamic player modelling: a framework for player-centered digital games. In: Proceedings of the international conference on computer games: artificial intelligence, design and education, pp 29–35

Charles D, McNeill M, McAlister M, Black M, Moore A, Stringer K, Kücklich J, Kerr A (2005) Player-centred game design: player modelling and adaptive digital games. In: Proceedings of the digital games research conference, vol 285

Chen J (2007) Flow in games (and everything else). Commun ACM 50(4):31–34

Conlan O, O'Keeffe I, Hampson C, Heller J (2006) Using knowledge space theory to support learner modeling and personalization. In: Reeves T, Yamashita S (eds) Proceedings of the world conference on E-learning in corporate, government, healthcare, and higher education 2006. AACE, Chesapeake, VA, pp 1912–1919

Crawford C (2004) Chris crawford on interactive storytelling. New Riders Press

Cronbach LJ (1967) How can instruction be adapted to individual differences. Learning and individual differences, pp 23–39

Csikszentmihalyi M (1990) Flow: the psychology of optimal experience. Harper and Row, New York, NY

Doignon JP, Falmagne JC (1999b) Knowledge Spaces. Springer, Germany

Encarnação M (2009) On the future of serious games in science and industry. In: Proceedings of the CGames, pp 9–16

Fabricatore C (2000) Learning and videogames: an unexploited synergy. Unpublished manuscript

Fairclough CR, Cunningham P (2003) A multiplayer case-based story engine. In: 4th international conference intelligent games and simulation, EUROSIS

Field S (1988) The screenwriter's workbook. Dell Publishing Company, New York

Figueiredo R, Brisson A, Aylett R, Paiva. (2008) Emergent stories facilitated: an architecture to generate stories using intelligent synthetic characters. In: Proceedings of the 1st international joint conf interactive digital storytelling 2008, LNCS, vol 5334. Springer, pp 218–229

Freytag G (1863) Die Technik des Dramas. Verlag: S. Hirzel, 1863. 310 Seiten

Fu D, Houlette R (2002) Putting AI in entertainment: an AI authoring tool for simulation and games. IEEE Intell Syst 17(4):81–84

Gee JP (2005) Learning by design: good video games as learning machines. E-Learning Digital Media 2(1):5–16

Göbel S, Malkewitz R, Becker F (2006) Story pacing in interactive storytelling. LNCS, vol 3942. Springer, p 419

Göbel S, Salvatore L, Konrad R (2008) StoryTec: a digital storytelling platform for the authoring and experiencing of interactive and non-linear stories. In: automated solutions for cross media content and multi-channel distribution, 2008. AXMEDIS'08. IEEE, pp 103–110

Göbel S, Mehm F, Radke S, Steinmetz R (2009) 80Days: adaptive digital storytelling for digital educational games. In: Proceedings of the 2nd international WS story-telling and educational games, vol 498, no 498

Göbel S, Wendel V, Ritter C, Steinmetz R (2010) Personalized, adaptive digital educational games using narrative game-based learning objects. Entertainment for education, digital techniques and systems. Springer, Berlin, pp 438–445

Göbel S, Mehm F, Wendel V (2012) Adaptive digital storytelling for digital educational games. In: Kickmeier-Rust MD, Albert D (eds) An alien's guide to multi-adaptive educational computer games. Informing Science Press, Santa Rosa, pp 89–104. http://books.google.at/books/about/An_Alien_s_Guide_to_Multi_Adaptive_Educa.html

Grasbon D, Braun N (2001) A morphological approach to interactive storytelling. In Proceedings of the CAST01, living in mixed realities. Special issue of Netzspannung. Mag Media Product Inter-media Res 337–340

Heller J, Steiner C, Hockemeyer C, Albert D (2006) Competence-based knowledge structures for personalised learning. Int J E-Learning 5(1):75–88

Hendrikx M, Meijer S, Van Der Velden J, Iosup A (2013) Procedural content generation for games: a survey. ACM Trans Multimedia Comput Commun Appl 9(1):1

Hoffmann A, Göbel S, Schneider O, Iurgel I (2005) Storytelling-based edutainment applications. E-learning and virtual science centers, pp 190–214

Houlette R (2004) Player Modelling for Adaptive Games. AI Game Programming Wisdom II, pp 557–566

Kaukoranta T, Smed J, Hakonen H (2003) Understanding pattern recognition methods. AI Game Programming Wisdom 2:579–589

Kickmeier-Rust MD, Albert D (eds) (2012) An Alien's guide to multi-adaptive educational computer games. Informing Science

Kickmeier-Rust MD, Albert D (2012c) Educationally adaptive: balancing serious games. Intl J Comput Sci Sport 11(1):15–28

Kickmeier-Rust MD, Albert D (2013) Using Hasse diagrams for competence-oriented learning analytics. In: Human-computer interaction and knowledge discovery in complex, unstructured, big data. Springer, pp 59–64

Korossy K (1999) Modeling knowledge as competence and performance. Knowledge spaces: Theories, empirical research, and applications, pp 103–132

Kriegel M, Aylett R (2008) Emergent narrative as a novel framework for massively collaborative authoring. Intelligent virtual agents. Springer, Berlin, pp 73–80

Law ELC, Mattheiss E, Kickmeier-Rust MD, Albert D (2010) Vicarious learning with a digital educational game: eye-tracking and survey-based evaluation. In: Leitner G, Hitz M, Holzinger A (eds) LNCS, vol 6389. Springer, Berlin, pp 471–488

Laws RD (2002) Robin's laws of good game mastering. Steve Jackson Games

Lazzaro N (2004) Why we play games: four keys to more emotion without story, 2004. http://www.xeodesign.com/whyweplaygames/xeodesign_whyweplaygames.pdf. Accessed 06 Feb 2015

Lindley CA (2004) Narrative, game play and alternative time structures for virtual environments. In: Göbel et al (eds) Technologies for interactive digital storytelling and entertainment, LNCS, vol 3105. Springer

Louchart S, Swartjes I, Kriegel M, Aylett R (2008) Purposeful authoring for emergent narrative. In: Spierling U and Szilas N (eds) Proc ICIDS 2008. Springer LNCS, vol 5334, pp 273–284

Louchart S, Aylett R (2003) Solving the narrative paradox in VEs—lessons from RPGs. In: Rist T, Aylett, R and Ballin D (eds) Proceedings of the intelligent virtual agents, 4th Intl WS IVA2003, LNAI 2792. Springer, pp 244–248

Louchart S, Aylett RS (2004) Narrative theory and emergent interactive narrative. Int J Continuing Eng Educ Life-long Learning (special issue on narrative in education) 14(6):506–518

Machado I, Paiva A, Brna P (2001) Real characters in virtual stories—promoting interactive story creation activities. LNCS 2197:127–134

Mateas M, Stern A (2003) Façade: an experiment in building a fully-realized interactive drama. In: Game developers conference, game design track

Mateas M, Stern A (2007) Façade, an artificial intelligence-based art/research experiment in electronic narrative. http://www.interactivestory.net/. Accessed 5 Feb 2007

McKee R (1997) Substance, structure, style, and the principles of screenwriting. HarperCollins, New York

McKenna K, Lee S (2003) A love affair with MUDs: flow and social interaction in multi-user-dungeons. http://www.websm.org/uploadi/editor/McKenna_Sangchul_2004_MUDs_love_affair. doc. Accessed 06 Feb 2015

Mehm F, Göbel S, Radke S, Steinmetz R (2009) Authoring environment for story-based digital educational games. In: Proceedings of the 1st international open workshop on intelligent personalization and adaptation in digital educational games, vol 1, pp 113–124)

Mehm F, Wendel V, Göbel S.Steinmetz R (2010) Bat cave: a testing and evaluation platform for digital educational games. In: Proceedings of the 3rd European conference on games based learning, pp 251–260

Mehm F, Göbel S, Steinmetz R (2013) An authoring tool for educational adventure games: concept, game models and authoring processes. Intl J Game-Based Learning 3(1):63–79

Nandi A (2004) Frames: At the Edge and Beyond. In: Hagebolling H (ed) Interactive Dramaturgies: new approaches in multimedia content and design other information. Springer, Berlin

Propp V (2010) Morphology of the Folktale, vol 9. University of Texas Press

Riedl MO, Sugandh N (2008) Story planning with vignettes: toward overcoming the content production bottleneck. Interactive storytelling. Springer, Berlin, pp 168–179

Ryan ML (2008) Interactive narrative, plot types, and interpersonal relations. Interactive storytelling. Springer, Berlin, pp 6–13

Schwarz D, Oleggini L, Steiner CM, Stoecker M (2012) The 80Days game. Published in Kickmeier-Rust MD, Albert D (eds) (2012) An Alien's guide to multi-adaptive educational computer games. Informing Science, pp 191–232

Schell J (2008) The art of game design: a book of lenses. Taylor & Francis US

Seger L (1997) Das Geheimnis guter Drehbücher. Alexander Verlag, Berlin

Smith AM, Lewis C, Hullet K, Sullivan A (2011a) An inclusive view of player modeling. In: Proceedings of the 6th international conference foundations of digital games. ACM, p 301–303

Smith AM, Lewis C, Hullett K, Smith G, Sullivan A (2011b) An inclusive taxonomy of player modeling. Technical report UCSC-SOE-11-13, University of California, Santa Cruz

Spronck P, Ponsen M, Sprinkhuizen-Kuyper I, Postma E (2006) Adaptive game AI with dynamic scripting. Mach Learn 63(3):217–248

Steinmetz R, Nahrstedt K (2004) Multimedia applications. Springer

Stern A (2008) Embracing the combinatorial explosion: a brief prescription for interactive story R&D. Interactive storytelling. Springer, Berlin, pp 1–5

Sweetser P, Wyeth P (2005) GameFlow: a model for evaluating player enjoyment in games. Comput Entertain (CIE) 3(3):1–24

Szilas N (2004) Stepping into the Interactive Drama. In: Göbel et al (eds) Technologies for interactive digital storytelling and entertainment, LNCS vol 3105. Springer

Tobias RB (1999) 20 Masterplots. Zweitausendeins, Frankfurt am Main

Trevino LK, Webster J (1992) Flow in computer-mediated communication electronic mail and voice mail evaluation and impacts. Commun Res 19(5):539–573

Torrente J, Moreno-Ger P, Fernandez-Manjon B (2008) Learning models for the integration of adaptive educational games in virtual learning environments. In: Pan Z, Zhang X, El Rhalibi A, Woo W, Li Y (eds) Technologies for E-learning and digital entertainment, LNCS, vol 5093. Springer, Berlin, pp 463–474

Vassileva D, Bontchev B (2009) Adaptation engine construction based on formal rules. In: Proceedings of the international conference on computer supported education (CSEDU)

Vogler C (1998) A Writer's Journey. Mythic Structure for storytellers and Screenwriters. Wiese Productions, Studio City, California

Vorderer P, Hartmann T, Klimmt C (2003) Explaining the enjoyment of playing video games: the role of competition. In: Proceedings of the 2nd international conference entertainment computing, Carnegie Mellon University, pp 1–9

Westra J, van Hasselt H, Dignum F, Dignum V (2009) Adaptive serious games using agent organizations. Agents for games and simulations. Springer, Berlin, pp 206–220

Yannakakis GN, Maragoudakis M (2005) Player modeling impact on player's entertainment in computer games. User Modeling 2005. Springer, Berlin, pp 74–78

Yee N (2006) Motivations for play in online games. CyberPsychol Behav 9(6):772–775

Zimmermann B (2008) Pattern-basierte Prozessbeschreibung und -unterstützung: Ein Werkzeug zur Unterstützung von Prozessen zur Anpassung von E-Learning- Materialien. PhD thesis, TU Darmstadt - Elektrotechnik und Informationstechnik - Multimedia Kommunikation

Multiplayer Serious Games

8

Viktor Wendel and Johannes Konert

Abstract

This chapter covers the topic of multiplayer serious games. Multiplayer games are discussed in terms of game types and forms, genres and techniques, as well as their impact on the use of multiplayer games. Based on that, this chapter will show how different types of multiplayer genres and techniques can be used for various serious game purposes. This chapter further provides an introduction to the topic of collaborative learning and collaborative multiplayer games—and their use for game-based collaborative learning. We discuss how collaborative learning concepts are inherently used by some massive multiplayer online games, and how those concepts can be used more thoroughly by using the multiplayer paradigm for game-based collaborative learning. Further, it is shown how various multiplayer design aspects like number of players, persistency, matchmaking, interaction, or social aspects need to be considered in the design phase of a multiplayer game.

8.1 Introduction

A game is called a *multiplayer game* when two or more players play it together—either against each other, together in teams against other teams, or completely cooperatively against the computer.

V. Wendel (✉)
Technische Universität Darmstadt, Darmstadt, Germany
e-mail: viktor.wendel@gmail.com

J. Konert
Beuth University of Applied Sciences Berlin, Berlin, Germany

© Springer International Publishing Switzerland 2016
R. Dörner et al. (eds.), *Serious Games*, DOI 10.1007/978-3-319-40612-1_8

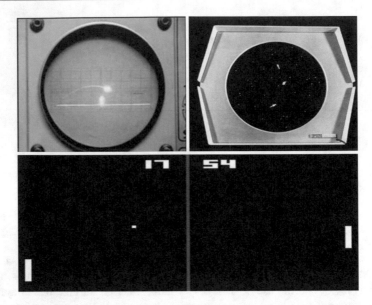

Fig. 8.1 *Upper left Tennis for Two* (1958) played on an oscilloscope. *Upper right Space Invaders* (1961). *Bottom Pong* (1972)

The concept of multiplayer games is not an invention of digital games. Rather, is as old as mankind itself. Children play with their parents and start playing with other children at a very young age although the rules defining the game are often rather lax. Even among animals—especially those living in herds or packs (e.g., wolves or lions)—playing can be observed especially among young animals, which is often considered a form of training for their later lives.

So, what makes people want to play with each other? Obviously, there are various components which (can) improve a game with other players compared to playing alone. One of them is the *social component*, as playing multiplayer games comprises interaction with other people (e.g., debating about team strategies, praising each other, etc.). On top of this, there is the *competitive element* that makes playing with other human players challenging.

When looking at the history of digital games, *Tennis for Two* (1958) or *Spacewar* (1961) were two of the early digital games—both are multiplayer games. They are shown in Fig. 8.1.

In the early years of digital gaming with limited hardware resources, AI players were hardly an option. Hence, most games were designed as player versus player games. In later years, with upcoming arcade game consoles, more and more single-player games were developed with multiplayer variants being mostly played in split-screen or shared-screen mode, like *Pong* (1972), see Fig. 8.1.

With the arrival of the Internet, game technology made a big step towards more multiplayer-centered games. Network technology via LAN or wide-area networks enabled game modes where many players could be part of one game, with each player having his/her own screen. The split-screen or shared-screen mode was no longer necessary. Popular multiplayer genres developed, from First-Person-Shooter (FPS) games over multiplayer Real-Time-Strategy (RTS) games, or round-based strategy games towards Massive Multiplayer Online (MMO) games. The first popular MMO games were MMO role-playing games (MMORPGs), with popular representatives like *World of Warcraft* (WoW) or *EverQuest*. Other MMO games were more focused on an open online world (e.g., *SecondLife*) or made use of social components, like the recent generation of Facebook games (e.g., *Farmville*). Most recently, Massive Online Battle Arenas (MOBAs) (e.g., *League of Legends, DotA*) have emerged as the latest MMO genre.

The increasing role of multiplayer games in today's games market, as shown by the success of MOBAs like *League of Legends* or *DotA2*, prove the fascination of multiplayer games. In 2014, *League of Legends* created revenues of $946 million USD (Statista 2014) and had more than 67 million active players per month (Statista 2014). On average, players in the US spent 107 min/day playing online games in 2013 (97 min in Europe) (Statista 2013). Apart from MOBAs, there are FPS (*Modern Warfare*), RTS games (*StarCraft, World of Tanks*), roleplay games (*WoW*), or other emerging genres like card-based games (*Hearthstone*).

Multiplayer games offer—by playing with or against other human players—competition (Mitchell and Savill-Smith 2004; Vorderer et al. 2003), cooperation, and other forms of social interaction (Manninen 2003), which might be the main reason for their popularity (see Sect. 8.2 for more details on various forms of multiplayer serious games). This social component is one major argument for using multiplayer concepts and technology for serious games (Ducheneaut and Moore 2004). Multiplayer technology can also be used very well in serious game application areas today; in fact, many of the above examples have been used for multiplayer serious game applications. Multiplayer serious games can offer the inclusion of a social component on top of the serious games principle and hence engage players on a social level. Moreover, principles from the collaborative learning paradigm can be used in multiplayer serious game scenarios. This enables players to learn in groups, thus making use of established group learning principles and mechanisms (see Sect. 8.3).

There is another aspect in games that appears to be very present in multiplayer games, especially MMORPGs. Players tend to spend considerable time learning a game, often even without playing it. It is a frequently observed phenomenon that players visit wikis, forums, or other websites dedicated to the MMO they like to improve their gameplay with, or learn something new about, the game (Voulgari and Komis 2008; Gee 2003; Yee 2005; Dickey 2007). There are theoretical results as to why players spend so much time learning a game, and how this motivation can be used in serious games (Gee 2003; Garris et al. 2002; Prensky 2006). This inherent motivation might be one more driver for the use of multiplayer serious games.

The concept of competition might also be a main motivation for multiplayer serious games. When players can learn from a game, this effect might be improved when players play the game against a human opponent, because competition is more real when there is a real (human) opponent. It has been shown that one learns best when the challenge is optimal (Sweetser and Wyeth 2005). Hence, suitable opponents are required to optimize the learning process. However, AI-based opponents are often limited—both in their skills and in their strategic variability and adaptability. Whereas players can train reflexes in shooter games, they can become more elaborated when playing against human opponents as those intelligent opponents tend to develop new strategies and change their behavior. For the same reason, human opponents can be better opponents in strategy games. Generally, human opponents are considered to be more challenging whenever an AI-based opponent is pushed to its limits. However, the question of finding an opponent best suited for a given player is not trivial; this will be elaborated below.

Learning theories (behaviorism, cognitivism, constructivism) highlight the important role of social interaction in different ways, but all agree on the supportive effect such *peer education* has for learning (Piaget 2003; Doise et al. 1975; Vygotsky 1997; Bandura 2002). More recently, George Siemens received attention in the field of technology-enhanced learning with his theory of connectivism, which focuses more on *know-where* instead of *know-what* (Siemens 2005). With a focus on serious games, the question in terms of social interconnection is not only to find team members or opponents of a similar competitive strength, but also with capabilities—like prior knowledge and personality traits—that lead to maximum learning progress for all players. Some aspects of this *learning group formation problem* and their potential of peer education are nicely described and analyzed by (Damon 1984). Initial algorithmic solutions are compared by (Konert et al. 2014). A literature review of relevant matching criteria for learning group formation can be found in (Konert 2014a). To mention one example, (Paredes et al. 2010) found out that homogeneous groups perform better on specific tasks, whereas heterogeneous groups perform better on broader tasks. These and other aspects have to be taken into consideration when designing team matching and group tasks in games.

Apart from finding a good match for players and opponents, other major challenges for multiplayer games comprise the heterogeneity of players and learners in general. As players have different preferences and affectations for games, genres, and ways of playing, it is almost impossible to create games that are equally appealing to all players. Also, in terms of learning, there are differences between the players (e.g., learning style, state of knowledge, etc.) that need to be considered. This constitutes a major challenge of using multiplayer serious games and leads to the research field of adaptation and adaptivity. Moreover, in collaborative learning scenarios, the role of the instructor needs to be considered, as the instructor plays a vital role the learning process. This special role needs to be considered both during game design and at runtime (see Sect. 8.3).

8.2 Forms of Multiplayer Serious Gaming

As explained above, multiplayer serious games offer a multitude of application fields due to multiplayer benefits that can be utilized in various forms. In this section, the different types and forms will be elaborated. As a first step, different types of multiplayer games will be described from a technical perspective, explaining technical possibilities and limitations and their implications.

After that, game types are discussed in relation to the type of player interaction, i.e., in terms of competition, cooperation, and collaboration. Implications for the games will be discussed and fields of applications derived.

8.2.1 Multiplayer Types and Techniques

Generally, there are different types of multiplayer techniques that impact the way players use a screen.

Players can play a multiplayer game using *one computer,* subsequently using one screen. Traditional multiplayer games—from the time when networking did not exist—had to rely on this technique. When only one screen is available, it needs to be decided in which way information is presented to the players. The method of sharing strongly depends on the game genre itself. If players play consecutively, there is no need to share screen space; players just take turns at the same computer. All players are usually around the screen where a player takes his/her turn. Therefore, from a gameplay perspective, it is very difficult to display sensitive/private information to a specific player (e.g., tactical advice), as the other players might also get that information.

If, on the other hand, players play simultaneously on one machine, the available screen space needs to be shared or divided among the players. Again, depending on the genre of the game, this can be done in various ways.

The most traditional way is the so-called *split screen*. This technique is used to split the available screen in (usually two or four) equal parts, depending on the number of players. As the screen space is limited, it appears to be not advisable to split the screen in more than four parts, as this would result in too small pieces for each player. Hence, this limits the number of players. An example for the split-screen approach is shown in Fig. 8.2.

A different way for displaying the screen for multiple players is a *shared screen*. Here, all the players are displayed on one screen at the same time. Although this is a very simple concept, it comprises some very important limitations regarding the game design. As there is only one screen for all players, the game design needs to reflect all player movements. The simplest idea is to restrict the level itself to a certain size so that it can be displayed completely in one screen. The players cannot leave the screen. If, however, the level needs to be larger, strategies need to be used

Fig. 8.2 Splitscreen for three players in the game *Sonic & All-Stars Racing Transformed* (PC version; screenshot created by the authors)

Fig. 8.3 Shared screen in the video game *Castle Crashers* (PC version) (screenshot created by the authors); all four players share one screen

to prevent players from leaving the screen. This can be done either by forbidding a movement towards a screen edge when other players are too far away (e.g., *Trine*, *Spelunky*), or by zooming out when players move in different directions (e.g., Xbox game *Teenage Mutant Ninja Turtles*, see Fig. 8.3). This, however, is limited by a maximum zoom distance—which again is defined by a minimum size of game objects on the screen.

Multiplayer types are defined by the number of players in a game and how the players access the game. In terms of presentation, players might use one device per player or share a device via split screen, shared screen, or by taking turns. For networked multiplayer games, network issues like latency, jitter, or packet loss are more or less relevant depending on the game genre.

With the arrival of network technology, and especially the Internet, a new multiplayer paradigm emerged. As it is now possible to interconnect computers, players can now participate with more than one computer in a game, with each player playing on one computer and thus on one screen. Although this solves the problem of how to best use the screen, it imposes new challenges.

The core issue with networked games is latency, which is mainly a problem with players using the Internet rather than players in a local area network. The topic of latency, also with a focus on games, is a major research area in the field of computer science. As there is a lot of literature on this problem (Armitage et al. 2006), it will not be elaborated further here.

Also, in terms of game design, Armitage et al. (2006) provides an exhaustive overview on how to minimize the effect of latency by lossless (Welch 1984) and delta compression, player and opponent prediction, time manipulation, interest management, or update aggregation.

When designing a multiplayer serious game, it should be considered from the beginning how much the gameplay relies on real-time execution. Depending on the game genre, there are different requirements for latency. For a realtime strategy game (RTS) or a first person shooter (FPS), for example, low latency is very important. For MMORPGs, the tolerance for a higher latency is bigger. And for round-based games, even higher latency is tolerable.

In many European schools, for example, Internet access is still mediocre or bad. This results in major latency issues, especially when 20+ computers share a narrow-band Internet connection.

8.2.2 Multiplayer Game Genres

As shown in the previous section, the game genre has a major impact on multi-player game design. Clearly, different game genres are appropriate for different application areas. Whereas FPS-like games might be applicable to train a player's reaction, interactive simulations might be the best choice when the goal of the game is to teach about a complex process. How can different multiplayer genres be used for serious purposes? This is mainly motivated from successful serious game examples:

First Person Shooters (FPS) are games relying heavily not only on quick reaction times and good reflexes, but also on knowledge about the level and on strategic thinking, especially in coordination within the team. Hence, FPS

Fig. 8.4 Screenshot of the serious first person shooter game *Re-Mission* (Kato et al. 2008)

mechanics can be used to train motor skills like reflexes, and to train aspects of teamwork. However, there are also examples of FPS mechanics used for educational games (e.g., *MathShooter, DimensionM, WordDomination*) or for informing and motivational shooters (e.g., *Re-Mission*, see Fig. 8.4).

> Multiplayer genres can be classified by aspects like the number of players, the dependency on technical aspects like latency, the importance of controls and input devices, and the importance of consistency of the game state or the game world. Other aspects refer to the game speed, i.e., whether the game is played in real-time, in a turn-based fashion or at varying speed. Resulting genres cover strategy games (chess), real-time strategy games (*Star Craft*), 4X games (*Civilization*), first-person shooters (*quake*), simulation games (*crusader kings*), asynchronous browser games (*Travian*), multiplayer online games (*World of Warcraft*), virtual worlds (*Second Life*), and multiplayer online battle arenas (*League of Legends*). Adventure games or interactive movies are one significant exception, as they are mainly designed for single-player use.

Strategy games are usually based on tactical and strategic thinking, which is related to problem solving. As many strategy games use *war* as a narrative setting, they often are set in a historical context. This makes them well suited for teaching history-related content, if the latter is well integrated into the game. Further, they can be used to train teamwork, especially on a more resource-based foundation, with players using different resources in one team and hence becoming dependent on each other. There are many examples of games that fall under the 4X category, like *Sid Meier's Civilization*.

Real-time strategy (RTS) games are a special class of strategy games in which the game is played in real-time as opposed to turn-based. As this genre is among the most popular ones, it is discussed separately. Similar to strategy games, RTS games can be used for training of strategic and tactical thinking, as well as teamwork aspects. Moreover, due to real-time gameplay, time pressure can be used to assess how well players react in stressful situations. Examples are the *Command & Conquer series, Company of Heroes, or StarCraft*.

Massively Multiplayer Online Roleplaying games (MMORPGs) are games in which players play a fictional character in a fantasy world. An important feature of MMORPGs is that usually thousands of players experience the game within one instance (i.e., world). Hence, this type of game heavily relies on player interaction. Although often major parts of a game are in so-called player versus environment (PvE) mode where the player mainly interacts with the game environment, another major part is player versus player (PvP), where players play against other players. Also, even the PvE parts of a game are often played in groups of players, as it is easier to overcome difficult obstacles and enemies in a team. Hence, it can be assumed that MMORPGs heavily rely on player interaction and team play, and this is what existing MMORPGs are typically used for in a serious games context. Delwiche (2006) performed learning units of an undergraduate communication course using the MMORPG *Everquest* and the sandbox game *Second Life*. Childress and Braswell (2006) investigate the use of MMORPGs to foster communication and interaction and to facilitate cooperative learning. Steinkuehler (2004) addresses social aspects of learning of learning with and within MMORPGs. However, it should be noted that due to the enormous game development effort and the costs of maintaining an MMORPG infrastructure, it can hardly be recommended to create a serious MMORPG from scratch. Rather, it stands to reason to use existing MMORPGs or available modifications of those for serious game scenarios. Examples for this are described by Childress and Braswell (2006) and Herz (2001). If the modding tools are powerful enough, it might well be possible to include serious content in a mod, e.g., a historically plausible, playable epoch of a historical setting.

Simulation games describe a genre of games in which the focus is on illustrating a complex system, situation, or mechanism as realistically as possible by simulating it. In most traditional simulation games, this leads to insights into the complex interrelationships and interdependencies between different parameters of a system—while playfully testing the system and experiencing how the change of parameters influences it. This mechanism perfectly fits into a serious game context to demonstrate difficult systems or mechanisms, and lets players experience them in a playful environment without the consequences of failure. Examples for this are *Sid Meier's Civilization, Sim City,* and *TechForce* (see Fig. 8.5).

Adventure games are games which focus on a strong story line. Usually, gameplay is limited to experiencing a story and solving puzzles and riddles along the way. Often, player decisions decide the future course of the narration. The oldest adventure games used only text to set the scene and tell the story, giving players limited decision options. Later, adventures were typically 2D games with a static background image, limited interaction possibilities (usually based on an inventory system and combining and using items), and choices for each scene.

Fig. 8.5 Screenshot of the serious game *TechForce*

Prominent examples are *Monkey Island* or *Maniac Mansion*. In recent years, 3D technology is used to increase immersion, but the core concept is still the same. Hence, adventure games can be used to wrap serious game content in a story to be interactively experienced by the players with a rather limited technical effort. It should be mentioned that most adventure games are single-player games, although there are some new multiplayer adventures (Lester 2013; Reuter et al. 2012).

Browser games emerged during the last decade. Although basically all game genres exist in the form of browser games, one specific type of games emerged from the use of browsers as the technical platform: *Social network games* (Casual Connect Research 2012). As no installation on the client machine (typically a PC or a smartphone) is necessary, casual gamers can easily be implemented because the technical hurdle is low. Browser games emerged with a huge community of active users. *FarmVille* from Zynga, to name an example, gained over 80 million players in 2010.[1] The rise and fall (server shutdown) of several such games, like *SimCity Social* or *Sim Social*, underline the challenge from a business model perspective: The games are offered for free, using the freemium revenue model (Runge et al. 2014). This means that the game itself is available for free, but players can be premium items, abilities, bonuses, etc., which give them an advantage. Usually, those advantages can also be gained by investing time in the game, but often there are bonuses that are exclusively available for purchase. Without a huge user base, operation of the central game servers is not profitable. As serious games can be considered more as niche products, rather than addressing a very large target group, such a revenue model seems to be impractical.

With the potential of social network games for educational purposes in mind, the design of a serious game could consider the following characteristics to be utilized to increase knowledge exchange among playing peers (Konert 2014a):

---

[1]http://mashable.com/2010/02/20/farmville-80-million-users.

- *Asynchronous play*: Multiplayer games are designed for social media-based interactions. Thus, players exchange items or manipulate the game environment, but do not have to be online at the same time. Everyone can play at her own pace and intensity without being dependent on other players.
- *Casual multiplayer*: As a virtual third place providing meaningful experiences, the game provides a multiplayer atmosphere with awareness of other players' activities (e.g., seeing their playground or avatars), but allows a rather independent single-player game play.
- *Competition*: Competition is only comparative by provided leaderboards or achievements; however, players cannot directly influence the game of other players. A "save private playing area" feature exists, in this state, the game cannot be damaged by other players (e.g., while the player is offline). Cooperative interactions allow for faster game progress, stimulating players to provide favors to others.
- *Beneficial social media interaction*: The three characteristics above are supported by an integration of social media interactions among players. These interactions can be categorized in four groups: Posting (new items, content), sharing (existing items or content with other players), discussing (opinions, decision making), and networking (neighborhoods, friendships, private networks). Some games use the network structure of existing online social networks such as Facebook, Twitter, or others for this purpose.

Thus, "a serious game satisfying all criteria mandatory for a social game" is called a *social serious game* (Konert 2014b).

The social aspects of a game can be such a strong motivational factor that game play is not the major reason for playing (Wohn et al. 2011). For further aspects see as well Sect. 8.4.7 on social issues in multiplayer game design.

8.2.3 Multiplayer Interaction

We now take a closer look at the interaction between players in a multiplayer scenario. Basically, players can play against other players (competitive), either with other players (cooperative, collaborative) or in a mixture of both (e.g., teams of players playing against each other). Each of these types has special features that can be utilized in a serious context.

Competitive. This type of gameplay is based on players in competition with each other to win the game. This competition can be direct, i.e., when players fight each other, or indirect, i.e., when players compete only via points they win, i.e., on a high score list.

In a direct competition, other players are considered opponents. Therefore, usually victory for one player means defeat for the opposing player. This results in the players' strategy to be directed towards defeating the opposing player(s). This means that a player or a team needs to play the game better than the opposing player or team. Here, "better" refers to gameplay in two dimensions—mechanical skills and knowledge about the game. An example for the first is the ability to quickly aim and shoot in an FPS, whereas an example for the latter is the knowledge of which weapon to use in which situation, e.g., regarding distance. The motivation to defeat the opponent hence can be seen as the driving force for a player to improve in both of those dimensions. In a serious context, this can be used if the characterizing goal can be integrated into the gameplay in a way such that the game's relevant (mechanical) skills and game knowledge conform with the characterizing goal.

Apart from that, there are various features that can be used to improve competition, like the already mentioned highscore list or in-game achievements. Both of these are even more effective if they can be combined with a player's social environment, i.e., friends. Using social networks in games enables game designers to reinforce competition by showing achievements and highscores to the friends of a player, thus challenging them to improve in the game. Examples for this method are friend lists in Steam or UPlay, which are used in games like *Farcry 3* to show when a player outperformed another player on his/her friend list.

Cooperative. In cooperative games, the gameplay is designed in a way such that players play in teams, i.e., they win or lose together. Hence, in cooperative games, the motivation is based on social dependency. Players can perceive a feeling of success by good team play, which again is based on good communication and common strategic planning. During the last two decades, this game mode was often included in games as a coop mode for the single player campaign, in which two or more players could play the single player campaign together, with limited or no changes to the game itself. This game mode was often criticized for a lack of game depth, as players were often merely playing next to each other instead of with each other.

However, cooperative gaming also takes place when players play in a real team with each other. Dillenbourg (1999) defines cooperation as follows: "In cooperation, partners split the work, solve sub-tasks individually and then assemble the partial results into the final output." In contrast, Roschelle and Teasley (1995) define collaboration as "a coordinated, synchronous activity that is the result of a continued attempt to construct and maintain a shared conception of a problem." Hence, when players are not mutually exchangeable and depend on each other (e.g., by filling different roles or by having resources to which others do not have access), gameplay is clearly collaborative.

Collaborative. In collaborative gaming, players do not merely play next to each other, but gameplay is based on those players to complement (the skills, knowledge, abilities, or resources of each other. There is an extensive review on how collaborative games work by Zagal et al. (2006). They show elements which are critical for collaborative games to work and pitfalls that should be avoided. The key points are:

- *Lesson 1*: "To highlight problems of competitiveness, a collaborative game should introduce a tension between perceived individual utility and team utility."

- *Lesson 2*: "To further highlight problems of competitiveness, individual players should be allowed to make decisions and take actions without the consent of the team."
- *Lesson 3*: "Players must be able to trace payoffs back to their decisions."
- *Lesson 4*: "To encourage team members to make selfless decisions, a collaborative game should bestow different abilities or responsibilities upon the players."
- *Pitfall 1*: "To avoid the game degenerating into one player making the decisions for the team, collaborative games have to provide a sufficient rationale for collaboration."
- *Pitfall 2*: "For a game to be engaging, players need to care about the outcome, and that outcome should have a satisfying result."
- *Pitfall 3*: "For a collaborative game to be enjoyable multiple times, the experience needs to be different each time, and the presented challenge needs to evolve."

> Interaction between players in multiplayer games is mainly categorized as competitive, cooperative, or collaborative. In competitive games, players (or teams) play against each other; in cooperative games they build teams, and either the whole team wins or loses. In collaborative games, players are usually depending on other players (who may or may not build a common team) and need to help each other, i.e., collaborate in order to advance in the game. There are also mixed forms of these three categories.

Collaborative games, as they are heavily based on interaction between the players—focusing on teamwork, coordination, and supplementing each other—and are are well suited as serious games to teach, train, or assess exactly those social skills. However, assessment of teamwork and quality of teamwork is a rather complex task still being researched.

The concept of collaborative gaming is closely related to the concept of collaborative learning. Hence, this type of games is well suited for game-based collaborative learning in multiplayer (serious) games.

8.3 Collaborative Learning in Multiplayer Serious Games

In the literature, different definitions for the term *collaborative learning* can be found.

A different definition as the one of Roschelle and Teasley (1995) is provided by Thomson et al. (2009): "Collaboration is a multidimensional, variable construct composed of five key dimensions, two of which are structural in nature (governance and administration), two of which are social capital dimensions (mutuality and norms), and one of which involves agency (organizational autonomy)."

8.3.1 Collaborative Learning

Using those definitions of collaboration, the concept of collaborative learning will be elucidated next. Dillenbourg defined collaborative learning as "a situation in which two or more people learn or attempt to learn something together." This definition for itself is rather weak, as the term "together" does not specify what is special about the collaboration when learning. Therefore, Dillenbourg (1999) further states that it is necessary to trigger various specific learning mechanisms in order for learning to happen. Those refer to individual activities, but also to the interaction activities between the learning partners, such as explanation or disagreement. Those activities again are meant to trigger different cognitive mechanisms. However, it cannot be guaranteed that those interactions occur. Therefore, Dillenbourg also specifies four categories of methods, which aim to increase the probability of the interactions to occur in collaborative learning scenarios to:

- setup initial conditions (e.g., group size and composition)
- over-specify the collaboration contract with a scenario based on roles (e.g., reciprocal teaching)
- scaffold productive interactions by encompassing interaction rules in the medium (e.g., provide semi-structured interfaces)
- monitor and regulate interactions (e.g., teacher as facilitator, providing hints, redirecting group work)

> Collaborative learning is a situation in which two or more people learn, or attempt to learn, something together with various specific learning mechanisms.

An important aspect for the success of collaborative learning is both group size and composition of the group of learners. When forming learning groups for knowledge exchange, a variety of criteria need to be taken into account, including personality traits and level of proficiency. Moreover, some of these criteria need to be matched homogeneously (all members of a group are as similar as possible, e.g., in age), and other citeria need to be matched heterogeneously (members of the group are different and amend each other, e.g., in prior knowledge of topics). Moreover, the relevance of criteria and which of them need to be similar (homogeneous) and different (heterogeneous) within the group, depends on learning targets and the learning scenario (Konert 2014a). Learning group formation is therefore an active research area in the interdisciplinary field of technology-enhanced learning (TEL) (Inaba et al. 2000; Cavanaugh and Ellis 2004; Gogoulou et al. 2007; Ounnas et al. 2008; Paredes et al. 2010; Konert et al. 2014).

Moreover, various circumstances need to be met according to Johnson and Johnson (1999) in order for cooperation[2] to happen in collaborative learning scenarios. Those are:

- *Positive interdependence*: knowing to be linked with other group members in a way so that one cannot succeed alone. Positive interdependence results from mutual goals. In this context, interdependence includes resource, role and task interdependence. There is evidence about the effects of positive interdependence in collaborative learning scenarios as summarized by Johnson and Johnson (2009), e.g., when players depend on other players due to their role (i.e., a player needs another player's help because only that player has a certain resource).
- *Individual accountability and personal responsibility*: individual assessment of each group member's performance, communicated to both the group and the individual. "Individual accountability exists when the performance of each individual member is assessed and the results are given back to all group members to compare against a standard of performance" (Johnson and Johnson 1999).
- *Promotive interaction*: Promoting each other's success by e.g., helping, encouraging and praising. Promotive interaction occurs when group members encourage each other, help, or facilitate each other's efforts towards the group goal.
- *Appropriate use of social skill*: Interpersonal and small group skills are vital for the success of a cooperative effort. Appropriate use of social skills means that group members need to possess and be able to use various soft skills like communication, supporting each other, or being able to resolve conflicts.
- *Group processing*: Group members discuss their progress and work relationships together. Group processing is the act of reflecting on the group members' actions as individuals and as a group in order to evaluate their effort (Dillenbourg 1999).

A vital role in many collaborative learning scenarios is taken by the instructor (e.g., teacher, trainer) who has various important roles before, during, and after a collaborative learning session. The instructor usually has tasks in preparation of the collaborative learning session, like selecting learning goals, setting up motivation strategies, planning the learning scenario, activating attention, or reactivating prior knowledge. Furthermore, the instructor performs important tasks during the collaborative learning session, such as coaching or moderating, observing the learners and the learning process, and helping or redirecting. Finally, the instructor guides through the process of concluding and evaluating the results, and he/she performs a post-session assessment.

---

[2]Cooperation is used as a synonym for collaboration in the work of Johnson and Johnson.

The role of the instructor imposes a critical challenge for digital collaborative learning scenarios, as it is not trivial to enable the instructor to perform all those tasks appropriately in a digital learning environment. However, the use of digital learning or gaming technology also includes new chances for preparation, control, and evaluation and assessment of the collaborative learning scenario.

8.3.2 Computer-Supported Collaborative Learning

Computer-supported collaborative learning (CSCL) is the transfer of the collaborative learning paradigm to digital media, in most cases the computer. In the early years of CSCL, the "primary form of collaboration support is for the computer [...] to provide a medium of communication" technology (Stahl et al. 2006). Hence, mainly Wikis, forums, discussion boards, newsgroups, chat rooms, instant messaging tools, video messaging, or email were used (Larusson and Alterman 2009). Later, more elaborate tools for CSCL were designed. Their fields of application are more focused on coordination, cooperation in groups, and cooperative learning rooms (especially virtual learning rooms) (Haake et al. 2004). Other collaborative learning tools and environments focus on group formation (Haake et al. 2004; Konert et al. 2014), collaborative document management, discussion groups, distributed classrooms (Konert et al. 2012), or virtual classrooms (Westera and Wagemans 2007; Denny et al. 2008). Whereas early virtual learning rooms were CSCL applications specifically designed for CSCL—often integrating a chat system and a shared screen—later versions used existing virtual worlds like *Second Life* or MMORPG worlds (Eustace et al. 2004). Moreover, there are platforms for knowledge exchange, collaborative knowledge access, student monitoring, or team-based learning.

8.3.3 Game-Based Collaborative Learning

Combining the collaborative learning paradigm with the advantages of computer technology and gaming principles and mechanisms appears to be a promising new way of creating game-based collaborative learning scenarios. If the mechanisms proposed by Johnson and Johnson and the requirements postulated by Dillenbourg can be incorporated in a multiplayer game design, digital game-based applications can be created—with the benefits of a motivating, fun environment and the assessment and evaluation tools coming from computer technology. On top of that, if the game incorporates the instructor in an appropriate way, it becomes possible to improve the instructor's work in a collaborative learning scenario. The mechanisms for collaborative fun gaming are very well suited for a game design, which fosters collaborative learning as the characterizing goal. They provide design guidelines to split the work among players/learners, to develop heterogeneous resources, to assign distinct tasks and abilities within the learning context, and to supply methods to foster communication and teamwork.

Fig. 8.6 Screenshot of Escape From Wilson Island of players carrying a palm tree together

Hence, in recent years, the first CSCL serious games have been designed and implemented. They incorporate CSCL principles and combine them with serious games mechanics, resulting in multiplayer serious games for collaborative learning (Zea et al. 2009). Hämäläinen (2011) describes an approach of a collaborative game for vocational learning, focusing on design elements essential for collaboration. Reuter et al. (2012) describe an approach for designing and authoring multiplayer adventures for collaborative learning, deriving concepts for puzzle design in multiplayer games. Other examples are the collaborative multiplayer serious games *Escape From Wilson Island* (Wendel et al. 2012) (see Fig. 8.6), and the serious game for teamwork workshops *TeamUp* (TeamUp 2015).

Yet, the lack of game-based collaborative learning applications in the market suggests that there are still obstacles and challenges to overcome. The design of teamwork, a component which is central to collaborative learning, is still not very well understood. Quantifying the amount and quality of teamwork and collaboration is challenging. In the literature, different performance measures are proposed. Bowers et al. (1992) use coordination as a measure for teamwork. They created a list of coordination behaviors based on seven behavioral dimensions. Those are: Communication, situational awareness, leadership, assertiveness, decision making, mission analysis, and adaptability. They are used to assess the frequency and quality of coordination. Paris et al. (2000) created a taxonomy of variables with an influence on team performance, providing the relevant factors with examples and applicable interventions to train those factors. They are grouped into contextual factors (e.g., culture, education system and information system), structural factors (e.g., physical environment, organizational arrangements and technological systems), team design factors (e.g., task interdependence, team size and composition and leadership), process factors (e.g., performance norms, communication, team interactions and team spirit), and contingency factors (e.g., team mission, resource availability, rules of operation, managing and decision-making). For each of those factors, they define a set of applicable interventions:

- Contextual factors: team selection, task design, training
- Structural factors: team design, training
- Team design factors: team selection, task design, training
- Process factors: team selection, task design, training
- Contingency factors: task design, training.

In addition to such parameters and factors, other metrics have also been proposed. A cooperative performance metric concept is described by El-Nasr et al. (2010). It contains the following six metrics (measuring positive and negative aspects) to measure teamwork, all relying on observation, with game sessions being recorded, observed, analyzed, and annotated:

- laughter or excitement together (pos.)
- worked out strategies (pos.)
- helping (pos.)
- global strategies (pos.)
- waited for each other (pos.)
- got in the way of each other (neg.)

Shapiro et al. (2008) provide an overview over metrics for team performance for simulation-based training in the domain of healthcare. They distinguish four types of metrics: Event-based measurements, behavioral observation scales, behaviorally anchored rating scales, and self-report measures. One of their main results is the fact that "there is no standard team performance metric or set of metrics [...] across the healthcare disciplines."

Another problem lies in the social component of multiplayer games and collaborative learning scenarios. As those scenarios involve a group of players/learners—even in a small group—the problem of *free riding* exists. Technical possibilities such as event logging, observation, etc. allow to counter this problem. Generally, it is assumed that learners and players feel that their contributions are more crucial to the progress of the team in smaller groups than in larger groups (Kidwell and Bennett 1993; Hindriks and Pancs 2002). Considering an optimal group size, Hare (1981) suggests a size of five, and states that for larger groups, individual group members might have fewer opportunities to contribute to the progress of the team.

Furthermore, the role of the instructor, while undoubtedly crucial to the collaborative learning process, presents a challenge for game design. Usually, this role does not exist in other games, except perhaps in role-playing games. The concept of role-playing games has been ported to computer and video games, yet without the role of the so-called Game Master: His/her role is similar to the role of an instructor in collaborative learning scenarios. Hence, in this context there exists research on how to utilize the concept of a Game Master in a digital game (Tychsen et al. 2005; Tychsen 2008; Wendel et al. 2012).

Nevertheless, there is still a lack of concepts on how to generally include instructors in multiplayer collaborative games such that they are able to perform their tasks as well as possible, supported by modern technology. This might be a major obstacle for using collaborative multiplayer games in training or teaching. In general, reluctance can be observed among many teachers in many European countries to use game technology—or even just computer technology in general— in class. This reluctance results from two main problems: Lack of familiarity with the medium and fear of loss of control when using a game technology without a Game Master.

8.4 Multiplayer Game Design

Generally, the same game design guidelines, hints, and pitfalls valid for single-player games also apply to multiplayer games. Those were already discussed in the earlier chapters of this book. The focus here will be on those features that are specific for multiplayer games.

When designing a serious game, one of the first steps is to define the target group and the characteristic goal of the game. In multiplayer games, it additionally needs to be decided how many players are supposed to play the game—whether they participate simultaneously or in an asynchronous way, if they play together in teams, against each other in a competitive way, or a combination of the two. In this context, it is relevant whether the game world is persistent or if games are played in (short) sessions. In competitive scenarios, matchmaking—matching opponents as fair as possible—is an important aspect. Moreover, the speed and flow of the game need to be taken into account. Further, it needs to be considered what influence communication, or the lack of it, might have on the gameplay. Social issues like grieving, mobbing, or toxic behavior of the players also needs to be considered, especially in a classroom environment. Finally, it needs to be considered to what extent the game will depend on hardware and network infrastructure in terms of latency (see before, not in focus here). Hence, the following characteristics have an impact on the game design:

- Number of players
- Persistency
- Matchmaking
- Competitive versus Collaborative
- Game speed and flow
- Influence of communication on gameplay
- Social issues (Grieving, Mobbing, Toxic behavior)

8.4.1 Number of Players

As discussed in Sect. 8.2, different multiplayer game genres are inherently appropriate for different numbers of players. Whereas an FPS is well suited for many players but possibly rather boring if played by only two players, the opposite is valid for strategy games—both round-based or real-time simulation (RTS) games. Round-based games tend to become boring due to long waiting times with an increasing number of players, and RTS games are limited in the number of players due to issues of overview and balancing. Hence, the number of desired players impacts the suitability of genres for the serious game to be designed.

8.4.2 Persistence

Another characteristic to be considered is persistence. Depending on the game type, there might be a persistent game world, or the game only persists during game sessions. The former is an example for most of the big roleplaying game worlds today, like *WoW, EverQuest*, etc. Those worlds exist continuously, independent of a player being in the game or not. Examples for the latter are FPS, strategy games, or simulations. In those genres, the games have a clearly defined start (when all players have joined the game) and end (usually when a winner is determined or the session is aborted). In most such games, the session continues or is paused if a player leaves the game (due to connection problems, etc.). If no pause is possible, the game continues without the player until the end condition (victory/loss) is reached. However, there is no persistent game world whatsoever between game sessions. A persistent world is always present and accessible. Hence, players can join the game whenever they wish, and players spending more time in the game world might have an advantage compared to players just joining. This needs to be considered in the game design. For example, in social network games, persistence is a prerequisite for the characteristics of asynchronous play and casual multiplayer access. For a non-persistent game, it needs to be considered that it usually can only be played when the required number of players is available.

8.4.3 Matchmaking

For competitive games, fairness is a central issue. If games are unfair or players with unequal skill are matched against each other, this might have a serious impact on the game experience and fun.

Hence, *matchmaking*—the automated process that matches a player to and against other players in games—is used in most of today's competitive games. This term should not be confused with the term matchmaking in computer science which describes the marriage problem. The general idea of matchmaking in games is to represent a player's relevant skill(s) for a game by a (set of) number(s) and match players according to those.

The most prominent matchmaking concept is the ELO concept, which originally was designed by Elo (1978) to match chess players according to their skill level. In the Elo system, each player has a skill value R assigned to him/her. Comparing two skill values R_A and R_B of players A and B gives an indication of what the probabilities for each of those players is to win the game. The following formula gives the win probability E_A for player A:

$$E_A = \frac{1}{1 + 10^{(R_B - R_A)/400}}$$

After a game, the Elo value of both players is updated according to the following formula:

$$R'_A = R_A + k \cdot (S_A - E_A)$$

Here, R'_A is the new value for player A, R_A is the old value for player A, S_A is the result of the game (1 for a win, 0.5 for a draw, 0 for a loss), and E_A is the win probability for player a. k is a weighting constant that usually changes according to the number of games played—such that the Elo value changes more heavily for new players, and less heavily for players after many games.

The ELO concept has since been extended to various competitive games (e.g., *League of Legends*, *DotA2*, etc.). However, the specific enhancements are not publicly available.

Elo was originally designed for a 1:1 setting, and this is where it works best. Elo has weaknesses in team scenarios, especially when a team does not consist of a fixed set of players. If teams are built in an ad hoc fashion, which is often the case in team-based multiplayer games as new players often join alone, such games need mechanisms to form teams with the available players in a fair matchup.

The Glicko system (Glickman 1995) uses a Gaussian approach where skills are assumed to lie within a variance σ^2 around mean value μ. Hence, the basic idea is that the initial estimated skill value lies within an interval that can be narrowed with every additional game played, thus making the estimation more and more accurate.

In contrast to the Elo system, Glicko can make an assumption of how accurate the current rating of a player is by using the variance, which should be smaller for players with many games and larger for new players. Moreover, it can measure consistency in player performance.

The TrueSkill model, developed by Microsoft Research for the Xbox, match-making system uses a Bayesian approach to estimate the skill of a player in a team (Herbrich et al. 2006). A factor graph is used to determine a team's strength based on its players' skills.

All of those models, however, do not consider different roles. Yet, in many team-based multiplayer games, different players usually take different roles, like e.g., damage dealer, healer, tank, etc. The success of a team depends on:

- a good composition, i.e., a team of five damage dealers might be inferior to a team with a well-tuned ratio of damage dealers, tanks, and healers)
- the players' skill in the role they are playing

The second condition can be problematic as the players' skill for each position can vary. Hence, players can be stronger on some positions and weaker on others. This can be compared to the different *roles*, i.e., *positions* in soccer, like striker, defense player, or goalkeeper. Usually, a good striker is not necessary equally good when he needs to play as goalkeeper. This problem can be circumvented if the matchmaking can make sure that each player plays in his/her preferred position, which is usually the case in teams with fixed members. However, in multiplayer games where players join the game alone and then get assigned to a team, it is very likely that players need to play a role which they are not good at.

The TrueSkill-ext rating by Zhang et al. (2010) is an extended version of TrueSkill. It uses a multivariate Gaussian model, where an m-dimensional vector is used describing m different contexts (one for each role) of a player. It should be mentioned that this only works if role selection is made before the team is assembled.

Besides fairness, in learning games, maximizing learning outcomes for each player is a major aspect. Thus, based on insights from learning theory, the learning group formation algorithms that emerged not only take into account skill level, but also how well team members complement each other and harmonize in their group roles, personality traits, learning style preferences, etc.

As analyzed by Konert (2014a), from an algorithmic perspective two major groups of approaches exist: Semantic matchmakers and analytic optimizer algorithms. The former have their strength in respecting manifold boundary conditions while matching learners based on an ontology of their knowledge domain; see also (Inaba et al. 2000) or (Ounnas et al. 2008). A major disadvantage is the need for a formalized ontology of the knowledge domain and/or the boundary conditions if a logic solver is used.

Analytic optimizers, on the contrary, have no detailed information about the interdependency of the manifold criteria to match. They operate on vector representations and use a limited set of boundary conditions, such as the maximum group size or the minimum group formation quality, based on a suitable metric for quality calculation, often called the fitness function. Paredes et al. (2010) match learners homogeneously by cluster analysis, but this appears to be limited in case learners are heterogeneous in their skills, e.g., to complement each other in the field of expertise and learn from each other the most. For this case, Cavanaugh and Ellis (2004) use an iterative approach to build learning groups for cooperative tasks. Gogoulou et al. (2007) provide several algorithms for the homogeneous, heterogeneous, and the mixed approach when some criteria have to be homogeneously matched, while others should be heterogeneous among the group members. Additionally, they have identified visual feedback for teachers (or instructors) as a valuable component in order to allow manual group adjustment and feedback about formed group quality. Based on the analysis of these approaches, in (Konert et al. 2014) the GroupAL algorithm is proposed that allows to use weighted homogeneous and heterogeneous criteria, while taking into account that all formed groups should be rather similar in their combined group quality. The key idea behind the GroupAL algorithm is to use the distance in criteria vectors K^1, K^2 between all possible pairs of members. The smaller the distance between two vectors is, the more similar two members are. For each criterion a weight is considered. A vector W represents the weights for all the criteria. For homogeneous criteria (K_{het}) this vector distance should be minimal, while for heterogeneous criteria (K_{hom}) the distance needs to be maximized. This is considered in the following equation for the so called Pair Performance Index which reached its maximum value, if the *homSum* is minimized and the *hetSum* is maximized):

$$PPI(K^1, K^2, W) = hetSum(K^1_{het}, K^2_{het}, W) - homSum(K^1_{hom}, K^2_{hom}, W)$$

In following steps, *PPI* is normalized to a value space in the interval $[0, 1]$, and a group performance index is calculated using the normalized standard deviation of *PPI*. To find the best combination of members for a group (i.e., maximize PPI over all groups) is a combinatory problem, which can be solved by optimization algorithms using *PPI* as the metric to judge how good is a new build group. If the result not good enough, new combinations are built and kept—if the resulting *PPI* values for all pairs of group members are better than before. To keep the algorithmic runtime performance manageable, GroupAL (like other algorithmic optimization approaches) starts with pivot elements as first group members and then searches for the next best candidate to add as long as not all groups are filled (or all participants have a group). Such optimization approaches generate reasonable results in scenarios with up to a few thousand learners to match (Konert et al. 2014). Suitable algorithmic solutions for larger scenarios are subject to ongoing research.

8.4.4 Competitive Versus Collaborative Gameplay

Another aspect impacting game design is the question of whether the game will be played competitively, cooperatively, or collaboratively. Special game design decisions need to be made to enable cooperative or collaborative gameplay. Especially for collaborative gameplay, design guidelines for collaborative gaming by Zagal et al., as well as the collaboration-related design guidelines by Dillenbourg and by Johnson and Johnson (see Sect. 8.3.1), need to be considered; see Sect. 8.2.3.

For competitive gameplay, fairness (matchmaking) needs to be considered for pairs of adversaries. Moreover, incentives like leaderboards, high scores, etc. can be used to motivate players.

For both competitive and collaborative games, it should be considered if and how different roles can be included into the game design. For competitive games, this might be a way to create team-based competitive games. For collaborative games, this might help to implement the advised guidelines for collaborative play, for example by providing heterogeneous resources.

A mixture of both, using the concept of *coopetition*, can be achieved if casual multiplayer concepts are implemented, as in social serious games (see Sect. 8.2.2).

8.4.5 Game Speed and Flow

Game speed and flow should be considered as early as possible in the design phase. Depending on the characterizing goal, the best genres can be found based on these criteria. Yet, for each genre, there are various kinds of games with a different gameplay, which impact how the serious game will work. If, for example, it was decided that a strategy game is the best choice, it needs to be decided if the game is going to be turn-based, real-time, or have a variable speed, if it should be possible to pause the game, etc. Those decisions might be influential regarding the learning content. For example, if it is required that players reflect on the learning content while playing, a slower-paced game (e.g., turn-based or with pausing) might be more appropriate than a real-time simulation.

8.4.6 Communication Between Players

Communication is another core element of multiplayer games that greatly impacts how the game is played. There are various ways of enabling communication between the players. They can be classified into three main categories:

1. in-game signs
2. chat
3. voice communication

In-game signs are a method of communication which is not based on text or speech; instead, it uses available mechanisms of the game to draw another player's attention to a relevant event. Examples are so-called pings, where a player marks an object or location in the game world (often on a map) to tell another player that something important is happening there. This is often used in team-based strategy games. Another example is avatar-based gestures, which are common in role-playing games where players are represented by an avatar. Those gestures can be used to mediate affections, feelings, or expressions without the use of language.

Chat is probably the most common way to communicate in a game. By chat, we mean digital chat tools for the exchange of short messages. While they are very simple and powerful, they require that players speak a common language and are able to express themselves in written form, possibly under time pressure. Hence, chat might not be the right communication solution in multiplayer games, depending on the target group (e.g., too young or international players) or the game type (in RTS games there is often not enough time to type complex phrases in a chat tool). Therefore, a slightly different and simpler way of chat-based communication is to use predefined commands such as *help*, *well done*, *come here*, or *do X* with just one mouse click. While this is more restrictive than a regular chat, it is quickly accessible, and it limits the misuse of a chat for off-topic discussions.

Voice-based communication is the third alternative. Here, players can communicate simply by talking to each other. Trivially, this is possible if all players are together in one room. If this is not feasible, voice communication tools like Skype can be used. Today, many such tools are available that are specialized in team-based communication for online games, like TeamSpeak, Mumble, RaidCall, or Curse Voice. Moreover, many online games have built-in voice communication. While due to its wide availability, voice communication is not a technical challenge for a game designer; however, it needs to be considered that voice communication is available to the players whether intended by the game designer or not. So, unless it cannot be assured that players do not use voice communication (like in a classroom setting), one should assume that players will use voice communication. This might impact various design decisions. For example, in a shooter game, a player who was eliminated from the game (i.e., was killed) can still talk to his/her teammates via a third party voice communication tool and give valuable hints.

8.4.7 Social Issues: Toxic Behavior and Virtual Property

Apart from communication, other social issues can have an influence on a multiplayer serious game.

In online games with persistence, there are usually players who are more experienced than other players. Those players have an advantage in game knowledge, and if gameplay is based on leveling up virtual characters, those players are probably more advanced in the game and hence more powerful than new players. Therefore, the game designer needs to think about problems of power imposition, namely using the fact that one player is stronger in order to negatively impact another player's game experience, e.g., repeatedly killing that player's character. There are various countermeasures, like so-called safe areas where player versus player combat is not possible, or mentoring systems where experienced players help new players. Apart from being more powerful, other forms of grieving (annoying other players on purpose) are verbal harassment, scamming (breaking promises), ninja looting (stealing loot from a player before that player can pick it up), leaving a game to prevent a loss, account sharing (sharing an account with other players to have advantages), multi accounting (having more than one account to boost the primary account), and many more. It needs to be considered to which extent this toxic behavior can occur in the serious game to be created.

There are some countermeasures against toxic behavior in existing online multiplayer games. Most of them provide their players with an option to report toxic players to administrators. They can judge if those players should get a penalty. In other games, this decision is given back to the player base for players who have been reported by several others too many times. The community then decides if those reports were justified, and if the player should be penalized. However, a study by Riot games (Lin 2013, 2014) showed that penalizing negative behavior alone is not sufficient to deal with toxic behavior in online multiplayer games. They suggested that positive reinforcement, in addition to the negative reinforcement, should be used. Hence, they gave players an option to honor fellow and opposing players for good teamwork and sportsmanlike behavior. They also showed the importance of visibility, i.e., that both the players themselves and other players can see if a player is positive.

Apart from this, virtual property is a problem the comes with state of the art online multiplayer games. In some of these games, players can own virtual property (e.g., a valuable magic sword). Usually, this is acquired by playing the game for a long time. However, as they usually can be traded between players, and players are willing to pay rather than spending a lot of time, those virtual items get a real monetary value. Until recently, virtual property has led to a lot of problems in gaming communities. On the one hand, virtual property is still considered a legal grey area as many legal institutions do not consider virtual property as legal property. For example, theft of virtual property is not covered by the law. Even real murders connected to virtual property were reported. This shows that game designers need to carefully consider if, and in which form, they include virtual property in their games.

On the other hand, virtual property can be a very powerful and beneficial aspect of game design, when players are empowered to create their own game elements. So called user-generated content allows players to personalize their game, be creative, and share their ideas with others. If used properly by game designers, user-generated content is a way to allow an endless amount of new content, quests, and tasks to be added to the game (e.g., new levels in Sony's *Little Big Planet,* or creatures in Electronic Arts' *Spore*). Especially for serious games with a limited budget, this seems to be an attractive option. Obviously, efficient quality control mechanisms have to be added to prevent content containing incorrect facts, low quality content, or illegal content to be spread via the game. From a didactic perspective, support for user-generated content allows for deep learning experiences as players not only solve predefined problems, but also ask questions create quests and provide proper new solutions. These abilities are part of the high-level problem-solving skills that are very suitable to be taught via games (Gee 2009).

8.5 Summary and Outlook

This chapter provided an overview of multiplayer serious games. Starting with an historical view on digital multiplayer games, we considered the development of multiplayer games and covered many facets of multiplayer gaming.

The chapter shows how multiplayer games can be classified in terms of game types, used techniques, genres, and interaction forms. This covers the use of various technologies like shared screen or split-screen, appropriateness of game genres for various serious gaming purposes, and which interaction form(s) can be used in a serious games context.

Further, this chapter covered the topic of collaborative learning, especially focusing on the relationship between collaborative gaming and collaborative learning. It is shown how the concepts and paradigms of collaborative learning can be naturally used in multiplayer games, and how they can be further utilized to improve collaborative learning in multiplayer games.

Finally, multiplayer game design issues were discussed, looking at the various dimensions of multiplayer gaming that impact the design process, and hence should be considered from the very beginning. Those are: Number of players, persistence of the game world, matchmaking, competitive versus collaborative gaming, game speed and flow, communication, social issues like toxic behavior, and user-generated content.

Check your understanding of this chapter by answering the following questions:

- Why were many of the oldest digital games multiplayer games?
- How are multiplayer games today different from multiplayer games in the 1970s and 80s?
- What forms of multiplayer games do you know about?
- What multiplayer genres do you know, and how are they appropriate for serious game purposes?
- What different kinds of communications do you know in multiplayer games?
- Why do multiplayer games offer great potential when it comes to collaborative learning?
- What collaborative learning concepts are used in multiplayer games, especially MMORPGs?
- What are important rules and pitfalls when designing collaborative multiplayer games?
- How do the number of players, game world persistence, or game speed and flow influence the design of multiplayer serious games?
- What is the role of matchmaking in multiplayer games? Why is this important for MMOGs? Why and under which circumstances might this be important when designing multiplayer serious games? Why is it even more complex to match players in serious games?
- What influence on the design of a multiplayer serious game does in-game communication have?
- Why are social issues relevant when designing multiplayer serious games, and what are current problems in MMOGs related to social aspects? Which counter-measures exist?

Recommended Literature

Adams E. (2014) *Fundamentals of game design*. Pearson Education. *"Chapter 2: Online gaming" is a comprehensive introduction to online gaming with a focus on online gaming design issues like persistency*

Armitage G, Claypool M, Branch P. (2006) *Networking and online games: understanding and engineering multiplayer Internet games*. John Wiley & Sons. *This book covers the history of online and multiplayer games and discusses more closely current multiplayer game types like FPS, RTS games, or MMOGs. It further details the influence of technology and Internet architecture on networked multiplayer games*

Habgood J, Overmars M (2006) Game Design: Balance in Multiplayer Games, book chapter in The Game Maker's Apprentice, Apress, 211–222. *An introduction to designing multiplayer games with a focus on balance and meaningful choices*

McGonigal, J. (2011) *Reality Is Broken: Why Games Make Us Better and How They Can Change the World.* The Penguin Press HC. *The book illustrates manifold examples of well-designed game prototypes, which use multiplayer concepts and real-world interactions. As such, the book is a strong inspiration for quest design, rule balancing, and dynamics when multiple players depend on each other. Most examples serve as proof of how social interactions in games can not only lead to benefits for the gamers, but also for the real world around them*

Huizinga, J. (2014) *Homo Ludens: A Study of the Play-Element in Culture.* Martino Fine Books— *If not recommended in other chapters already, this book needs your full attention. It is not an educational book in a classical meaning, but a classical book about humans faible for playing, the socio-cultural integration of play and the meaning for each individual's development. As such, the book highlights the multiplayer aspect from a totally non-technical perspective, which leads to fresh insights for everyone with technical mindsets when designing multiplayer games*

References

Armitage G, Claypool M, Branch P (2006) Networking and online games: understanding and engineering multiplayer Internet games. Wiley, Chichester

Bandura A (2002) Social foundations of thought and action. In: Marks DF (ed) The health psychology reader, chapter 6, pp 94–106. SAGE. ISBN 0761972706

Bowers C, Salas E, Prince C, Brannick M (1992) Games teams play: a method for investigating team coordination and performance. Behav Res Methods Instrum Comput 4(4):503–506

Casual Connect Research (2012) Social network games 2012—casual games sector report

Cavanaugh R, Ellis M (2004) Automating the process of assigning students to cooperative-learning teams. In: Proceedings of the 2004 American society for engineering education annual conference & exposition

Childress MD, Braswell R (2006) Using massively multiplayer online roleplaying games for online learning. Distance Educ 27(2):187–196

Damon W (1984) Peer education: the untapped potential. J Appl Dev Psychol 5(4):331–343. ISSN 01933973

Delwiche A (2006) Massively multiplayer online games (MMOs) in the new media classroom. Educ Technol Soc 9(3):160–172

Denny P, Luxton-Reilly A, Hamer J (2008) The PeerWise system of student contributed assessment questions. In: Proceedings of the tenth Australasian computing education conference (ACE2008). Wollongong, Australia, pp 69–74

Dickey MD (2007) Game design and learning: a conjectural analysis of how massively multiple online role-playing games (MMORPGs) foster intrinsic motivation. Educ Technol Res Dev 55 (3):253–273

Dillenbourg P (1999) What do you mean by collaborative learning? In: Dillenbourg P (ed) Collaborative-learning: cognitive and computational approaches. Elsevier, Oxford, pp 1–19

Doise W, Mugny G, Perret-Clermont AN (1975) Social interaction and the development of cognitive operations. Eur J Soc Psychol 5(3):367–383

Ducheneaut N, Moore RJ (2004) The social side of gaming: a study of interaction patterns in a massively multiplayer online game. In: Proceedings of the 2004 ACM conference on computer supported cooperative work (CSCW'04), ACM, New York, NY, USA, pp 360–369

El-Nasr MS, Aghabeigi B, Milam D, Erfani M, Lameman B, Maygoli H, Mah S (2010) Understanding and evaluating cooperative games. In: Proceedings of the SIGCHI conference on human factors in computing systems, pp 253–262, ACM

Elo AE (1978) The rating of chessplayers, past and present. Arco Pub, ISBN 0-668-04721-6

Eustace K, Lee M, Fellows G, Bytheway A, Irving L (2004) The application of massively multiplayer online role playing games to collaborative learning and teaching practice in schools. In: Atkinson R, McBeath C, Jonas-Dwyer D, Phillips R (eds), Beyond the comfort zone: proceedings of the 21st ASCILITE conference

Garris R, Ahlers R, Driskell JE (2002) Games, motivation, and learning: a research and practice model. Simul Gaming 33(4):441–467

Gee JP (2003) What video games have to teach us about learning and literacy. Comput Entertain 1 (1):20–20

Gee JP (2009) Deep learning properties of good digital games. In: Ritterfeld U, Cody MJ, Vorderer P (eds) Serious games: mechanisms and effects. Routledge, New York, pp 67–82

Glickman M (1995) The glicko system. Boston University, Boston, pp 1–5

Gogoulou A, Gouli E, Boas G, Liakou E, Grigoriadou M (2007) Forming homogeneous, heterogeneous and mixed groups of learners. In: Brusilovsky P, Grigoriadou M, Papanikolaou K (eds) Proceedings of workshop on personalisation in e-Learning environments at individual and group level, 11th international conference on user modeling, pp 33–40

Herbrich R, Minka T, Graepel T (2006) Trueskill™: a bayesian skill rating system. In: Advances in neural information processing systems, pp 569–576

Haake J, Schwabe G, Wessner M (2004) CSCL-Kompendium—Lehr- und Handbuch zum computerunterstützten kooperativen Lernen. Oldenbourg Wissenschaftsverlag

Hare AP (1981) Group size. Am Behav Sci 24(5):695–708

Hämäläinen R (2011) Using a game environment to foster collaborative learning: a design-based study. Technol Pedagog Educ 20(1):61–78

Herz J (2001) Gaming the system: what higher education can learn from multiplayer online worlds. EDUCAUSE Publications from the Internet and the University Forum, The Internet and the University: Forum, pp 169–291

Hindriks J, Pancs R (2002) Free riding on altruism and group size. J Public Econ Theor 4(3):335–346

Inaba A, Supnithi T, Ikeda M, Mizoguchi R, Toyoda J (2000) How can we form effective collaborative learning groups? In: 5th international conference on ITS. Springer, Montreal, Canada, pp 282–291

Johnson DW, Johnson RT (1999) Making cooperative learning work. Theory Pract 38(2):67–73

Johnson DW, Johnson RT (2009) An educational psychology success story: social interdependence theory and cooperative learning. Educ Res 38(5):365–379

Kato M, Cole SW, Bradlyn AS, Pollock BH (2008) A video game improves behavioral outcomes in adolescents and young adults with cancer: a randomized trial. Pediatrics 122(2):305–317

Kidwell RE, Bennett N (1993) Employee propensity to withhold effort: A conceptual model to intersect three avenues of research. Acad Manag Rev 18(3):429–456

Konert J (2014a) Related work. In: Interactive multimedia learning: using social media for peer education in single player educational games. Springer, Heidelberg, pp 11–48. ISBN 9783319102566

Konert J (2014b) Approach and concept for social serious games creation. In: Interactive multimedia learning: using social media for peer education in single player educational games. Springer, Heidelberg, pp 49–60. ISBN 9783319102566

Konert J, Richter K, Mehm F, Göbel S, Bruder R, Steinmetz R (2012) PEDALE—A peer education diagnostic and learning environment. J Educ Technol Soc 15:27–38

Konert J, Burlak D, Steinmetz R (2014) The group formation problem: An algorithmic approach to learning group formation. In: Rensing C, de Freitas S, Ley T, Muñoz-Merino PJ (eds) Proceedings of the 9th european conference on technology enhanced learning (EC-TEL). Springer, Berlin, Graz, Austria, pp 221–234

Larusson JA, Alterman R (2009) Wikis to support the collaborative part of collaborative learning. Int J Comput Support Collab Learn 4(4):371–402

Lester J (2013) The cave interview| Ron Gilbert on cavernous depths & the state of adventure games. http://www.dealspwn.com/ron-gilbert-interview-cave-125244. Accessed 03 Aug 2015

Lin J (2013) The science behind shaping player behavior in online games. Talk at GDC 2013. http://gdcvault.com/play/1017940/The-Science-Behind-Shaping-Player. Accessed 05 Aug 2015

Lin J (2014) Enhancing sportsmanship in online games. Talk at GDC 2014. http://www.gdcvault. com/play/1020389/Enhancing-Sportsmanship-in-Online. Accessed 05 Aug 2015

Manninen T (2003) Interaction forms and communicative actions in multiplayer games. Game Stud 3(1)

Mitchell A, Savill-Smith C (2004) The use of computer and video games for learning: a review of the literature. Learning and Skills Development Agency London, Great Britain

Ounnas A, Davis H, Millard D (2008) A framework for semantic group formation. In: Eighth IEEE international conference on advanced learning technologies, pp 34–38

Paredes P, Ortigosa A, Rodriguez P (2010) A method for supporting heterogeneous group formation through heuristics and visualization. J Univ Comput Sci 16(19):2882–2901

Paris CR, Salas E, Cannon-Bowers JA (2000) Teamwork in multi-person systems: a review and analysis. Ergonomics 43(8):1052–1075

Piaget J (2003) Meine Theorie der geistigen Entwicklung. Beltz GmbH, Julius. ISBN 3407221428

Prensky M (2006) Don't bother me, mom, I'm learning!: How computer and video games are preparing your kids for 21st century success and how you can help!. Paragon house, New York

Reuter C, Wendel V, Göbel S, Steinmetz R (2012) Multiplayer adventures for collaborative learning with serious games. In: Felicia P (ed) Proceedings of the 6th european conference on games-based learning, Academic Conferences Limited, pp 416–423

Roschelle J, Teasley SD (1995) The construction of shared knowledge in collaborative problem solving. In: O'Malley C (ed) Computer-supported collaborative learning. Springer, Berlin, pp 69–97

Runge J, Gao P, Garcin F, Faltings B (2014) Churn prediction for high-value players in casual social games. In: 2014 IEEE conference computational intelligence Games, pp 1–8

Shapiro MJ, Gardner R, Godwin SA, Jay GD, Lindquist DG, Salisbury ML, Salas E (2008) Defining team performance for simulation-based training: Methodology, metrics, and opportunities for emergency medicine. Acad Emerg Med 5(11):1088–1097

Stahl G, Koschmann T, Suthers D (2006) Cambridge Handbook of the learning sciences, chapter computer-supported collaborative learning: an historical perspective. Cambridge University Press, Cambridge, pp 409–426

Statista (2013) Average daily time spent playing online games worldwide in April 2013, by region (in minutes) http://www.statista.com/statistics/261264/time-spent-playing-online-games-worldwide-by-region/. Accessed 25 November 2015

Statista (2014) Leading massively multiplayer online (MMO) games worldwide from January to September 2014, by revenue (in million U.S. dollars). http://www.statista.com/statistics/343075/mmo-games-revenue/. Accessed 25 November 2015

Steinkuehler CA (2004) Learning in massively multiplayer online games. In: ICLS'04: proceedings of the 6th international conference on learning sciences. International Society of the Learning Sciences, pp 521–528

Sweetser P, Wyeth P (2005) GameFlow: a model for evaluating player enjoyment in games. Comput Entertain (CIE) 3(3):1–24

TeamUp (2015) TeamUp http://thebarngames.nl/teamup/. Accessed 25 November 2015

Thomson AT, Perry JL, Miller TK (2009) Conceptualizing and measuring collaboration. J Publc Adm Res Theor 19(1):23–56

Tychsen A (2008) Tales for the many: Process and authorial control in multiplayer role-playing games. ICIDS'08: proceedings of the 1st joint international conference on interactive digital storytelling. Springer, Heidelberg, pp 309–320

Tychsen A, Hitchens M, Brolund T, Kavakli M (2005) The game master. In: Proceedings of the second Australasian conference on interactive entertainment. Creativity & Cognition Studios Press, pp 215–222

Vorderer P, Hartmann T, Klimmt C (2003). Explaining the enjoyment of playing video games: The role of competition. In: Proceedings of the second international conference on Entertainment computing. Carnegie Mellon University, pp 1–9

Voulgari I, Komis V (2008) Massively multi-user online games: the emergence of effective collaborative activities for learning. In: DIGITEL'08: proceedings of the 2008 second IEEE international conference on digital game and intelligent toy enhanced learning, IEEE Computer Society, pp 132–134

Vygotsky LS (1997) Interaction between learning and development. Readings on the development of children, pp 29–36

Welch TA (1984) A technique for high performance data compression. IEEE Comput 17(6):8–19

Wendel V, Göbel S, Steinmetz R (2012) Game mastering in collaborative multiplayer serious games. In: Göbel S, Müller W, Urban B, Wiemeyer J (eds) e-Learning and games for training, education, health and sports—LNCS, vol 7516. Darmstadt, Germany, Springer, pp 23–34

Westera W, Wagemans L (2007) Help me! Online learner support through the self-organised allocation of peer tutors. In: Abstracts of the 13th international conference on technology supported learning & training. ICEW GmbH, Berlin, pp 105–107

Wohn DY, Lampe C, Wash R, Ellison N, Vitak J (2011) The "s" in social network games: Initiating, maintaining, and enhancing relationships. In: 2011 44th Hawaii international conference system science, pp 1–10

Yee N (2005) Motivations of play in MMORPGs

Zagal J P, Rick J, His I (2006) Collaborative games: lessons learned from board games. Simul Gaming 37(1):24–40

Zea NP, Sánchez JLG, Gutiérrez FL (2009) Collaborative learning by means of video games: an entertainment system in the learning processes. In: ICALT'09: proceedings of the 2009 ninth IEEE international conference on advanced learning technologies. IEEE Computer Society, Washington, DC, USA, pp 215–217

Zhang L, Wu J, Wang ZC, Wang CJ (2010) A factor-based model for contextsensitive skill rating systems. Proc Int Conf Tools Artif Intell ICTAI 2:249–255

Player Experience

9

Josef Wiemeyer, Lennart Nacke, Christiane Moser
and Florian 'Floyd' Mueller

Abstract

In computer science, the concept of user experience has proven to be beneficial in order to improve the quality of interaction between software and its users, by taking users' emotions and attitudes into account. In general, user experience focuses on interaction. As not only interaction (e.g., good usability) is of importance for players, this chapter discusses how the concept of user experience can not only be applied to serious games, but also how it can be extended in order to cover the characteristics of games as a special software. For this refined concept, the term *player experience* has been coined. First, the concept of player experience is introduced in this chapter. The adequate conceptualization of player experience requires differentiating specific dimensions like (game-) flow, immersion, challenge, tension, competence, and emotions. Because of the individual nature of player experience, psychological models need to be used for the conceptualization as they are able to reflect this multidimensional structure. In addition, interdisciplinary models are needed in order to address the various factors influencing player experience. This ensures a holistic approach. Second, the question how to measure player experience is discussed. Here, different levels

J. Wiemeyer (✉)
Technische Universität Darmstadt, Darmstadt, Germany
e-mail: wiemeyer@sport.tu-darmstadt.de

L. Nacke
University of Waterloo, Waterloo, Canada

C. Moser
University of Salzburg, Salzburg, Austria

F. 'Floyd' Mueller
RMIT University, Melbourne, Australia

© Springer International Publishing Switzerland 2016
R. Dörner et al. (eds.), *Serious Games*, DOI 10.1007/978-3-319-40612-1_9

have to be distinguished: Behavior, physiological reactions, and subjective experience. Finally, it is shown how knowledge about player experience can be employed to develop serious games systematically and to improve their quality.

9.1 Introduction

According to their double mission characterized in Chap. 1, serious games have to accomplish at least two goals: on the one hand entertainment and on the other hand the characterizing goal(s). The entertainment goal will be addressed in this chapter, whereas Chap. 10 will deal with the characterizing goal(s). Experiencing a serious game as a "game" is a personal and individual matter. According to Huizinga (2013), playing games has a different meaning in different cultures. In Chap. 1, gaming or ludus (rule-based) has been distinguished from playing or paidea (free). The individual and personal experience of gaming comprises numerous aspects, for example, intrinsically motivated actions (free of external determination), performing symbolic or fictional actions in a quasi-real context constrained by the rules of a game, ambivalence and openness to both procedure and outcomes, presence and immersion etc. All these aspects refer primarily to the (socio-)psychological experience of the players. Therefore, (socio-)psychological factors play an important role in the research on player experience. On the other hand, personal experience is accompanied by more or less specific observable behavior (like laughing, smiling or frown) and physiological reactions (like increased heart rate or blood pressure). Accordingly, three levels of player experience need to be distinguished:

- The (socio-)psychological level (individual experience)
- The behavioral level
- The physiological level

Because the individual (socio-)psychological level is the constituent aspect of player experience this aspect will be emphasized in this chapter.

The uniqueness of gaming experience is one important reason for the great success of digital games in general. The goal of serious games is to exploit this fascination of players to enhance engagement, in order to foster the acquisition of the characterizing goal(s). Therefore, it is important to know how player experience is structured to systematically address mechanisms that elicit player experience. In a strict sense, *player experience* is the more appropriate term as compared to *game experience,* because it is the person of the player who makes this specific experience. Therefore, player experience (PE) will be used in this chapter whenever possible. Player experience has to be distinguished from player types. Whereas the former denotes a transient and dynamic construct (state), the latter denotes a more or less stable and static construct or trait. For a recent approach to player types, see (Nacke et al. 2014).

This chapter is divided into four main parts. First, the concept of user experience will be discussed as a kind of precursor of player experience. Second, psychological models of player experience are discussed to clarify the mechanisms and components of player experience. Third, integrative models of player experience are addressed. These models integrate the findings of numerous scientific disciplines, e.g., (neuro-) physiology, psychology, and sociology to explain the factors contributing to player experience. Often, these models are dedicated to a specific domain, e.g., exergames or educational games. In the last part of this chapter, guidelines and recommendations are given to foster player experience.

9.2 User Experience as a Precursor of Player Experience

In the past decade, we have seen a surge of interest in the emotional and affective aspect of user experience (UX), especially in entertainment media, such as video games. Before it became a field of its own, games user research (GUR) was often done informally within the development team or with players that were close friends of the developers. Today, GUR is a formal process with its own set of techniques that is aimed at finding the desired experience for a game together with the design team. Classic usability testing is not sufficient for testing games, since its standard metrics, such as effectiveness measured as task completion or efficiency measured as error rates, do not map directly to evaluating games. Developers of user interfaces for desktop software are primarily concerned with functionality, while games need to be evaluated with a strong focus on the human aspect—the player—in mind. Traditional usability metrics remain relevant in GUR, but they are subsidiary means that can supplement other forms of evaluation of digital games.

User experience is a concept that has been misunderstood for years, because the shift of research from a focus on functionality toward creating an aesthetically pleasing experience was done slowly. Similarly, we have seen quality assurance and simple functionality tests in game development for years, but during the past decade, the choice toward creating entire games user research departments became obvious for many game developers. The focus on humans as part of evaluating technology is now the de facto standard for many evaluation approaches within human-computer interaction (HCI) and has led to prominence of user experience (UX) research over usability research. For video games, understanding and attempting to measure player experiences (PE) has become a core aspect of GUR. Thereby, PE describes the qualities of the player-game interactions and is typically investigated during and after the interaction with games (Nacke et al. 2009).

Along these lines, it might be useful to distinguish between different GUR concepts, such as playability, game usability, and player experience. There are even more definitions in the literature that refer to different types of player experiences. However, for the sake of our understanding of PE in games, we can distinguish between different levels of perception of gameplay for players. Nacke (2010) introduced a core understanding of these perceived layers of experience within video games. Evaluating the technology is fundamentally different from evaluating the higher level concepts of experience for players within a given context (Engl and Nacke 2013). The ideas behind playability and game usability seem to be more relevant for ensuring a good experience for players on a technological level, which serves as the foundation for creating good player experiences subsequently.

> Whereas *playability* and *game usability* refer to the technological level, *player experience* denotes the individual and personal experience of playing games. Player experience describes the qualities of the player-game interactions and is typically investigated during and after the interaction with games.
>
> Analogous to HCI, where a shift took place from *usability* to *user experience (UX)*, in games research *player experience (PE)* has gained importance rather than *game experience (GX)*.

In the related literature, we find a number of different understandings regarding PE in games. By reviewing these, we can move toward a better definition of PE in games.

Brown and Cairns (2004) have noted that players choose games they play according to their mood, and it is to be expected that people especially seek games that elicit appreciated emotional responses. Therefore, it is necessary to get to know the player better (e.g., how they play, what motivates them to play, or what creates aversion towards certain game forms; Mäyrä 2008a, b). Ravaja et al. (2008) evaluated emotional response (e.g., emotional valence, arousal, and discrete emotions like joy, pleasant relaxation, anger, fear, and depressed feelings) and sense of presence as potential criteria in games from the point of view of UX.

Gerling et al. (2011) state that the term player experience "in video games describes the individual perception of the interaction process between player and game," and is derived from the phenomenon of UX (defined in ISO 9241-210:2010) describing how a person perceives and responds to the interaction with a system—both highlighting the subjective, psychological nature of the phenomenon and focusing on the interaction process.

Lazzaro (2008) argues that UX and PE are not the same. For her, UX is the experience of use (i.e., how easily and well suited is the system to the task or what the person expects to accomplish in order to advancing the usability), while PE is the experience of play (i.e., how well the game supports and provides the type of fun the player wants to have). She claims that UX looks at what prevents the ability to play, and PE looks at what prevents the player from having fun.

Nacke and Drachen (2011) introduce a framework to investigate player experience based on existing UX research and the differences between games and other applications. For them, PE is related to the user experience in the context of digital games. They claim that current PE research is aimed at investigating emotional, social, and cognitive components of the experience emerging from the interaction between players and a game. In contrast to most UX research, they also want to take into account PE before, during and after interacting with a game (inspired by Law et al. 2007). Schell (2008) noted that games enable PE through interaction with game elements and/or other players, but the imagined (i.e., anticipated) player experience is the reason for people to play.

Many of these papers use definitions of player, gameplay, gaming, playing, or player experiences without establishing what such a construct would actually mean. The most useful for a shared understanding of PE is, therefore, to think about how these terms can provide a useful vocabulary for GUR when trying to improve video game design. This remains challenging as new models of PE are being developed and tested.

Furthermore, the concept of PE is divided to reflect specific aspects of play, such as challenge, tension or anxiety, and immersion within the game world. Immersion is of particular interest when discussing novel interactive technologies and control paradigms, as designers strive to enhance realism and meaningful interaction within games. The integration of new technologies can have a multitude of differing impacts on PE, affecting the ability of players to understand their role in the game world and to effectively complete game objectives. Ultimately, the effects of any one system element on the entire player experience is composed of an intricate collection of relationships between the factors defining PE. For a better understanding of these elements, we have to turn to psychological models of human motivation and behavior to create a holistic picture of PE.

9.3 Psychological Models of Player Experience

In principle, the experience of gaming is a personal experience. Therefore, psychological models try to explain the structure of player experience as well as the factors contributing to this experience. In this section, models that address player (or game) experience are discussed. Unfortunately, as has been argued in the previous section, there is no general agreement on player experience. Therefore, various models are introduced and discussed first. In a next step, the components and factors addressed by the models are summarized.

Psychological models can be divided into two categories: *Generic models* that have been developed for a wide range of application areas including gaming, and *domain-specific models* that have been developed especially for the game domain. Generic models range from simple behaviorist frameworks (like instrumental conditioning by Skinner) over cognitivist or information processing approaches to constructivist approaches. Due to limited space, this section will not be able to cover all psychological models that are relevant to understanding and explaining player experience. Rather, selected approaches are analyzed that attempt to explain the particular appeal of player experience.

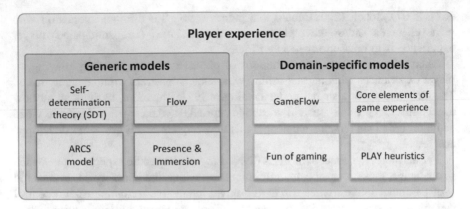

Fig. 9.1 Models relevant to player experience

The following models will be discussed (see Fig. 9.1):

- Self-determination theory (SDT)
- Attention, relevance, confidence, satisfaction (ARCS)
- Flow
- GameFlow
- Presence and immersion
- Fun of gaming (FUGA)
- Core elements of game experience (CEGE)
- PLAY heuristics

Self-determination Theory (SDT)

Player experience is a positive experience including intrinsic motivation. There are numerous models that try to explain how intrinsic motivation arises. One very influential approach is the theory of self-determination (SDT) proposed by Ryan and Deci (2000). According to SDT people have three basic needs: competence, autonomy and relatedness.

The concept of *competence* means that people like to feel being able to meet the requirements of tasks they have to or want to complete. However, it is important to attribute the outcome to one's own engagement or talent. This perceived internal "locus of causality" (Ryan and Deci 2000, p.70) confirms intrinsic motivation as opposed to external attributions, e.g., to chance or support by others. One important source of intrinsic motivation is intrinsic rewards like success. On the other hand, intrinsic motivation can be undermined by all forms of extrinsic reward (for a taxonomy of rewards see Phillips et al. 2013), like money or praise (e.g., Deci et al. 1999).

Furthermore, people want to feel *autonomous* in selecting their individual goals, choosing the means to reach these goals, and evaluating the causes of success or failure. External control is detrimental to intrinsic motivation, for example, resulting in decreased engagement and curiosity.

Beyond competence and autonomy, a third aspect is important for intrinsic motivation, i.e., *relatedness*. Being integrated in various interpersonal settings like parent-child, inter-sibling, or peer-to-peer seems to establish a sense of security to start and maintain exploratory behavior.

For player experience, this means that playing games should support competence (i.e., by appropriate level design and feedback), autonomy (i.e., by experiencing internal control of gaming), and relatedness (i.e., by establishing a game community for communication and collaboration).

Ryan et al. (2006; see also Rigby and Ryan 2007) extended the SDT to the *Player Experience of Need Satisfaction* (PENS) model. The PENS approach includes five dimensions:

- *PENS in-game autonomy*: This dimension denotes the experience of the players to feel free to make decisions and choices in the game.
- *PENS in-game competence*: This dimension concerns an appropriate balance between the challenges of the game and the competence level of the players.
- *PENS in-game relatedness*: In-game relatedness means, how much the players are feeling connected to other players in the game.
- *PENS presence*: This dimension is subdivided into three subdimensions, i.e., physical, emotional, and narrative presence.
- *PENS intuitive controls*: This dimension concerns the ease of control in the game, e.g., by easy-to-remember control keys.

Attention, Relevance, Confidence, Satisfaction (ARCS)

Keller (1987, 2009) developed a model that includes four main strategies to elicit and maintain motivation: Attention, relevance, confidence, and satisfaction (ARCS).

Attending to information is a widely accepted prerequisite of information processing. Information that is not in the focus of attention goes unrecognized and will not be processed. Attention plays a role in many models of human behavior. There seems to be an optimum of attention. This implies that an appropriate balance has to be established on the continuum of extremely low and extremely high attention. Possible means to attract attention in a game are a surprising event, a loud noise, or a quiet pause.

Relevance means that the activity should be considered purposeful and meaningful from the perspective of the player. Therefore, the player should be able to immediately recognize the functional significance of every in-game activity.

Confidence or expectancy of success means that the players have the persuasion to be successful if they show sufficient engagement. The level of confidence has important consequences for several aspects—for example, causal attribution in case of success (ability and effort rather than good luck), increased and sustained engagement, and self-efficacy.

Satisfaction means that people "feel good about their accomplishments" (Keller 1987, p.6). Analogous to intrinsic motivation mentioned in the previous subsection, intrinsic satisfaction and personal enjoyment can decrease if the activities are externally controlled.

Flow

Flow is a particular state that emerges when people perform intrinsically motivated or *autotelic* activities, i.e., activities bearing their rewards in themselves (see also Chap. 1). The state of flow has the following characteristics (Nakamura and Csikszentmihalyi 2002): Increased and focused attention on the current activity, merging of action and awareness, loss of reflective self-consciousness, sense of control over one's actions, distortion of time experience, and experience of the activity as intrinsically rewarding.

According to Jackson and Marsh (1996), the flow experience has the following nine dimensions: Balance of challenge and skill level, merging of action and awareness (i.e., things happen automatically), clearly defined goals, unambiguous, i.e., clear and immediate, feedback, concentration on task at hand, sense of control, loss of self-consciousness, transformation of time, and autotelic experience. The authors could confirm this nine-scale structure by a confirmatory factor analysis.

GameFlow

Sweetser and Wyeth (2005) applied the concept of flow to gaming in order to explain enjoyment in games. Their concept of *GameFlow* consists of eight elements: concentration, challenge, skills, control, clear goals, feedback, immersion, and social interaction. Table 9.1 maps the elements of GameFlow proposed by Sweetser and Wyeth (2005) to the elements of Flow proposed by Jackson and Marsh (1996).

Furthermore, the authors deliver numerous criteria to assess the eight elements of GameFlow. For example, concerning the control dimension players should feel a sense of control over the actions of their characters, their interfaces, the game shell (i.e., starting, stopping, saving), and their strategies.

Presence and Immersion

Presence is a concept that has a close relationship to flow experience on the one hand and to immersion on the other hand. People experiencing presence in media-controlled environments like virtual reality or digital games have the feeling of "being there," i.e., actually being in the scene regardless of the notion that the scene is artificial. Whereas *presence* denotes a specific personal experience, *immersion* is suggested as an umbrella term by Nacke (2009a, b) which incorporates presence and flow as certain stages. There are several connotations of presence (Lombard and Ditton 1997), and the concept is considered a multi-faceted phenomenon. A common distinction is made between social and physical (i.e., spatial) presence (Schultze 2010).

Table 9.1 Mapping elements of GameFlow (Sweetser and Wyeth 2005) to elements of flow (Jackson and Marsh 1996)

GameFlow element (Sweets and Wyeth 2005)	Flow element (Jackson and Marsh 1996)
Concentration	Concentration on task at hand
Challenge	Balance of challenge and skill level
Skills	
Control	Sense of control
Clear Goals	Clearly defined goals
Feedback	Unambiguous, i.e., clear and immediate, feedback
Immersion	Loss of self-consciousness
	Transformation of time
Social Interaction	–
–	Autotelic experience
–	Merging of action and awareness

According to the process model of spatial presence proposed by Wirth et al. (2007), spatial presence evolves according to two consecutive stages. First, a spatial situation model is established depending on attentional processes, which are influenced by both media and user factors. Second, a spatial presence experience emerges depending on involvement and suspension of disbelief. The authors developed and validated an eight-scale spatial presence questionnaire (Wirth et al. 2008).

Takatalo et al. (2011) try to integrate presence and flow. In their *Presence-Involvement-Flow Framework (PIFF²)*, they state that on the one hand presence and involvement in a game are influenced by the (interactive) way the player establishes a relationship with the game (adaptation); on the other hand, the level of flow influences the cognitive evaluation and the emotional outcomes of playing.

Furthermore, the authors distinguish ten subcomponents of player experience: Skill and competence, challenge, emotions, control, autonomy and freedom, focus and concentration, physical presence, involvement, meaning and curiosity, story, drama and fantasy, social interaction and interactivity, controls, and usability.

Fun of Gaming (FUGA)

Based on focus groups, expert interviews and questionnaire studies, Poels et al. (2008) developed a seven-factor model of player experience. The seven factors are specified as follows: Sensory and imaginative immersion, tension, competence, flow, negative affect, positive affect, and challenge. Note that the presence dimension was subsumed under the immersion dimension. Negative and positive affects denote unpleasant and pleasant emotional responses, respectively.

Core Elements of the Gaming Experience (CEGE)

Calvillo-Gámez et al. (2010) proposed a "theory of the Core Elements of the Gaming Experience (CEGE)." This model was developed using qualitative methods. It identifies two essential factors influencing the experiences of immersion, flow and presence when playing digital games: puppetry and video-game perception.

The term *puppetry* denotes the player's interaction with the game. This interaction is shaped by the player's *sense of control*, e.g., operating controllers and memory load, and *ownership*, e.g., personal goals, actions, and rewards. Furthermore, facilitators like aesthetics, previous experience, and playing time moderate the interaction process.

The term *video-game (perception)* denotes how the player experiences the game depending on the environment, i.e., graphics and sound, and game-play, i.e., rules and scenarios.

Using an unconventional terminology, this approach includes many concepts from the above-mentioned generic models like competence.

PLAY Heuristics

Desurvire and Wiberg (2009) proposed a framework for evaluating the playability of games. The framework consists of three categories: Gameplay, coolness/entertainment/humor/emotional immersion, and usability and game mechanics. Many of the 116 proposed heuristics directly address aspects of player experience: Enduring play, challenge, immersion, sense of control, and positive emotions.

Combining the Results

The approaches discussed in this section address the process of player experience from different perspectives. One type of model transfers the concepts in general psychology to games. Another type of model starts from the perspective of either the players themselves, or the perspective of game developers and researchers. To combine the results, the following (social-)psychological elements of player experience are reported:

- Competence
- Autonomy and control
- Immersion, (spatial and social) presence, flow, and GameFlow
- Involvement and (enduring) engagement
- Social relatedness and social interaction
- Challenge
- Tension
- Curiosity
- Fantasy
- Positive and negative emotions
- Intrinsic goals
- Feedback and evaluation

However, it has also become clear that some of the elements are hardly separable. Furthermore, the approaches state that there are complex interactions between the elements of player experience. In addition, the particular elements themselves are often structured into different components, e.g., flow and presence. Finally, there are numerous moderators influencing the interactions.

9.4 Integrative Models of Player Experience

In this chapter, the multidimensional nature of player experience has been emphasized several times. Therefore, purely psychological model are not able to cover all aspects of this multi-faceted construct. Rather, models integrating the various disciplinary aspects are required, e.g., psychological, sociological, physiological, and biomechanical perspectives (see Fig. 9.2). Due to the double mission of serious games and the domain-specific interrelations of influencing factors in specific application fields, there is a need for the adaptation of generic models (for an example in the field of exergames for persons with disablties, see Wiemeyer et al. 2015).

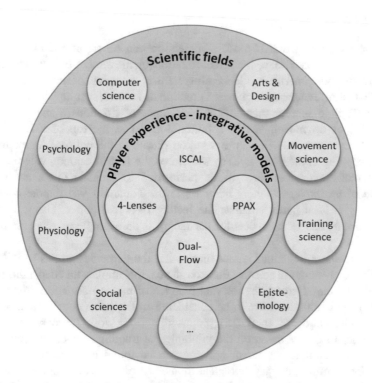

Fig. 9.2 Integrative models of player experience

In this section, selected integrative models are discussed. The following models will be addressed:

- ISCAL model
- Dual-flow model (DFM)
- Four-lens model (4LM)
- Play Patterns And eXperience (PPAX) framework

In a strict sense, these models are not pure models of player experience. However, they address specific features of serious games design that are deemed important for player experience.

ISCAL Model

Zhang et al. (2011) proposed a model for the design of exergames. This model claims that five characteristics are important to establish high-quality exergames:

- Immersion
- Scientificalness
- Competitiveness
- Adaptibility
- Learning

According to the ISCAL model, immersion can be supported by the use of sensor-based feedback, e.g., force, acceleration or movement trajectories, and by naturally mapped interfaces. Concerning natural mapping of interfaces, Skalski et al. (2011) differentiate four types: Directional, kinesic, incomplete tangible and realistic tangible natural mapping. An example of *directional mapping* is the assignment of up movements to a button located at the top of a keyboard or gamepad, and down movements to a button placed at the bottom. An example of *kinesic mapping* is the Sony EyeToy system or the Kinect camera, where gestures without realistic devices have to be performed to indicate one's actions. An example of *incomplete tangible mapping* is the Nintendo Wii remote controller, which may at least partly simulate the feeling of a real object. Using a steering wheel, throttle, and brake pedals for car racing is an example of *realistic tangible mapping*.

Scientificalness of serious games means that the game design has to follow the current state-of-the-art in science. For exergames, this implies that depending on the objective and target group, the relevant theories of motor learning, training, health science, or rehabilitation have to be considered in the game development process. For example, Hardy et al. (2015) proposed a framework for personalized and adaptive health games based on the principles of training science. An example of scientific substantiation of motor learning can be found in Wiemeyer and Hardy (2013). Furthermore, the psychological models of player experience mentioned in the previous section should also be considered.

Competitiveness means that serious games should include comparison to others, either real players or virtual non-playing characters (NPC). However, competitiveness has its limits. Results in several fields show that competition in serious games is not always the best way to enhance player experience. Often, cooperation is a better way to motivate players—for example, in the fields of learning and rehabilitation (e.g., Hattie 2009; Marker and Staiano 2015).

Adaptibility means that the game must be able to perform dynamic adjustments to the more or less static as well as dynamic characteristics of the player. A serious game that does not adapt may lead to a decline of player experience due to overload or underchallenge. Examples for adaptive systems are proposed by Hocine et al. (2014) for motor rehabilitation and by Hoffmann et al. (2014) for individualized aerobic training. This aspect will also be addressed in Chap. 10.

Learning about the environments of serious games is also a feature which may add to the attractiveness of games. Zhang et al. (2011), for example, included learning of knowledge about Chinese and Olympic culture in their function and design framework of a digital Olympic museum. However, knowledge to be learned should always be relevant to the context of the serious games to avoid demotivation due to externally enforced learning of irrelevant information. At the very least, game developers have to consider whether players may actually be interested in the learning subject.

Zhang et al. (2011) applied the model to an exergame for aerobic training. A sample of 20 players (undergraduate students; age: 17 to 22 years; gender: 7 females, 13 males) played this exergame for 15 consecutive days. The ISCAL model was able to differentiate between different playing modes (tour, training, and competition). Furthermore, the study revealed a high level of player experience, i.e., the score was always about 7.5 on a 10-point scale. However, PE was assessed by asking just one question (scale: 1–10). Interestingly, the female player experience initially increased logarithmically, followed by a plateau and small decline, whereas the male player experience started at a high level followed by a gradual decrease. In contrast to this, subjective satisfaction with training effects showed a logarithmical increase in females and males.

Dual Flow Model (DFM)

To address the double mission of serious games, Sinclair (2011) proposed a dual-flow model (DFM). This model differentiates two main objectives: Attractiveness and effectiveness of serious games.

The *effectiveness* of serious games means that the characterizing goal is actually achieved. This requires that serious games are based on sound scientific ground. In exergames, for example, the appropriate load parameters like intensity, duration, density, volume, and frequency have to be considered—as well as the principles of progression, adaptation, and individualization. To ensure optimal effectiveness the load parameters have to be adapted to the physical or psychic capacity of the player. Effectiveness will be impaired if the load imposed by the game leaves the "corridor" of optimal matching. If load is too high, maladaptations and overload will result; if load is too low, no or sub-optimal adaptations will be the consequence.

Attractiveness means that the "system needs to make people want to play the game or games, in order to motivate the user to exercise" (Sinclair 2011, p.38). Following the findings of Malone (1980, 1982), Sinclair claims that attractiveness is supported predominantly by challenge, curiosity, and fantasy. However, the appropriate balance of challenge, curiosity, and fantasy seems to be dependent on the individual characteristics of the player. Furthermore, Sinclair includes the concepts of flow and GameFlow mentioned above, as well as the individual zones of optimal functioning model (IZOF; Hanin 2007) and the *Yerkes-Dodson law* (Yerkes and Dodson 1908). Whereas the flow and GameFlow model relate skill level to challenge, the other two models relate emotions and arousal to performance. In this context, it should be noted that in their original work Yerkes and Dodson already identified task difficulty as a moderator of the arousal-performance relationship. Their experiments indicated that the more difficult the task is the lower is the stress level yielding peak performance. This result is often neglected when referring to the Yerkes-Dodson law as a general inverted-U-shaped relation of stress or arousal and performance. To ensure the attractiveness of serious games, Sinclair (2011) also calls for efficient dynamic difficulty adjustment in order to keep the players in the zone of flow and optimal functioning.

Sinclair (2011) tested his dual-flow model by manipulating the control of intensity (effectiveness) and challenge (attractiveness) on a sample of 21 subjects (age: 21 to 41 years; gender: 8 males, 13 females). Using a repeated-measures design, the subjects played a bike-based exergame under four conditions: Dynamic challenge control and dynamic intensity control, dynamic challenge control only, dynamic intensity control only, and no dynamic control at all. Concerning player engagement assessed by three questions (interest, time perception), the control of intensity evoked a lower level of engagement, whereas there was no differential effect of challenge control. On the one hand, this result illustrates the interrelation of load and attractiveness; on the other hand, the dual-flow model has to be reworked concerning control of challenge.

Four-Lens Model (4LM)

Mueller et al. (2011) proposed a four-lens model of exergames design. Although the model has been particularly developed for exergames, it can easily be transferred to serious games in general. In this model, they distinguish four levels of players' reaction to exergames:

- The responding body
- The moving body
- The sensing body
- The relating body

The *responding body* denotes changes of internal states as a consequence of playing games. Strictly speaking, every system of the human body responds to playing games: Central nervous system, cardiovascular, respiratory, endocrine (hormone), metabolic, neuro-muscular, etc. Therefore, the body's physiological and biochemical responses can be measured to estimate the psychophysical strain or the impact of serious games on player experience. This aspect will be addressed in Sect. 9.5. The responses of the body can be more or less transient (functional adaptations) or permanent (structural adaptations).

The *moving body* means that game (inter)actions are always accompanied by spatio-temporal changes of the whole body or at least of body parts (e.g., fingers). These changes can be quantified by biomechanical sensors. Therefore, trajectories, translational velocity, acceleration, angular displacement, velocity, and acceleration as well as forces, torques, work, and energy can be determined to quantify movements. Biomechanical signals can be used to identify either distinct types of actions, e.g., a backhand stroke in tennis, or action parameters, e.g., force, timing, and direction of a stroke. To support the player experience, sensor signals should be mapped naturally to the game (e.g., Skalski et al. 2011); there should also be a close temporal relationship of player actions and game reactions (feedback) (e.g., Spelmezan 2012). Beyond quantitative characteristics of movement, there are also qualitative aspects like rhythm, speed, fluency, or structure. These features can also be used to control games.

The *sensing body* describes information processing of the players. When playing games, players perceive, make decisions, and solve problems. The game environment, including real or virtual objects, considerably influences these subjective experiences. Therefore, experiences can be more or less realistic or virtual. Both variants bear specific advantages and disadvantages. For example, interacting with virtual environments offers much more degrees of freedom compared to realistic environments. On the other hand, virtual environments may lack the persuasive power of realism—and may even lead to discomfort when signals from different senses do not match. In virtual environments, the phenomenon of "simulator sickness" is well known (e.g., Kolasinski 1995).

The *relating body* means that players interact with, or communicate to, other players. These interactions and communications are mediated by game technology. Mueller et al. (2011) emphasize the fact that social interactions are extremely diverse. Different roles as well as modes of interaction (e.g., cooperation versus competition) determine player experience. Maier et al. (2014) report preliminary results regarding the influence of social relations on gaming. They could find a tendency that social gaming enhanced engagement and motivation to play a rehab game. Furthermore, social relations are a strong factor determining adherence to activities, e.g., gaming or health-related behavior.

Play Patterns And eXperience (PPAX) Framework

The PPAX framework was developed by Cowley et al. (2013) to connect player experience to game design and game context. The model relies predominantly on physiological measures of player experience. This data is the ingredient for computational analysis of higher level relationships. The hierarchical model distinguishes four basic links within a hierarchic framework: Game-player links, design-pattern–personality links, play pattern-reaction pattern links, and game event–play reaction links.

Concerning the personality of the player, general and domain-specific states and traits are distinguished. Furthermore, the model does not only consider single links of game events and play reactions, but also patterns of play-reaction links.

Integrative Models—Summary

To conclude, the integrative models described in this section extend the view on player experience by adding important perspectives, e.g., social and (neuro-) physiological aspects. This knowledge contributes to the quality of serious games design. In particular, the relationship between different disciplinary perspectives has to be considered. Therefore, the development of serious games requires interdisciplinary teamwork. Considering the multi-faceted and interdisciplinary nature of player experience, the question arises as to how the different components and dimensions can be assessed. This issue will be addressed in the following section.

9.5 Measuring Player Experience

Comprehending the interactive relationship that exists between human beings and game systems is a complex and challenging area of ongoing games research within HCI. To obtain an accurate understanding of PE, a plethora of factors must be considered relating to psychological characteristics, gameplay performance, and human emotion. The measurement of these factors is achieved through the use of a number of experimental techniques involving behavioral (e.g., reaction time, and game logs), physiological (e.g., sensors monitoring heart rate, muscle activity, and brain waves) and subjective (e.g., questionnaires and interviews) methods.

Game researchers are thus tasked with the experimental analysis of large groups of interrelating experience factors, often through the manipulation of discrete characteristics of the game system (such as difficulty, control scheme, and sensory feedback) or the context in which the game is played (for a comparison of laboratory and home, see Takatalo et al. 2011). Through the careful manipulation of these variables, researchers attempt to quantify the specific effects of any given change or design decision in a game system. There are several methods that are commonly used in games user research to assess player experiences.

Some of the methods used to access individual player experience are (Nacke et al. 2010a, b; see also Fig. 9.3):

- *Psychophysiological player testing*: Controlled measures of gameplay experience with the use of physical sensors to assess user reactions.
- *Eye tracking*: Measurement of eye fixation and attention focus to infer details of cognitive and attentional processes.

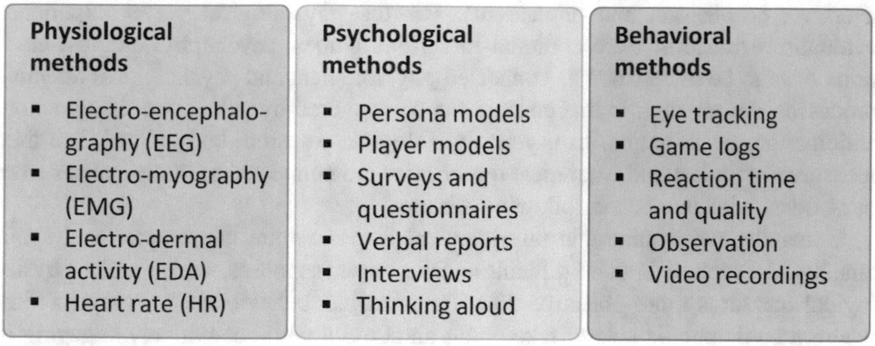

Physiological methods	Psychological methods	Behavioral methods
<ul><li>Electro-encephalo-graphy (EEG)</li><li>Electro-myography (EMG)</li><li>Electro-dermal activity (EDA)</li><li>Heart rate (HR)</li></ul>	<ul><li>Persona models</li><li>Player models</li><li>Surveys and questionnaires</li><li>Verbal reports</li><li>Interviews</li><li>Thinking aloud</li></ul>	<ul><li>Eye tracking</li><li>Game logs</li><li>Reaction time and quality</li><li>Observation</li><li>Video recordings</li></ul>

Fig. 9.3 Selected methods for the assessment of player experience

- *Persona modelling*: Constructed player models.
- *Game metrics behavior assessment*: Logging of every action the player takes while playing, for future analysis.
- *Player modeling*: AI-based models that react to player behavior and adapt the player experience accordingly.
- *Qualitative interviews and questionnaires*: Surveys to assess the player's perception of various gameplay experience dimensions.

In this section, we focus primarily on some of the most common evaluation techniques of physiological evaluation and player surveys. For more detailed introductions to measuring player experience with physiological sensors, see Nacke (2013, 2015).

9.5.1 Physiological Evaluation

In pursuit of increasingly complex and fulfilling player experiences, researchers and designers have collaborated to create games that are capable of interfacing with human physiology on an intuitively responsive level. Specifically, evaluation and interaction frameworks are being investigated that enable direct communication between computer systems and human physiology. Beyond the traditional application of such technologies in the medical field, games researchers are finding that the advanced technologies underlying these systems can be leveraged to create player experiences that are more meaningful.

The measurement of physiological activity that is used for evaluating these games is based mainly on sensors that are placed on the surface on the human skin to make inferences about players' cognitive or emotional states.

Most emotion theories distinguish between two basic concepts: Discrete states of emotion (often referred to as basic emotions like surprise, fear, anger, disgust, sadness, and happiness) or biphasic emotional dimensions (arousal and valence, but the dimensions often differentiate between positive and negative, appetitive and aversive, or pleasant and unpleasant). For the physiological player experience evaluation studies that are common in serious games, psychophysiological emotions have to be understood as connected physiological and psychological affective processes. An emotion in this context can be triggered by perception, imagination, anticipation, or an action. In psychophysiological research, body signals are then measured to understand what mental processes are connected to the responses from our bodies with one of the following sensors.

Generally, we assume that physiological responses are unprompted and spontaneous. As such, it is quite difficult to fake these responses, which make physiological measures more objective than, for example, behavioral gameplay metrics, where a participant is able to fake doing an activity while cognitively engaging in another. When using physiological sensors for evaluating player experiences, we need to have a controlled experimental environment, because physiological data is volatile, variable, and can be difficult to correctly interpret. For example, when participants talk during an experiment, this might influence their heart rate or respiration, resulting in altered physiological signals. As games user researchers, we also have to understand the relationship between how our mind processes information and the information responses that our body produces. The psychological effect or mental process is not always in a direct relationship to the underlying brain response. As such, we need to be aware that we cannot map physiological responses directly to a discrete emotional state. However, we can make inferences about emotional tendencies using physiological measures.

Unfiltered physiological signals measured from electrodes on the human skin are not more than positive or negative electrical voltage (Nacke 2013). These signals are generally characterized by their amplitude (the maximum voltage), latency (i.e., time from stimulus onset to occurrence of the physiological signal), and frequency (i.e., the number of oscillations in a signal). Before the signals become useful for analysis, they are usually processed and filtered. More intense experiences yield more intense responses in the physiological signals. There are some minor differences between some of the major physiological signals.

Electroencephalography (EEG)

EEG is currently not yet a common measure to analyze player experiences, because the brain wave activity that it records is hard to process and analyze. The resulting data can be very insightful into the cognitive processes of players, but it might also not be as actionable as other physiological data, because inferences depend largely on the experimental setup. EEG analyzes responses from a human's central nervous system, but it is less complicated to set up and less invasive than other measures, such as magnetic resonance imaging (MRI) or positron emission tomography (PET) scans. The temporal resolution of EEG is rather high compared to other techniques, which makes it especially useful for real-time feedback during gameplay. However, its spatial resolution is lower than other methods, resulting in low signal-to-noise ratio and limited spatial sampling.

Electromyography (EMG)

EMG sensors measure muscular activity on human tissue. This has many useful applications, but the main area of interest for games user researchers is facial muscle measurement. Our facial expressions are driven by muscle contractions and relaxations, which produce differences in electrical activity on the skin or isometric tension. This can then be measured by an EMG electrode. Our muscles contract, for example, as a result of brain activity or other stimuli, which makes them a primary indicator of peripheral nervous system activities. In game research, studies focus on brow muscle (*corrugator supercilii*) to indicate negative emotion and on cheek muscle (*zygomaticus major*) to indicate positive emotion (Hazlett 2006; Mandryk and Atkins 2007; Nacke et al. 2010a, b; Nacke and Lindley 2010).

Electrodermal Activity (EDA)

In physiological player evaluation, EDA measures the passive electrical conductivity of the skin that is regulated via increases or decreases in sweat gland activity (Nacke 2015). When a participant gets aroused by an external stimulus, their EDA will increase. The fluctuations of EDA are indicative of the excitement a player feels during gameplay. Often EDA is used to analyze the responses of players to direct events during a game; however, when we analyze those events, the delay of the signal has to be taken into account. So, studies often look at a 5–7 s window after an event has occurred to see what the physiological response indicates.

Physiological measures are powerful tools for analyzing player experience, but they are most useful when used in tandem with interviews or surveys to find out more about the subjective reasons behind the body responses recorded.

9.5.2 Surveys

The assessment of player experience by means of post-play surveys or interviews is the easiest and least expensive approach; however, it has some drawbacks. Since it relies on a player's memory, information may be lost in the delay between action (gameplay) and recall (interview or questionnaire).

The *Game Experience Questionnaire (GEQ)* developed by the FUGA group (Poels et al. 2008) consists of 36 items representing 7 scales: competence, immersion, flow, tension, challenge, positive and negative affect. The authors also offer shorter versions like the post-game experience questionnaire (PGQ; 17 items) and the in-game experience questionnaire (iGEQ; 14 items).

The *MEC spatial presence questionnaire (MEC-SPQ)*, by Vorderer et al. (2004), consists of 103 items and nine scales that measure attention allocation, spatial situation, spatial presence (in terms of self location and possible actions), higher cognitive involvement, suspension of disbelief, domain specific interest, or the visual spatial imagery.

The *Spatial Presence Experience Scale (SPES)*, by Hartmann et al. (2015), builds on the theoretical model of spatial presence (Wirth et al. 2007). It consists of

20 items and two scales that measure self-location (i.e., the users' feelings of "being there") and possible action (i.e., sense of being able to carry out actions and manipulate them).

The *Social Presence in Gaming Questionnaire (SPGQ)*, by de Kort et al. (2007), is based in part on the Networked Minds Measure of Social Presence (Biocca et al. 2001). It consists of 21 items and three scales that measure psychological involvement (empathy, psychological involvement), negative feelings, and behavioral involvement.

The *Game Engagement Questionnaire (GEnQ)*, by Brockmyer et al. (2009), serves as an indicator of game engagement. The questionnaire identifies the players' level of psychological engagement when playing video games, assuming that more engagement could lead to a greater impact on game playing. It consists of 19 items that measure absorption, flow, presence, and immersion.

The *EGameFlow*, by Fu et al. (2009), measures the learner's cognition of enjoyment during the playing of e-learning games. It consists of 56 items and eight scales that measure concentration, goal clarity, feedback, challenge, autonomy, immersion, social interaction, and knowledge improvement.

The *Core Elements of the Gaming Experience Questionnaire (CEGEQ)*, by Calvillo-Gámez et al. (2010), is used to assess the core elements of the gaming experience. It builds on the CEGE model described before and consists of 38 items and 10 scales that measure enjoyment, frustration, CEGE, puppetry, video-game, control, facilitators, ownership, gameplay, and environment.

Wourters et al. (2011) developed a questionnaire to measure perceived curiosity of players regarding serious games. The questionnaire contains seven items. The items were used as a single index for curiosity.

The *extended Short Feedback Questionnaire (eSFQ)*, by Moser et al. (2012), is used to assess the player experience of children aged 10–14 years. It consists of different parts to quickly measure the enjoyment, curiosity, and co-experience.

9.6 Fostering Player Experience

The previous sections articulated various ways on how to understand and examine player experience. This allows serious game creators to obtain insights into their game design; for example, a serious game designer might have created a game and consequently measured the player experience, gaining a better understanding of the overall product. However, she/he might then realize that the game does not achieve its objectives, i.e., it does not facilitate the desired player experience. The question is then, what does the serious game creator do?

One approach is to redesign the game, hoping that the measurements improve in a subsequent evaluation. However, such a redesign does not need to start from scratch. Like with the creation of the original design, there are several ways available to designers that can guide the design process to facilitate the desired player experience. For example, designers interested in facilitating a desired player experience can:

- learn from prior games. Game creators can look at (and play) other games and learn from bad as well as good examples.
- read post mortems as often published by game studios in industry publications, learn from them, and use them to inspire a (re)design.
- examine academic papers from serious game projects in a university or research organization setting. These academic papers often describe detailed learnings when it comes to fostering player experience and what the authors would do differently in future game designs.
- learn from books on game design.

Examining such guidance is worthwhile in the design and any redesign of a game. Furthermore, this guidance is applicable to both entertainment and serious games. It is important here that to address the serious component, game creators can look at specific guidance to complement the items detailed above. With the advancement of serious games, there will be more specific serious games guidance emerging to foster player experience. For now, however, we provide a couple of examples that aim to foster desired player experiences for specific serious game scenarios.

Fostering Player Experience: Example 1

Creators of serious games that aim to foster a desired player experience in movement-based games (for example, to facilitate positive health benefits) can look at the movement-based game guidelines developed by Isbister and Mueller (2014). These movement-based game guidelines emerged out of game design practice and research, and were developed with the help of industry game designers and user experience experts that were involved in some of the most popular commercial movement-based games to date—such as Dance Central, Your Shape and Sony's Eyetoy games.

The movement-based game guidelines are articulated in detail here, along with a website (http://movementgameguidelines.org/), and include examples and explanations. In this section, we highlight the key overarching points in order to inspire the reader to examine the guidelines further through these external references when needed.

The movement-based game guidelines are aimed to support creators of games where movement is at the forefront of the player experience. These games have been made popular by game consoles and movement-focused accessories such as the Nintendo Wii, Microsoft Xbox Kinect and Sony Playstation Move, however, they also apply to mobile phone developments that make use of sensing equipment that can detect movement or other technological advancements that enable movement-based games.

The guidelines are articulated in the form of heuristics, i.e., they are not required "must-dos," but rather guidance that designers should know about. As such, designers can break these rules; but first, they need to know the rules before they can break them.

The movement-based game guidelines can be grouped into these three categories:

- Movement requires special feedback
- Movement leads to bodily challenges
- Movement emphasizes certain kinds of fun

Each category has 3–4 specific guidelines:

Movement requires special feedback

- Embrace ambiguity
- Celebrate movement articulation
- Consider movement's cognitive load
- Focus on the body

Movement leads to bodily challenges

- Intend fatigue
- Exploit risk
- Map imaginatively

Movement emphasizes certain kinds of fun

- Highlight rhythm
- Support self-expression
- Facilitate social fun

To provide an example of the guidelines, we explain the first one, *embrace ambiguity*, in more detail. "Embrace ambiguity" suggests that "instead of fighting the ambiguity of movement, embrace it." Ambiguity in movement-based games arises from the fact that (a) no two movements are the same and (b) most sensor data is messy. Therefore, trying to force any precision might only frustrate the player and make the sensor limitations obvious in an un-engaging way. Therefore, the guideline suggests that instead of trying to eliminate the ambiguity, to work with it in a way so players can enjoy the uncertainty and figure out optimal strategies to cope with it.

The guideline also provides do's and don'ts; here, it proposes a very practical don't for the development process: don't use buttons during the early development phase (even if it seems easier), as the designer might miss opportunities that might arise from dealing with ambiguity (Mueller and Isbister 2014).

Fostering Player Experience: Example 2

Another example of guidance for facilitating a certain player experience is the work on applying game design knowledge to the creation of more playful jogging experiences. The work draws from the "non-serious" knowledge on designing games as articulated in the game design workshop book by Fullerton et al. (2004) and examined how it could be applied to the design of games that are situated in a jogging context. The authors draw on their prior experiences of designing jogging systems that aim to rekindle the playful aspect in jogging, and adopt the game design guidance to make it applicable to the design of such jogging systems.

The original game design workshop book proposes that game designers need to consider two key aspects (there are more, but we focus on these for now) in every game: *formal elements* and *dramatic elements*. Formal elements provide the underlying structure of the game (considering aspects such as objectives, rules, and outcomes) whereas dramatic elements are concerned with the visceral excitement that unfolds throughout the player experience. When applied to jogging, the authors describe how a look at formal elements can describe the "usability" tools in the designer's toolkit, whereas the dramatic elements make the "aesthetics" of jogging, describing the experiential tools in the designer's toolkit. These dramatic elements are important, as they allow the creator of the serious game to see the jog beyond a series of strides towards gaining a view on the overall physical activity experience.

Some examples of formal elements are: "the social jogger," which asks "who is involved in the jog?" and "the joggers' objective" that examines "what is the jogger striving for?" The "jogger's conflict" asks "what is in the jogger's way?" while "the jogger's resources" asks "what assets can the jogger use to accomplish the objective?"

Some examples of the dramatic elements are: "the premise of the jog" asks "how to support the setting of the jog" "the jogger's character" asks "who is the jogger?" and "the story of the jog" examines "how to support the jog as a narrative?"

By considering both the formal and dramatic elements, creators will be guided in their endeavor to facilitate the player experience they are striving for in their design.

Fostering Player Experience: Example 3

Another example of how to foster player experience in serious games is through considering the game features Reeves and Read (2013) articulate in their book "Total Engagement: How Games and Virtual Worlds are Changing the Way People Work and Businesses Compete." In this book, the authors propose that companies can draw on games to advance their business, a typical scenario for serious games. In order to guide the creators of such games, they list "ten ingredients of great games" and articulate why they are particularly important for businesses. These ten game features "to guide real work" are:

- Self-representation with avatars
- Three-dimensional environments
- Narrative context
- Feedback
- Reputations, Ranks, and Levels
- Marketplaces and Economies

- Competition under rules that are explicit and enforced
- Teams
- Parallel communication systems that can be easily reconfigured
- Time pressure

Each of these game features has a specific set of aspects to consider; for example, "Three-dimensional environments" are described further with the following aspects:

- Virtual space works like real space: No instruction necessary
- Three-dimensional space helps you remember where stuff is
- Special properties of virtual space (referring to the ability to go beyond copying the real world)
- Opportunities to explore
- The use of three-dimensional space can organize and inspire work

Overall, it should be noted that these features as well as their associated aspects are no guarantee for an engaging player experience. As Reeves and Read point out, they can guide creators of serious games based on the author's knowledge and as suggested by prior research. However, they might not work in other, novel settings and contexts. Nevertheless, they provide a good starting point for creators of serious games when considering player experience.

Furthermore, it should be noted that not all of the features need to be present together, they can be considered individually and independently. The same applies to the suggested features and proposed guidelines described in the other examples: They are no guarantee for success. However, their articulation based on existing practice suggests that they can aid creators of serious games to facilitate the desired player experience.

9.7 Summary and Questions

Research on user experience as well as player experience has turned from usability and playability to the person of the user or player, respectively. Player experience is located at three interacting levels: the (socio-)psychological, behavioral, and physiological level. Player experience as an individual experience goes beyond playability and game usability. Psychological responses comprise cognitive, perceptual and emotional experiences like immersion, flow, challenge, curiosity, tension, positive and negative affects. Playing behavior includes all possible actions in and interactions with the game. Physiological responses range from peripheral reactions like changes in EDA and EMG to central reactions like EEG changes. Whereas psychological models of player experience focus on the multi-dimensional structure of individual player experience, integrative models address the holistic and interdisciplinary structure of player experience integrating the findings of numerous scientific disciplines, e.g., (neuro-)physiology, psychology, and sociology. The most useful for a shared understanding of PE is, therefore, to think about how these terms can provide a useful vocabulary for GUR when trying to improve video game design. This remains challenging as new models of PE are being developed and tested.

Guidelines and recommendations to foster player experience can be either derived from theory or from practice.

Check your understanding of this chapter by answering the following questions:

- What is the difference between usability and user experience?
- What is the difference between game usability, playability, and player experience?
- How can player experience be measured at the psychological, behavioral, and physiological level?
- What are the advantages and disadvantages of physiological compared to psychological measures of player experience?
- What are the advantages and disadvantages of psychological models of player experience?
- What are the basic assumptions of the following models: Self-determination theory (SDT), Attention, relevance, confidence, satisfaction (ARCS), Flow, GameFlow, Presence and immersion, Fun of gaming (FUGA), Core elements of game experience (CEGE), and PLAY heuristics?
- What are the characteristics of player experience?
- What are the added values of holistic models of player experience?
- What are the basic assumptions of the following models: ISCAL model, Dual-flow model (DFM), Four-lens model (4LM), Play Patterns And eXperience (PPAX) framework?
- How can player experience be fostered?
- What are the sources for guidelines to foster player experience?

Recommended Literature[1]

Bernhaupt R (ed) (2010) Evaluating user experience in games – Concepts and methods. Springer, London—*This book addresses both game researchers and developers. The book provides an overview of methods for evaluating and assessing player experience before, during, and after playing games*

---

[1]Issues of player experience are addressed at many conferences, ranging from the Games and Serious Games conferences mentioned in Chap. 1 to more specific conferences on usability, user experience, computer-human interaction (CHI) etc. Papers concerning player experience can be found in journals addressing human-computer interaction (e.g., Interacting with computers, Computers in Human Behavior, and International Journal of Human-Computer Studies), as well as journals specifically addressing games and serious games (e.g., Journal of gaming and virtual worlds).

Bernhaupt R (ed) (2015) Game user experience evaluation. Springer International Publishing, Cham—*This book is an update of the previously mentioned edition. Current developments in the assessment and evaluation of player experience are covered*

Fairclough SH (2009) Fundamentals of physiological computing. Interact Comput 21(1–2): 133–145—*This article gives a comprehensive overview of psychophysiological methods used for assessment of the current state of users and players, as well as their integration into adaptive systems. In addition, selected ethical issues are addressed*

Kivikangas JM, Chanel G, Cowley B, Ekman I, Salminen M, Järvelä S, Ravaja N (2011) A review of the use of psychophysiological methods in game research. JGVW 3(3):181–199—*This article gives a comprehensive overview of the psychophysiological measures typically used in game research. It also provides valuable information about the theories behind psychophysiological measurement*

Mäyrä F (2008) An introduction to game studies. SAGE Publications, London—*This textbook introduces students to the research field of studying games. The book delivers historical facts about (digital) games as well as basic knowledge concerning research methods for game studies*

Nacke LE (2009) Affective ludology: Scientific measurement of user experience in interactive entertainment. Blekinge Institute of Technology, Doctoral Dissertation Series No. 2009:04—*This dissertation is a comprehensive example of how the player experience can be investigated in practice. Various methods are thoroughly discussed concerning their research quality and systematically applied to selected research issues*

References

Biocca F, Harms C, Gregg J (2001) The networked minds measure of social presence: pilot test of the factor structure and concurrent validity. In: 4th annual international workshop on presence, Philadelphia, PA, 1–9

Brockmyer JH, Fox CM, Curtiss KA, McBroom E, Burkhart KM, Pidruzny JN (2009) The development of the game engagement questionnaire: a measure of engagement in video game-playing. J Exp Soc Psychol 45:624–634

Brown E, Cairns P (2004) A grounded investigation of game immersion. In: CHI conference proceedings/conference on human factors in computing systems. CHI conference. ACM, New York, pp 1297–1300

Calvillo-Gámez EH, Cairns P, Cox AL (2010) Assessing the core elements of the gaming experience. In: Bernhaupt R (ed) Evaluating user experience in games. Springer, London, UK, pp 47–71

Cowley B, Kosunen I, Lankoski P, Kivikangas JM, Järvelä S, Ekman I, Kemppainen J, Ravaja N (2013) Experience assessment and design in the analysis of gameplay. Simul Gaming 45: 624–634

Deci EL, Koestner R, Ryan RM (1999) A meta-analytic review of experiments examining the effects of extrinsic rewards on intrinsic motivation. Psychol Bull 125(6):627–668

Desurvire H, Wiberg C (2009) Game usability heuristics (PLAY) for evaluating and designing better games: the next iteration. In: Ozok AA, Zaphiris P (eds) Online communities and social computing. LNCS 5621, Springer, Berlin, pp 557–566

Engl S, Nacke LE (2013) Contextual influences on mobile player experience—a Game User Experience Model. Entertainment Computing 4(1):83–91

Fu FL, Su RC, Yu SC (2009) EGameFlow: a scale to measure learners' enjoyment of e-learning games. Comput Educ 52(1):101–112

Fullerton T, Swain C, Hoffman S (2004) Game design workshop. Morgan Kaufmann, Amsterdam

Gerling KM, Klauser M, Niesenhaus J (2011) Measuring the impact of game controllers on player experience in FPS games. Proceedings of the 15th international academic mindtrek conference: envisioning future media environments (MindTreck'11). ACM, New York, pp 83–86

Hanin YL (2007) Emotions and athletic performance: individual zones of optimal functioning model. In: Smith D, Bar-Eli M (eds) Essential readings in sport and exercise psychology. Human Kinetics, Champaign, IL, pp 55–73

Hardy S, Dutz T, Wiemeyer J, Göbel S, Steinmetz R (2015) Framework for personalized and adaptive game-based training programs in health sport. Multimed Tools Appl 74:5289–5311

Hartmann T, Wirth W, Schramm H, Klimmt C, Vorderer P, Gysbers A, Böcking S, Ravaja N, Laarni J, Saari T, Gouveia F, Sacau AM (2015) The spatial presence experience scale (SPES). JMP. doi:10.1027/1864-1105/a000137

Hattie J (2009) Visible learning: A synthesis of over 800 meta-analyses relating to achievement. Routledge, London

Hazlett RL (2006) Measuring emotional valence during interactive experiences. Proceedings of the SIGCHI conference on human factors in computing systems. ACM, New York, pp 1023–1026

Hocine N, Gouaich A, Cerri SA (2014) Dynamic difficulty adaptation in serious games for motor rehabilitation. In: Goebel S, Wiemeyer J (eds) Games for training, education, health and sports. Springer International Publishing, Cham, pp 115–128

Hoffmann K, Wiemeyer J, Hardy S, Göbel S (2014) Personalized adaptive control of training load in Exergames from a sport-scientific perspective. In: Goebel S, Wiemeyer J (eds) Games for training, education, health and sports. Springer International Publishing, Cham, pp 129–140

Huizinga J (2013) Homo ludens, 23rd edn. Rowohlt, Reinbek

Isbister K, Mueller F (2014) Guidelines for the design of movement-based games and their relevance to HCI. Hum-Comput Interact 30(3–4):366–399

Jackson SA, Marsh HW (1996) Development and validation of a scale to measure optimal experience: the flow state scale. J Sport Exercise Psy 18(1):17–35

Keller JM (1987) Development and use of the ARCS model of instructional design. JID 10(3): 2–10

Keller JM (2009) Motivational design for learning and performance: the ARCS model approach. Springer Science & Business Media, New York

Kolasinski EM (1995) Simulator sickness in virtual environments, Technical report, DTIC Document. U.S. army research institute for the behavioural and social sciences, Alexandria, VA

Kort YA de, IJsselsteijn WA, Poels K (2007) Digital games as social presence technology: Development of the social presence in gaming questionnaire (SPGQ). In: Proceedings of PRESENCE, 195203

Law E, Vermeeren APOS, Hassenzahl M, Blythe M (2007) Towards a UX manifesto. Proceedings of the British HCI group annual conference. British Computer Society, London, pp 205–206

Lazzaro N (2008) The four fun keys. In: Isbister K, Schaffer N (eds) Game usability: advancing the player experience. Elsevier, Burlington, pp 315–344

Lombard M, Ditton TB (1997) At the heart of it all: the concept of presence. J Comput-Mediat Comm 3(2)

Maier M, Ballester BR, Duarte E, Duff A, Verschure PF (2014) Social integration of stroke patients through the multiplayer rehabilitation gaming system. In: Goebel S, Wiemeyer J (eds) Games for training, education, health and sports. Springer International Publishing, Cham, pp 100–114

Malone TW (1980) What makes things fun to learn? Heuristics for designing instructional computer games. Proceedings of the 3rd ACM SIGSMALL symposium and the first SIGPC symposium on small systems. ACM, New York, New York, pp 162–169

Malone TW (1982) Heuristics for designing enjoyable user interfaces: lessons from computer games. Proceedings of the 1982 conference on human factors in computing systems. ACM, New York, New York, pp 63–68

Mandryk RL, Atkins MS (2007) A fuzzy physiological approach for continuously modeling emotion during interaction with play technologies. Int J Hum-Comput St 65(4):329–347

Marker AM, Staiano AE (2015) Better together: Outcomes of cooperation versus competition in social exergaming. Games Health J 4 (1):25-30

Mäyrä F (2008b) An introduction to game studies. SAGE Publications, London

Moser C, Fuchsberger V, Tscheligi M (2012) Rapid assessment of game experiences in public settings. Proceedings of the 4th international conference on fun and games (FNG'12). ACM, New York, pp 73–82

Mueller F, Isbister K (2014) Movement-based game guidelines. Proceedings of the SIGCHI conference on human factors in computing systems. ACM, New York, pp 2191–2200

Mueller F, Edge D, Vetere F, Gibbs MR, Agamanolis S, Bongers B, Sheridan JG (2011) Designing sports: a framework for exertion games. In: CHI'11: proceedings of the SIGCHI conference on human factors in computing systems, Vancouver, Canada

Nacke LE (2009) Affective ludology: scientific measurement of user experience in interactive entertainment. Blekinge Institute of Technology, Doctoral Dissertation Series No. 2009:04

Nacke LE (2010) From playability to a hierarchical game usability model. Proceedings of future play 2010. ACM, New York, pp 11–12

Nacke LE (2013) An introduction to physiological player metrics for evaluating games. In: Seif El-Nasr M, Drachen A, Canossa A (eds) Game analytics: maximizing the value of player data. Springer, London, pp 585–619

Nacke LE (2015) Games user research and physiological game evaluation. In: Bernhaupt R (ed) Game user experience evaluation. Springer International Publishing, Cham, pp 63–86

Nacke LE, Lindley CA (2010) Affective ludology, flow and immersion in a first-person shooter: Meas Player Exp Loading… 3(5):1–12

Nacke LE, Drachen A (2011) Towards a framework of player experience research. In: Proceedings of the second international workshop on evaluating player experience in games at FDG'11. ACM, New York

Nacke LE, Drachen A, Kuikkaniemi K, Niesenhaus J, Korhonen HJ, Hoogen VDW, Poels K, IJsselsteijn WA, Kort Y (2009) Playability and player experience research. In: Proceedings of DiGRA 2009, DiGRA, Tampere, pp 1–5

Nacke LE, Drachen A, Göbel S (2010a) Methods for evaluating gameplay experience in a serious gaming context. Int J Comp Sci Sport 9(2):40–51

Nacke LE, Grimshaw MN, Lindley CA (2010b) More than a feeling: measurement of sonic user experience and psychophysiology in a first-person shooter game. Interact Comput 22(5): 336–343

Nacke LE, Bateman C, Mandryk RL (2014) BrainHex: a neurobiological gamer typology survey. Entertain comput 5(1):55–62

Nakamura J, Csikszentmihalyi M (2002) The concept of flow. In: Snyder CR, Lopez SJ (eds) Handbook of positive psychology. Oxford University Press, New York, pp 89–105

Phillips C, Johnson D, Wyeth P (2013) Videogame reward types. Proceedings of the first international conference on gameful design, research, and applications. ACM, New York, pp 103–106

Poels K, de Kort YAW, IJsselsteijn WA (2008) FUGA—The fun of gaming: measuring the human experience of media enjoyment. Deliverable D3.3: game experience questionnaire. TU Eindhoven, Eindhoven, The Netherlands

Ravaja N, Salminen M, Holopainen J, Saari T, Laarni J, Järvinen A (2008) Emotional response patterns and sense of presence during video games: potential criterion variables for game design. Proceedings of the 3rd nordic conference on human-computer interaction (NordiCHI '04). ACM, New York, pp 339–347

Reeves B, Read JL (2013) Total engagement: How games and virtual worlds are changing the way people work and businesses compete: Harvard Business Press, Boston, MA

Rigby S, Ryan R (2007) The player experience of need satisfaction (PENS): an applied model and methodology for understanding key components of the player experience. http://www.immersyve.com/?wpdmdl=8283. Accessed 18 Feb 2016

Ryan RM, Deci EL (2000) Self-determination theory and the facilitation of intrinsic motivation, social development, and well-being. Am Psychol 55(1):68–78

Ryan RM, Rigby CS, Przybylski A (2006) The motivational pull of video games: a self-determination theory approach. Motiv emotion 30(4):344–360

Schell J (2008) The art of game design: a book of lenses, 2nd edn. CRC Press, Boca Raton

Schultze U (2010) Embodiment and presence in virtual worlds: a review. J Inform Technol 25(4):434–449

Sinclair J (2011) Feedback control for exergames. Dissertation, Edith Cowan University, Mount Lawley

Skalski P, Tamborini R, Shelton A, Buncher M, Lindmark P (2011) Mapping the road to fun: Natural video game controllers, presence, and game enjoyment. New Media & Society 13(2):224–242

Spelmezan D (2012) An investigation into the use of tactile instructions in snowboarding. Proceedings of the 14th international conference on human-computer interaction with mobile devices and services. ACM, New York, New York, pp 417–426

Sweetser P, Wyeth P (2005) Game flow: a model for evaluating player enjoyment in games. ACM CIE 3(3):Article 3A

Takatalo J, Hakkinen J, Kaistinen J, Nyman G (2011) User experience in digital games: differences between laboratory and home. Simul Gaming 42(5):656–673

Vorderer P, Wirth W, Gouveia FR, Biocca F, Saari T, Jäncke F, Böcking S, Schramm H, Gysberg A, Hartmann T, Klimmt C, Laarn, J, Ravaja N, Sacau A, Baumgartner T, Jäncke P (2004) MEC spatial presence questionnaire (MEC-SPQ): short documentation and instructions for application. Report to the European community, project presence: MEC (IST-2001-37661)

Wiemeyer J, Hardy S (2013) serious games and motor learning—concepts, evidence, technology. In: Bredl K, Bösche W (eds) Serious games and virtual worlds in education, professional development, and healthcare. IGI Global, Heshey, PA, pp 197–220

Wiemeyer J, Deutsch J, Malone LA, Rowland JL, Swartz M, Xiong J, Zhang FF (2015) Recommendations for the optimal design of exergame interventions for persons with disabilities: challenges, best practices, and future research. Games Health J 4(1):58–62

Wirth W, Hartmann T, Böcking S, Vorderer P, Klimmt C, Schramm H, Saari T, Laarni J, Ravaja N, Gouveia FR, Biocca F, Sacau A, Jäncke L, Baumgartner T, Jäncke P (2007) A process model of the formation of spatial presence experience. Media Psychol 9:493–525

Wirth W, Schramm H, Böcking S, Gysbers A, Hartmann T, Klimmt C, Vorderer P (2008) Entwicklung und Validierung eines Fragebogens zur Entstehung von räumlichem Präsenzerleben. In: Matthes J, Wirth W, Fahr A, Daschmann G (eds) Die Brücke zwischen Theorie und Empirie. Operationalisierung, Messung und Validierung in der Kommunikationswissenschaft, Halem, Köln, pp 70–95

Wourters P, Oostendorp HV, Boonekamp R, Spek EVD (2011) The role of game discourse analysis and curiosity in creating engaging and effective serious games by implementing a back story and foreshadowing. Interact Comput 23:329–336

Yerkes RM, Dodson JD (1908) The relation of strength of stimulus to rapidity of habit-formation. J comparative neurology and psychology 18:459–482

Zhang M, Xu M, Liu Y, He G, Han L, Lv P, Li Y (2011) The framework and implementation of virtual network marathon. IEEE international symposium on virtual reality innovation 2011, 19–20 March. Singapore, IEEE, New York, pp 161–167

Performance Assessment in Serious Games

10

Josef Wiemeyer, Michael Kickmeier-Rust
and Christina M. Steiner

Abstract

In every digital game, players both act in and interact with the game. They use the options of game mechanics to achieve goals. For example, players move a controller to steer the motions of an avatar, or they press buttons to trigger certain actions. These actions and interactions lead to certain results like a successful finish of a quest, solving a problem, or increasing a score. Both the quality and results of actions and interactions are subsumed under the term *performance*. Assessment of player performance is required for several purposes, for example for in-game or online adaptation and for offline evaluation. This chapter addresses the issue of performance assessment in serious games. Performance is a complex concept comprising results and processes of actions and interactions of the players in and with the game. First, generic and domain-specific models of performance are introduced to illustrate the variety of approaches. Based on this knowledge, online and offline assessments of performance are discussed. Finally, the integration of online and offline performance assessment into the process of game adaptation is described.

10.1 Introduction

Imagine playing an educational serious game in physics where you try to solve tasks according to various quests. You take action and realize that you are unable to solve the tasks. Even worse, you do not get any hints or instructions to guide you to

J. Wiemeyer (✉)
Technische Universität Darmstadt, Darmstadt, Germany
e-mail: wiemeyer@sport.tu-darmstadt.de

M. Kickmeier-Rust · C.M. Steiner
Graz University of Technology, Graz, Austria

© Springer International Publishing Switzerland 2016
R. Dörner et al. (eds.), *Serious Games*, DOI 10.1007/978-3-319-40612-1_10

the solution. As a consequence, you feel angry or even disappointed. Further, imagine making progress in the game (after spending a long, hard time gaming). With increasing expertise, the tasks offered by the game may become very easy to solve. Therefore, you get increasingly bored. Obviously, the game does not offer tasks that are balanced enough—in the sense of establishing optimal difficulty according to your current competence and mood state—to challenge you. The game could have done much better if your current performance had been assessed continuously in order to use this information for appropriate adaptation and personalization. Perhaps the game would have realized your specific problem with a missing competence component, e.g., lacking knowledge about refraction. Furthermore, the game could have also determined your personal learning styles or preferences, and adapted the offered information accordingly.

Performance assessment in serious games is important for several reasons (see also Bellotti et al. 2013). First, as illustrated by the previous example, to maintain player experience and keep the players within the corridor of game flow the game has to be adaptive considering the current performance of the player. Second, to deliver feedback in the form of instructions, hints, score or awards the current performance of the player needs to be assessed. Third, to improve the game, information concerning the performance of all players is required, either for formative or summative evaluation. Fourth, summative evaluation is also required to deliver evidence for the effectivity and efficiency of the final version of the game.

Evaluation of serious games can be formative or summative. *Formative evaluation* is used during development and aims at testing and improving the serious game or parts of the game iteratively to eliminate all the weaknesses before finishing and releasing. *Summative evaluation* is the evaluation of the final serious game and aims at testing the end product according to certain guidelines, principles or standards.

To serve the above-mentioned goals, performance assessment has to be performed either online, i.e., during gameplay ("in-game" or "stealth"), or offline, i.e., after having finished playing the game (Ifenthaler et al. 2012a, b).

In this chapter, the issue of performance assessment in games is addressed. First, concepts and measures of game performance are introduced. Based on these conceptual fundamentals, advantages and challenges of online and offline assessment will be addressed. Finally, the relation of game assessment and game adaptation is discussed.

10.2   Performance in Games—Concepts and Measures

Performance in games is a complex concept. First, performance is always a process that evolves over time. For example, solving a problem may start with facing a problem, followed by thinking of possible solutions, and finally choosing and realizing one solution deemed appropriate. Second, performance brings forth observable or measurable results. Performance results or outcomes are specific to the particular application domain. Therefore, performance can mean solved tasks, change of health-related behavior or knowledge, awarded scores, knowledge gains, improved perceptual or motor skills or abilities, changed attitudes, etc. Whereas performance outcomes can be measured or observed easily, the processes lying behind these outcomes are often not as easily measurable or observable. For example, the correct or incorrect solution of a game task can be easily measured. However, the reasons for success or failure are not that obvious. In case of failure, the player may not have been motivated, or she may lack knowledge required to solve the task. Another possible reason may be that knowledge existed, but appropriate hints were missing to activate this knowledge. A further reason could be that the player was inattentive. Therefore, there are several possible reasons for a particular performance outcome. As a consequence, serious games require an explicit definition of performance to ensure appropriate assessment of both results and process of performance.

> Performance in games comprises both the *processes and the results of actions and interactions* of the player(s) in the game. Equal performance results can be established by different processes. Different levels, components, and stages of performance can be distinguished. Performance measures are specific to the domain of application.

In general, human performance is organized on different levels. First, performance is observable or measurable at the social, behavioral and physiological level. Second, psychological processes like perception and cognition, as well as motivation, emotion, and volition, play an important role in the control of human performance; unfortunately, psychological processes are not available for direct measurements in the strict sense. However, they can be either inferred from behavioral and physiological data or assessed by asking the players to report (see also Chap. 9).

There are numerous models that attempt to identify the building blocks of human performance. One type of models addresses the structure of *movements* as spatio-temporal or neurophysiological phenomena, whereas other models analyze the structure of *actions* as goal-directed, and intentionally organized human-environment interactions including cognitive, motivational, emotional, and volitional processes (see Fig. 10.1). The structure of movement is usually analyzed by means of methods

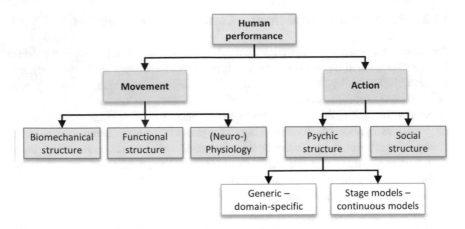

Fig. 10.1 Approaches to the structure of human performance

used in natural sciences like mathematics, physics, and biology. The structure of action is usually analyzed by psychology.

> Human performance can be considered as movement or action. The term *movement* denotes the spatio-temporal and neurophysiological aspects of human-environment interactions, whereas *action* denotes the socio-psychological aspect of goal-directed and intentionally organized human-environment interactions, including cognition, motivation, emotion, and volition.

According to models of movement structure, game movements can be divided into different components, e.g., preparatory, main and end phase, supportive or main functional phases, or action-effect relations (e.g., Wiemeyer 2003). These concepts are very important for exergames, where complex movements have to be learned. For example, for an evaluation and correction of errors it is important to know which error is most important and how errors are associated and interrelated. An error in movement preparation may lead to a subsequent error in the main phase that can easily be corrected when addressing the preparation error.

The neurophysiological aspects of movements comprise neural functions of the central nervous systems, particularly of the brain and spinal cord. Specific parts of the brain are responsible for controlling movement and action, e.g., the primary sensory and motor cortex, the supplementary and premotor cortex, the basal ganglia, and the cerebellum. In the spinal cord, several sensory-motor reflexes are organized (e.g., Houk and Wise 1995; Buschman and Miller 2014).

Psychological models of performance structure can be divided into general and domain-specific models. Another distinction is made between stage or process models and continuous models (e.g., Schwarzer 2008). Whereas stage models distinguish different phases of human performance regarding long-term or short-term control, continuous models distinguish different components of human performance, irrespective of stages. An example of a long-term stage model popular in health sciences is the transtheoretic model proposed by Prochaska et al. (2008). This model distinguishes six stages in the process of behavioral change: precontemplation, contemplation, preparation, action, maintenance, and termination. An example of a short-term stage model is the Rubicon model by Heckhausen (1991). This model tries to integrate motivational and volitional components in the preparation, initiation, maintenance, and evaluation of actions. Thus, stage models contribute to the understanding of the whole health process. They explain what happens in the respective phases and how phase transitions are established.

Examples of continuous models are the theory of planned behavior (TPB; Ajzen 1991), the self-determination theory (SDT; Ryan and Deci 2000), the social-cognitive theory (SCT; Bandura 1991), and behavioristic models, e.g., operant conditioning (OC; Abraham and Michie 2008; Lieberman 2001; Michie et al. 2011). Whereas the TPB emphasizes the influence of attitudes, subjective norms, self-efficacy, and perceived behavioral control on human intentions and behavior, SDT explains that human intrinsic motivation is substantially influenced by the human need for autonomy, competence, and social relatedness. Social relatedness is also addressed by SCT, which emphasizes the significance of role models for human behavior. Finally, OC stresses the importance of reinforcements and rewards for human behavior.

There are also attempts at integrating stages and components. A well-known example in the health domain is the health-action process approach (HAPA) by Schwarzer (2008). In this model, direct and indirect effects of outcome expectancies, risk perception and different forms of self-efficacy (i.e., concerning the initiation, maintenance, and recovery of actions) on intending, planning, and performing actions are described.

Another important type of general psychological models of human performance is proposed by action theory (e.g., Schack and Hackfort 2007). On the one hand, these models claim to be interdisciplinary in the sense that they try to integrate the above-mentioned monodisciplinary perspectives on human performance. For example, these models address social, physical, and psychological systems (respective levels) of human performance. On the other hand, human performance is analyzed based on both stage and continuous models. The basic stage model distinguishes three main stages of human performance: preparation or anticipation (including planning and calculation), realization (including processing and tuning), and interpretation (including evaluation and controlling). The cyclic nature of human action is illustrated in Fig. 10.2. The continuous model identifies three main constraints of action: Person, task and environment. This means: When an action is performed, there is a complex interaction of person, task, and environment. For example, if a person has to solve a task, the relations of the properties of the task (e.g., complexity), the person (e.g., competencies and motivation) and the environment (e.g., supportive vs. hostile) determine whether the attempt is successful or not. In case of failure, a person's competencies may not have been sufficient, the task was too difficult for the person, or the environment did not support (or even

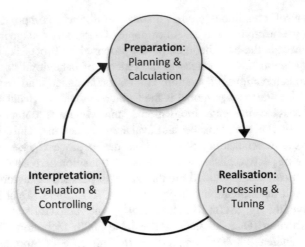

Fig. 10.2 Cyclic organization of human actions

impeded) a successful solution. The correct evaluation of these complex interactions is an important prerequisite of adequate adaptation in serious games.

Human performance can be generally analyzed from different perspectives (Fig. 10.1). On the one hand, natural sciences primarily analyze the *structure of movements*, whereas psychology analyzes the *structure of actions*. On the other hand, psychological models distinguish between *general* and *domain-specific* models as well as *stage* and *continuous* models of action.

Beyond generic aspects of human performance, every application field of serious games, every characterizing goal has its specific characteristics. Therefore, either the generic models mentioned above are adapted to the respective field, or new domain-specific performance models are developed. Taking the example of serious games for health: When the objective of the serious game is to change health-related behavior—for example, to stop or reduce smoking, to reorganize nutrition, to perform safer sexual practices or to increase habitual physical activity—the above-mentioned behavioral models are applied to derive game interventions (e.g., Lieberman 2001). Furthermore, in the area of health, numerous models have been developed addressing human behavior in particular. Examples are the Health Belief Model (HBM; Becker et al. 1977), the Health Action Process Approach (HAPA; Schwarzer 2008), and models explaining sustainable adherence to regular exercising (SARE; Wagner 2000; Fuchs et al. 2011; Williams and French 2011). Whereas the HBM explains the influences of individual cognition and motivation and modifying factors (i.e., demographic and sociopsychological variables) on the probability to initiate and maintain health-related actions, the HAPA model described above also considers intentions and planning activities. SARE models differentiate cognitive, motivational, and volitional variables influencing human intentions and behavior in early and late(r) stages of health activities. From these models, specific concepts can be derived for online (ingame) and offline assessment, for example subjective perceptions of benefits, risks, and barriers regarding health and health-related behavior, self-efficacy, or social support by friends, other players, or relatives.

For the domain of learning, education, and training: Generic learning approaches like behavioristic, cognitive, or constructivistic models are relevant for assessment (for a review, see Kearsley 1993). An interesting approach that has been successfully integrated into educational games is the theory of micro-adaptability (Kickmeier-Rust and Albert 2010, 2012a, b). This approach is based on competence-based knowledge space theory (CbKST); this approach separates observable behavior from non-observable constructs, i.e., skills or competencies. This approach will be addressed later in this chapter.

An important model for assessment in exergames and exertion games is the structural model of sport performance. This model is illustrated in Fig. 10.3.

Figure 10.3 shows that sport performance has several components. The components that can be addressed by exergames are mainly coordination (specific skills and general abilities), condition (endurance, strength, speed, and flexibility), as well as psychological and tactical competencies. Endurance regards cardiovascular fitness. Examples of coordinative abilities are balance, sensory differentiation, and spatial orientation.

Assessment in serious games has to consider the particular genre or field of application. Therefore, either generic models are adapted to the respective field or domain-specific models are used. From these models, measures can be derived for direct or indirect online and offline assessment.

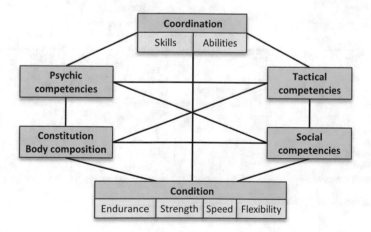

Fig. 10.3 Structure of sport performance

On the one hand, performance measures are very specific to the domain of the respective serious game. On the other hand, there are also generic performance measures.

At the spatio-temporal level the following measures can be assessed by means of biomechanical measurements (Fig. 10.4; e.g., Hay 1985; Bartlett 2007):

- *Kinematic measures*: trajectory or displacement, velocity, acceleration, joint angles, angular velocity, angular acceleration
- *Kinetic measures*: torque, angular momentum, force, work, power, and energy
- *Electrophysiological measures*: Electromyogram (EMG)

At the (neuro-)physiological level there are numerous measures located at the central or peripheral level (Fig. 10.5; Kivikangas et al. 2011; Bellotti et al. 2013):

- *Brain activation*: Electroencephalogram (EEG), Electrocorticogram (ECoG), Magnetoencephalogram (MEG), functional magnetic resonance imaging (fMRI)
- *Cardiovascular system*: electro-cardiogram (ECG), heart rate (HR), heart rate variability (HRV), blood pressure (BP)
- *Respiratory system*: breathing rate, inspiratory volume, oxygen uptake, ventilatory thresholds (VT1, VT2), respiratory exchange ratio (RER)
- *Skin*: electrodermal activity (EDA), skin conductance response (SCR), skin conductance level (SCL)
- *Visual system*: pupil diameter, pupil response

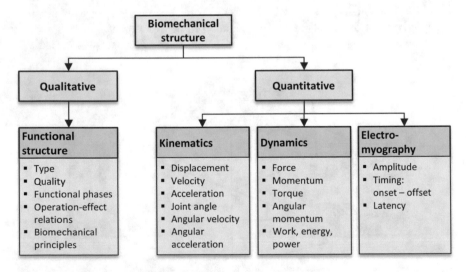

Fig. 10.4 Biomechanical analysis of human movements

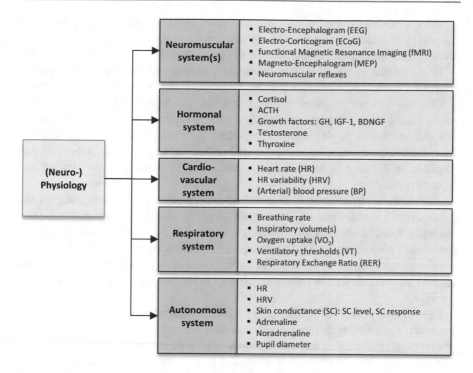

Fig. 10.5 (Neuro-)physiological measure of human performance

At the socio-psychological level, observable relations and interactions between people can be categorized, like making contact, withdrawing from contacts, cooperation, or conflicts, as well as communication behavior.

Specific performance measures pertain to the respective domain of the serious game. In Table 10.1, selected performance measures of selected domains of serious games are illustrated.

Table 10.1 Examples of domain-specific performance measures

Domain	Measures (examples)
Educational games	knowledge, attitude, skill level
Games for Health	knowledge, health-enhancing physical activity (HEPA), health-related behavior, health outcomes, attitude, fitness level
Reha(b)games	activities of daily living (ADL), various clinical scales and scores
Sport games	skill level, ability level, knowledge, sport performance
Advergames	knowledge, attitude, purchase
Persuasive games	persuasion, knowledge, attitude
Simulation and training games	"real world" behavior (transfer), strategic knowledge

In *educational games*, the educational impact is most important. Depending on the particular educational goal, performance can be measured by the application of knowledge or skill tests. Another commonly used method is attitude questionnaires.

In *games for health*, the most important performance measure is the specific impact on the respective health indicator. For example, in cardiovascular diseases (CVD), the relevant measures are heart rate, oxygen uptake, blood pressure, respiratory parameters, blood parameters, and energy expenditure. In addition, specific risk and protection factors are also important performance indicators. For CVD, these factors comprise adequate level of regular physical activity, smoking, and nutrition. In the area of health, often a distinction is made between primary and secondary outcomes.

The field of *reha(b)games* shows a considerable variety. According to the International Classification of Diseases (ICD-10; WHO 1992), numerous diseases can affect specific anatomical regions or functions of the human body. Therefore, the primary performance measures are specific to the particular disease. As already mentioned with games for health, primary and secondary risk and protection factors can be measured, as well as the components of health, according to the definition of the WHO.

Due to the variety of sports, *sport games* also comprise numerous relevant measures. Considering the performance model illustrated in Fig. 10.3, numerous measures of conditioning and coordination can be distinguished.

Advergames aim at advertising a product or a company. Therefore, all aspects relevant to product or company marketing are candidates for measures. Of course, the most important measure is purchases of the product. Secondary performance measures are publicity, knowledge of, and attitude towards the product or company.

Persuasive games aim primarily at changing attitudes and subsequently behavior. Persuasive games can address many application fields like politics, history, social sciences, and life sciences. Beyond attitude and behavior, knowledge measures are also often applied.

Simulation and training games aim at managing a particular situation or task under time pressure. Therefore, the most important performance measure is the successful transfer to real-world behavior. Often, specific declarative and strategic knowledge is required for and acquired in simulation and training games, e.g., if-then rules for decisions.

> For the adequate choice of a relevant performance measure, there is no "one size fits all" solution. Rather, either specific measures exist for particular groups—e.g., children versus adults, or healthy versus ill people—or generic measures are used, e.g., mood or motivation questionnaires. In addition, in many application domains there is no common agreement on a "gold standard." Therefore, choosing the correct measure is not at all trivial.

10.3 Online Assessment

Online assessment refers to the idea to ground assessment on the data that can be pulled out of games, primarily the log file data. The analysis of such data, however, is not trivial. Basically, there are two challenges that must be addressed. On the one hand, there is the problem that a large amount of information coming from the game—such as movements, actions, interactions with the game world and perhaps with other players—must be analyzed in real time (cf. Koidl et al. 2010). On the other hand, there is the perhaps even more difficult challenge to interpret the data in a valid and relevant way. There have been various attempts to draw specific conclusions about motivation, or sentiment, however, the results of research are unclear, and concrete applications are still sparse (Mattheiss et al. 2010).

The main focus of online assessment in the educational community is on learning performance. This naturally leads to the concepts of *Learning Analytics* (LA) (e.g., Ferguson 2012; Siemens 2012) and *Educational Data Mining* (EDM; EDM 2015). The concepts are paired with a real-time analysis of data coming from games. The main idea is to interpret the assessment results, which often have limited utility in an educational sense, in a formatively-inspired way. This means that the aim is to make the step from diagnosing to finding the right treatment. All this is closely related to the notion of intelligent tutorial technologies that, in turn, rely on robust assessment.

EDM has been defined as "an emerging discipline, concerned with developing methods for exploring the unique types of data that come from educational settings, and using those methods to better understand students and the settings which they learn in" (International Society of EDM, EDM 2015).

Baker and Yacef (2009) provided an extensive overview of EDM applications, developments, and definitions. EDM originates from many research areas, such as statistics, data mining, machine learning, visualization, and computational modeling, and aims to automatically discover patterns and models in huge and growing datasets. While in the beginnings of EDM, most data were retrieved from experimental learning sets that did not last longer than a few weeks. Today, such data are often tracked over the duration of an entire course and can last up to one year of studying. Collected data are further analyzed to gain valuable insights into learning processes. With these enormous amounts of data, new challenges arise, especially with regard to visualizing and modelling the information to make it readable and interpretable for human stakeholders.

While EDM aims to discover patterns and models in scaled data, learning analytics take into account the needs of different educational stakeholders and the strength of their judgement, in addition to computational measurements. Although EDM and LA focus on slightly different areas, they have similar goals that relate to improving educational technology and evaluating pedagogically sound instructional designs (Ferguson and Shum 2012). In particular, LA emphasizes supporting pedagogical approaches by providing assistance to teachers with practical issues (e.g., the quality of the learning material or the engagement of students in specific exercises). Data gained by LA tools can be used to evaluate pedagogically-sound instructional designs in classroom settings. In most cases, this mainly involves monitoring learner actions, and interactions with learning tools and learning peers (Lockyer and Dawson 2011). Many attempts have been made of visualizing such learning traces either to make significant relationships explicit or to allow stakeholders to discover such relationships independently. Research on using dashboards in LAs was performed for example by Duval (2011). These dashboards are graphical representations of activities and performance data of learners. As known in other domains (e.g., sports), visualization of collected interaction training data and their comparison with data of like-minded peers may not only provide insights into poor and good practices, but also increase motivation due to the playful introduction of competitiveness.

Chatti et al. (2012) presented a reference model for LA in which they distinguished four main dimensions:

- *Who?—Stakeholders*: This dimension refers to the people targeted by the analysis.
- *Why?—Objectives*: This dimension refers to the motivation for or goals of doing the analysis.
- *What? - Data and environment*: This dimension refers to the kind of data that is gathered, managed and used for analysis.
- *How?—Methods*: This dimension relates to the techniques and tools used for performing the analysis of collected data.

In addition to these main dimensions for the domain and application of LA, Greller and Drachlser (2012) identified two additional dimensions in their approach of defining a generic framework for LA:

- *External limitations*: This dimension refers to conventions (ethics, personal privacy, socially motivated limitations) and norms (legal and organisational constraints).
- *Internal limitations*: This dimension refers to relevant human factors, like competence (e.g., interpretation, critical thinking) and acceptance that may conflict with or complicate LA.

In principle, the objectives for using LA are in line with the different views of its stakeholder groups. Chatti et al. (2012) identified the following main objectives; these certainly have overlaps, and usually a specific application of LA will serve several of them (see Fig. 10.6).

- *Monitoring and analysis*: tracking and checking the learning process, which is then used by teachers or educational institutions as a basis for taking decisions, e.g., on future steps, the design of new learning activities, improving the learning environment.

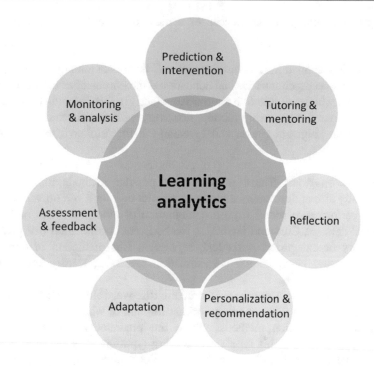

Fig. 10.6 Objectives of learning analytics

- *Prediction and intervention*: estimating learners' future knowledge or performance in terms of finding early indicators for learning success, failure, and potential dropouts, to be able to offer proactive interventions and support for learners in need of assistance.
- *Tutoring and mentoring*: helping learners with and in their whole learning process, or in the context of specific learning tasks or a course, providing guidance and advice.
- *Assessment and feedback*: supporting formative and summative (self) assessment of the learning process, examining efficiency and effectiveness of learning, and providing meaningful feedback of results to teachers and learners.
- *Adaptation*: Finding out what a learner should do or learn next and tailoring learning content, activities, or sequences to the individual. This idea of carefully calculated adjustments corresponds to the central aim and component of adaptive learning environments and intelligent tutoring systems.
- *Personalization and recommendation*: Helping learners to decide their own learning and learning environment, and what to do next by providing recommendations while leaving the control to the learner.
- *Reflection*: Prompting and increasing reflection or self-reflection on the teaching and learning process, learning progress and achievements made; providing

comparison with past experiences or achievements between learners, across classes, etc.

The methods applied in LA consider methods from data mining and analytics in general, as well as psychometrics and educational measurement as the main sources of inspiration, which fall into five main classes (see Fig. 10.7): prediction methods, structure discovery, relationship mining, discovery with models, and distillation of data for human judgment (Baker and Inventado 2014; Adomavicius and Tuzhilin 2005).

- *Prediction methods*: These are the most popular methods in EDM. They essentially aim at developing a model to predict or infer a certain variable (e.g., mark, performance score) from a combination of other indicators of the educational data set. Common prediction methods are classification (for prediction of binary or categorical variables), regression (for prediction of continuous variables), and latent knowledge estimation (assessing learner knowledge or skills).
- *Structure discovery*: Algorithms of structure discovery aim at detecting structure in educational data without an a priori assumption of what should be found (in contrast to prediction methods, where the predicted/dependent variable is known). Methods of this type are clustering (splitting data sets into clusters), factor analysis (finding dimensions of variables grouped together), and domain structure discovery (deriving the structure of knowledge in an educational domain).
- *Social network analysis* (SNA) is another method from this class, which is quite popular in LA (Siemens 2012). It allows one to analyze relationships and interactions between learners in terms of collaboration and communication activities, information exchange, etc. SNA uncovers the patterns and structure of interaction and connectivity, which can then be visually illustrated and provide the possibility of quantification (e.g., via centrality measures), to identify learners that are very important, represent "hubs," or are in isolation (Romero 2010).
- *Relationship mining*: The aim of this group of methods is to find out relationships between variables, and how strong those relationships are. Concrete

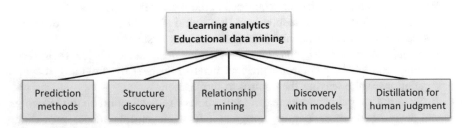

Fig. 10.7 Methods of learning analytics and educational data mining

methods are association rule mining (finding *if-then* rules), correlation mining (finding positive or negative linear correlations), sequential pattern mining (finding temporal associations between events), and causal data mining (finding out whether one observation is the cause of another).

- *Discovery with models*: This class does not denote a specific group of techniques but refers to the general approach of using the results of one analytics method within another analysis. A popular way of doing this is, for instance, to use a prediction model within another prediction model; however, there are a variety of other ways for conducting discovery with models.

- *Distillation of data for human judgment*: This is an approach quite common in LA, in a narrower sense, but not considered as a method of EDM, since it consists in providing teachers immediate access to reports and visualisations of the learner data for their interpretation, judgement and to support decision making and pedagogical action. Examples are learning curves or heat maps (Homer 2013; Baker et al. 2007).

Typically, LA is used to support teachers and instructors with deeper insights into learning processes. Games may serve as an ideal data source for LA. A crucial question is how to harness and make sense of this data in an effective and efficient manner. LA is currently in the process of initiating the elaboration of analytics that can be used for serious games. By using and combining ideas from gaming analytics, web analytics, and learning analytics, it is possible to establish meaningful analytics on data from games for educational purposes.

A great challenge with learning analytics in educational games is the wide variety of different games available, which complicates the development of analytics tools that are applicable to all games. To overcome this, Serrano-Laguna et al. (2012) propose a two-step generic approach to apply learning analytics in educational games, which is applicable to any kind of game. First, generic traces are gathered from gameplay, including game traces (start, end, and quit), phase changes (game chapters), input traces like mouse movements or clicks, and other meaningful variables like attempts or scores (depending on the game). This data gives rise to reports with general and game-agnostic information, like the number of students who played the game, the average playing time, game phases in which users stopped playing, etc. This information can be visually reported and may provide initial useful information on how learners interacted with the game. In a second step, additional information may be extracted by letting teachers define game-specific assessment rules based on and combining the generic game trace variables to obtain new information (e.g., setting maximum time thresholds, comparing actual and expected/required values of variables). These rules clearly need to be closely defined in line with each game to match the educational objectives; however, since the building blocks of these kinds of rules are elements from the basic set of traces, the creation and provision of template rules to support teachers in defining their own is conceivable.

To make use of learning analytics in educational games, a game platform needs to be used that allows the collection of the relevant data, and that holds a representation of game variables. The data for learning analytics will likely need to be stored and processed separately and remotely. To technically implement such analytics in an educational game, the definition of a learning analytics model and implementation of a learning analytics engine—which is separate from the game engine but communicates with it—has been proposed (Homer 2013). The learning analytics engine is conceived as comprising a set of modules enabling the different steps of the learning analytics process, from capturing data via aggregating and reporting, to evaluating in terms of transforming information into educational knowledge.

Assessment in a learning game may have two main purposes. First, just measuring the success of the student will serve to provide teachers and students with the derived information as a basis for action, like selecting new educational resources, deciding on additional support or learning tasks, etc. Second, the derived information may be used for realizing dynamic adaptation during game time through an adaptation model, and adapter (part of the learning analytics framework) communicating with the game engine.

An example of using learning analytics in a serious game has been presented by Baker et al. (2007); see also Miller et al. (2014). The authors also realized skill assessment in an educational action game by using game events (e.g., attacking and fleeing from an enemy) as evidence for users' mathematical skills. The authors deployed exponential empirical learning curves to determine player improvement in accuracy and speed. This approach proved useful for formative assessment in educational games, and may also be used to inform the redesign and improvement of intelligent tutoring systems. Another very recent LA attempt has been made towards elaborating an automated detector of engaged behavior in a simulation game (Stephenson et al. 2014). Their goal was to identify and model learner actions that give evidence of user engagement and, in the end, are predictive for success in the game. An integration of the engagement detector in the game will enable to report the results back to learners and teachers for reflection.

An approach to consider the structure of competencies was introduced by Kickmeier-Rust and Albert (2010); it is based on the notions of so-called competence-based knowledge space theory (CbKST) (cf., Kickmeier-Rust and Albert 2012a, b). The principal idea is to monitor each activity of a learner or a group of learner's exhibits, and to interpret the behavior in terms of available or lacking competencies or cognitive states such as motivation. Originally, this concept was developed in the European ELEKTRA project (ELEKTRA 2014) (and advanced in the following 80Days project (80Days n.d.). In the following, generic Web services have been developed around the micro-adaptation framework. The service-oriented architecture (as described by Carvalho et al. 2015) is based on a set of recommendations, policies, and practices for the design of software architectures which implements business processes, and it is using loosely coupled components that are arranged to deliver a certain level of service or set of functionalities (Hurwitz et al. 2007). The services are (partly) available and accessible through the service catalog platform of the Serious Games Society (Serious Games Society n.d.).

The service approach has been implemented and evaluated, for example, in primary level maths games. One example is the *Sonic Divider* (Kickmeier-Rust and Albert 2013a), a tool to practice the formal sequence of solving divisions at the level of third grade. In this case, the micro-adaptation framework builds upon a domain model that includes about 100 atomic competencies (including number dimensions, knowledge about sequences, rounding of numbers, etc.). The system identifies correct and incorrect actions of the learners and updates an underlying probability model of available competency states (in the sense of CbKST). This kind of believe model is then used to trigger highly targeted interventions (such as guidance or feedback), matching the competency levels of the learners well. The approach was also successfully applied to a multiplication game, named the *1 × 1 Ninja* which is based on a domain model for second grade multiplication skills including the number dimensions for multiplicand and multipliers. The tool can give tailored feedback, and it automatically adapts the difficulty level of the multiplication tasks to the performance of the learners. In school studies, we could show that suitable and individualized interventions are superior to no, non-individualized, or simple right/wrong statements.

A highly interesting application of the micro-adaptation framework and LA was realized in the context of the European Next-Tell project (Next Tell 2015). In this example a full teacher control suite that allows realizing educational sessions in virtual worlds (such as Second Life or OpenSim) has been developed. The tool analyzes the log files from the virtual world in real-time and—in greater detail— post hoc, and provides teachers with activity statistics, chat summaries, probabilities over competencies and competence states (based on heuristic-based analyses of activities), and real time messages (e.g., in case of unwanted activities such as using inappropriate language). In example studies with Norwegian and Austrian children who met and learned English together in an OpenSim environment, it was demonstrated that an appropriate feedback based on LA resulted in clear benefits for the teacher, who had the opportunity to monitor and document activities and, more importantly, to review language competencies (Kickmeier-Rust and Albert 2013b).

Learning Analytics (LA) and *Educational Data Mining (EDM)* aim at using activity and performance data from a game to draw educationally relevant conclusions. Their purposes are primarily providing learners with feedback, providing teachers and instructors with insight and overview, and allowing an adaptation of the game.

10.4 Offline Assessment

Whereas online assessment has to face challenges like real-time diagnostics and non-intrusiveness, offline assessment is much less challenging in this regard. Playing activities can be paused or finished before methods of offline assessment are administered. However, offline assessment also has to meet specific requirements. The most important requirement is to fulfill quality standards in the respective field or discipline. Unfortunately, in many application fields there is no consensus on one assessment method that represents the gold standard. Rather, many different methods are in use. Therefore, in this section the options in selected application domains of serious games are discussed without recommending particular methods. Depending on the structure of the respective field performance, knowledge, attitude and other psychological variables may be assessed on a qualitative or quantitative scale. The following fields will be addressed: health and rehabilitation, learning and education, sports and exercise, and training and simulation.

In principle, offline assessment can be qualitative or quantitative (see Fig. 10.8). Available methods comprise measurements, tests, observations, questionnaires, and (written or verbal) self-reports. Whereas measurements, tests and observations can be considered more or less direct methods of assessment, questionnaires and self-reports assess performance indirectly.

Offline Assessment in Games for Health

Due to the complexity of the health domain, numerous assessment methods are used. These methods are either based on specific health models or on a general understanding of health as a state of physical, psychological, and social well-being. Health and health-related behavior addressed in games for health comprise (regular) physical activity, nutritional behavior, perceptual-motor skills (e.g., falls, spatial vision) and abilities (e.g., balance and reaction), stress management, smoking, drug (mis-)use, asthma prevention, and safer sexual behavior (Baranowski et al. 2008; Lager and Bremberg 2005). In this section, we focus on assessment in prevention. Therapy and rehabilitation will be addressed in the next section.

In general, in the health domain the current health status has to be assessed. This can be done either by laboratory diagnostics, field tests or surveys. Well-known laboratory diagnostics are measurements of arterial blood pressure, biochemical

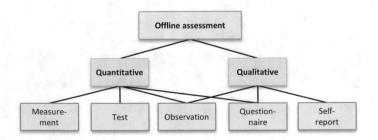

Fig. 10.8 Overview of methods for offline assessment

blood parameters like hemoglobin, liver enzymes, and other biochemical markers of organic functions. Concerning cardiorespiratory fitness, a broadly accepted indicator is the maximum oxygen uptake (VO_2max; for an overview of physiological methods, see Maud and Foster 2006). This measure indicates the aerobic capacity of the cardiorespiratory system. Normally, VO_2max is determined by a stepwise ergometer protocol (either cycle ergometer or treadmill). Starting from a low initial load (e.g., 25 or 50 W), the load is increased stepwise until certain criteria for exhaustion are reached. For example, in the WHO protocol for children, the initial load of 25 W is stepwise increased by 25 W every two minutes (Finger et al. 2013; see also Andersen et al. 1971). Furthermore, ramp tests exist that require less time for assessment (e.g., Poole et al. 2008).

Another indicator of physical activity (PA) that has often been assessed in videogames is energy expenditure (EE; e.g., Biddiss and Irwin 2010; Peng et al. 2011, 2013; Sween et al. 2014; Deutsch et al. 2015). EE can be measured as oxygen uptake (l/min), burned calories (kcal/h) or METs (metabolic equivalents). A well accepted finding is that active videogames increase EE at a low to moderate level, both in healthy and diseased populations (Fig. 10.9).

As another instrument to assess physical activity accelerometers are often used (Reilly et al. 2008). This instrument allows for objective assessment of PA over a longer period. Furthermore, activity logs or diaries (e.g., Garcia et al. 1997) as well as specific questionnaires exist for assessing regular PA (e.g., Baecke et al. 1982; for a critical review see Shephard 2003; Prince et al. 2008). For example, the Baecke questionnaire consists of 16 items addressing PA at work, in sport, and

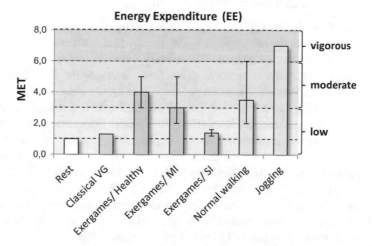

Fig. 10.9 Energy Expenditure (EE, in METs) while playing different kinds of video games versus performing locomotion activities (mean ± minimum/maximum). *Legend VG*—Video-games; *MI*—Mild neurological impairment; *SI*—Severe neurological impairment

during leisure. Based on these items three scores are calculated: work index, sport index, and leisure time index.

Concerning individual health, an often-applied instrument is the health status questionnaire for medical outcomes studies (MOS SF-36; McHorney et al. 1993; Ware and Sherbourne 1992; Ware 2000). The MOS SF-36 consists of 36 items and eight scales representing mental and physical health. It has been developed for self-administration by persons at the age of 14 years and older and for administration by trained interviewers. There also exists a short version (SF-12) with 12 items.

Nutritional knowledge and/or behavior can also be assessed by questionnaires for adults (Parmenter and Wardle 1999) and children (Wilson et al. 2008). The nutrition questionnaire for adults comprises 50 items addressing knowledge about food and nutrition, whereas the questionnaire for children consists of 14 items addressing actual nutrition behavior. A shorter 20-item questionnaire has been validated by Dickson-Spillmann et al. (2011). There also exists a computer-supported interview tool for assessing nutrition (Bakker et al. 2003). Furthermore, nutrition can be documented over a certain time period in a nutrition log or diary.

Health-related indicators of physical fitness like motor skills and abilities can be measured by specific field tests like balance, jump, or run tests. Bös (2001) gives an overview of about 700 single tests. According to Fig. 10.3 these tests can be used to assess elementary and complex motor skills, motor abilities, or conditioning abilities like strength, power, endurance, speed, and flexibility—as well as complex combinations of coordination and condition. As in the other areas, questionnaires exist asking the players to self-estimate their physical fitness level (e.g., Strøyer et al. 2007; Bös et al. 2002; Knapik et al. 1992).

Offline Assessment in Therapy and Rehabilitation

Offline assessment in therapy and rehabilitation depends on the specific disease. Beyond the primary outcomes targeted by the therapy further effects can be assessed. For example, in neurorehabilitation, the primary outcome is the improvement of mental and sensorimotor functions. Therefore, instruments like Fugl-Meyer assessment (FMA), Postural Assessment Scale (PASS), the Assessment for Motor Ability (AMA), Wolf Motor Function Test (WMFT), Stroke Impact Scale (SIS), and the Functional Independence Measure (FIM) are applied. For example, the FMA is a 226-point scale comprising five domains (motor function, sensory function, balance, joint range of motion, and joint pain; Gladstone et al. 2002). There are also domain-specific instruments like the Berg Balance Scale (for a review, see Blum and Korner-Bitensky 2008). The Berg Balance Scale has been widely used in stroke rehabilitation. The scale consists of 14 items rated from 0 to 4. The above-mentioned instruments have also been applied in the evaluation of serious games in neurorehabilitation (reviews: Staiano and Flynn 2014, Wiemeyer 2014).

Another important therapy field is cancer. In order to establish a good primary outcome, patients have to adhere to long-lasting and strenuous therapy, often including periods of self-medication and chemotherapy. Compliance to therapy can be assessed by subjective methods like self-reports and questionnaires, or by

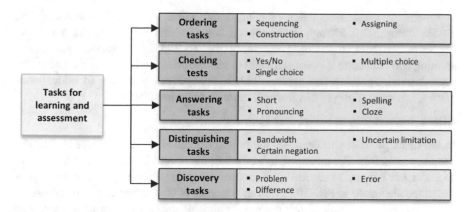

Fig. 10.10 Taxonomy of tasks for assessing learning effects (according to Meder 2006)

objective measures like blood assays and clinic visit attendance. An example of a successful application of these assessment methods is given by Kato et al. (2008), who could prove that playing a cancer-related videogame (*Re-mission*; Hope Labs 2015) has positive effects both on subjective and objective assessment scores.

Offline Assessment in Learning and Education

The primary outcome of serious games in learning and education is increased knowledge and skills. Knowledge can be declarative, e.g., the successful recall of facts, or procedural, e.g., drawing a circle or constructing a triangle. Therefore knowledge and skill tests are appropriate assessment methods. There are many approaches for assessment of learning and education in pedagogy and psychology. Three mainstreams in learning theory have already been mentioned: Behaviorism, cognitivism, and constructivism (Kearsley 1993; Egenfeldt-Nielsen 2006). Whereas *behaviorism* focusses on learning by stimulus-response connections supported by repetitions and reinforcement, *cognitivism* analyzes the information processing during learning supported by instruction and feedback. *Constructivism* states the importance of authentic learning environments and social communication. As an example of a cognitive approach, the Component Display theory by Merrill (1983) distinguishes between four types of learning content (fact, concept, procedure, principle) and three types of use (remember, use, find). From these 10 meaningful content combinations,[1] a use can be derived that can be assessed, e.g., remembering facts, using concepts or principles, or finding new procedures or principles. A similar approach comprising four types of learning content (fact, concept, procedure, meta-cognition) and six type of use (remember, understand, apply, analyze, evaluate, create) has been proposed by Krathwohl (2002). Another approach is to distinguish different kinds of tasks. In his "Web-Didaktik," Meder (2006) develops a hierarchical taxonomy of tasks (see Fig. 10.10).

---

[1]Note that two combinations have been removed because they do not make sense, i.e., finding and using facts.

Prominent application fields of educational games are learning mathematics, physics, geography, history, health-related behavior and languages (for a review, see Egenfeldt-Nielsen 2006). Concerning the assessment of serious games for learning and education it is not sufficient to test the primary outcomes, i.e., what has been learned by using the games. Rather, the secondary effects of educational games, i.e., how a player has learned, deserve scientific attention.

Offline Assessment in Sport and Exercise

In the fields of sport and exercise, the primary outcome is performance in specific sports or exercises. For example, in basketball the scored baskets and in soccer the scored goals can be assessed. Furthermore, according to the model of sport performance illustrated in Fig. 10.3, various subareas of competencies can be assessed: conditioning, coordination, tactics, psychological, and social competencies. For example, numerous tests for strength, endurance, flexibility, and speed as well as for tactical behavior, coordinative abilities, and sport skills have been developed. For example, commonly used performance measures of endurance are the time needed to run a certain distance (e.g., 3,000 m), or the distance covered within a prescribed time (e.g., 12 min in the Cooper test). An example of a power test is the jump-and-reach test, where the task is to jump as high as possible from a standing position.

Furthermore, sport psychology has validated many generic or sport-specific tests for cognition, perception, emotions, motivation and volition (e.g., Tenenbaum and Eklund 2007).

Particularly sensorimotor skill and knowledge tests have been assessed in studies on serious games in sport and exercise (for a review, see Wiemeyer and Hardy 2013).

Offline Assessment in Training and Simulation

In a way, training and simulation is a specific form of learning. Training denotes all measures aiming at the systematic, purposeful and sustainable change of human competencies and behavior. Simulations are manipulations applied to a physical or computational model. Simulations are used when it is too expensive, unethical or simply impossible to perform experiments with the original. Therefore, the most important outcome of learning and training with simulations is the transfer to the "real world" situation. This transfer can be direct, i.e., showing the behavior acquired in the simulation immediately in the real world situation, or indirect, i.e., gaining knowledge about principles or strategies to facilitate the transfer. As a consequence, methods for direct and indirect assessment of training and simulation can be applied. Unfortunately, existing reviews and meta-analyses do not distinguish between these two kinds of assessment (Lee 1999; Vogel et al. 2006). However, they prove that appropriately instructed, engaged, and playful use of simulations may enhance performance.

Offline assessment of human performance is specific to the respective application field of serious games. In this regard, many assessment methods exist ranging from measurements via tests and observations to reports and surveys. In many fields, no "gold standard" has been agreed upon. Therefore, the great challenge is to select the method(s) that meet best the requirements for the particular offline assessment.

10.5   Performance Assessment and Game Adaptation

As pointed out in the chapter introduction, performance assessment serves numerous functions in serious games. One important function is the adaptation of the game to changes in the current performance of the player (see also Chap. 7). First, adaptation of a game has to consider more or less static characteristics of the player like age, gender, experience level, level of expertise, etc. In addition, rehabilitation games have to adapt to the degree of impairment. This type of adaptation is called *macro-adaptation* (e.g., Kickmeier-Rust and Albert 2012a, b). A second type of adaptation is much more dynamic and depends on the current state of the game. This type of adaptation, called *micro adaptation*, depends very much on online performance assessment. In Fig. 10.11, the relation of performance assessment and micro adaptation is illustrated.

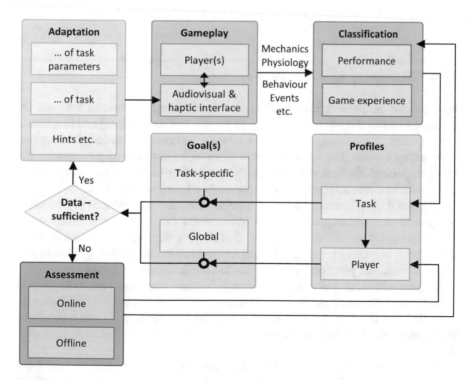

Fig. 10.11 The relation of performance assessment and adaptation in serious games

During gameplay the player interacts with the audiovisual and haptic interface of the game. Depending on the sensors used, different sensory information can be recorded as a result of the player-game interaction. For example, the kinematics and dynamics of the player's movements like forces or acceleration can be measured, as well as the physiological reactions like heart rate or energy expenditure. Furthermore, events like pressed buttons or keys can be registered. This sensor data can be used both for performance classification and player experience classification (see Chap. 9). For example, the biomechanical data may signify a particular movement error that has to be corrected. Or the physiological data may indicate that the emotional arousal of the player is decreasing. Based on the results of the classification, the task profile—and consequently the player profile—can be updated. These profiles are then compared to the task-specific and global goals, respectively. If the data suggests an adaptation of the game, decisions have to be taken whether to change the task as such, adjust task parameters, or to use other means of adaptation, e.g., hints or encouragements. If the data is not sufficient for an adaptation, a decision has to be made whether to initiate further online, i.e., in-game assessment, or off-line assessment. In order to not disrupt the game, online assessment is preferred. However, the options for online assessment may be not sufficient to get valid information concerning the current performance state. For example, this may happen in serious games for rehabilitation when the performance of the patient does not improve. To identify potential causes of the stagnation, a thorough clinical examination may be required.

10.6 Summary and Questions

Performance assessment in serious games is important for several reasons, for example to adapt the game dynamically to progress of the player(s) and to evaluate game quality. Performance denotes the process and result of actions and interactions within a game. The numerous approaches to the structure of performance can be distinguished into movement-based versus action-based approaches. Furthermore, different levels, stages, and components of performance regulation can be distinguished. Assessment of different aspects of human performance can be based on generic or domain-specific models. Assessment can be performed online, i.e., during gameplay, or offline, i.e., at the end of playing the game. Due to the different levels and components of performance, biomechanical, (neuro-)physiological, observational, and psychological methods are available for assessment.

Online assessment poses major challenges because assessment has to be done in realtime and without disturbing the ongoing game. Using the example of games for education and learning, the approaches of learning analytics (LA) and educational data mining (EDM) have been introduced to illustrate the demands on online assessment.

Offline assessment has to consider the methodological standards in the respective application field. In the health domain, specific options of measuring, observing, testing, or self-reporting health-related activities and knowledge are available.

In education and learning domains, as well as in simulation and training domains, the most important requirement is to assess learning and transfer, respectively. In sport and exercise domains, assessment focuses on the whole or parts of the complex structure of sport and exercise performance.

Check your understanding of this chapter by answering the following questions:

- What does the concept of "human performance" mean?
- What is the difference between movement-oriented and action-oriented approaches to human performance?
- Which stages are distinguished by the action theory of human performance?
- Which components are distinguished in the generic model of sport performance?
- Which metrics are assessed by biomechanical analysis of performance?
- Which metrics are assessed by (neuro-)physiological analysis of performance?
- What does the term "learning analytics" mean?
- What is meant by "educational data mining?"
- What are the objectives of learning analytics?
- What are the methods of learning analytics and educational data mining?
- What are the specific challenges in online assessment?
- What are the options for offline assessment in the field of health?
- What are the options for offline assessment in the field of rehabilitation?
- What are the options for offline assessment in the field of learning and education?
- What are the options for offline assessment in the field of training and simulation?
- What are the options for offline assessment in the field of sport and exercise?
- How can online and offline assessment be integrated in the adaptation of serious games?

Recommended Literature

GALA (ed) (2014) Learning analytics for and in serious games. http://css-kmi.tugraz.at/mkrwww/leas-box/downloads/ectel14_booklet.pdf. Accessed 18 Feb 2016—*This booklet gives an overview of current issues and methods in the field of learning analytics in serious games*

Ifenthaler D, Eseryel D, Ge X (eds) (2012) Assessment in game-based learning: Foundations, Innovations, and Perspectives. Springer, New York—*This book provides an overview of assessment in games. Different assessment methods and methodologies are introduced and discussed concerning their specific strengths and weaknesses. Technological and methodological approaches are addressed, as well as issues of practical application of assessment in games and game-based learning*

Larusson JA & White B (eds) (2014) Learning Analytics—From Research to Practice. Springer, New York—*This book is an introduction to learning analytics: Methods, theory, and practical applications are addressed*

References

80Days (n.d.) 80Days—Around an inspiring virtual learning world in eighty days. www. eightydays.eu. Accessed 18 Feb 2016

Abraham C, Michie S (2008) A taxonomy of behavior change techniques used in interventions. Health Psychol 27(3):379–387

Adomavicius G, Tuzhilin A (2005) Toward the next generation of recommender systems: a survey of the state-of-the-art and possible extensions. IEEE Trans Knowl Data Eng 17:734–749

Ajzen I (1991) The theory of planned behaviour. Organ Behav Hum Dec 50:179–211

Andersen KL, Shephard RJ, Denolin H, Varnauskas E, Masironi R (1971) Fundamentals of exercise testing. WHO, Geneva

Baecke JA, Burema J, Frijters JE (1982) A short questionnaire for the measurement of habitual physical activity in epidemiological studies. Am J Clin Nutr 36(5):936–942

Baker R, Inventado PS (2014) Educational data mining and learning analytics. In: Larusson JA, White B (eds) Learning analytics: from research to practice. Springer, New York, Germany, pp 61–75

Baker R, Yacef K (2009) The state of educational data mining in 2009: a review and future visions. JEDM 1(1):3–17

Baker RS, Habgood MJ, Ainsworth SE, Corbett AT (2007) Modeling the acquisition of fluent skill in educational action games. Proceedings of User Modeling 2007. Springer, Berlin, pp 17–26

Bakker I, Twisk JWR, Van Mechelen W, Mensink GBM, Kemper HCG (2003) Computerization of a dietary history interview in a running cohort: evaluation within the Amsterdam growth and health longitudinal study. Eur J Clin Nutr 57(3):394–404

Bandura A (1991) Social cognitive theory of self-regulation. Organ Behav Hum Dec 50 (2): 248–287

Baranowski T, Buday R, Thompson DI, Baranowski J (2008) Playing for real: video games and stories for health-related behavior change. Am J Prev Med 34(1):74–82

Bartlett R (2007) Introduction to sports biomechanics: analysing human movement patterns, 2nd edn. Routledge, London

Becker MH, Haefner DP, Kasl SV, Kirscht JP, Maiman LA, Rosenstock IM (1977) Selected psychosocial models and correlates of individual health-related behaviors. Med Care 15(5): 27–46

Bellotti F, Kapralos B, Lee K, Moreno-Ger P, Berta R (2013) Assessment in and of serious games: an overview. Adv Hum-Comput Interact 2013:136864. doi:10.1155/2013/136864

Biddiss E, Irwin J (2010) Active video games to promote physical activity in children and youth: a systematic review. Arch Pediat Adol Med 164(7):664–672

Blum L, Korner-Bitensky N (2008) Usefulness of the berg balance scale in stroke rehabilitation: a systematic review. Phys Ther 88(5):559–566

Bös K (ed) (2001) Handbuch motorische tests. [Handbook of perceptual-motor tests] Hogrefe, Göttingen

Bös K, Abel T, Woll A, Niemann S, Tittlbach S, Schott N (2002) Der Fragebogen zur Erfassung des motorischen Funktionsstatus (FFB-Mot). [Questionnaire for assessing the state of motor functions]. Diagnostica 48(2):101–111

Buschman TJ, Miller EK (2014) Goal-direction and top-down control. Philos Trans R Soc B 369 (1655):0130471

Carvalho MB, Bellotti F, Berta R, De Gloria A, Gazzarata G, Hu J, Kickmeier-Rust M (2015) The journey: a service-based adaptive Serious Game on probability. Entertainment Comput 6:1–10

Chatti MA, Dyckhoff AL, Schroeder U, Thüs H (2012) A reference model for learning analytics. IJTEL 5:318–331

Deutsch JE, Guarrera-Bowlby P, Myslinski MJ, Kafri M (2015) Is there evidence that active videogames increase energy expenditure and exercise intensity for people poststroke and with cerebral palsy? Games Health J 4(1):31–36

Dickson-Spillmann M, Siegrist M, Keller C (2011) Development and validation of a short, consumer-oriented nutrition knowledge questionnaire. Appetite 56(3):617–620

Duval E (2011) Attention please! Learning analytics for visualization and recommendation. In: Proceedings of 1st international conference on learning analytics and knowledge. ACM, New York, pp 9–17

Egenfeldt-Nielsen S (2006) Overview of research on the educational use of video games. Digital kompetanse 1(3):184–213

EDM (2015) International data mining society. http://www.educationaldatamining.org/. Accessed 18 Feb 2016

ELEKTRA (2014) ELECTRA—Enhancing learning in ENPI countries through clean technologies and research related activities. http://kti.tugraz.at/css/projects/elektra/. Accessed 18 Feb 2016

Ferguson R (2012) Learning analytics: drivers, developments and challenges. IJTEL 4(5/6): 304–317

Ferguson R, Shum SB (2012) Social learning analytics: five approaches. In: Proceedings of 2nd international conference on learning analytics and knowledge. ACM, New York, pp 23–33

Finger J, Gößwald A, Härtel S, Müters S, Krug S, Hölling H, Kuhnert R, Bös K (2013) Measurement of cardiorespiratory fitness in the German health interview and examination survey for adults (DEGS1). Bundesgesundheitsbl 56:885–893

Fuchs R, Goehner W, Seelig H (2011) Long-term effects of a psychological group intervention on physical exercise and health: The MoVo concept. J Phys Act Health 8(6):794–803

Garcia AW, George TR, Coviak C, Antonakos C, Pender NJ (1997) Development of the child/adolescent activity log: a comprehensive and feasible measure of leisure-time physical activity. Int J Behav Med 4(4):323–338

Gladstone DJ, Danells CJ, Black SE (2002) The Fugl-Meyer assessment of motor recovery after stroke: a critical review of its measurement properties. Neurorehab Neural Re 16(3):232–240

Greller W, Drachsler H (2012) Translating learning into numbers: a generic framework for learning analytics. JETS 15:42–57

Hay JG (1985) The biomechanics of sports techniques. Prentice Hall, New Jersey

Heckhausen H (1991) Volition: Implementation of intentions. In: Heckhausen H (ed) Motivation and Action. Springer, Berlin, pp 163–188

Homer BD (2013) Overview. Introductory Talk to the Learning Analytics and Educational Data Mining Workshop," CREATE Lab, New York University, April 2013 http://create.nyu.edu/wordpress/wp-content/uploads/2013/04/01.HOMER_.LEARNING.ANALYTICS. WORKSHOP.04.04.13.pdf. Accessed 18 Feb 2016

Hope Labs (2015) Re-Mission. www.re-mission.net. Accessed 18 Feb 2016

Houk JC, Wise SP (1995) Distributed modular architectures linking basal ganglia, cerebellum, and cerebral cortex: their role in planning and controlling action. Cereb Cortex 5(2):95–110

Hurwitz J, Bloor R, Baroudi C, Kaufman M (2007) Service oriented architecture for dummies. Wiley, Indianapolis

Ifenthaler D, Eseryel D, Ge X (eds) (2012b) Assessment in game-based learning: foundations, innovations, and perspectives. Springer, New York

Kato PM, Cole SW, Bradlyn AS, Pollock BH (2008) A video game improves behavioral outcomes in adolescents and young adults with cancer: a randomized trial. Pediatrics 122:e305–e317

Kearsley G (1993) Hypertext as a tool for the metatheoretical analysis of learning theories: the TIP database. JCHE 4(2):43–56

Kickmeier-Rust MD, Albert D (2010) Micro adaptivity: protecting immersion in didactically adaptive digital educational games. J Comput Assist Lear 26:95–105

Kickmeier-Rust M, Albert D (2012a) Educationally adaptive: balancing Serious games. Int J Comput Sci Sport 11(1):15–28

Kickmeier-Rust MD, Albert D (eds) (2012b) An Alien's guide to multi-adaptive educational games. Informing Science Press, Santa Rosa, CA

Kickmeier-Rust MD, Albert D (2013a) Gamification and intelligent feedback mechanisms for a division learning tool. In: Escudeiro P, de Carvalho CV (eds) Proceedings of 7th European conference on games based learning, Oct 2–3, 2013, Porto, Portugal, pp 290–296

Kickmeier-Rust MD, Albert D (2013b) Learning analytics to support the use of virtual worlds in the classroom. In: Holzinger A, Pasi G (Eds) Human-computer interaction and knowledge discovery in complex, unstructured, big data. lecture notes in computer science, 7947, Springer, Berlin, pp 358–365

Kivikangas JM, Chanel G, Cowley B, Ekman I, Salminen M, Järvelä S, Ravaja N (2011) A review of the use of psychophysiological methods in game research. JGVW 3(3):181–199

Knapik JJ, Jones BH, Reynolds KL, Staab JS (1992) Validity of self-assessed physical fitness. Am J Prev Med 8(6):367–372

Koidl K, Mehm F, Hampson C, Conlan O, Göbel S (2010) Dynamically adjusting digital educational games towards learning objectives. In: Proceedings of 3rd European Conference on Game Based Learning (ECGBL), October 2010

Krathwohl DR (2002) A revision of Bloom's taxonomy: an overview. Theor Pract 41(4):212–218

Lager A, Bremberg S (2005) Health effects of video and computer game playing. A systematic review. Swedish National Institute of Public Health, Stockholm

Lee J (1999) Effectiveness of computer-based instructional simulation: a meta analysis. Int J Instr Media 26(1):71–85

Lieberman DA (2001) Management of chronic pediatric diseases with interactive health games: theory and research findings. J Ambul Care Manage 24(1):26–38

Lockyer L, Dawson S (2011) Learning designs and learning analytics. In: Proceedings of 1st international conference on learning analytics and knowledge. ACM, New York, pp 153–156

Mattheiss E, Kickmeier-Rust MD, Steiner CM, Albert D (2010) Approaches to detect discouraged learners: assessment of motivation in educational computer games. In: Proceedings of eLearning Baltics (eLBa) 2010, July 1–2, 2010, Rostock, Germany

Maud PJ, Foster C (2006) Physiological assessment of human fitness. Human Kinetics, Champaign, Illinois

McHorney CA, Ware JE Jr, Raczek AE (1993) The MOS 36-item short-form health survey (SF-36): II. Psychometric and clinical tests of validity in measuring physical and mental health constructs. Med Care 31(3):247–263

Meder N (2006) Web-Didaktik—Eine neue Didaktik webbasierten, vernetzten Lernens. [Web didactics—a new didactics of web-based networked learning] Bertelsmann, Bielefeld

Merrill MD (1983) Component display theory. In: Reigeluth CM (ed) Instructional-design theories and models: an overview of their current status. Erlbaum, Hillsdale, NJ, pp 279–333

Michie S, Ashford S, Sniehotta FF, Dombrowski SU, Bishop A, French DP (2011) A refined taxonomy of behaviour change techniques to help people change their physical activity and healthy eating behaviours: the CALO-RE taxonomy. Psychol Health 26(11):1479–1498

Miller WL, Baker RS, Rossi LM (2014) Unifying computer-based assessment across conceptual instruction, problem-solving, and digital games. Technol Knowl Learn 19:165–181

Next Tell (2015) Next-Tell. Next generation teaching, education and learning for life. http://next-tell.de/. Accessed 18 Feb 2016

Parmenter K, Wardle J (1999) Development of a general nutrition knowledge questionnaire for adults. Eur J Clin Nutr 53(4):298–308

Peng W, Lin J-H, Crouse JC (2011) Is playing exergames really exercising? A meta-analysis of energy expenditure in active video games. Cyberpsychol Behav Soc Netw 14(11):681–688

Peng W, Crouse JC, Lin JH (2013) Using active video games for physical activity promotion: a systematic review of the current state of research. Health Educ Behav 40(2):171–192

Poole DC, Wilkerson DP, Jones AM (2008) Validity of criteria for establishing maximal O_2 uptake during ramp exercise tests. Eur J Appl Physiol 102(4):403–410

Prince SA, Adamo KB, Hamel ME, Hardt J, Gorber SC, Tremblay M (2008) A comparison of direct versus self-report measures for assessing physical activity in adults: a systematic review. Int J Behav Nutr Phys Act 5(1):56

Prochaska JO, Redding CA, Evers K (2008) The transtheoretical model and stages of change. In: Glanz K, Lewis FM, Rimer BK (eds) Health behavior and health education, 4th edn. Jossey-Bass, San Francisco, pp 97–121

Reilly JJ, Penpraze V, Hislop J, Davies G, Grant S, Paton JY (2008) Objective measurement of physical activity and sedentary behaviour: review with new data. Arch Dis Child 93(7): 614–619

Romero C (2010) Educational data mining: a review of the state of the art. IEEE Trans Syst Man Cybern C 40:601–618

Ryan RM, Deci EL (2000) Self-determination theory and the facilitation of intrinsic motivation, social development, and well-being. Am Psychol 55(1):68–78

Schack T, Hackfort D (2007) Action theory approach to applied sport psychology. In: Tenenbaum G, Eklund RC (eds) Handbook of sport psychology, 3rd edn. John Wiley and Sons, New York, pp 332–351

Schwarzer R (2008) Modeling health behavior change: how to predict and modify the adoption and maintenance of health behaviors. Appl Psychol 57(1):1–29

Serious Games Society (n.d.). Serious games web services catalog. http://services. seriousgamessociety.org/. Accessed 18 Feb 2016

Serrano-Laguna A, Torrente J, Moreno-Ger P, Fernández-Manjón B (2012) Tracing a little for big improvements: application of learning analytics and videogames for student assessment. Procedia Comput Sci 15:203–209

Shephard RJ (2003) Limits to the measurement of habitual physical activity by questionnaires. Br J Sports Med 37(3):197–206

Siemens G (2012) Learning analytics: envisioning a research discipline and a domain of practice. In: Proceedings of international conference on learning analytics and knowledge, ACM, New York, pp 4–8

Staiano AE, Flynn R (2014) Therapeutic uses of active videogames: a systematic review. Games Health J 3(6):351–365

Stephenson S, Baker R, Corrigan S (2014) Towards building an automated detector of engaged and disengaged behavior in game-based assessments. In: Poster, annual conference on games + learning + society

Strøyer J, Essendrop M, Jensen LD, Warming S, Avlund K, Schibye B (2007) Validity and reliability of self-assessed physical fitness using visual analogue scales. Percept Mot Skills 104 (2):519–533

Sween J, Wallington SF, Sheppard V, Taylor T, Llanos AA, Adams-Campbell LL (2014) The role of exergaming in improving physical activity: a review. J Phys Act Health 11(4):864–870

Tenenbaum G, Eklund RC (eds) (2007) Handbook of sport psychology. Wiley, New York, NY

Vogel JJ, Vogel DS, Cannon-Bowers J, Bowers JC, Muse K, Wright M (2006) Computer gaming and interactive simulations for learning: a meta-analysis. J Educ Comput Res 34(3):229–243

Wagner P (2000) Aussteigen oder Dabeibleiben? [Drop out or continue?] Wissenschaftliche Buchgesellschaft, Darmstadt

Ware JE Jr (2000) SF-36 health survey update. Spine 25(24):3130–3139

Ware JE Jr, Sherbourne CD (1992) The MOS 36-item short-form health survey (SF-36): I. Conceptual framework and item selection. Med Care 30(6):473–483

Wiemeyer J (2003) Function as constitutive feature of movements in sport. Int J Comput Sci Sport 2(2):113–115

Wiemeyer J (2014) Serious games in neurorehabilitation—a review of recent evidence. SeriousGames'14, Proc. ACM international workshop on serious games. ACM, New York, pp 33–38

Wiemeyer J, Hardy S (2013) Serious games and motor learning—concepts, evidence, technology. In: Bredl K, Bösche W (eds) Serious games and virtual worlds in education, professional development and healthcare. IGI Global, Heshey, PA, pp 197–220

Williams SL, French DP (2011) What are the most effective intervention techniques for changing physical activity self-efficacy and physical activity behaviour—and are they the same? Health Educ Res 26(2):308–322

Wilson AM, Magarey AM, Mastersson N (2008) Reliability and relative validity of a child nutrition questionnaire to simultaneously assess dietary patterns associated with positive energy balance and food behaviours, attitudes, knowledge and environments associated with healthy eating. Int J Behav Nutr Phys Act 5(1):5

World Health Organization [WHO] (1992) The ICD-10 classification of mental and behavioural disorders: Clinical descriptions and diagnostic guidelines. World Health Organization, Geneva

Serious Games—Economic and Legal Issues

11

Stefan Göbel, Oliver Hugo, Michael Kickmeier-Rust
and Simon Egenfeldt-Nielsen

Abstract

Serious games are fascinating, not only as a popular research field, but also as a relevant economic factor for the prospering game industry. The use of advanced gaming concepts and game technology applied to non-leisure contexts (e.g., education, training, health) is a logical and promising approach, but acceptance by the gaming industry itself (game developers, publishers), intermediaries (e.g., training departments in a company investing into recruiting or qualification programs), and consumers (individuals, groups; private persons, customers, employees and trainees) is low so far, and a market breakthrough of serious games is still missing. What are the reasons for this? The reasons are manifold, ranging from (a) low development budgets and poor quality of existing serious games to (b) the complexity and cost-intensive, multidisciplinary development of serious games matching the needs of individuals and groups and (c) missing scientific evidence that proves beneficial effects of serious games. Further, legal and security issues such as intellectual property rights, data protection, and privacy—particularly in the context of personalized educational games, or games for health improvement and behavior change—represent major challenges in the complex field of serious games. This chapter tackles the economic side of serious games and explains major challenges and obstacles that currently hinder

S. Göbel (✉)
Technische Universität Darmstadt, Darmstadt, Germany
e-mail: stefan.goebel@kom.tu-darmstadt.de

O. Hugo
University of Applied Sciences in Aschaffenburg, Aschaffenburg, Germany

M. Kickmeier-Rust
Graz University of Technology, Graz, Austria

S. Egenfeldt-Nielsen
Serious Games Interactive, Copenhagen, Denmark

© Springer International Publishing Switzerland 2016
R. Dörner et al. (eds.), *Serious Games*, DOI 10.1007/978-3-319-40612-1_11

303

a market breakthrough. It starts with an overview of the current status quo of the serious games market. Then, economic insights and trends, business and distribution models, and legal issues are discussed.

11.1 Introduction: Status Quo of the Serious Games Market

As the European Commission states in its call *ICT 21–2014: Advanced digital gaming and gamification technologies* (EU ICT21 2014)—which is part of the *LEIT—Information and Communication Technologies* sector (EU LEIT 2020) within the Horizon 2020 program (EU Horizon 2020)—on one hand, advanced gaming concepts are seen as both a promising innovative technology and a key driver of creative industries in Europe. This explicitly includes serious games as those using game concepts and game technologies in an application area beyond entertainment. On the other hand, the call addresses the field's current complexity, variety, and diversity, resulting in a *scattered industry*. Serious games are implemented in manifold application areas (Sawyer and Smith 2008) with different stakeholders involved as well as specific technological and socio-economic characteristics. The following statement by organizers of an international survey for the status of digital games research underlines the complexity of the field:

> Digital games research is a young, growing, multidisciplinary field of study. It spans disciplines as diverse as arts, humanities, social sciences, psychology, design, computer science, engineering, and others. This diversity and richness is part of its strength—but also one of its challenges.

The above-mentioned survey was initiated by the Digital Games Research Association (http://www.digra.org/), the Digital Games Research Temporary Working Group of the European Communication Research and Education Association, and the Games Studies special interest group of the International Communication Association (http://www.icahdq.org/).

This situation particularly becomes true in the context of serious games, which strive to follow both the principles of entertainment games and the additional characterizing goal of a serious game in a specific application field. Here, further subject-matter experts—such as educators, coaches, medical doctors, and therapists—are involved in the development process.

Compared to the entertainment industry's well-established business processes, funding schemas, and distribution models, the motivation for developing a serious game differs enormously. Typically, serious games production is initiated either by a customer—such as a company aiming to introduce game-based learning and training (rather than an idea of a game developer or game publisher serving the anticipated needs and interests of the gamers' community)—or represents a byproduct of collaborative research projects in form of a *proof of concept* for new technical achievements in (mostly technology-driven) research initiatives.

A major drawback of many *research-driven* serious games—often initiated by research organizations with minor game development expertise—is often confirmed by the low quality of resulting games in terms of bad (or even missing) game design, limited complexity and quality of gameplay, game environments and game experience. In these serious games, the characterizing goal (e.g., an intended learning effect) as the *serious* part clearly dominates the "game" portion. Consequently, these serious games usually do not go beyond a research prototype status; successful technology transfer to a commercial (serious) game is far away.

Conversely, industry-driven serious game productions are more promising in terms of their proposed outcomes. This is due to involving both professional game developer studios (optional additional groups such as subject matter experts or research institutions for scientific evaluation) and a user-centered approach, starting with the motivation and (more or less) clear requirements of the customer. Therefore, two obstacles often hinder a fluent project implementation: First, customers are not really aware about games and underlying game development processes. Similarly, game developers are not aware of subject-specific application areas. This causes a need for increased communication among developers, customers, and other stakeholders, in contrast to production of entertainment titles. Second, customers, such as training units in large companies, often have inadequate expectations in terms of quality and cost. They expect the same quality as entertainment titles (with development budgets of at least $1 million USD) at a fraction of the cost (five to six digit amounts) which are common investments for existing eLearning/Web-based training solutions. Further, potential customers seek best-practice examples that clearly indicate the effects of serious games—before making the final decision to invest in a serious game as a new learning and training paradigm.

As underlying model for a *search tool* for identifying and retrieving appropriate serious games, Göbel et al. (2011) developed a serious games metadata format. This format provides quality criteria and further descriptive data about serious games in a formalized way, enabling information retrieval tools to find an appropriate serious game for a specific user (group) with dedicated user requirements. This format was further cultivated in the context of the EU funded project ALFRED (http://alfred.eu/). Solid scientific evaluation studies have shown the potentials and limitations of serious games in different application areas. Among others, Backlund and Hendrix (2013), Egenfeldt-Nielsen (2005), Malone and Lepper (1987), Prensky (2001), de Freitas (2006), and Connolly et al. (2012) indicate the benefit of serious games for playful learning, learning effectiveness, and learning motivation in the educational sector. In the healthcare domain, Baranowski et al. (2008), Kato et al. (2008), Lund and Jessen (2014), Larsen et al. (2013), LeBlanc et al. (2013), Maddison et al. (2007), and Wiemeyer and Kliem (2012) analyze the effects of game-based approaches in the direction on health-related behavior changes, e.g., healthier nutrition choices, increased physical activity, or a better understanding of cancer and the willingness to fight against it.

Chapter 12 provides a set of best-practice examples of serious games in selected application areas.

11.2 Economic Issues—Market Analysis and Business Models

As outlined in the previous section, serious games are very promising, not only as research field but also as a *proven methodology* (in singular evaluation studies to date) and a potential economic factor in the *advanced gaming industry*.

11.2.1 Market Analysis

In 2010, the US research institute Apply Group predicted serious games to be the next evolution wave in computer-based learning, with 135 of the world's largest companies using serious games in upcoming years. The IDATE study from 2010 titled *Serious Games—A 10 billion euro market in 2015* (IDATE 2010). However, this only represents a fractional amount compared to the overall gaming industry as the fastest-growing market of the media sector with an estimated average growth per year of 9.1 %. Latest studies by the market research and predictive analytics company Newzoo conclude that the worldwide games market will jump from $83.6 billion USD in 2014 to $91.5 billion USD in 2015, which represents an increase of 9.4 % year by year (Newzoo 2015). Further, Newzoo forecasts in its 2015 Global Games Market Report that the global games market will reach $113.3 billion USD by 2018, which would imply a compound annual growth rate of +7.9 % from 2014 to 2018.

Developers' and publishers' efforts to professionally create and sell digital games, serious and otherwise, to consumers give rise to a range of distinct market information requirements. Typically, the most critical information requirements relate to data about (1) hardware and software sales performance, (2) the size of installed hardware base, (3) the structure of the installed base along with (4) the characteristics of associated users. We will address each of these in turn, and provide an overview of the most important methodologies used to collect such data in practice.

Yet first, let us clarify why companies should bother with elaborate market analysis at all. After all, one might argue, the success of a digital game can be measured simply in terms of the sales, downloads and, more recently, the volume of in-game or in-app purchases it manages to generate. Indeed, such performance metrics should be readily available to those who have developed and, in particular, published and marketed the game in question. Isn't that enough? No.

Physical product sales as well as downloaded data provide an important but myopic view, which limits the potential for targeted product development and market opportunity exploitation. Four deficits are readily apparent: (1) sales data reflect the result of a product and campaign after these have been created and implemented (and are thus not useful for ex ante planning and control), (2) sales data represent a partial view (lacking a perspective on the whole market, i.e., excluding non-buyers), (3) global sales data alone does not provide insight on the demographic structure of existing and potential buyers and players, and (4) for products sold physically through retailers or other distribution channels not fully controlled by the developer or publisher, sales data does not necessarily represent actual sales to consumers.

Professional market analysis data plays a crucial role in supporting developers in targeted development of new titles and their effective marketing. It contributes to answering questions like:

- Who are we developing for?
- How big is the target group and sales potential?
- Who are our competitors and what are their key strengths?
- What kind of attitudes and beliefs does the target group hold?
- By which means can we best communicate our product to the target group?

Estimates of market sales and installed bases for software and hardware are typically generated using a variety of different methodologies. These include:

- Consumer panels, such as those run by GfK in Germany
- Retail panels, such as those by Media Control in Germany and Chartrack in the UK
- Consumer surveys, such as those implemented by NewZoo and GameVision

Analysts such as IHS/ScreenDigest and Parker Consulting maintain historical records and apply basic modelling techniques to predict the lifecycle of hardware sales.

However, just as important as sheer sales figures and the size of installed bases are the structures of their owners or, more specifically, their users. This type of data can be collected through consumer panels, bespoke surveys and, increasingly, customer registration and loyalty/reward programs.

The advent of digital distribution and delivery is having a significant impact on the game industry's ability to collect and analyze sales and player data. While it would seem to be easier to track key figures (due to the absence of middlemen), in some ways it has become more difficult to create a coherent, aggregate view of total market performance. New agreements between hitherto unrelated players are required, and new companies are emerging to meet this need (e.g., AppAnnie for apps).

A key deficit of most market analysis endeavors, however, is the neglect of non-players or potential product buyers. Serious digital games can especially be assumed to have significant potential for expanding the population of digital game users by offering them a—to them—novel and perhaps unexpected degree of utility that exceeds that of conventional gaming products.

As far as we can tell, market analysis for serious games not targeted to consumer markets is still in its infancy. A number of problems make such an effort complicated. First of all, the serious games industry is highly fragmented. Second, corporations that employing serious games for the purposes of i.e., training, may view such technology as proprietary and not reveal information about their use cases. Third, serious games are often highly customized, reflecting very specific user requirements—which limits marketability to a wider audience.

We conclude that market analysis for serious digital games will encounter different challenges, thus giving rise to different methodological requirements that depend on the type of target market. While consumer markets can be tracked with a wide range of existing instruments, valid market monitoring for serious digital games in a business-to-business (B2B) context will be more difficult.

11.2.2   Job Market and Qualification Programs

According to recent market studies by Gartner (Gartner Inc. 2013), the gaming industry is also becoming one of the largest job creators in the IT sector. For instance, 43,000 professionals in 2014 were involved in the art and business of making games in the US, with an additional 12,200 professionals in Canada. Almost 600 game companies operate in North America alone. An estimated 10,400 + game-related organizations and businesses exist in 74 countries. According to a 2015 estimate by the German Association for Interactive Entertainment, the gaming industry employs approximately 13,000 people in Germany. The computer and video game industry sells an incredible rate of nine games every second. In contrast, the percentage of serious games titles and number of game developer studios focused on serious games is quite low so far. As an example, approximately 10 percent of German developer studios in G.A.M.E. (the German game developer association) tackle serious games as their core business—whereby the percentage serious games compared to entertainment games is continuously increasing. Similarly, few positions in developer studios (ranging from designers to programmers or content producers) have real experience in serious games production. This is also caused by the fact that international qualification programs for game development and game design (both private or in academia) are rare. Second, existing Masters degree programs, offered by European and US universities among others (e.g., Copenhagen, Utrecht, Salford, and Skövde in Europe, or Michigan State, Georgia Tech, University of California Santa Cruz, and North Carolina State in the US), rarely address the complex and interdisciplinary field of serious games development. Similarly, numerous qualification programs offered by universities of applied sciences (e.g., in Germany, 156 study programs are available to prepare students for entry into the multi-faceted gaming industry; refer to the education compass provided by the BIU association for game publishers: http://www.biu-online.de/en/) focus on (the use of) digital media (tools) and media informatics aspects—rather than research, development, and production process of games and serious games.

11.2.3   Market Access

Hence, from a game developer perspective serious games so far only represent a niche market in the gaming industry. The key question is how to access the serious games market and how to make profitable business out of it?

As Founder and CEO of Serious Games Interactive Simon Egenfeldt-Nielsen states, the most likely simplest route for mainstream (entertainment) developers will be adapting existing titles to non-leisure uses. As there are no specialized design and communication tools in this area—with most of the evaluation of a game's chance of success coming from experience—creating new titles from scratch will likely be beyond many developers in the short- to medium term.

> A significant problem faced by all actors in this area is the lack of publishers/distributors in the field, and no specialists. Some CBT (Computer-based training) publishers have 'dipped their toe in the water' but no one has made a serious move in this space to date.

Nevertheless, serious games—either in the form of contractual work or as part of collaborative research projects with even smaller development budgets—provide a good opportunity for developer studios to cross-finance their own technology development or to bridge time between big(ger) entertainment productions eventually popping up due to unforeseen events, such as problems with a (bankrupted) publisher—unfortunately not that unrealistic in the fast-moving gaming industry.

11.2.4   Funding Schemes

The difficulty for market studies in serious games also originates from the variety of serious games described above—with their broad range of application areas as well as the diversity of underlying business models and funding schemes. Contrary to the entertainment sector, serious games usually are not mass-market products; typically, it is not possible to buy them in a store or to download from online distribution platforms. Only in extremely rare cases do professional game developers create a serious game (one not contracted by a customer) directly addressed to players as consumers, with similar distribution models analogous to entertainment titles. In most cases, serious games are developed either in the course of contractual work or research-driven innovation projects.

In the case of contractual work, customers commission a game developer to develop a serious game. This contractual work are typically private 1:1 projects with one serious game and one customer—such as a company or nonprofit social-professional organization—where the organization distributes the game among its employees or respective member institutions (and their staff). Usually, the amount of customer investment for these kinds of serious game productions does not become public (cf. the best practice examples *Mega Airport* (series), *Sharkworld,* or *Oil for Quest* in Chap. 12).

In the case of serious games as byproducts in the course of research projects, the overall funding rate typically is public, but it is quite hard to determine and calculate the cost for dedicated serious game development—as the research project is minor, serving primarily as proof-of-concept of new research achievements (e.g., 80 Days or *Dance with ALFRED* in Chap. 12).

A third funding resource for serious games represents foundations, which support the development of serious games following the mission of the foundation. Popular examples for that include health games such as *Remission*, funded by the Hope Lab foundation, as well as social awareness games such as *Mission for Life*, where a foundation wants to raise public awareness about a topic relevant for society. Since foundations usually aim to reach as many people as possible, the games are typically distributed for free. The amount of sponsorship for individual projects is often available in a foundation's annual reports.

Another (philosophic) discussion considers the question which games belong to serious games and where is the border to pure entertainment titles? For instance, Nintendo does not explicitly classify its products *Wii Sports* and *Wii Fit* or *Dr. Kawashima's Brain Jogging* as health or educational games, but as entertainment games that new target groups such as families, silver gamers, etc.

All of these aspects and varying funding schemas, business, and distribution models make it difficult to create profound market studies for serious games.

11.2.5 Business and Distribution Models for the Entertainment Sector

In the entertainment sector, the games industry currently uses several business models, including premium payment and free to play (see Fig. 11.1).

The traditional model contains a value chain from game developers on the production side over publishers, distributors, and retailers, to players on the consumer side. Developers are contracted by publishers, which serve as an investor for the games. Publishers own the rights of the game and offer it to distributors and

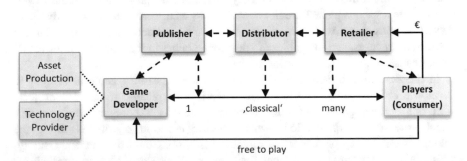

Fig. 11.1 The business model for Entertainment Games from the value chain of the traditional distribution model (*upper*) to premium and free-to-play models (*lower*). The *dashed arrows* indicate different options within the traditional value chain. The *dotted* connections on the left side indicate development tasks optionally subcontracted by game developers to additional parties, such as individual freelancers or specialist (game) service providers

retailers with different distribution channels (e.g., distribution platforms or geographic regions). Finally, consumers buy the titles in a store or download it from a platform. In this model, by example, the royalties are distributed as follows: Let's assume a consumer pays 50 EUR for a game in a store. From that, the retailer keeps 10 EUR, and 40 EUR go to the distributor. The distributor keeps 14 EUR; 16 EUR are passed to the publisher. From that, finally 4 EUR reach the game developers. Therefore, game developers also need to finance their different departments and (optionally contracted) content producers or additional technology providers.

Based on that situation, developers have a vital interest to increase their revenue and percentage of royalties. For that, recently, simplified, unburdened value chains have become more and more popular, i.e., value chains from game developers over distributors directly to players, or even a direct connection from the game developers to the consumers (players). This implies that game developers also take the publisher role and (in the latter case) distribute the games on their own, using platforms such as *Steam* (http://store.steampowered.com). Accordingly, the percentage of royalty dramatically increases, e.g., the game developer keeps 10 EUR from a 15 EUR expensive title (5 EUR go to a distributor), or a game developer gets the full price for a title in the case of a direct link with the customer.

With respect to premium and free-to-play models (refer to arrow from Player to Game Developer in the lower part of Fig. 11.1), a premium payment implies that content is paid in advance by the end user through the actual purchase of the game, e.g., a boxed game in a shop, or a game available for download via a distribution platform. In contrast, in the context of the software-as-a-service idea (Papazoglou 2003) the games industry has also developed the *free-to-play model*: In this model, the gamer has the possibility to access the game for free and then, later, different monetization strategies are applied during gameplay on a voluntary basis—i.e., the player pays only for extras such as shortcuts, additional power, points and coins, or similar advantages.

11.2.6 Business and Distribution Models for Serious Games

Compared to business models and value chains in the entertainment sector, the typical scenario in serious games is slightly different (see Fig. 11.2): Here, domain experts enter the stage and bring in another dimension—the *serious* part. Also, customers typically initiate and finance serious game development (i.e., contract game developers for customized solutions and distribute the game for free for training purposes among company employees, or among school-age children in educational settings). The majority of best practice examples provided in Chap. 12 also follow this business and distribution model. Only a few examples exist, where consumers (players) directly purchase a game. Therefore, the overall question is whether players/consumers are willing to pay for serious games in general. Do they want to personally invest in education or health as private individuals (cf. regular visits to fitness studios with a subscription model and monthly fees)—or is the general mindset that societally relevant areas are fully covered by public services,

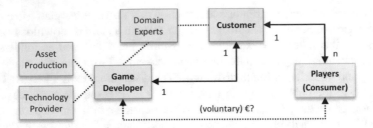

Fig. 11.2 The business model for serious games

and serious games—as instruments for those public areas—should be offered for free/without cost to consumers? A second interesting point is whether premium or free-to-play models might be promising models for serious games at all.

11.2.7 Cost-Benefit Aspects

With respect to necessary development budgets and the cost-benefit ratio of serious games, a commercially highly relevant issue considers IPR (intellectual property rights) and license issues: Whereas some big(ger) developer studios rely on their own technologies, a lot of smaller studies and startups make use of available (third party) technology. For instance, Unity (https://www.unity3d.com) is very popular and widespread—not only in the academic community, but also by the game companies. This is due to low license costs and easy-to-use authoring tools and additional game middleware. Previously available only to large game development studios due to their high licensing fees, both the CryEngine and the Unreal Engine (http://www.cryengine.com, http://www.unrealengine.com) are now available for a small monthly fee, with the Unreal Engine additionally providing full source code access. These changes allow everyone—from smaller developers to research projects, or even student projects—to use the same state-of-the-art tools as some of the largest game developers in the industry.

Another aspect referring to the applicability and acceptance of serious games in industry considers the technology used in the games paired with legal and compliance issues in industry: Many corporate customers do not allow the use of plugins in their company intranets. Due to this fact, there is an ongoing trend towards technology solutions without the need of any plugins. For instance, there is a joint effort by Epic Game studio and Mozilla to show the potential of WebGL. Epic Games ported the Unreal engine (actually an effort to cross-compile c/C++ to Javascript). Also, Mozilla and Unity want to bring the Unity Game Engine to WebGL.

Chapter 12 provides numerous best-practice examples of serious games, including relevant cost-benefit aspects: Economic information about the development costs and funding models, quality information about the intended effects and benefit for consumers, as well as technical information about supported platforms.

11.3 Legal Issues—Ethics, Gender, Data Protection and Privacy

A major goal of many serious games is to provide personalized gaming environments in order to support individuals in achieving a proposed serious purpose, i.e., a learning outcome or improved health. For that, the collection of personal data is necessary to apply adaptation and personalization mechanisms that match the needs of individual users. This has different pros and cons and directly leads into the topic of ethics and legal issues—including ethical issues and privacy and data protection issues. In the following section, these legal aspects are discussed in the context of educational games.

11.3.1 Sensitive Ethical Aspects

Individual data to be collected and analyzed by smart game-based learning technologies—in particular, data about learning competencies and abilities, independent of age or occupation—may raise sensitive ethical questions concerning privacy and data protection issues. When conducting experimental research (during research and development projects and/or as a preliminary step for educational game development), international ethical standards and requirements of (psychological) empirical research, as emphasized by the American Psychological Association or the British Psychological Society (http://www.bps.org.uk/what-we-do/ethics-standards/ethics-standards), need to be obeyed. This includes (a) justifying the reasons why people need to involved in research activities, (b) applying to national and local administrative bodies (if applicable), (c) obtaining agreement from children's legal representatives (if applicable), (d) providing no financial or other inducement for participating, (e) allowing children to voluntarily participate in the research protocol, (f) providing an appropriate environment, (g) avoiding any risks or harm, (h) providing age-appropriate and complete information about the research protocol, (i) recording a minimum amount of personal biographical data, (j) performing data analyses on an anonymous basis, and (k) providing participants with the possibility to retrieve feedback on subsequent research results.

11.3.2 Privacy and Data Protection

The main idea of smart educational assessment and personalization services for serious games is that the understanding of a learner's activities and learning trajectories are key elements for intelligent game mastering, game control, and game adaptations and they are advantageous for the individual, instructor and educational provider. It appears obvious that a better understanding of a single student and an entire student cohort as well as the learning designs and interventions to which they best respond would be of importance to improve education, or the "educational success rate."

Of course, schools and educational/training organizations collect and analyze data about their students all the time, but with the increasing number of electronic devices, a new dimension has been reached (cf. Oblinger 2012). Collecting data of students and their activities, weaknesses, achievements, failures, and successes on a large scale bears a number of severe and significant ethical challenges, including issues of location and interpretation of data; informed consent, privacy and the de-personalization of data; and the classification and management of data (Slade and Prinsloo 2013), which is specifically true when data are passed to web services in the cloud. Some researchers have suggested approaches to the perils of learning analytics. In the US, as an example, Bienkowski et al. (2012) suggested a code of conduct or Creagh et al. (2012) published a *good practice guide*. In a recent paper, Slade and Prinsloo (2013) identify principles of an ethical framework for learning analytics that (1) highlights the moral dimension, (2) involves students as collaborators instead of recipients, (3) demands awareness that all learning analytics results are only of temporary/momentary nature, (4) demands awareness that achievements are extremely multidimensional and therefore analytics are only a snapshot of that, and (5) requires transparency. However, this framework concludes (6) that schools [our educational system] cannot afford not to use the data to improve the effectiveness and efficiency of educational measures.

Similar ethical and privacy issues become obvious in the field of personalized health games—in particular, in the context of AAL (Ambient Assisted Living) settings that primarily address the elderly and their social environment. Here, ethical questions arise, such as "Who should know that a person has mild cognitive impairment, only doctors…or relatives, neighbors, and other professional/non-professional care givers as well?" or "Who can support an older person with limited IT skills to register online for a Web-based cognitive training program? Which information is necessary for registration?" Similarly, "Which information about individuals and their health status is necessary before a health insurance company accepts the costs for a game-based training program?" And, closely connected: "Are health games generally accepted as instrument for therapies—does it fall under the Medical Devices Act? Which processes are necessary for certification?" These aspects are tackled by Manzeschke et al. (2015) in their study about ethical issues in the context of AAL systems and applications.

Other legal aspects independent from dedicated serious game application areas include gender issues as well as violence in games.

11.3.3 Gender Aspects

In the context of computer games, particularly those used for serious purposes, gender aspects play a crucial role. Everyone working in this area must be aware of these issues, and that each game potentially may increase a gender gap (cf. Rabasca 2000). Current studies yield a variety of gender differences in terms of preferences and gaming behavior. In general, however, the variance within one gender can be considered larger than the variance between genders (e.g., Boyle and Connolly 2008 or Hsu and Noble 2007). Still, gender aspects and factors of gender-fair design in educational technology and educational games (i.e., discussed in Kickmeier-Rust et al. 2007) need to be an integral part of design and development efforts. For that, an equal representation of both genders should be considered in early game design phases (in the context of user requirement analyses) to achieve better coverage. In general, educational game productions should account for existing gender differences in visual, gaming, and learning preferences—to provide gender-fair design at all levels.

11.4 Summary and Questions

The gaming industry is the driving factor of the creative industry in general, and not only in Europe: Market studies estimated the worldwide games market to be $91.5 billion USD in 2015, and forecast an increase up to $113.3 billion USD by 2018. Serious games represent a promising part of the advanced gaming industry—using game technology and game concepts for additional purposes beyond pure entertainment—and the topic of serious games is well accepted in society.

The current state of technology allows for global distribution of products with relative ease. The booming games industry of recent years was driven by casual games, which turned tens of millions of people around the wourld into gamers. Today's generation of 30–40 year-olds are the first to grow up with computer games; hence, this is the first time the world has seen a large number of gamers who are well into their 30s—with much larger spending budgets than ever before. Due to that fact these people will start to look for more serious challenges than casual Facebook games and, as stated earlier, games closer to real-world topics (e.g., business topics being most relevant to office workers).

Funding schemes and distribution models of serious games are quite different from entertainment ones: Serious game projects are typically not produced for the mass market, but for individual customers—such as a company introducing game-based training for internal qualification programs. Further, additional stakeholders such as the actual customer (i.e., a company's Human Resource department, which is responsible for employee training) and subject-matter experts are involved in the development process. For that, the authors of this chapter introduce a new illustration for business and distribution models (see Fig. 11.2) for serious games based on the experience from academia (serious games group at TU Darmstadt, cognitive science group at TU Graz) and industry (GAME developer association, Serious Games Interactive and former personal experience from Nintendo).

A major drawback in the serious games market is that (so far) most serious game productions have small development budgets (which are one to two dimensions lower compared to entertainment titles), coupled with wrong expectations of customers: there is generally a discrepancy between expected quality—compared to successful entertainment productions—and low budgets—compared to existing eLearning solutions. This not only regularly leads to a low quality of serious games—which results in low user acceptance—but also hinders professional entertainment game developers to enter the market and to produce high-quality serious games both entertaining users and fulfilling a characterizing goal in a serious games application domain. Examples such as Re-Mission underline the need for appropriate development budgets (>$1 million USD, comparable to successful entertainment games) to create successful serious games that are well-received and accepted by customers and consumers, both entertaining users and showing the intended serious purpose—for example, positively changing patient attitudes towards strict adherence to chemotherapy, as shown in the study by Kato et al. (2008).

In sum, the serious games market is promising and fascinating in terms of research and development; however, it also represents a scattered industry with a variety of application areas and characteristics. As of today, there is no serious games market breakthrough. Reasons for these grand challenges in serious games include socio-economic aspects (development costs, quality, cost-benefit ratio), legal aspects (data protection and privacy), and a number of research and technical development related issues. Issues in the latter category range from effective game creation to adaptive control and adaptation mechanisms—along with evaluation aspects to prove the effects and benefit of serious games.

One possible way for a serious games market breakthrough would be certified serious games with significant evaluation studies that prove benefits to a potential customer. For instance, certified health games subsidized by the health industry might provide necessary development budgets. This could encourage game developers to both investigate the serious games market and develop high-quality, entertaining, customized health games—both convincing customers in terms of its proposed effects and affordability.

With respect to legal issues, on the one side detailed user profile information—such as the knowledge background of a learning subject, or a user's health status—will help to configure appropriate game-based learning and training environments (e.g., a personalized cardio-training program with specific duration, intensity, and frequency according to the user's health status). On the other side, that kind of personalized information in principle might lead to misuse, too. It is always the question of who gets what information and what happens with it. For instance, in the field of healthcare and ambient assisted living, who should be aware of the health status of an elderly person: Doctors, therapists, caregivers, the family, health insurance companies? For that, appropriate data protection mechanisms are essential.

Check your understanding of this chapter by answering the following questions:

- Why is it so difficult to analyze and calculate the serious games market?
- Which funding schemas, business and distribution models are common practice in serious games production?
- What is the difference between business and distribution models in the entertainment industry and in serious games?

- What are the possibilities and obstacles for professional game developers to enter the serious games market?
- Which ethical and legal issues arise in the context of educational games or health games?

References

Backlund P, Hendrix M (2013) Educational games—are they worth the effort? A literature survey of the effectiveness of serious games. In: 5th international conference on games and virtual worlds for serious applications (VS-GAMES), pp 1–8. doi:10.1109/VS-GAMES.2013.6624226

Baranowski T, Buday R, Thompson DI, Baranowski J (2008) Playing for real. Video games and stories for health-related behavior change. Am J Prev Med 34(1):74–82

Bienkowski M, Feng M, Means B (2012) Enhancing teaching and learning through educational data mining and learning analytics: An issue brief. U.S. Department of Education Report

Boyle E, Connolly T (2008) Games for learning: Does gender make a difference? In: Connolly T, Stansfield M (eds) Proceedings 2nd european conference on games based learning (pp 227–236), 16–17 October 2008, Barcelona, Spain. Reading, UK: Academic Publishing Limited

Connolly TM, Boyle EA, MacArthur E, Hainey T, Boyle JM (2012) A systematic literature review of empirical evidence on computer games and serious games. Comput Educ 59(2):661–686

Creagh TA, Nelson KJ, Clarke JA (2012) Development of a good practice guide to safeguard student learning engagement. In: 15th international first year in higher education conference. http://eprints.qut.edu.au/50075/2/50075.pdf

de Freitas S (2006) Using games and simulations for supporting learning. Learn Media Technol 31 (4):343–358

Egenfeldt-Nielsen S (2005) Beyond edutainment: exploring the educational potential of computer games. Ph.D. thesis, IT-University Copenhagen

EU Horizon (2020) HORIZON 2020—The EU framework programme for research and innovation. http://ec.europa.eu/programmes/horizon2020/en/what-horizon-2020. Accessed 23 Jul 2015

EU ICT21 (2014) Advanced digital gaming/gamification technologies. https://ec.europa.eu/research/participants/portal/desktop/en/opportunities/h2020/topics/279-ict-21-2014.html. Accessed 23 Jul 2015

EU LEIT (2020) Leadership in enabling and industrial technologies. http://ec.europa.eu/programmes/horizon2020/en/h2020-section/leadership-enabling-and-industrial-technologies. Accessed 23 Jul 2015

Gartner Inc. (2013) Forecast: video game ecosystem, worldwide, 4Q13. http://www.gartner.com/newsroom/id/2614915. Accessed 23 Jul 2015

Göbel S, Gutjahr M, Steinmetz R (2011) What makes a good serious game—conceptual approach towards a metadata format for the description and evaluation of serious games. In: Proceedings european conference games based learning, pp 202–210

Hsu D, Noble R (2007) Warriors from mars, archers from venus?–gender differences in massively multiplayer online role playing games. In: Zauchner S, Siebenhandl K, Wagner M (eds) Gender in e-Learning and educational games. A reader. Studien Verlag, Innsbruck, pp 263–280

IDATE (2010) Serious games—A 10 billion euro market in 2015. http://www.idate.org/en/News/Serious-Games_643.html. Accessed 23 Jul 2015

Kato PM, Cole SW, Bradlyn AS (2008) Pollock BH (2008) A video game improves behavioural outcomes in adolescents and young adults with cancer: a randomized trial. Pediatrics 122 (2):305–317

Kickmeier-Rust MD, Albert D, Roth R (2007) A methodological approach to address individual factors and gender differences in adaptive eLearning. In: Siebenhandl K, Wagner M, Zauchner S (eds) Gender in e-Learning and educational games: a reader. Studien verlag, Innsbruck, pp 71–84

Larsen LH, Schou L, Lund HH, Langberg H (2013) The physical effect of exergames in healthy elderly—a systematic review. Games Health Res Dev Clin Appl 2(4):205–212

LeBlanc AG, Chaput J-P, McFarlane A, Colley RC, Thivel D et al (2013) Active video games and health indicators in children and youth: a systematic review. PLoS ONE 8(6):e65351

Lund HH, Jessen JD (2014) Effects of short-term training of community-dwelling elderly with modular interactive tiles. Games Health Res Dev Clin Appl 3(5):277–283

Maddison R, Ni Mhurchu CN, Jull A, Jiang Y, Prapavessis H, Rodgers A (2007) Energy expended playing video console games: an opportunity to increase children's physical activity? Pediatr Exerc Sci 19(3):334–43

Malone TW, Lepper MR (1987) Making learning fun: a taxonomy of intrinsic motivations for learning. in: aptitude, learning an instruction: III. Conative and affective process analyses. In: Snow RE, Farr MJ (eds) Hilsdale. Erlbaum, NJ, pp 223–253

Manzeschke A, Weber K, Rother E, Fangerau H (2015) Ethical questions in the area of age appropriate assisting systems. German Federal Ministry of Education and Research, VDI/VDE Innovation + Technik GmbH

Newzoo (2015) 2015 global games market report. https://newzoo.com/insights/articles/global-games-market-will-grow-9-4-to-91-5bn-in-2015/. Accessed 06 Feb 2015

Oblinger DG (2012) Let's talk analytics. EDUCAUSE Review. http://www.educause.edu/ero/article/lets-talk-analytics. Accessed 06 Feb 2015

Papazoglou MP (2003) Service-oriented computing: concepts, characteristics and directions. In: Proceedings IEEE web information systems engineering, pp 3–12

Prensky M (2001) Digital game-based learning. McGraw-Hill, New York

Rabasca L (2000) The Internet and computer games reinforce the gender gap. Monit Psychol 31(9)

Sawyer B, Smith P (2008) Serious games taxonomy. Game developers conference 2008. http://www.dmill.com/. Accessed 6 Feb 2015

Slade S, Prinsloo P (2013) Learning analytics ethical issues and dilemmas. Am Behav Sci 57 (10):1510–1529

Wiemeyer J, Kliem A (2012) Serious games in prevention and rehabilitation—a new panacea for elderly people? Eur Rev Aging Phys Act 9:41–50

Serious Games Application Examples

12

Stefan Göbel

Abstract

Serious games are useful in a broad spectrum of application domains—ranging from educational games for younger audiences, to collaborative training and simulation environments for industry, or games for health and behavior change. Other examples include games for culture and tourism, marketing and advertising, participation and planning for public awareness, and social impact games covering societal relevant topics such as security, religion, climate, or energy. This chapter starts with a technology-driven approach to the broad field of serious games and an introduction of the most relevant application areas of serious games, with a rough summary of their characteristics in terms of domain-specific economic and technical aspects. Then, a set of selected best-practice examples per serious game application area is provided. Hereby, a coherent description format is used based on a first version of a metadata format for serious games introduced by Göbel in 2011, which considers typical descriptive elements for games used in game archives and game rating systems. Description elements contain the title of a serious game, its application area and target user group, its characterizing goal and a short description of the gameplay (including a snapshot), distribution info (including access to the game, supported platforms, and price), economic information (business model and development costs), quality information (evaluation studies, certificates, ratings, awards), and further information (point of contact, website, developer, publisher). Combining economic and quality information provides valuable indicators for potential customers about the cost-benefit ratio of the serious games.

S. Göbel (✉)
Technische Universität Darmstadt, Darmstadt, Germany
e-mail: stefan.goebel@kom.tu-darmstadt.de

© Springer International Publishing Switzerland 2016
R. Dörner et al. (eds.), *Serious Games*, DOI 10.1007/978-3-319-40612-1_12

12.1   Introduction

Serious games can be considered as playful instruments to achieve a desired goal, i.e., learning or training effect or a better health status. Figure 12.1 illustrates the basic understanding and technology-driven approach to serious games: In the center, game design methods, game concepts, and game principles are used in analogy to the development and design of entertainment games. These concepts, technologies, and principles are combined with further information and communication technologies, as well as domain-specific methodologies and technologies with regard to the characterizing goal of the serious game. Typical ICT technologies, among others, include mechanisms of artificial intelligence for automated game control, aspects of human-computer interaction considering game controller and I/O devices, usability and game experience features, multimedia aspects with a focus on computer graphics and audio or sensor technology to retrieve (user/player-related) context information—in order to build and process personalized adaptive serious games. Domain-specific methodologies—apart from application-specific knowledge and content—include aspects such as didactic and pedagogic concepts for educational settings, or psychophysiological mechanisms to monitor vital status in healthcare applications.

Fig. 12.1 Serious games: game concepts and game technology combined with further application-relevant concepts and technologies, applied in a broad range of serious games application areas

Application fields of serious games include, but are not limited to, game-based training and simulation, digital educational games ranging from kindergarten to university, vocational or workplace training, marketing and advertisement games, health games for prevention and rehabilitation, or social awareness and impact games covering societal relevant topic such as politics, security, religion, energy, or climate. A comprehensive overview of serious games application areas is provided by the *Serious Game Classification System* published by Ludoscience (http://serious. gameclassification.com/) and the serious games directory (http://www. grandmetropolitan.com/) provided by the Serious Games Association (education, healthcare/medical, corporate, military/government, games for good) as well as the serious games taxonomy introduced by Sawyer and Smith (2008). Considering these classification systems and underlying serious games categories (cf. Sect. 12.7), the authors of this chapter have identified a set of best practice examples for serious games in different application domains (see outer circle in Fig. 12.1). Hereby, the characteristics of serious games in the different application areas show a great variety in terms of their economic potential, its underlying business and distribution models (cf. Chap. 11), used concepts and technology, involved stakeholders and user acceptance.

Serious Games for Training and Simulation

Training and simulation games (cf. Sect. 12.2) might represent the biggest and economically most relevant application area for serious games. Examples among others include: Single and multiplayer simulation and training programs for military forces (e.g., *America's Army*, see https://www.americasarmy.com/ or *Lost Earth*, see Sect. 12.2.2) and civil relief organizations (e.g., *VIPOL* for police officers), virtual training environments for service staff in various service sectors (e.g., bus drivers, train conductors, pilots and flight attendants, sales staff, supermarket cashiers) or business and management games (cf. *learn2work* and *Sharkworld*). In some cases, serious games in those areas are not only used for internal training purposes, but also as a marketing instrument for recruitment (e.g., *America's Army*, (Games and Knight 2002; Nieborg 2005)).

Whereas training and simulation environments for industrial (in-house) training are typically built by game developers in contractual work ordered by individual companies in the form of corporate games (e.g., *VIPOL*, *3DSim@GBT*, *Sharkworld*, or *Houthoff Buruma*), different simulator genres such as flight simulators, farming simulators, railway or ship/rescue simulators are produced not necessarily for professional users, but also for the public games market, i.e., enthusiasts and fan communities interested in this game genre. For instance, the *MegaAirport.. (series)* was produced both for professional users (airport management, planning, pilots) and non-professional users; the *Ship Simulator: Maritime Search and Rescue* is used by younger and older "hobby sea rescuers" who are fascinated by playing rescue simulators.

Technology-wise, these virtual training and simulation environments were built on the basis of desktop VR technology in former times. Nowadays game engines (see Chap. 6) by default provide improved, high-quality rendering facilities, support network communication for multiplayer scenarios, and offer cross-platform publication for Web-based and mobile training.

Digital Educational Games

Serious games for education—digital educational games (DEG), discussed in Sect. 12.3—are very similar to serious games for training and simulation referring to their overall purpose and characterizing goal, i.e., playful acquisition and transfer of knowledge and skills and competence development. The main difference concerns the target user groups of children, students, trainees, families, and silver gamers (i.e., elderly players)—instead of employees in companies, or soldiers and police officers in military and civil forces. Examples for serious games in education and vocational training include:

- *Techforce*, a game-based training and learning environment for trainees in the field of electro- and metal industries (http://www.techforce.de, see also (Unger 2013))
- Game mods of *Civilization* (http://civilization.com/, see also (Squire and Barab 2004)), *The Elder Scrolls*: *Oblivion* (http://www.elderscrolls.com/oblivion, see also (Martin 2011)), or *Roma Nova* to teach history in higher education
- The authoring tool *gamemaker*, originally provided by Mark Overmars to enable pupils and students both to create their own game and simultaneously have game-based access to object-oriented programming (Habgood and Overmars 2006)—meanwhile, gamemaker has been commercialized (http://www.yoyogames.com/).

For younger audiences, numerous educational games exist, which can be used either at school or as supplementary learning material for the "afternoon market." This includes: The physics games *Ludwig* and *PhysikusHD*[2], the geography game *Feon's Quest* (80Days), or the game-based learning platform *scoyo* (covering the complete curriculum of subjects in Germany up to Grade 7 for math, German, English, biology, physics, chemistry, and art; see http://www-de.scoyo.com.

Many digital educational games originate from research projects (e.g., *80Days* in the field of technology-enhanced learning funded by the European Commission). A characteristic of these "by-products" of research projects is that they on the one hand typically provide excellent new, innovative concepts such as automated personalization and adaptation mechanisms—but on the other hand less matured, appealing gameplay and content. Other commercial products such as the game classic *The Incredible Machine* (https://www.mobygames.com/game-group/incredible-machine-series, http://www.crazy-machines.com), Nintendo's *Dr. Kawashima brain jogging*, or *Yes or Know* (combining classical board games with smart play) are less focused on a dedicated target user group such as kids and pupils with a specific age. In contrast, these products were introduced for the public and enjoy great popularity especially among casual gamers, families (serving as party games), and silver gamers.

Often, educational games also have a direct link to social awareness games (e.g., *Internet Hero*, drawing attention to the risks of Internet use), health games (e.g., *Meister Cody* tackling the issue of dyscalculia), or pervasive games in the field of culture and tourism (e.g., *REXplorer*). Digital educational games are also often associated with serious games at first; however, it needs to be emphasized that this is only one (broad) application area in the broad spectrum of serious games.

Health Games

The third big application field of serious games represents games for health (cf. Sect. 12.4), covering prevention (e.g., *Play Forward* for HIV prevention) or rehabilitation (e.g., *Respir Games* for asthma therapy), physical exercises (exergames such as *ErgoActive* for cardio training and *BalanceFit* for balance, coordination, and strength training (Göbel et al. 2010a)) or *Dance with ALFRED* motivating people for collaborative dancing in a group, cognitive training (e.g., Nintendo's *Brain Jogging* or *NeuroVitAALis* tackling mild cognitive impairment) or any other form of games aiming to support health in general and to enforce a behavior change towards a better, more active and healthier lifestyle (including a better nutrition). The contemporary "hype" on health games is also motivated by the fact that the global health care system has to develop new concepts to tackle demographic changes, a widespread sedentary lifestyle including physical inactivity, and increasing costs in the health-care sector (Göbel et al. 2011a, b).

Similar to educational games, there are numerous health games available, either as commercial products or game prototypes that were a result from research projects. Commercial products such as Nintendo's *Wii*™ system with *Wii Fit* or *Wii Sports* are dedicated to a broader audience with an emphasis on entertainment issues (for casual users, families, silver gamers, etc.) rather than an intended health effect or behavior change. This is the case for other small(er) health games and game prototypes, which usually represent user-tailored solutions optimized for a smaller user group with a specific user characteristic and user needs (e.g., the autism games *KickAss* and *Zirkus Empathica* for adolescents and children, respectively).

Recently, the most prominent example of health games with numerous citations represents the third-person shooter *Re-Mission* (http://www.re-mission.net/), which encourages young patients with cancer to fight against their disease and to strictly adhere to chemotherapy schedules. Re-Mission is also one of a few serious games that successfully proved its positive effects in a clinical study (Kato et al. 2008). On the other side, Re-Mission also represents one of a few examples of serious games with a higher development budget (>$1 million USD) compared to many other serious games, whether ordered in contractual work or funded in research projects.

One of the first health games (Lieberman 2001) with profound underlying scientific methods and evaluation studies was *Packy & Marlon* for diabetes self-management (Brown et al. 1997), published in 1994 by Raya Systems. Packy & Marlon is a side-scrolling adventure game for the Super Nintendo console, targeted to children and adolescents with Type 1 diabetes (ages 7–18). The health game aims to reduce diabetes-related urgent care and emergency medical visits; further goals of the game include improvements in diabetes knowledge, self-efficacy for diabetes self-management, communication with family and peers about diabetes care and emotions related to care, diabetes self-care behavior, clinical utilization, and health outcomes. The game simulates 4 days in the lives of two diabetic characters who must keep their blood glucose under control with insulin and proper nutrition, while engaging in challenging adventures. The game has 24 levels (each level involves a meal or snack, with three meals and three snacks per day) and is designed to improve players' diabetes self-management skills and behaviors (Fig. 12.2).

The design, user testing, production, and outcomes research for this game were supported by grants to Debra Lieberman, principal investigator, from the National Institute of Diabetes and Digestive and Kidney Diseases (NIDDK) of the U.S. National Institutes of Health (NIH). A 6-month randomized controlled trial with Type 1 diabetes patients from Stanford University Medical Center and Kaiser-Permanente clinics provided a Super Nintendo console to all 59 participants, and randomly assigned them to take home either Packy & Marlon or an entertainment video game with no diabetes content. They were encouraged to play their game as much or as little as they wished, as long as they followed their parents' rules about when and for how long they were allowed to play video games. At the start of the study, both groups averaged about 2.5 urgent care and emergency visits per child per year. After 6 months, participants who took home Packy & Marlon reduced their diabetes-related emergency and urgent-care visits by 77 %, on average, down to 0.5 visits per child per year; while those who took home the non-diabetes entertainment video game had no reduction in diabetes-related emergency and urgent-care visits, and remained at 2.5 visits per child per year. Several improvements contributed to this outcome. Players of Packy & Marlon gained knowledge about diabetes, improved their self-efficacy for diabetes self-management, increased their communication with family and peers about diabetes self-care and related emotional issues, and improved their self-care behaviors. Results of the randomized controlled trial were published in peer-reviewed scientific publications (Brown et al. 1997) and in the Yearbook of Medical Informatics (Brown et al. 1998).

In the context of Packy & Marlon and other health games produced in the nineties, the Los Angeles Times stated in its column *The cutting edge/personal technology* on December 15, 1997:

Fig. 12.2 *Packy & Marlon* box cover, gameplay, glucose testing, and story line screenshots (from *left* to *right*)

Video Games Turn Health Issues Into Child's Play. Medicine: Firm's products use diabetic heroes and asthmatic dinosaurs to educate kids and help them manage their diseases. Packy and Marlon, plucky pachyderms in a children's video game, charge through summer camp and blast peanuts at their enemies. And every now and then, they stop to measure their blood glucose level...Over the last five years, 40,000 copies of the games have been distributed, teaching children about diabetes, asthma, smoking and AIDS, and in some cases helping them manage their diseases.

Other press articles such as "Spiel macht glücklich—klinisch getestet" (English: *Playing makes happy—clinically tested*) by the German newsticker *Heise* summarize reports from the British Medical Journal, which point out that youth with depression can expect as good healing results by specialized computer therapies as by personal talk therapy with a doctor—as a result of studies by researchers from the University of Auckland with 187 youths aged 12 to 19 years with symptoms of moderate depression. This study took place for 3 months at 24 randomly selected medical institutions in New Zealand, where half of the test persons received the traditional treatment by personal talk therapy, and the other half used the game *SPARX* (http://sparx.org.nz/). *SPARX* was initiated and funded by the health ministry from New Zealand and realized as 3D fantasy game. Within the game, a customizable virtual character is available, which tackles seven tasks like the detection of unfavorable thoughts. The researchers figured out that the youth people not only enjoyed the game, but that 44 % of the test persons who succeeded in solving at least four out of seven tasks, could be classified as entirely healed after play. This was a great success compared to the equivalent success rate for conventional therapy with 26 %.

Social Awareness and Impact Games

Apart from educational, training and health games, social awareness and impact games (cf. Sect. 12.5), persuasive games or so-called *games for good* represent another classical segment of serious games. This pillar is characterized by the fact, that those games address public, societal relevant issues such as:

- *Politics and history*: e.g., *Utopolis, which* addresses and simulates a democracy, or *Lotte* a mobile serious game accompanied by a short film aiming at remembering the Holocaust to young adults in a media format appropriate for the target group.
- *Religion*: e.g., *Global Conflicts: Palestine* (see http://globalconflicts.eu/), putting players into the roles of the different sides in the conflict and offering an insight into the different perspectives.
- Epidemic plague—e.g., *The Great Flu*, tackling the flu virus H5N1.
- Sexism and racism—e.g., tackled within *Purpose*
- Security awareness games—e.g., see http://mindfulsecurity.com/2010/09/14/security-awareness-games/
- Climate—e.g., *imagine earth*, see http://www.imagineearth.info/
- Energy—e.g., *Enercities*, a serious game to stimulate sustainability and energy conservation, see http://www.enercities.eu

That kind of serious games are usually implemented in the course of public funded (science meets business) projects (e.g., *Enercities*) or financed by charity institutions (e.g., the World Health Organization initiated and funded the game *Food Force* for increasing awareness about world hunger crisis, or *Missio for Life*, tackling world's social problems, funded by the Missio foundation). Sometimes industry also invests into these societally relevant issues—primarily in the context of image campaigns (e.g., *GreenSight City* originated by Daimler Chrysler, see http://www.emercedesbenz.com/autos/mercedes-benz/corporate-news/greensight-city-is-a-new-simulation-game-developed-by-daimler-ag-and-zone-2-connect/).
Hereby, the type of social awareness and impact games usually is very similar to educational games, i.e., within the games the users/players can learn something and get awareness about societal relevant issues in a playful manner.

Similarly to health games, certain persuasive games have also been validated (e.g.,, Enercities, see Knol and De Vries (2010, 2011) and De Vries and Knol 2011).

Pervasive Gaming, Cultural Heritage and Tourism

The idea of pervasive games is to integrate games and game-based concepts into daily processes and activities, especially in the context of mobility, whether the way to work or during Nordic walking and jogging in leisure time. Hereby, game concepts are combined with wearables and mobile technologies available in smartphones such as positioning systems, audio, camera, and accelerometer or additional biosensors (e.g., heart-rate sensors) to consider the context and health status of users in mobile settings. Popular examples include the research prototype *Ere Be Dragons*, using both mobile devices with GPS and additionally incorporating heart-rate sensors (Davis et al. 2006); Nike's *Nike + Running App* (http://www.nike.com/) using GPS and audio on smartphones opt further wearables; and *Zombies, Run* (http://www.zombiesrungame.com) chasing users to run away from zombies, and focusing on GPS and audio.

Further, often augmented reality technology is used, especially within pervasive games for cultural heritage. One of the first examples in that direction was the project *GEIST* (English: ghost) funded by the German Ministry for Education and Science in the field of VR/AR, which combines mobile edutainment, interactive storytelling, and VR/AR in order to explore a segment of Heidelberg's culture and history (Göbel et al. 2004). Research into theoretical and practical aspects for the development and exploration of pervasive games also has been investigated within the EU-funded Integrated Project on Pervasive Gaming (IPerG, see http://iperg.sics.se/). Among others, tangible outcomes have been the game prototypes *Can you see me now?* (Benford et al. 2006) and Epidemic Menace—described in the AR handbook (Wetzel et al. 2011). These concepts have been further elaborated resulting in the pervasive game Tidy City (http://totem.fit.fraunhofer.de/tidycity, see also (Wetzel et al. 2012)), which also enables users to integrate their own content as new missions in the game.

Similar mobile, pervasive technologies are used within *REXplorer*, where users have been able to actively explore the city of Regensburg as well as in *FreshUp*, which offers a campus environment as playground for interactive, pervasive exploration of campus life, processes, orientation, and navigation. Both examples are described in the best practice Sect. 12.6 on pervasive games, cultural heritage, and tourism.

Oppermann (2009) summarizes the different forms of pervasive games (cf. Sect. 12.6) within his Ph.D. thesis entitled "Facilitating the Development of Location-based Experiences." Magerkurth et al. (2005) and Magerkurt and Roecker (2007a, b) provide an overview of fundamentals in pervasive gaming, and Wetzel et al. (2011) provide insight into the design of mobile augmented reality systems. Mortara et al. (2014) provide an overview for learning cultural heritage by use of serious games. Walz and Deterding (2014) provide further examples how serious gaming and gamification (might) pervade the daily life in a playful world.

Apart from transporting a certain message in one direction—as in social awareness games or educational games—mobile pervasive games are also used to collect data in the back channel: For instance, location-based data such as pictures, environmental data (e.g., pollution) or user-centric data such as how people feel at different places are used to create mood maps or other visualizations (opt enhanced by user-generated content such as geo-referenced images) as basis for urban planning processes. On the commercial side, the same pervasive data collection mechanisms are used by Google's massive multiplayer online role-playing game *Ingress* (http://www.ingress.com), where Google attracts millions of users to annotate geographic locations on a voluntary basis.

Marketing and Advergames

Further application areas of serious games that not further tackled in detail within this book include marketing and advertisement games (or *advergames*), which typically are used to advertise a product or (company's) brand.

For instance, *Quest for Oil* described in Sect. 12.7 is a serious game used for branding the Maersk corporation, recruiting, and providing internal corporate communication. Another prominent example represents McDonald's as a game (http://www.mcvideogame.com/), where players get insight into the processes at McDonald's (i.e., the work life at a McDonald's restaurant and insights about the production chain of burgers, including background information such as the point of origin of food).

Best Practice Serious Games—Overview

Table 12.1 shows the selected serious games from different serious games application fields that will be described in the following sections.

The description of the serious games follows the following structure, which is based on a first version of a metadata format for serious games introduced by Göbel et al. (2011a, b):

Table 12.1 Overview of the serious games described in this chapter

Section	Application field	Titles
12.2	Training and simulation (10 titles)	*ViPOL* (virtual training for police forces) *Lost Earth 2307* (image interpretation, military) *3DSim@GBT* (planning, railroad construction) *Mega Airport.. (series)* (visualization, flight simulators) *Ship Simulator: Maritime Search and Rescue* *SchaVIS* (flooding simulation and prevention) *Seconds* (supply chain management) *Learn2work* (company simulation and training) *Sharkworld* (project management training) *Houthoff Buruma* (recruitment and assessment)
12.3	Learning and education (9 titles)	*Ludwig* (educational game for physics) *Physikus HD* (learn adventure for physics) *80Days* (adaptive educational game for geography) *Roma Nova* (teaching history with brain interfaces) *Uni Game* (insights to universities and campus life) *Internet Hero* (learning the pros & cons of the internet) *Yes or Know* (family quiz game) *Bionigma* (science game for protein exploration) *Meister Cody* (educational game for dyscalculia)
12.4	Health (8 titles)	*Play Forward* (HIV prevention) *Respir Games* (asthma therapy) *BalanceFit* (balance, coordination and strength training) *Dance with ALFRED* (collaborative dancing) *NeuroVitAALis* (personalized cognitive training) *KickAss* (autism game for adolescents) *Zirkus Empathica* (autism game for children) *SPARX* (mental health game for youths & adolescents)
12.5	Societal and public awareness games (6 titles)	*Missio for Life* (exploring the world's social problems) *Friend Ship* (holocaust remembrance) *Purpose* (racism and sexism) *Utopolis* (democracy simulation) *The Great Flu* (awareness game for the flu virus) *Global Conflicts series* (tackling social problems)
12.6	Pervasive games, heritage and, tourism (3)	*FreshUp* (pervasive gaming in a campus environment) *REXplorer* (sightseeing game) *Jogging over a Distance* (healthy, pervasive gaming)
12.7	Marketing games (1)	*Quest for Oil* (branding game)

- Title of a serious game
- Application area(s)
- Target user group
- Characterizing goal
- Short description and gameplay (including a snapshot)
- Distribution info (including access to the game, supported platforms and the price)
- Economic information (business model and development costs)
- Quality information (evaluation studies, certificates, ratings, awards)
- Further information (point of contact, website, developer, publisher).

Combining economic and quality information also provides valuable indicators for potential customers about the cost-benefit ratio of serious games.

12.2 Games for Training and Simulation

12.2.1 VIPOL—Virtual Training for Police Forces

Author: Markus Herkersdorf

Title: ViPOL® (Virtual Training for Police Forces)

Application areas: Police forces, tactical training, team training, virtual live exercise

Target user group: Police Officers

Characterizing goal: Enable police forces to train scenarios that are too expensive, complex, or dangerous for live exercises

Short description and gameplay: ViPOL enables mission training in a virtual world of 150 km^2 urban and rural terrain. It is designed as a multiplayer, simulation-based training solution to be operated in a secure police intranet environment.

Every tactical scenario/team mission is prepared by a police trainer in advance. A scenario editor allows him or her to set the time of day, choose weather conditions (e.g., rain, fog), place all active roleplaying avatars or objects (like cars) to their initial position, and populate the scenario with AI-driven autonomous agents. The trainer assigns roles to the participants of a training session (Fig. 12.3).

Trainees join missions directly from their workplace computers, wherever they are. After an initial mission briefing, they start to act in a free play mode according to the given information and orders (e.g., bank hold-up, two suspects on the run, all patrols available commence search activities). Every roleplaying trainee is represented by an avatar and experiences the virtual world out of the ego-sight of its avatar. Avatars can walk, drive cars, run, jump, crawl, lie down, or use personal equipment like weapons, radios, flashlights, etc. Special voice and radio communication is realized by integrated VoIP.

Fig. 12.3 Snapshot of VIPOL—collaborative training of police operations

While the trainee screen has a purpose of maximum immersion and as complete a sense of reality as possible, the trainer screen provides a lot of tools to prepare, supervise, analyze, and debrief training sessions. Two powerful tools are full camera and full communication control. The trainer can join any team communication and directly address single or all players with instructions. Taking over any perspective (overview, trainee, suspect, etc.) allows optimal monitoring of all action during the free play phase. A second trainer (or a member of the police helicopter squadron) operates (in a simplified way) a police helicopter as an additional tactical air component and supports ground forces, e.g., by infrared camera information. As all action (including communication) is recorded, a replay of the full training is available for team debriefing. Also in the replay (no video), the trainer has full camera control and can make the trainees re-experiencing situations out of any suitable perspective (including change of perspective). Trainer comments (written or spoken) during live play, linked to time markers, allows one to jump right to the interesting or critical scenes for an efficient debriefing. Additionally, the trainer can draw onto a screen overlay that is visible for all trainees, to visualize and illustrate oral comments directly in the scene.

Debriefings can take place right after the training or any time later. The combination of free play action in a realistic scenario (including mistakes and suboptimal individual and team approaches) and subsequent self-, team- and trainer-reflection (including change of perspective) makes ViPOL a means of training with effective and sustainable learning transfer.

Distribution info: ViPOL is a non-public product, developed for special use in police training organizations.

Economic information: ViPOL was developed by TriCAT GmbH, Ulm, Germany, and is available for licensing by police forces. Development costs are >500,000 EUR. A first prototype/pilot was supported by the Police of Baden-Württemberg and MFG Baden-Württemberg.

Quality information: ViPOL has been developed in close cooperation with specialists of the Police of Baden-Württemberg. 2010/2011 a prototype version was evaluated by the Knowledge Media Research Center (KMRC), Tübingen, together with the University of Tübingen, Department of Applied Cognitive Psychology and Media Psychology, as part of a dissertation (J. Bertram) on Knowledge Building in Virtual Online Worlds. Three training groups (one with standard training, one with virtual training, one control group with no special training) were compared on knowledge acquisition and learning transfer. Findings were: the virtual training was accepted, both training groups show a significant increase in gain of knowledge, the personal value of the standard training subjectively was estimated as higher by the trainees, measurements demonstrate a higher learning transfer for the virtual training, virtual training appears as effective means of training. The project was discussed on international conferences worldwide and published in scientific journals (Moskaliuk et al. 2013a, b).

ViPOL is has received multiple awards, including the 2011 Innovation Award from the German Federal Institute for Vocational Education and Training (BIBB).

Further information: Scientific information are available on the website of the KMRC (http://www.iwm-kmrc.de; > Projects > Virtual Training), project information on the TriCAT website http://www.tricat.net. For direct questions, please contact Markus Herkersdorf (TriCAT).

12.2.2 Lost Earth 2307—A Serious Game for Image Interpretation

Authors: Daniel Szentes, Alexander Streicher

Title: Lost Earth 2307

Application areas: image interpretation, military, surveillance

Target user group: The field of remote sensing and image interpretation is a highly specialized community. One of the main training facilities for this field in Germany is the Air Force Training Centre for Image Reconnaissance of the German Armed Forces. This school has to handle very heterogeneous groups of students varying in age, education, and technical background. The target group is students, mainly from Generation Y, who are eager to play and will be trained as image interpreters.

Characterizing goal: The serious game should motivate students to achieve better and sustainable learning results, and to ultimately achieve sound and reliable image interpretation results.

Short description and gameplay: *Lost Earth 2307* is a 4X strategy game for training purposes in the field of remote sensing for image interpretation. The explorative and exploiting characteristics are mirrored in its game mechanics and are congruent to the job description of an image interpreter. This encompasses the systematic identification all kinds of objects in challenging imagery data from various sensor types. The game is set in mankind's future, placed in space throughout our galaxy. The player is part of a rebellion which strives to liberate human colonies from a hostile, oppressing, technophobic cult. As part of a liberation mission, the player has to fulfill an image interpretation task and produce a sound and valid report. Depending on the quality of the report, the mission is successful and the colony is free, or it will still be under the influence of the cult. The quality of the report also influences the morale on the liberated colony, which leadis to more or less resources (credits, matter, or science). A set of real imagery data for each colony (i.e., mission) is provided, i.e., optical, infrared or radar images. The cult's dogma of no technology development explains why no science-fictional imagery data is shown, but just real images from today. In a strategy game setting, the player has to build sensors, units, and structures (e.g., drones, recce airplanes, barracks, ground control stations, etc.) to defend colonies—or to attack colonies of the hostile cult. The fog of war concept (Crawford et al. 1988) perfectly represents the fact, that interpreters generally don't see the world in real time —they only see the latest shot of an area. The sensors, units, and structures operate along the classic rock-paper-scissors concept (Moore 2011). Each sensor, unit, or structure has some strengths and weaknesses, which can analogously be found in real world advantages and disadvantages of mimicked sensors and platforms (Fig. 12.4).

Distribution info: Lost Earth 2307 is available to all image interpreter students, as well as fully trained personnel of the German Armed Forces. Typically the game is played while in school (blended learning) in a free play mode. This mode can be edited by a tutor to fit the current curriculum. A campaign mode allows for solo trainings. The game is developed in C++ with the Havok Engine and runs on Microsoft Windows. The rationale for this engine is, amongst others, its flexibility and capability to realistically visualize (render) detailed specific imagery effects of infrared and radar sensors.

Economic information: The Fraunhofer Institute of Optronics, System Technologies, and Image Exploitation IOSB developed the game for the German Armed Forces' Air Force Training Centre for Image Reconnaissance (AZAALw). Established expertise in image interpretation and various sensor types have been key aspects of the collaboration, and are crucial for the ambitious development of this kind of customized game (with a six-figure budget).

Quality information: The development of the game has been in close cooperation with the customer and the target group. Wherever possible, the game world is abstract from the real world, so the players can immerse themselves in the game. Only when it comes to specific requirements of the learning objectives, the game is as close to the real world as didactically necessary. The basis for the game design has been the *6–11 framework* (Dillon 2010). After a thorough requirements analysis

Fig. 12.4 *Lost Earth 2307*—main bridge (*top left*), screenshots of a galaxy map and dialogue for image analysis and reporting (*top right*), strategy game component with optical and infra-red views (*bottom*)

phase and with a coordinated written Game Design Document, game mechanics were refined step by step to match the requests of the target group. Evaluations were conducted continuously throughout development by testing with user groups. The game will be part of the regular curriculum at AZAALw starting from 2016.

Further information: Further general and scientific information can be found at the Fraunhofer IOSB website, http://www.iosb.fraunhofer.de/servlet/is/11/. For direct questions, please contact Daniel Szentes from Fraunhofer IOSB.

12.2.3 3DSim@GBT—Planning, Simulation and Training

Authors: Markus Herkersdorf

Title: 3DSim@GBT

Application areas: Railway companies, competence training, team training, virtual live exercise

Target user group: Train personnel, tunnel maintenance personnel, intervention personnel

Characterizing goal: 3DSim@GBT is a web-based and fully interactive 3D simulation to (a) make personnel familiar with the Gotthard-Basis-Tunnel and (b) to train personnel to safely operate trains in the tunnel including adequate handling of minor and major incidents (e.g., mass evacuation in the tunnel due to fire).

Short description and gameplay: In December 2016, the world longest railway tunnel—the Gotthard-Basis-Tunnel in Switzerland—will be put into operation. For the Swiss Railway company SBB (Schweizerische Bundesbahnen SBB), this causes a huge and complex challenge to qualify nearly 4000 persons in 200 different roles in highly safety-related issues by practical training—in a very short period of time and with very limited access to the tunnel. SBB decided to go for a sophisticated Web-based interactive 3D simulation, consisting of a Virtual World representing the tunnel environment, a 3D model-based representation of all trains (6 different types), an avatar-based representation of the personnel and an authoring tool to create plenty of different missions for single- or multi-player (team) training, by their own training staff members on a graphical plug-and-play basis (without any additional coding). By means of this authoring tool, a mixed team of didactical and SBB training experts in a first step set up dedicated training scenarios by choosing train types (maybe rearranging the wagons), placing them on initial positions inside or outside the tunnel, defining the route, adding (AI-controlled) passengers to the wagons plus the trainee's avatars, and preparing some incident items (e.g., a garbage can which can be inflamed). In a second step, dynamic behavior is predefined by a node-based system of action elements, conditions, and transitions (e.g., the fire will be inflamed after 10 min and will get out-of-control, if not extinguished within 3 min by anyone). The whole scenario can be exported as single-player training (with instructions and automatic feedback to the trainee's action) or as multi-player team training (Fig. 12.5).

Team training exercises usually are supported by two trainers, who will supervise the free play action and role-play all external roles and communication (e.g., the train operation center). Trainer and operator are in full control of the simulation, but will be—for workload reasons—assisted by the system. E.g., fire will inflame automatically as predefined by the flow logic, without any need for the trainer to take action, but he can intensify the fire, if he does not want the trainee to succeed in extinguishing it. The system also helps track all trainee action and provides a report on defined action items at the end. The trainer has full camera control, so he or she can take any perspective (tunnel/train overview with zoom-in/out, trainee (ego or

Fig. 12.5 Snapshot of 3DSim@GBT: simulation and training environment around the Gotthard tunnel in Switzerland

third person)). He also has full control of the communication means (train radio, tunnel telephony, cellular) and can talk to all (briefing/debriefing) or just to a single person. Trainees observe the situation from the ego-perspective of their avatars. According to their assigned role, they can drive the train, care for the passengers, or perform tunnel maintenance. They are expected to act along the given rules and procedures, but are not limited in their action by the system. Special voice and communication by the technical means is available by VoIP. The huge mass of passengers is AI-driven and reacts context-sensitive to situations and incidents (fire, train evacuation). The trainer can take over passenger control, either by interacting with the AI-system or by directly controlling a single avatar. The record/replay capability of the system allows to debrief the entire training out of any desirable camera perspective, including all communication and interaction.

3DSim@GBT not only helps SBB to achieve necessary staff qualification for the Gotthard-Basis-Tunnel, but also provides the organization with complete new opportunities to plan and deliver competence-based training in terms of flexibility, cost-efficiency, resource preservation, and learning transfer.

Distribution info: 3DSim@GBT will be available by end of 2015 for internal use by SBB only.

Economic information: 3DSim@GBT has been developed by the TriCAT GmbH, Ulm, Germany. Overall development costs are >1 Mio CHF.

Quality information: The project 3DSim@GBT started with an Europe-wide request for quotation. After a pre-selection process, four companies had to go for a proof-of-concept including a functional demonstrator. Based on exact specifications the winner then had to elaborate a very detailed concept on didactics, technical issues, methods of development, operation model, train-the-trainer and quality management. The application itself is being developed in an agile process in close cooperation with

SBB specialists in the field of didactics, train simulators, train material, train operation and infrastructure (tunnel). Several quality gates were established.

Very important was an early fully functional prototype to enable the various specialists to experience their requests in a live system and then provide qualified input for the further development. An intensive evaluation phase with all relevant peer groups was included to assess acceptance, performance, training benefit and learning transfer. Beside quality, time is absolutely crucial, because 3DSim@GBT is part of the fixed, unshiftable schedule until opening the tunnel for passenger traffic in December 2016.

Further information: Further project information is available at the TriCAT website http://www.tricat.net. For direct questions, please contact Markus Herkersdorf (TriCAT).

12.2.4   Mega Airport—Realistic Airport Visualizations

Authors: Winfried Diekmann

Title: Mega Airport.. (series)

Application areas: Add-ons for use in Microsoft Flight Simulator X or X-Plane 10

Target user group: (1) Games market—flight simulation enthusiasts, pc-pilots, customers of simulation games; customized versions for specific user groups with dedicated needs, and (2) professional simulation—aircraft manufactures to use the airports within their training devices. Manufacturers of flight simulators or visuals to use the airports as a database in their products. Companies running a commercial flight simulator which can be rented by private and commercial customers.

Characterizing goal: Land an aircraft as good as possible on one of the airport runways.

Short description and gameplay: The gameplay is 100 % similar to the gameplay of the flight simulator the add-ons are made for: primarily Microsoft Flight Simulator X, including its STEAM-version, and the flight simulator Prepar3D based on Microsoft's FSX and enhanced by Lockheed. These products are pure simulators, and customers mainly want to fly as real as possible from one airport to another with their favorite aircraft (Fig. 12.6).

Fig. 12.6 Snapshots of *Mega Airport.. (series)*: Zurich airport (*left*), London Heathrow (*right*)

Distribution info: *Mega Airport.. (series)* is available in German, English, and French. The product is accessible as a boxed version in retail store in Germany, Austria, Switzerland, the Netherlands, Belgium, and other countries, and for download at http://www.aerosoft.com/ and various other download platforms. The game-version for non-commercial purposes is available for approximately 25 EUR. Professional versions in commercial flight simulators without any changes cost between 250–500 EUR, and with changes mainly for professional use are between 5,000–25,000 EUR.

Economic information: For developing an airport, developers should have knowledge of aviation, of the airport itself, and of the simulator the add-ons it is made for. The most difficult part is getting airport information, and facility and aerial pictures. Depending on the quality of that information and of the size of the airport, development takes between 8 and 18 months for one developer.

Quality information: Product quality is always very close to reality: Complete airport lighting, all taxiways with all taxiway signs, and lighting and all buildings with all gates are on their correct place. Airport buildings are recreated in detail and buildings or landmarks in the surrounding areas are also done, if they are important for departure or in the final approach. Because of the high quality and number of details, thee products are also sold to companies from the aviation industry for various purposes.

Further information: Most products of the Mega Airports series are available as a box version in English and German, with some also in French and Spanish. The products are also available for download at the website http://www.aerosoft.com/ and other dedicated simulation online shops. Due to the fact that all products of the Mega Airport series are compatible with the flight simulator X-Plane, they are also available on STEAM.

12.2.5 Ship Simulator—Rescue Simulation for Enthusiasts

Author: Clemens Hochreiter

Title: Ship Simulator: Maritime Search and Rescue

Application areas: rescue simulation, ship simulation, action

Target user group: 10+, casual and core gamers

Characterizing goal: Become acquainted with the hard day-to-day life of a sea rescuer and make the high seas a little bit safer. The main goal of the game is to simulate the true life of sea rescuers based on true events and a lot of research. The simulation puts human stories and social interactions in the center and reduces the usual technical aspects that are normally found within simulation games.

Short description and gameplay: As a sea rescuer, the player puts his/her life on the line—to save the lives of others! Extinguish fires, salvage damaged ships, direct

Fig. 12.7 Snapshots of the *Ship Simulator*: the ships are modeled like the official boats of the German Maritime Search and Rescue team (*left*). Combined with real controls, players can imagine how it feels to be in command of a rescue ship (*middle*). Difficult weather, like this rainy, stormy scenario is an important part of the gameplay (*right*)

search and rescue operations, stay in constant radio contact with the Maritime Rescue Coordination Center, and save lives in 20 different missions. Together with the crew, the player will become acquainted with the hard day-to-day life of a sea rescuer and makes the seas a little bit safer (Fig. 12.7).

Distribution info: *Ship Simulator: Maritime Search and Rescue* was developed by Reality Twist GmbH and published by Rondomedia GmbH. It is available on Amazon and Steam since July 2014, currently for 18 EUR. It is distributed in the German retail market as well. The game is playable in four different languages: English, French, German, and Spanish.

Economic information: The game was primarily financed on a publisher-advanced-royalty-basis. Rondomedia financed one part of the game. Another part was achieved by the funding from FilmFernsehFonds Bayern with additional 55,000 EUR. Reality Twist invested into the game itself as well. The business model is thus soley based on sales and revenue. The German Maritime Search and Rescue Service (DGzRS) was chosen to serve as a brand partner for the game.

Quality information: A large research phase has been passed before development. The development team spent time on a rescue cruiser and talked to real sea rescuers to get a feeling for the subject. Furthermore, they talked to all people involved in the sea rescuing business on land (e.g., radio operators). Afterwards, real cases of distress at sea have been researched and stories from both sea rescuers as well as castaways collected. Thus it was assured that all actions portrayed stuck to reality. To furthermore assure the content, the whole productions was supported and supervised by the German Maritime Search and Rescue Service (DGzRS). They assured that all actions within the game are within their modus operandi. The game has been nominated for the German Game Developer Award.

Further information: Information about publishing aspects are available at astragon Sales & Services, the successor of rondomedia: http://www.astragon.de/. Information about the development is available at Reality Twist: http://www.reality-twist.com. Information about the utilization of a brand within a serious game can be achieved by contacting the German Maritime Search and Rescue Service: http://www.seenotretter.de/en/who-we-are/

12.2.6   SchaVIS—Flooding Simulation and Prevention

Author: Ralf Dörner

Title: SchaVIS

Application areas: prevention, public awareness

Target user group: people who live in an area close to a river that is prone to flooding.

Characterizing goal: The characterizing goal of the game is to raise people's awareness that they should be well prepared for the event of a flooding. People should know which strategies to adopt in order to reduce the amount of damage in their homes and the environment. Moreover, they should have experience how to avoid life-threatening situations (Fig. 12.8).

Short description and gameplay: The basic storyline of the game is that a player has agreed to look after the house of a friend who is on vacation. The player is surprised to learn that the house is located close to a river which is suspected to burst its banks. The player has only a couple of hours to react before severe flooding will occur.

In a first phase, the player is able to explore the house, the garage and the gardens in a 3D environment. To allow inexperienced players to navigate in a 3D environment, a special navigation technique has been used: the user can only move between pre-defined waypoints that are visualized as beacons. The user can only navigate from one beacon to another by simply selecting a beacon. Then, the user is moved automatically along a pre-defined path to the beacon selected. That reduces a complex 3D navigation task to a simple selection task. In the user tests, this has proved to be a crucial element for inexperienced users to play the game. In the second phase, the player has to decide which actions to take. For instance, the player can move all furniture freely in the house, make a trip to a local hardware store and buy equipment, install restraints for the oil tank in the cellar, or turn off electricity. Although the player is not put under time pressure to make the decisions, each action is associated with a temporal duration. If a player chooses one action, its duration reduces the time budget available.

Fig. 12.8 Screenshots of the *SchaVIS* game. The "eye" denotes a waypoint that a user can select to navigate to this position

The second phase ends when the time budget is consumed or the players have put themselves in life-threating situation (e.g., if they forgot to secure doors properly and might become trapped).

In the third phase, the player can watch the water level in the house rising due to flooding. Simultaneously, the amount of damage rises as well. This amount is determined by a realistic underlying simulation. As a result, the score of the game is the sum of money that puts a figure on the flooding damage. The player with the lowest score wins.

Players are encouraged to repeat levels and use different strategies in order to reduce their score. In a fourth phase, the player can get some advice and crucial mistakes are pointed out. The game has four levels with different degrees of difficulty and sophistication of actions that can be carried out. In the levels, the focus changes from reactive to pro-active measures.

Distribution information: The game can be downloaded for free at a webpage of the German state of Rhineland-Palatinate: http://www.hochwassermanagement.rlp. de/servlet/is/174900/ The game is available in German, for Windows 7 only.

Economic information: Protecting citizens from personal and economic risks, and reducing harm to the local economy due to flooding, are important tasks for a regional government. Thus, public money has been invested in the production of the game. A public bidding process took place. The cost for producing the game was over $250,000 USD, including distribution costs. A campaign was conducted and the game was presented at fairs in order to draw the target group's attention to the game. The game itself is free to play.

Quality information: SchaVIS has been successfully in use since 2010. In informal interviews with users, the tension to see the house being flooded and the damage raising was one of the most fun and motivating aspects of the playing this serious game. In addition, surprises were described as most memorable, e.g., seeing the amount of damage jump from $20,000 USD to $200,000 USD, although the water level was increased by only 2 cm. This left players wondering what the underlying cause was and fostered active exploration. In comparison to more traditional means to raise awareness such as flyers or brochures, the activation of the user can be assumed beneficial for a lasting change in behavior. For the success of the game, the distribution strategy proved to be crucial. One promising strategy is to play this game with schoolchildren during lessons, and have them take the game home where they motivate their parents to play the game with them. Obviously, applying their knowledge, children had fun beating their parents.

Further information: The game was produced by the RheinMain University of Applied Sciences at Wiesbaden, Germany who provided expertise in serious games (Prof. Ralf Dörner) and hydraulic engineering (Prof. Ernesto Ruiz-Rodriguez, Sonja Baumeister). The game concepts and the implementation were realized by Matthias Heckmann and Benjamin Reppmann, the co-founders of the company mindtrigger. The point of contact for SchaVIS is message@mindtrigger.de.

12.2.7 Seconds—Supply Chain Management

Author: Jannicke Baalsrud-Hauge

Title: Seconds

Application areas: Supply Chain Management, manufacturing, collaborative work

Target user group: vocational training and higher education in manufacturing, logistics, and supply chain management

Characterizing goal: Decision-making, supply chain management, distributed production

Short description and gameplay: *Seconds*, developed at the University of Bremen (Germany), is used to train students in decision making on supply chains (SC), in distributed production environments, and enterprise networks in general. The gaming scenario evolves as the players play the game. The players have to design their processes and make decision. Depending on production volume and time, players can gain experience and skills needed for producing higher quality (Fig. 12.9).

The scenarios are developed to give the students a high degree of freedom in their decision processes by providing each player with a starting role. Players are assigned to different companies having different functions in the supply chain. The role and company description includes information on products and production, company history, current locations, and vision when starting the game. Based on this and an analysis of the market opportunities, students start with developing different possible scenarios using scenario and SWOT analysis and establish the company strategy, which they will have to follow during gameplay. Thus, the player decides where and what to produce and how the production process is to be carried out. This requires a turn-based setup and long playing time (3–4 h, 5–6 rounds), followed by a 30–45 min debriefing and reflection session. Seconds was developed by a multidisciplinary team using the SCRUM approach, and partly considering guidelines for balanced game design and the MDA framework (Hunnicke et al. 2004). The underlying assumption is that from a designer's perspective, the game mechanics will generate the dynamics of the game, which again generate the aesthetics; the players' perspective is opposite. Based on the deployment context of Seconds, the main interaction within the game arises from the

Fig. 12.9 *Seconds* main GUI, production GUI, and configuration toolbox (from *left* to *right*)

communication and collaboration (both possible, depends on players' strategies). The dynamic in the game results from the interaction among the players as well as from the interaction with the underlying simulation model. In addition, the dynamic is further increased by the use of key performance indicator (KPI) triggered events (Azadegan et al. 2014). The interaction between players leads to the evolvement of the narrative story and is thus different for each game play, even though the starting scenario might be the same. The role-playing mechanism is important for assigning students to take specific roles in the supply chain, in order to simulate a typical environment for decision-making in multi-stakeholder supply networks. Due to the fact that the game scenario has to cover the main stakeholders in a supply network, the game should not be played with fewer than 12 participants.

The client application functions more or less as a viewer of the current game state of the active players and delegates the performed actions to the server application using a self-defined event based command protocol. Most of the internal game elements (such as game instances, user accounts, companies, bank accounts, resources, sites, relations between them, etc.) can be edited, added, or removed via the Seconds toolbox editor. The Seconds data model is based on an SQL database; the game scenario can be altered by simply modifying this database. This makes it less technically demanding to adapt and configure different business scenarios to a specific business case, allowing ease of integration in different teaching settings.

Distribution info: Seconds is available in German and English; a Spanish version is in progress. It is written in C#, is a server client application, running with any Windows operating system. Access to a playable standard scenario can be requested for free via *mail@biba-gaminglab.com*. The standard scenario offers between 12 and 18 roles. Customized versions for institutions can be implemented as contractual work (projects), costs depending on the user-specific requirements. For direct questions please contact Jannicke Baalsrud Hauge; *baa@biba. uni-bremen.de*.

Economic information: Seconds was developed at BIBA—Bremer Institut für Produktion und Logistik by a team of researchers and research assistants. Seconds evolved from the experience gained with a different game developed in the EU funded project PRIME. Later versions have been further elaborated for the use in a gamebased learning course on decision making in supply chain management at the University of Bremen.

Quality information: Seconds have been in use for educational purposes since 2007. It has been regularly used at the University of Bremen (Germany) and University of Nottingham (UK) in different settings. So far, around 550 players have played Seconds. The evaluation of the learning outcome on risk awareness and management showed that the students were able to identify risks, apply risk assessment and management methods, as well as reporting that the game helped them to apply their theoretical knowledge and to develop suitable strategies within Supply Chain Management. Applying risk management successfully requires that the participants know the steps of the process, thus the game train also procedural knowledge and competence development by letting the players carrying out risk assessment and management. The tests show that the players are able to apply the theory and to use different methods for risk mitigation and decision-making in supply network (Baalsrud-Hauge et al. 2013). The tests also show that the longer the participants play, the better they get in identifying and assessing the different types of risks at an early stage. However, if we compare the mid test with the final test, the results show that the level increases more after the game than after the introduction. The participants mentioned two main challenges (provoked by the game); first, they lost the overview and did not manage to deal with the user interface and what was happening. Second, they found it difficult to identify hidden risks. The results show that for students without any, or with a little knowledge of risk management, it is important to make their task more visible in the first game level. Furthermore, it was seen that the process of playing one game, debriefing it, and then playing another game level helps to increase performance on the second game because of the transfer of knowledge from one game to another through debriefing (Baalsrud-Hauge and Braziotis 2013). Participants identified the risks, as well as developed strategies for reducing the collaboration risks to a much higher degree (Baalsrud-Hauge and Braziotis 2012). The continuous evaluation of learning effects demonstrates that the time required to transfer information into knowledge not only depends on the essential debriefing phase, but also relies on the participant's prior experience. This needs have to be taken into consideration at an early stage of the experimental setup, so that participants can be supplied with the necessary information on methods and approaches in advance.

Further information: Please contact Jannicke Baalsrud Hauge, Bremer Institut für Produktion und Logistik, BIBAGamingLab, *mail@gaming-lab.com*.

12.2.8   Learn2work—a Higly Adaptable Company Simulation

Author: Oliver Korn

Title: learn2work

Application areas: management training, business training, production management training

Target user group: skilled employees in production companies, management, economics students

Characterizing goal: On a general level, *learn2work* combines skill development and motivation and encourages entrepreneurial thinking and acting. On the content level the simulation focuses the skill areas of production planning and human resources.

Short description and gameplay: learn2work is an authentic and playful simulation of a small production company. The players' aim is to manage this company—either as individuals (i.e., as the CEO) or as a team with distributed roles (e.g., production, human resources and finance). Managing the company is a permanently challenging task: unpredictable events like market fluctuations, cases of illness, or machine breakdowns create a unique sense of realism. Thus on a general level, learn2work combines skill development and motivation and encourages entrepreneurial thinking and acting (Korn 2005, 2006) (Fig. 12.10).

An elaborate tutorial explains the basic relations and interdependencies to make the start easy. There also are three pre-configured and documented scenarios focusing on different management challenges: Changing the product and thus the production pipeline, re-structuring and qualifying the workforce, and surviving in a shrinking market.

Alternatively own scenarios and goals can be setup to meet the requirements of different groups. Also the level of realism and difficulty can be adapted in detail.

Within the game, the players of the team are briefed and receive the objective. Then they explore alternative ways to solutions, e.g., a shrinking market can be addressed by downsizing or by changing the product line. The simulation allows testing different strategies which then can be evaluated, compared and assessed. This is easy, as the serious game both tracks the level each objective is reached and attributes an overall score based on a simplified *balanced score card*.

While learn2work focuses on production planning, other departments like human resources, sales & marketing, and materials management are simulated as

Fig. 12.10 *learn2work* provides a bird eye's view of a small production company

well. General topics like soft skills, group dynamics, and ergonomics are also taken into account.

The following list provides an overview of activities in the serious game:

- choose profitable orders
- plan production
- manage stock and central buying
- manage sales and marketing
- plan finances
- observe market cycles and objectives
- train and motivate employees
- build teams
- explore strategies to resolve conflicts

Distribution info: learn2work is available as a Web service or alternatively on USB sticks. The serious game is localized in English, German, and Turkish. There also is an elaborate manual and workbook containing exercises and a glossary of relevant economic terms. The regular price for a 1-year license is 219 EUR and 849 EUR for a license with unlimited duration. Discounts for educational institutions like schools and universities apply. More information and the web service can be accessed on http://www.learn2work.de

Economic information: The game was developed by two full-time developers within 3 years. The development was financed by two grants (EXIST-SEED and Young Innovators). It was self-published and is distributed by Korion.

Quality information: learn2work received numerous awards: the *Education Innovation Award* by the German Chamber of Commerce, the *Innovation Award* of the German SME Initiative, and the *eLearning Award* in the category company simulations. Several major companies—among others, Siemens and Stihl—use learn2work in their training and further education departments.

Further information: Serious game: http://www.learn2work.de. More information on the developer: http://www.korion.de/.

12.2.9 Sharkworld—Professional Project Management Training

Authors: GAF van Baalen, Bruno Joordan

Title: Sharkworld

Application areas: Management training, corporate training, stakeholder management (PRINCE2)

Target user group: Employees with project management ambitions, students in business and/or technical programs

Characterizing goal: Introducing players to project management in a playful way, and letting them feel what it's like to deal with stakeholders in a project

Short description and gameplay: *Sharkworld* combines simulation elements with a story and characters, to create an engaging project management experience. With the help of picture and video material, players are taken on a trip to China. There, the main character must replace a project manager who has mysteriously fallen ill (Fig. 12.11).

Once there, players have to manage their project. Through conversation, chat and email, they have to take care of the interests of the boss, their client, and the team. They also make schedules and budgets. The choices that players make during the game decide whether the project becomes a success or turns into a disaster.

The game uses various media to give extra depth to the experience. When players are not behind the computer, they get text and voice messages from game characters on their mobile phones. The characters in the game also send emails.

Distribution info: Sharkworld is playable through a Web browser and needs Flash to run. http://www.sharkworld-game.com/.

Economic information: The game is sold online per license and in combination with institutional training packages.

Quality information: The game won the following awards: 2009 Japan Prize, 2008 European Innovative Games Award, 2008 Dutch Game Award 2008, and the 2009 Accenture Innovation Award.

Fig. 12.11 Snapshots of *Sharkworld*

Further information: The game was developed in cooperation with Otib and TenStep.

12.2.10   Houthoff Buruma—Recruitment and Assessment

Authors: Marcus Vlaar, Bruno Jordaan

Title: Houthoff Buruma—The Game

Application area: Law recruitment

Target user group: top-tier law graduates

Characterizing goal: Offer a selection tool for Houthoff Buruma to test new recruits on creativity, solution mindedness, stress resistance and social skills.

Short description and gameplay: Houthoff Buruma and ranj created a recruitment game in which participants can discover and experience legal practice from within. During an office visit, students are challenged to resolve a case study within 1.5 h, inside a rich multimedia setting. They work together in teams but are also in competition with rivals, which stimulates their motivation.

Each team works for Chinese Mining & Marine, a Chinese state-owned company. They assist in the take-over of the small Dutch offshore company, 't Hoen. This family business owns innovative technology that is essential for a prestigious Chinese offshore project to succeed (Fig. 12.12).

Using various media, teams discover fragmentary information about the interests and motives of different stakeholders, with which they can develop a successful acquisition strategy. Interviews with different game characters confront the teams with the human aspects of the case. The international context of the takeover demands political insight. The pressure increases because there are more issues than can be solved in limited time. The boundary between fiction and reality is intentionally blurred, continuously challenging the cognitive and analytic abilities of the students.

Fig. 12.12 Snapshots of *Houthoff Buruma*

After solving the case, a plenary session takes place. In this final round, the teams' solutions are compared and discussed. Subsequently, the winning team is announced.

Distribution info: The game is only playable within the Houthoff Buruma offices on a laptop.

Economic information: The game has been developed exclusively for Houthoff Buruma to be used as part of their recruitment process.

Quality information: The game won the following awards: 2011 E-Virtuosos Award, 2010 European Innovative Games Award, 2010 SAN Accent.

Further information: The game was developed in cooperation with Houthoff Buruma and made a significant contribution to the firm's election as 2010 Benelux Law Firm of the Year.

12.3   Educational Games

12.3.1   Ludwig—Digital Educational Game for Physics

Author: Michael Kickmeier-Rust

Title: Ludwig

Application area: Physics: renewable and sustainable energy

Target user group: The game is designed for the secondary education level, children aged 11 and up. The game is supposed to be used by teachers in secondary education.

Characterizing goal: Primarily, Ludwig follows the Austrian curriculum and covers aspects such as Fire (combustion, exhaust gases, etc.), Water (hydroelectric power, water cycle, or rivers), and Technology.

Short description and gameplay: Ludwig is an interactive 3D-adventure game built around a serious topic: Fossil and renewable energy (http://www.playludwig.com/). Players can explore the game world freely without any limitations given by the pedagogical design. The game was utilized and optimized gradually based on the feedbacks of participatory students and teachers. Usability, fun of play, motivational factors, and learning progress were investigated during the design process. A key element of the game and the project was to provide a convincing and competitive virtual 3D environment. The basic idea is that the learners explore the virtual environment and solve consecutive quests. The quests are designed as mostly 2D interactive experiments. In addition, the solving of quests and the degree to which a student explores the environment the more content of a *knowledge base* is unlocked. The knowledge base in turn is an in-game encyclopedia of the related topics (Fig. 12.13).

Fig. 12.13 Screenshot of *Ludwig*

Distribution info: The game is a Windows game for XP and higher systems. The game requires about 2 GB hard disk space and a performing graphics card. The game is distributed on CD and can be downloaded freely from the Ludwig website (http://www.playludwig.com/). In addition to the game itself, the package comes with additional information packages for teachers, as well as related worksheets for students.

Economic information: The project is a cooperation of the game studio Ovos in Vienna and various universities and school throughout Austria. The joint project was funded by the "sparkling science" initiative of the Austrian ministry of science, research, and economy and supported by various industry sponsors.

Quality information: The game was designed to have a high graphical standard that can compete with other commercial games, as well as convincing gameplay. This was one of the premises of the Ludwig project. In the context of the 2-year project, iterative design and development cycles as well evaluation studies have been conducted (Wernbacher et al. 2012; Wagner and Wernbacher 2013). The game received a number of awards, most recognizable the World Summit Award for e-content and creativity in 2013; this award is an initiative of the United Nations. Noteworthy is also the 2013 Austrian State Award (Staatspreis) for Multimedia.

Further information: All information about the project, the game, and evaluation studies is available on the game website (http://www.playludwig.com/).

12.3.2 Physikus HD—Learn Adventure for Physics

Author: Clemens Hochreiter

Title: Physikus HD^2

Application areas: adventure, puzzle, physical experiments, physical laws

Target user group: Primary: 9+ years, students and pupils as well as adventure players in general; secondary: All physics-interested casual gamers, teachers and instructors

Characterizing goal: *Physikus HD^2* is an adventure game with physics knowledge-based puzzles. Playing the game should spark interest in physics knowledge. Browsing through the knowledge part should be fun and allow players to solve adventure puzzles.

Short description and gameplay: In *Physikus HD^2*, a meteorite has hit a planet, causing it to stop rotating around its own axis. One half of the earth looks set to freeze solid in arctic conditions, while scorching heat is making life unbearable on the other half.

The gameplay is geared to classical First-person adventure games with beautiful graphics, exploration sequences, and machine and logic puzzles. These are connected to an appropriate didactical learning encyclopedia. Therefore, players are encouraged to work with the learning content in order to find and understand solutions to the different puzzles. Meanwhile, the storyline unfolds slowly, transporting the narrative and backstory mainly over objects like letters, machines, etc.

In this completely reworked version of the 90s classic, new storylines, different puzzles and new characters are added to the fascinating world of Physikus. No matter whether you know the original game or not: *Physikus HD^2* is a complete new experience for the iPad or iPhone (Fig. 12.14).

Distribution info: *Physikus HD^2* was released in December 2011 in multiple languages. The game was available in the AppStore for $3.99 USD for iOS devices. As of today, it is no longer available for purchase.

Fig. 12.14 Screenshots of Physics HD. A basic electric circuit explained (*left*), Stampy the roboter with various personalities, guides the player through the game (*middle*), still from cut-scene—the story is the motivation for landing and exploring the planet (*right*)

Economic information: *Physikus HD²* was developed by Reality Twist GmbH. The financing of the production was supported by funds of FFF Bayern (http://www.fff-bayern.de/) and the Bavarian state chancellery (http://bayern.de/) with 85,000 EUR. The game was published by Braingame Publishing.

The game itself is part of a very popular German educational adventure called *Physikus*, originally published by Braingame Publishing in German and English.

Developed in 1990, the successful learning adventure from Braingame is seen as the founder of German learning adventures and was now technically upgraded by Reality Twist. The game's given successful features, like an intuitive point & click interface and pedagogical learning, were extended by many modern features.

Quality information: Physikus|HD² was nominated at the German Developers Award show in 2011. The original Physikus has also won dozens of awards, including the Giga Maus in 2001, and the highest ranking possible in the educational guide book of Thomas Feible (Lern-Software-Ratgeber 2000, 2001). *Eltern for family*, a nationwide magazine for educational advices for parents, called the game *exemplary*.

Further information: Reality Twist GmbH (http://www.reality-twist.com/en) is the developer behind the portation of Physikus to iOS. The original creators can be reached at ARUS Media (http://www.arus-media.de/), the successor of Braingame Publishing.

12.3.3 80Days—Adaptive Game (Prototype) for Geography

Author: Michael Kickmeier-Rust

Title: Feon's Quest

Application area: Geography (the game follows a general European curriculum and basically covers European topography as well as environmental aspects)

Target user group: The game is designed for the secondary education level, for children from 12 to 14.

Characterizing goal: The game, in fact is a research prototype, developed in the context of the 80Days project (http://www.eightydays.eu), which was a European project funded by the European commission. The project ran from 2008 to 2010. Thus, the main goal of the game was to implement and demonstrate innovative research outcomes in terms of in-game adaptation, so-called micro-adaptivity (cf. Kickmeier-Rust and Albert 2010) and interactive storytelling (cf. Göbel et al. 2010b). From a learning perspective, the game is supposed to convey basic information about European countries as well as European capitals and major rivers. In addition, the goal is to teach environmental aspects such as the risk and impact of flooding (Fig. 12.15).

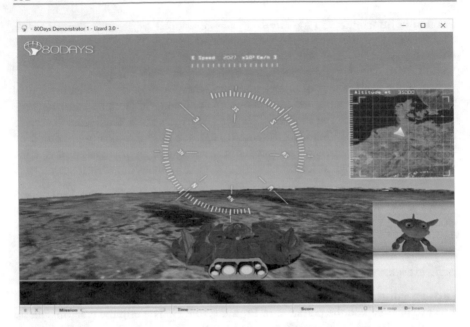

Fig. 12.15 Screenshot of the 80Days prototype *Feon's Quest—Feon explores Europe*

Short description and gameplay: In the game the learner takes the role of an Earth kid at the age of 14. The game starts when a spaceship lands in a backyard, and an alien named Feon contacts the player. Feon is an alien scout who was sent to collect information about Earth. The player wants to have fun by flying a spaceship, and in the story pretends to be an expert about planet Earth. He or she assists the alien to explore the planet, and to create a report about Earth and its geographical features. This is accomplished by the player by means of flying to different destinations on Earth, exploring them, and collecting and acquiring geographical knowledge. The goal is to send a report about planet Earth to the Alien mothership. At a certain point the player, finds out that the Aliens are not peaceful but plan to conquer Earth —using the found information about the planet. This reveals the "real" goal of the game: The player has to save the planet, and the only way to do it is to draw the right conclusion from the Earth report. The game is based on the idea that the real world is the playground where real geographical knowledge is learned. Gameplay and story are based on the metaphor of a "long zoom," which enables to approach geography and the Earth from different perspectives (i.e., a global view of the entire planet, a medium view of countries, cities, and landscapes, and a local view). The actual subject matter is enriched by meta-aspects such as environmental preservation.

Distribution info: The game is a Windows game for XP and higher systems. The game requires about 2 GB hard disk space and a performing graphics card. The game is distributed through the project website (http://www.eightydays.eu).

Economic information: The entire research project was carried out by seven partners and had a duration of 30 months. The entire project budget was about 3.3 million EUR; however, only a minor part was dedicated to game development.

Quality information: The game was designed with a high demand to graphical quality and quality of contents, in terms of learning contents as well as 3D assets. The environment, that is, the surface of Europe is rendered in real time on the basis of the real geographical data (provided freely by NASA). However, computational demands are comparably high and the game in itself is not complete (being a research demonstrator).

Further information: All information about the project, the game and, evaluation studies are available on the project website (http://www.eightydays.eu).

12.3.4 Roma Nova—Teaching History with CG and BCI

Author: Fotis Liarokapis

Title: Roma Nova

Application areas: Cultural heritage, history, crowd modeling, brain-computer interfaces

Target user group: Aims to teach history to 11–14 year-old students

Characterizing goal: The goal of the *Roma Nova* project was two-fold. Firstly, to test whether serious games that make use of high fidelity graphics can be an effective means of teaching history to children. The second goal was to test whether cheap and commercial brain computer interfaces can be used to fully control the same serious game.

Short description and gameplay: Roma Nova was built on top of the results of *Rome Reborn* project. The project aim was to develop a digital reconstruction of ancient Rome based on reliable archaeological evidence. 32 monuments were reconstructed at a very high detail. Roma Nova used these high resolution monuments and created a serious game aiming to teach history to young audiences by means of an original engaging experience where the player is immersed in a crowd of virtual Romans. Two different versions were developed. In the first version, players can interact with the Roma Nova game using three different ways based to the Levels of Interaction (LoI) framework (Panzoli et al. 2010a, b). The game allows for exploratory learning by immersing the learner/player inside a virtual heritage environment where they learn different aspects of history through their interactions with a crowd of virtual Roman avatars. LoI was designed to simplify the interactions between the players and artificial intelligence avatars. The first level of interaction offers a living background, enhancing the player's experience and immersion. The second level of interaction assigns characters automatically a more

Fig. 12.16 Brain-computer interaction using the NeuroSky MindSet (*left*), brain-computer interaction using the Emotive device (*right*)

realistic graphic representation and more complex behaviors. The last level of interaction uses an agent at the dialogue level to teach the learner (Fig. 12.16).

In the second version of the game, players control the avatar using only brainwaves. Two different commercial headsets were used (NeuroSky MindSet and the Emotiv) and a comparison between them was performed. Both systems are capable of fully controlling the avatar even if they have a completely different configuration and numbers of sensors. The NeuroSky MindSet uses only one sensor and players control the avatar by changing cognitive states such as meditation and attention. The Emotiv prototype has 14 sensors and requires prior training to operate the device which takes approximately 30–60 min depending on the adaptability of the user. Most players typically achieve their best results after training each action several times.

Distribution info: Roma Nova was developed in Unity 3D game engine and it is available in English. The software is not publically available since it was designed for research purposes only.

Economic information: The first version of Roma Nova was developed in 2010 as a collaboration between Coventry University (UK) and the University of Toulouse (France). The second version was completed in 2013 and was solely developed at Coventry University. All versions were funded internally and the overall cost of the whole project did not exceed 10,000 EUR.

Quality information: The final version of the Roma Nova game was evaluated with 62 participants in open-space laboratory conditions and conference demonstration areas. In respect to the first goal, all participants agreed that the use of high fidelity graphics can be an effective means of teaching history to children. Participants noted that realistic games can immerse the player fast and serious games should focus on that element. The use of the LoI was very interesting and adds another element of immersion to the players. On the other hand, the main negative point was that a much more concrete scenario was required. Also, for the LoI more dialogues were requested similar to commercial computer games.

In terms of the second goal (to test whether cheap and commercial brain computer interfaces can be used to fully control the same serious game), a lot of interesting results were recorded. For the NeuroSky MindSet device, participants were allowed 5 min to accommodate with controlling the avatar and around 3 min to complete the task of arriving at a particular destination. The prototype was tested with 31 users (60.65 % males and 39.35 % females), across the span of 2 months. In particular, testing was done at three sites: at a Coventry University computer games laboratory, the 3rd Phoenix Partner Annual conference, and the Archeovirtual 2012 International conference. Participants were drawn by the ease of use of the BCI device for controlling the virtual character via EEG technology. They viewed the concept as an interesting approach for future gaming scenarios, categorizing the whole experience as challenging, enjoyable and engaging. In particular, most participants were immediately engaged with the game and they wanted to explore the whole virtual city and interact with the artificial intelligent agents (which were controlled by the computer) to become more knowledgeable about the history of Rome (Liarokapis et al. 2014).

For the Emotiv device, 31 users (67.7 % male and 32.3 % females) were asked to provide comments on a questionnaire anonymously after playing the serious game. The testing was performed in an open-space environment at two locations at Coventry University: the Serious Games Institute (SGI) and the Department of Computing. Here, navigating into the game was much easier. It is a clear indication that it would be better for the training trial to include the components from the game for the user to get familiarized. Overall, the experience was reported as quite engaging and interesting regardless of certain issues of response time and accuracy. As soon as the participants had a profile, level interaction was very satisfactory—thus improving the learning process in respect to the serious game (Liarokapis et al. 2014).

In terms of quantitative analysis, the Emotiv device proved to be more effective for controlling the avatar into the serious game and for learning on how to use the interaction device, whereas the NeuroSky device performed better in terms of satisfaction of the player. Controlling the character using the Emotiv required less effort and the performance was also better for the Emotiv. The NeuroSky MindSet was considered more satisfying, perhaps owing to the immediate use of it due to the lack of setup as compared to the Emotiv. Learnability was also considered better for Emotiv, likely due to the same reasons as performance and effort.

Further information: For direct questions, please contact Fotis Liarokapis (*liarokap@fi.muni.cz*) from the HCI Lab (http://decibel.fi.muni.cz/wiki/) at Masaryk University.

12.3.5   Uni Game—Insights to Universities and Campus Life

Author: Helmut Hlavacs

Title: UniGame

Application areas: teaching, simulation, university, history

Target user group: school students, university students, anybody who wants to know about the inner workings of a university

Characterizing goal: learn about how a university works, but also about the multitude of research areas of the University of Vienna

Short description and gameplay: *UniGame* is a university manager game, created for the 650th anniversary of the University of Vienna (Austria). The player enters the role of a rector (president) of a large university and has to decide how to spend funding provided by the state (country). After haggling with the ministers, the rector has to agree to achieve certain goals, like creating new buildings, increasing the number of students, having more scientific discoveries, etc. Also he can hire researchers, who are supposed to teach students and do research. If there are not enough teachers compared to the number of students, both teachers and students get annoyed, and students leave the university, whereas teachers are less effective in research.

There are five major faculties, represented by knowledge graphs. The graphs consist of nodes and edges. The nodes and graphs represent by and large the research areas of the University of Vienna, and there are around 650 nodes. Each node represents a specific discovery, described by a small text. The task is now to schedule researchers such that they can discover these nodes, which at the start are hidden behind clouds representing the unknown future. After some time the next discovery can be made, and the players have to read the text and answer a question related to the text.

The task is now to detect all 650 discoveries taken from a vast amount of areas such as mathematics, computer science, social sciences, physics, astronomy, chemistry, law, psychology, etc. (Figure 12.17).

Distribution info: The game can be played free of charge at the website http://unigame.cs.univie.ac.at/

Economic information: the game was financed by the University of Vienna as part of its 650th anniversary

Quality information: First field tests in the form of qualitative studies have shown that the game is well received and provides a lot of fun for players.

Further information: The game was created at the Entertainment Computing research group at the Faculty of Computer Science of the University of Vienna. The game is available in German only.

Fig. 12.17 The start screen of the *UniGame*. Players can buy land and build faculty buildings (*left*). The main university building (*right*)

12.3.6   Internet Hero—Learning the Pros and Cons of the Internet

Author: Helmut Hlavacs

Title: Internet Hero

Application area: teaching, Internet, know-how, dangers

Target user group: children 8–12 years

Characterizing goal: The intention is to get to know how the Internet works, which dangers lurk, and which services can be used.

Short description and gameplay: The game consists of several minigames focusing a specific topic around the Internet. The minigames follow an adventure story of a young boy being dragged into the Internet; he is supposed to save the Internet, which is under attack by a bad character.

In each minigame, children first hear a short tutorial how the game works. Entangled to this information the actual information that should be learned is presented. After going through the tutorial, the respective minigame starts. Minigames are diverse and follow many different ideas and game mechanics. The next minigame is enabled only if a minimum level is achieved (Fig. 12.18).

Distribution info: The game can be played free of charge under http://www. internet-hero.at/

Economic information: The game was financed by two sequential stipends donated by the Austrian Internet Service Provider who funded NetIdee. It was created not only by specific students hired for the project, but also by newcomers as part of their bachelor degree theses.

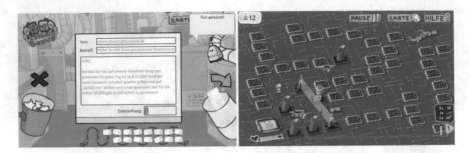

Fig. 12.18 Screenshots of *Internet Hero—The SPAM* minigame. The task is to decide whether an email is SPAM or not (*left*). In a tower defense game, children build defenses against viruses, worms and trojans (*right*)

Quality information: The game was tested with various audiences, and achieved a high level of entertainment.

Further information: The game was created at the Entertainment Computing research group at the Faculty of Computer Science of the University of Vienna. The game is available in German and English.

12.3.7 Yes or Know—Combining Board Games and Smart Play

Author: Clemens Hochreiter

Title: Yes or Know (Smart Play)

Application areas: quiz, board game, family game

Target user group: deliberately designed to target all ages, age 8 and up.

Characterizing goal: The idea behind "smart play:" Bring the whole family together to play together again. This is achieved by an intelligent and adaptive system that combines quiz games, board games, and mobile gaming (Fig. 12.19).

Short description and gameplay: The innovative system uses the intelligent smartphone, opening up an entirely new dimension of games. The user simply downloads the free app, puts the smartphone in the smartplay tripod and starts playing on the board. Thus, even elderly players only used to board game understand the principles. All activties are made on the board and the app only reacts to the inputs the player has given. In *Yes or Know*, quiz master Bob will lead you through the game and asks difficult questions. Players have to guess and estimate from ten different trivia categories, with more than 2,000 questions. There are tasks and questions for each age group, so children and teens have a fair chance amongst their parents, too. The smartplayer manages all points gathered. And the best: The whole interactive game show is fully and professionally voiced over.

Fig. 12.19 *Yes or Know*: combining board games with smart play. Official box (*left*), the smart play system with smartphone holder (*right*)

Distribution info: The game is distributed indirectly via the retail market: Players need to buy the board game in order to have the app work. The app itself is free. The game is available on the iOS AppStore and Android GooglePlay. The board game is produced and distributed by German market leader Ravensburger. The language is German only.

Economic information: The business model is centered around the idea of generating revenue by selling board games over retail. The developer itself developed without royalties on a purely work-for-hire basis. Development costs have been medium range.

Quality information: The game won the 2014 Award for *Best Family Game* at the German Developers Award Show.

Further information: A website about the smartplay concept available at http://www.ravensburger-smartplay.com/ (German only).

12.3.8 Bionigma—Science Game for Protein Exploration

Author: Martin Hess

Title: Bionigma

Application areas: Citizen Science, scientific games, puzzle games, bioinformatics, multiple sequence alignments

Target user group: Puzzle and casual gamers, as well as amateur scientists of any age

Characterizing goal: *Bionigma* aims at the optimization of Multiple Sequence Alignments of proteins by using human pattern recognition.

Short description and gameplay: Bionigma is a classical puzzle game. A puzzle consists of several colored tokens placed on a grid. The goal of the game is to align similar tokens to each other. The more similar the aligned tokens, i.e., color, shape, and texture, the higher the player's reward. The constraints are that tokens can only be moved left or right and that the order of tokens cannot be changed. In addition, gaps in the puzzle introduced by moving the tokens are penalized. In order to solve a puzzle by reaching a level-specific score, the player must find the optimal balance between rewards and penalties.

As a scientific game, Bionigma serves a specific purpose, namely the optimization of so called Multiple Sequence Alignments (MSA) of proteins. Game puzzles are abstract representations of these real world biological problems. Here, a row in the puzzle grid represents a single protein sequence and the colored tokens inside the corresponding amino acids. By aligning the tokens and maximizing their score, players help to discover similarities between the protein sequences, which can be used to analyze evolutionary effects such as coevolution (Fig. 12.20).

To encourage players both to play the game and to optimize their level scores, Bionigma features a global player ladder, which ranks players according to their puzzle performance. This performance is measured by the number of puzzles solved and especially by holding level high scores. Thus further improving puzzles to reclaim level high scores is very valuable and directly results in improved MSAs. In order to assist players in improving their alignments, Bionigma features several interaction and highlighting techniques. For example, players can easily select tokens by their type, align multiple tokens in a single step, or reset the puzzle to their highest scoring state. Additionally, similar tokens or those giving low rewards can be highlighted. While the first option helps to understand which tokens should be aligned for the highest reward, the latter aids in the identification of suboptimal aligned and thus improvable regions.

Distribution info: The game can be downloaded and played completely for free. Downloads for Windows, Mac OS X, and Linux are available on http://www. bionigma.de/. Supported languages are English and German. Further platforms and languages may be available in the future.

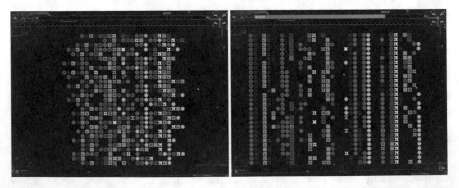

Fig. 12.20 Screenshots of *Bionigma*—a level at the beginning (*left*), solved and improved (*right*)

Economic information: Bionigma has been developed in cooperation with the groups Graphics, Capture and Massively Parallel Computing (GCC), Computational Biology and Simulation (CBS), and the Institute of Sport Science (IFS) at Technische Universität Darmstadt, Germany. The project was funded by a grant of the Forum for Interdisciplinary Research at Technische Universität Darmstadt, Germany.

Quality information: Bionigma was continuously evaluated during its development considering game mechanics and experience as well as usability. The first game prototype was tested in a study with 20 persons (6 female, 14 male; age 22–34; background in biology n = 11, computer science n = 8 and educational science n = 1; No prior experience in computer games n = 5). Results showed that the game is visually appealing, fun to play, and delivers a good game experience, but can still be improved especially regarding immersion and flow (Hess et al. 2014).

Building upon these results, Bionigma was further improved especially in its visual representation, game mechanics, and usability. Two follow-up studies showed that these improvements increased the game experience and the fun in playing the game.

Further information: For questions about the game, please email *info@bionigma. de*. Further scientific information about the underlying project *Serious Games for Bioinformatics*, as well as publications and contact information: http://www. bionigma.de/.

12.3.9 Meister Cody—Educational Game for Dyscalculia

Author: Markus Schütze, Ulrich Schulze Althoff

Title: Meister Cody—Talasia

Application areas: education, e-health

Target user group: elementary school students with math weakness/dyscalculia

Characterizing goal: identifying dyscalculia and therapeutically helping children master it (Fig. 12.21)

Short description and gameplay: *Meister Cody—Talasia* is an online screening test and learning game for second to fourth grade elementary school children with math weakness or dyscalculia. It is based on the CODY-project initiated by the University of Münster. First, the scientifically validated test is used to reliably identify dyscalculia and math weakness. Then children train in the magical world of Talasia. The wise leader character, Meister Cody, sends them on an epic journey to save the country. In order to proceed with the story, children will have to master a variety of over 20 therapeutic exercises. To make the training as efficient as possible, the game engine monitors children's improvement and delivers results to the parents, teacher and/or therapist. Depending on this data the level of difficulty of

Fig. 12.21 Screenshot of Meister Cody's story-based gameplay environment

each training session will constantly adapt daily to the child's personal skills. In addition, the data allowed researchers to identify four types of dyscalculia profiles and deliver all users a custom training experience and tutorials that automatically start when a child experiences a challenge.

Distribution info: Meister Cody is available as a download for Windows, Mac (Mac App Store), iPad (iTunes App Store), and Android devices (Google Play Store). The download and first training module (which also includes the screening test) are free. After the free trial, parents sign up for a monthly subscription. Schools purchase annual contracts that auto-renew.

Economic information: Meister Cody is based on a research project called CODY that is managed by the Institute of Psychology at University of Münster in Germany. Thanks to Prof. Dr. Heinz Holling (Institute of Psychology) and Dr. Christian Dobel (Institute for Biomagnetism and Biosignalanalysis) for receiving grants valued over 750,000 EUR. Financial support is provided by the German Ministry of Education and Research.

Quality information: Scientific evaluation of the learning outcomes that were achieved by playing the game was conducted and published by the Institute of Psychology, WWU Münster. In one study, 1,175 German elementary school children (grades 2–4) were administered the CODY test between September 2012 and September 2013. Four key training tasks were evaluated in a randomized controlled trial with three groups: (1) CODY training, (2) training for inductive reasoning, (3) control group. A group of children with dyscalculia was assigned at random to one of the following groups: (1) children who trained with the first CODY version for 30 days for 20 min per day, (2) completed 30 days of inductive reasoning training, (3) control group. A subset of these participants took part in an additional experiment to measure brain activity through Magnetoencephalography (MEG) at the time of number crunching.

A previous study of the CODY test took place with 68 German children. Results of the study are published (Kuhn et al. 2013).

While still in its beta phase, the game won the Vodafone Innovation Award 2013. The jury consisted of high-level experts from Vodafone and the IT sector who praised in particular the "innovative solution, which makes it possible to use and experience the potential of mobile communication and networking." In October 2014, Meister Cody—Talasia won Germany's prestigious GIGA-Maus award for "best math learning program for children from six to ten." The game also won "Best Multi-platform Title" and "Best Overall Game" at the 8th European Conference on Games Based Learning (ECGBL 2014). In 2015, the game was honored with the Silver Medal at the Serious Play Awards in the United States, the eco Internet Award (Best Game), and the Dyslexia Quality Award. The lead WWU researcher, Dr. Jörg-Tobias Kuhn, was editor of the Developmental Dyscalculia issue of Zeitschrift für Psychology (Magazine for Psychology). Two CODY articles are published in this academic magazine (Kuhn 2015; Kuhn et al. 2015). His team began a research study in German schools in Fall 2015. Meister Cody—Talasia is also being piloted by primary schools in Finland.

Further information: For development, marketing, sales, and/or distribution questions, please contact Markus Schütze at Kaasa health, +49 211 730 635 11, *markus.schuetze@kaasahealth.com* or visit http://www.meistercody.com. For scientific or research questions, please contact the CODY project team at WWU, +49 251 83 34320 or *cody@uni-muenster.de*.

12.4 Games for Health

12.4.1 Play Forward—HIV Prevention

Authors: Kimberly Hieftje, Lynn Fiellin

Title: PlayForward: Elm City Stories (PlayForward series)

Application areas: Risk behavior reduction, HIV/STI prevention in young adolescents

Target user group: young adolescents, age 11–14 years

Characterizing goal: aims to provide young adolescents the opportunity to acquire and practice skills for risk reduction and HIV/STI prevention (Fig. 12.22)

Short description and gameplay: *PlayForward* is an interactive, role-playing videogame designed for young adolescents to gain knowledge and practice skills needed to make good decisions related to alcohol, drugs, and sex. In the game, the player must guide their character, or *Aspirational Avatar*, that they have created

Fig. 12.22 PlayForward: Elm City Stories main screen

through middle and high school, while negotiating challenges that require them to make decisions that have both short and long-term effects on their Avatar's future. As the game progresses, the player is able to see how each decision affects their Avatar's life, and can subsequently go back in time, change their decision, and see how a different action might lead to a different outcome. *PlayForward* allows adolescents to experience negative consequences related to risk behaviors in a safe, virtual environment, while giving them the tools to acquire and practice skills needed to avoid or reduce the risk behaviors in real life.

Distribution info: *PlayForward* is available in English on iOS and Android tablets, PC, and Mac. Currently, the game is part of a large randomized controlled trial (RCT) and is not available to the public for purchase or download, but is expected to be available mid-year 2016. To learn more about this game and associated research studies, visit http://play2PREVENT.org.

Economic information: Funded by the Eunice Kennedy Shriver National Institute of Child Health and Human Development (USA) (NICHD R01 HD062080-01: Principal Investigator, Lynn Fiellin, MD), *PlayForward* was developed by the play2PREVENT Lab at Yale University School of Medicine (USA) in conjunction with Schell Games (schellgames.com) and DigitalMill (dmill.com).

Quality information: A multidisciplinary team of individuals with expertise in HIV, health behavior, addiction, pediatrics, community-based participatory research, community psychology, education, clinical psychology, social psychology, and serious and commercial videogame design and development contributed to the development of *PlayForward*. Additionally, the play2PREVENT Lab partnered with over a dozen community schools and after school programs in the greater New Haven, Connecticut area and has involved over a hundred young adolescents, school and after school program directors, community partners, teachers, and parents in the development of the game.

PlayForward is currently being evaluated in a large randomized controlled trial with 333 young adolescents aged 11–14 years old. The study is examining a range of outcomes including knowledge, intentions, self-efficacy and actual behaviors and data is being collected at baseline, 6 weeks, 3, 6, 12, and 24 months. The play2PREVENT team will examine these outcomes using an experimental group (adolescents playing *PlayForward*) compared with a control group (adolescents playing a set of off-the-shelf games). Data is currently being collected for the 24-month time period, with the study expected to be complete by June of 2016. Qualitative interviews were also conducted with adolescents that played *PlayForward*, and data was collected on their gameplay experience.

Preliminary data comes from an early cohort of 198 adolescents enrolled in the RCT, in which 161 had completed 6 weeks of gameplay and 125 had completed 3-month follow-up assessments. There were no significant baseline between-groups differences on a 22-item assessment of HIV risk-related knowledge. After 6 weeks of gameplay, the intervention group had higher knowledge scores (mean = 15, S.D. = 4.8) than the control group (mean = 12.5, S.D. = 4.5; $p < 0.001$) at 6 weeks and at 3 months (mean = 14.4, S.D. = 5.5 vs. mean = 12.5, S.D. = 4.7; $p < 0.04$). Analysis of 1,289,903 events in logfiles revealed that the number of game levels completed was positively correlated with knowledge gains measured at 6 weeks ($r = 0.32$; $p < 0.005$) and at 3 months ($r = 0.42$; $p < 0.001$).

Notably, the majority of teens reported enjoying playing the game (79 %), liked the way the game looked (84 %), and felt they would make decisions in life like they made them in the game (79 %) and felt responsible for the choices they made (88 %).

In 2013, *PlayForward* won the Gold Medal Award in the Healthcare/Medical category at the International Serious Play Conference at DigiPen Institute, the Pittsburgh Technology Council's DATA Award for the Joystick Category, and received a 3-year certification from the International Serious Play Award Program for meeting the criteria for titles having a high quality standard.

Further information: For more information regarding *PlayForward* and its associated research study or to learn more about other projects at the play2PREVENT Lab, visit play2PREVENT.org or contact the team at *play2PREVENT@yale.edu*.

12.4.2 Respir Games—Asthma Therapy

Author: Peter Bingham

Title: RespirGames™—Spirometer

Application areas: health game, exergame, breath awareness, respiratory muscle training, heart rate variability training, deep inspiration pacing, post-operative atelectasis

Target user group: Pediatric Asthma, Muscular Dystrophy, Chronic Obstructive Pulmonary Disease, Chronic Lung Disease, Breath Interoception training enthusiasts, athletes

Characterizing goal: Personalized improvement of pulmonary function and breath awareness/interoception

Short description and gameplay: RespirGames consists of software that can be used on mobile or desktop platform. The software is used with a separately purchased, off-the-shelf spirometer, a device that measures breath flow and volume, and that is used as the Respirgames controller. Depending on the health goal, the player competes against himself as he/she encounters one of three scored challenges: (1) *tracking*—track a moving target (or evade obstacles that move across the screen, or navigate a maze); (2) *forced exhalation*—exhale with maximum force in a single maneuver; or (3) *deep inspiration*—render a maximal inhaled volume from full exhalation. Depending on the challenge and associated game scenario, the player, by intentionally controlling or "maneuvering" his/her own breath flow rate, is paced through various breath "gestures" rendered as visual (on-screen) or acoustic events. In a breath-tracking accuracy scenario, the player is paced to increase the precision with which they track a moving "coach" object (Fig. 12.23).

Distribution info: RespirGames is not yet ready for commercial distribution. An English, iOS-compatible version will be accessible via download (free-$15/download).

Fig. 12.23 Clinical Spirometer adapted as a Bluetooth-enabled *Respirgames* controller—NIH/NHLBI Grant "Breath controlled Computer Game Controller for Asthma Therapy" R43HL103370 (*left*), Respirgames created with a grant from the Robert Wood Johnson Foundation for children with cystic fibrosis (*middle* and *right*). The game includes both Type 1, 2, and 3 challenges as outlined above

Economic information: RespirGames is a privately held, for-profit startup with an exclusive license to patented technology held by the University of Vermont (*Breath biofeedback Method and System, US Patent No. 7,618,378, November 17, 2009* is a patent held by the University of Vermont; Peter Bingham, Jason Bates, inventors). The technology was developed and tested through research at the University of Vermont, and with support ($500,000 USD) from the NIH (National Heart, Lung, Blood Institute) and from the Robert Wood Johnson Foundation (USA).

Quality information: RespirGames was initiated in a pilot study in 2011. 11 in-patient suffering from pulmonary exacerbations of cystic fibrosis engaged with a target tracking game (Type 1 Challenge as outlined above). This initial study demonstrated a novel type of learning that entails improved eye-breath coordination (Bingham et al. 2010). In a subsequent field trial with 19 subjects with cystic fibrosis, subjects engaged spontaneously with a game in their home environment of a ∼3 week period, and engaged more frequently with airway clearance breath maneuvers (forced exhalations) that had previously been recommended by respiratory therapists, and to which, at baseline, they had been chronically, poorly adherent (Bingham et al. 2012). Qualitative, interview explorations structured around Self Determination Theory with pediatric cystic fibrosis as well as asthma subjects have shown a positive alignment with users' knowledge, attitudes, and beliefs with values incorporated into RespirGames as a consumer product/health aide (Bingham and Meyer 2011).

Further information: See reference list. Inquiries may be directed to RespirGames Principal Dr. Peter Bingham at *Peter.Bingham@uvmhealth.org*.

12.4.3 BalanceFit—Balance, Coordination and Strength Training

Authors: Sandro Hardy, Stefan Göbel

Title: BalanceFit

Application areas: health game, exergames, balance training, fall prevention

Target user group: individuals/private persons at home; institutions such as hospitals, therapy studios, or elderly care houses

Characterizing goal: aims to improve the coordination, strength and balance of users (players, patients)

Short description and gameplay: BalanceFit resembles classic wooden maze-and-ball-games. The goal of the exergame is to navigate a ball through a maze into a target. The maze is presented on a screen and the player steers the game by moving the center of pressure (COP) of his body intentionally. The maze consists of walls which facilitate the task and game features which increase the difficulty of the game such as round and rectangle open spaces to fall through or bridges and narrow

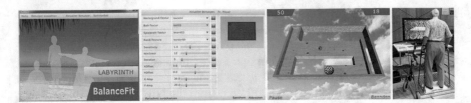

Fig. 12.24 *BalanceFit's* main menu, configuration tool, game level 50, setup (from *left* to *right*)

passages which need higher accuracy in steering. As input control, a regular Nintendo Wii Balance Board is used, which has four pressure sensors, one at each of its edges, which allows measuring the weight distribution of the player standing on the board. Optionally, the balance board is integrated into a robust installation offering more stability for users with gait impairments or difficulties in standing. Based on the weight distribution the COP is calculated. If the player moves in a specific direction, the COP also moves in this direction. Accordingly, the virtual maze is rotated into the same direction and the virtual ball follows (Fig. 12.24).

BalanceFit provides a configuration tool (for individual players or therapists) that allows game adaptation of visual style and difficulty (defined by the layout of the labyrinth and the sensitivity of the controller). Automatic difficulty adjustment of the game is offered in customized versions of BalanceFit for dedicated user groups. In general, the system can be used by agile and fit users as well as by gait-impaired users (with a standing frame as hardware to provide stability)—and even by wheelchair drivers (Hardy et al. 2013).

Distribution info: BalanceFit is available in German and English and runs on all platforms supporting Unity3D (users need to install the Unity plugin, available for free). The game is accessible for download at http://www.spielend-fit.de. A public version for non-commercial purposes is available for free. Personalized versions for institutions (e.g., elderly care houses, physiotherapy studio), associations, etc. are implemented as contractual work (projects) for ~10,000 EUR, depending on the user-specific requirements of customized version.

Economic information: BalanceFit has been developed by the Serious Games group located both at the Hessian Telemedia Competence Center (httc) and the Multimedia Communications Lab of Technische Universität Darmstadt (TUDA KOM) in Germany. The development of the first prototype version was supported by the Wilhelmine Thoss Foundation (10,000 EUR); later versions were further elaborated in the course of strategic research and education/practical courses at httc and TUDA KOM.

Quality information: BalanceFit was initiated in 2011 and tested with different users and user groups, among others student groups as well as seniors from the elderly care house "Emilstraße" an institution of "Klinikum Darmstadt" (hospital).

The influence of individual game features on the perceived difficulty posed on the player has been investigated within a study with 44 students (28 female, 16 male; age 18–42; background in psychology and computer science). Results showed a significant influence of single features on psychological (motivation, difficulty) and physiological constructs (performance, needed time) (Hardy et al. 2014a).

The acceptance of the prototype BalanceFit has been evaluated with 30 seniors from the Emilstraße (residents' home for elderly) for a time period for more than 1 year. Qualitative analyses (interviews and observations) underlined that the visual style and the sensitivity (difficulty level, sensitivity of control/pressure sensors) play an important role for the accessibility of the overall system. By changing the visual style and increasing the contrast, BalanceFit can be adapted for people with visual impairments. Adjusting the sensitivity of the control allows the game to be played by seniors with heterogeneous skills/impairments. This way, young and fit people, as well as people with small and bigger gait impairments, can play the game. Even wheelchair drivers are able to play BalanceFit as long as their legs are not completely paralyzed. The most important results of the study are that all participants enjoyed playing BalanceFit and had no major problems in using the system (Hardy et al. 2013). Another important outcome results from another study published by Hardy et al. (2014b) where both young and elderly people state that they would fully accept the game as an appropriate kind of training.

Further information: BalanceFit is available for download at the website http://www.spielend-fit.de hosted by httc. Further scientific information and publications are available at the KOM website http://www.kom.tu-darmstadt.de (research area on multimedia technologies and serious games). For direct questions, please contact Sandro Hardy and/or Stefan Göbel from the serious games group at httc and KOM.

12.4.4 Dance with ALFRED—Collaborative Dancing

Authors: Tim Dutz, Siavash Tazari, Stefan Göbel

Title: Dance with ALFRED (public version: Dancicians)

Application areas: Health game, exergame, social awareness

Target user group: although designed to be enjoyed by a wide variety of people, its primary target user group is the elderly.

Characterizing goal: aims to motivate those suffering from a lack of movement to accustom themselves to physical motion, in a manner that is considered social and entertaining. The social aspect of the game is underlined by a multi-player-centric game design, allowing participants to play side by side, cooperating and competing at the same time.

Short description and gameplay: In classic, non-serious game terminology, *Dance with ALFRED* is a rhythm-action game, where the player is challenged to execute moves in accordance to the rhythm of music. Aspects that set it apart as a one-of-a-kind serious game are considerations about accessibility, target audience capabilities and social interaction in close proximity. Accessibility is enhanced by developing Dance with ALFRED specifically for smartphones, which is, in this day and age, in possession of most people in most Countries. Player movement is registered via the accelerometer of the smartphone. No further device is required to play; though, a wireless internet connection is necessary for multi-player. Considering the capabilities of seniors, the game offers three difficulty settings, with the easiest setting suitable even for persons with low agility and capacity of reaction. Furthermore, there are five different songs available to dance along to; each from a different genre, not only to satisfy different tastes, but also to offer various rhythm-tempos to make the desired challenge even more customizable. Dance with ALFRED is especially geared towards playing with a group in the same room. Each participant is responsible for the sound of an instrument or a set of instruments—very similar to a music band—and with a bit of practice, they perform synchronized moves that resemble a group dance, which could even be entertaining for non-participants in the room (Fig. 12.25).

Gameplay evolves during dance moves at the right times in order to sustain the sound of each of the instruments of a song. In this regard, Dance with ALFRED is not only about dancing, but also about provoking the feeling of making music. Possible moves are stepping left, right, up or down, as well as half and full rotations. The set of moves is limited intentionally to facilitate accessibility. Player interaction is cooperative in the sense of trying to accomplish a good group performance, and competitive by enabling individuals to compare their scores with each other.

Distribution info: Dance with ALFRED is currently still in development, but the public version (*Dancicians*) is planned to be released soon on the Google Play Store for free. As part of the ALFRED project, Dance with ALFRED will be available on a personalized mobile device for assisting elderly people (more information about the ALFRED project at: http://alfred.eu/). Only the game menus are language-dependent. Although all menu options are originally defined in the English language, they automatically become translated to another language based on personal smartphone settings.

Economic information: Dance with ALFRED is being developed by the Serious Games group located at the Multimedia Communications Lab of Technische Universität Darmstadt (TUDA KOM) in Germany and is funded by the European

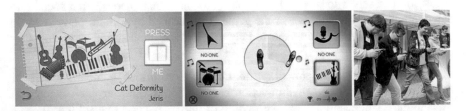

Fig. 12.25 *Dance with ALFRED* instrument selection, game instructions, play (*left* to *right*)

Commission. The project is funded with ~4 million EUR, but only a minor part (less than 50,000 EUR) is allocated for the development (and extension) of five (existing) health game apps provided by TUDA KOM.

Quality information: Dance with ALFRED was initiated in 2014 and tested with different users and user groups all across Europe, among others student groups as well as seniors. Test reports of initial feasibility studies indicated that almost all participants have been enthusiastic about the game. Comments have been positive about the provided motivational push to perform physical exercises. The younger users, besides delivering necessary feedback to improve the visual appeal of the game, have shown more interest towards the higher difficulty settings, whereas the older users, partially over the age of 80, preferred the medium to low challenge levels. Additional feedback has influenced the set of available moves, the transmission of information through the graphical user interface, the choice of colors and further visual aspects, among other qualities.

Further information: Complementing scientific information and publications are available at the KOM website http://www.kom.tu-darmstadt.de (research area on multimedia technologies and serious games). For direct questions, please contact Tim Dutz and/or Stefan Göbel from the serious games group at KOM.

12.4.5 NeuroVitAALis—Personalized Cognitive Training

Authors: Elke Kalbe, Christian Reuter, Stefan Göbel, Josef Kessler & Gisa Baller

Title: NEURO*vitAALis*

Application area: personalized cognitive training

Target user group: (1) healthy elderly people (2) patients with cognitive impairment, e.g., mild cognitive impairment or early dementia.

Characterizing goal: cognitive training to (1) prevent cognitive decline in healthy aging and (2) to treat cognitive impairment and prevent further cognitive decline

Short description and gameplay: NEURO*vitAALis* is a scientifically based, personalized cognitive training program that offers a guided training mode as well as the possibility to choose a combination of training tasks freely. Before training starts a cognitive screening test is conducted which results in recommendations on the type (three types of training are available with different combinations of tasks) and the starting level of the training.

The guided training mode includes a 6-week program with three training sessions per week, each one for 40 min. After these 6 weeks, all cognitive exercises are available, and the individual can choose them freely. The program includes five complex tasks with different difficulty levels (between 12 and 24 levels). The program adapts to the individual performance level so that the individual always trains at the personal limit, resulting in a maximum training success. It uses controlled randomization in order to reduce repetition during long term usage.

The tasks are *category memory* (matching and memorization of cards), *city plan* (putting a map together and finding the quickest route), *think differently* (recognizing shapes in a timely manner), *plan a day* (creating a schedule), and *word fluency* (finding fitting words). With these tasks, the program trains the age-sensitive cognitive domains learning and memory, working memory, planning and reasoning, word fluency, attention, and visuospatial processing. Besides these tasks, each training session includes a psycho-educational video with useful information, e.g., on the brain and brain functions or the optimization of higher cognitive functions, as well as advices for the everyday use of cognitive strategies. Importantly, for patients with mild dementia for which some of the regular task might be too demanding, the program offers the opportunity to conduct biography work. For example, individual photographs can be uploaded by relatives, and these pictures are transformed into puzzles with different complexity, so that the patient can train his or her memory and, at the same time, individual memories are activated. Several screenshots are depicted in Fig. 12.26.

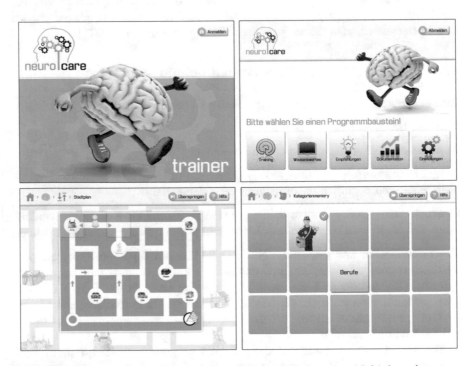

Fig. 12.26 *Upper row* (*left*) front page of the NEURO*vitAALis* program; (*right*) the main menu: a training task, a psycho-educational video, hints for improving everyday cognition, feedback on performance in the training tasks, or program adjustments can be chosen as options; *lower row*: (*left*) screenshot of the game *city plan* which trains planning abilities and visuospatial processing; (*right*) screenshot of the game *category memory* (e.g., the word "professions" corresponds to the picture of a postman) which trains learning and memory as well as executive functions (building associations)

Distribution info: The cognitive training program NEURO*vitAALis* is available as prototype for iOS in German and is currently being tested with end users in the course of the research project *NeuroCare*, funded by the German Ministry of Education and Science. Distribution information and availability for other platforms like Android or PC will be available at http://neurocare-aal.de/. The original (paper and pencil) version of the cognitive group training NEURO*vitalis* (Baller et al. 2010) is available at http://www.prolog-therapie.de ($\sim$230 EUR).

Economic information: NEURO*vitAALis* has been developed within the *Neuro-Care* project, at the University Clinic Cologne, Germany (Department of Medical Psychology & Center for Neuropsychological Diagnostics and Intervention; Department of Neurology) together with the Multimedia Communications Lab of Technische Universität Darmstadt, Germany, and Prolog GmbH. The exact price for the digital game will be negotiated among the partners of the NeuroCare project consortium involved in the development of the game.

Quality information: A randomized controlled trial (RCT) to examine the efficacy of *NEUROvitAALis* is currently being conducted at the Department of Medical Psychology, Cologne, Germany. Several studies exist that demonstrate the efficacy of the original group training program NEURO*vitalis* in enhancing cognition in patients with Parkinson's disease in the short-term (Petrelli et al. 2014) and the long-term (Petrelli et al. 2015) as well as in patients with mild cognitive impairment (Rahe et al. 2015a, b). Furthermore, a study comparing pure cognitive training with NEURO*vitAALis* with a variant that adds physical activity to the program (*NEU-ROvitAALis plus*) demonstrates that both variants lead to cognitive gains in healthy elderly subjects (Rahe et al. 2015a).

Further information: Website http://neurocare-aal.de/ for the NeuroCare project, personal contact: Elke Kalbe, Ph.D. (role: concepts, efficacy studies), *elke.kalbe@uk-koeln.de*, phone: +49 221 47896244; Gisa Baller (concepts), Josef Kessler (concepts/testing), Christian Reuter and Stefan Göbel, Ph.D. (TU Darmstadt, Serious Games group, development, http://www.kom.tu-darmstadt.de/serious-games), *christian.reuter@kom.tu-darmstadt.de*, Oliver Schmid, publisher, Prolog, http://www.prolog-shop.de/

12.4.6 KickAss—Autism Game for Adolescents

Authors: Roman Schönsee, Michael Bas, Rens van Slagmaat

Title: KickAss

Application areas: Online therapy, adolescents, autism

Target user group: Adolescents with autism

Characterizing goal: Support adolescents with autism spectrum disorder to better deal with difficult social situations; Provide peers of adolescents with autism

spectrum disorder with more insight and understanding about the goals and challenges of the player.

Short description and gameplay: This game is created by ranj and commissioned
by Cooperation E-lab Autism (Netherlands). The primary goal of this game is to
give adolescents with autism insight in their behavior in difficult social situations
and provide them with strategies to cope with these situations. The game provides
them with a safe environment in which they can experiment with how to react in
these situations and what the consequences of those reactions are (Fig. 12.27).

At first, the player creates a personal profile. This provides insight in their
planning, flexibility, control, and initiative skills. Based on this, they set their
personal learning goals.

During the game, the player is faced with different social situations and confronted with his or her choices straightaway. An evaluation moment asks the player
to share thoughts and feelings about the dilemma. At the end of the dilemma the
player sees an overview of the choices made during the situation and is asked if the
personal learning goal has been met. These situations can be replayed to experience
different outcomes and new insights in a safe environment.

A logbook will keep track of their activity, progression and lists achievements.
The log also lists likes and compliments from their peers. Peers themselves can also
keep track of a player's progression and can even experience the same social
situations the player played through. The player can decide who to nominate as
peer.

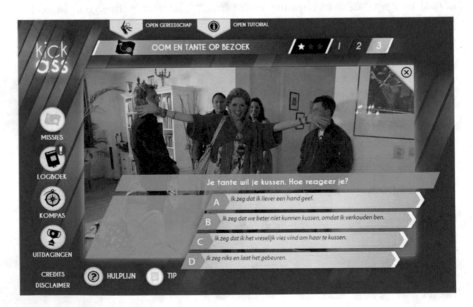

Fig. 12.27 KickAss—situational choice

Distribution info: The game is in Dutch. It is possible to get a demo version at https://www.mentaalbeter.nl/. Furthermore, it is possible for mental health care institutions to join this project and use this game online.

Economic information: The game is developed by ranj in co-operation with GGzE (mental healthcare organization), Leo Kannerhuis Nederland (centre for autism), and a group of adolescents. The game development has been supported by the health insurance company CZ.

Quality information: KickAss is linked to the E-Mental Platform used by therapists. Supervisors of the adolescents with autism spectrum disorder can use the Therapist module tool to get an insight into the activities and progression of the player.

Further information: http://www.ranj.com

12.4.7   Zirkus Empathica—Autism Game for Children

Authors: Simone Kirst, Dietmar Zoerner, Ulrike Lucke, Isabel Dziobek

Title: Zirkus Empathico

Application areas: psychology, emotions, empathy

Target user group: Children with autism

Characterizing goal: Training of socio-emotional competencies in pre- and elementary school children with autism to foster everyday social interaction and communication skills (Fig. 12.28).

Short description and gameplay: The mobile application *Zirkus Empathico* follows a holistic approach to effectively foster social behavior in autistic children. Different emotional and empathic competencies are trained separately in four training modules and generalization into daily life is aimed at with the app's fifth module. Naturalistic film clips showing dynamic emotional expressions of children and adults as well as emotional situations and events ("context films") are used to convey five basic emotions (joy, sadness, anger, fear, surprise) and one neutral state.

In Module 1, the user is asked to recognize and verbalize own emotional states, which are induced by the context films. The adequate processing of one's own emotions builds the foundation for the correct understanding of other's emotions and prosocial reactions, with these *empathic* capacities being explicitly trained in Modules 2 and 3. Addressing cognitive empathy, Module 2 strengthens the recognition of other's emotions from facial expressions. Module 3 complements this skill by training the understanding of emotional cues in contextual information (e.g., thunderstorms evoke fear; receiving a gift induces happiness). Finally, Module 4 focuses on emotional empathy: one's own emotional feeling elicited by somebody else's emotional state needs to be recognized (e.g., I feel sorry because

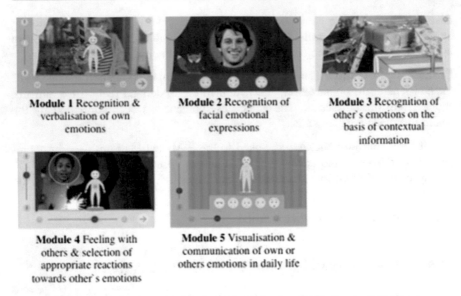

Module 1 Recognition & verbalisation of own emotions

Module 2 Recognition of facial emotional expressions

Module 3 Recognition of other's emotions on the basis of contextual information

Module 4 Feeling with others & selection of appropriate reactions towards other's emotions

Module 5 Visualisation & communication of own or others emotions in daily life

Fig. 12.28 *Zirkus Empathico*—Tasks of module *1–4* and generalization module (*5*)

another person is sad). In this module, the practicing child is also demanded to select an appropriate action in response to emotional states of self and other (e.g., console another person). Finally, Zirkus Empathico allows for transferring the targeted empathy skills into daily social life by providing a generalisation module, which aids in visualizing and communicating one's own and other's emotions.

Distribution info: Zirkus Empathico is in a pilot project phase. Currently, an evaluation with children with autism spectrum disorder is carried out in order to determine training efficacy and to analyze design issues. For a demonstration of the app please visit: http://www.zirkus-empathico.de/

Economic information: The software was developed as a psychological research instrument by the Social Cognition group of the Berlin School of Mind and Brain at Humboldt-Universität zu Berlin in cooperation with the Complex Multimedia Application Architectures group at the Department of Computer Science at the University of Potsdam, Germany. Based on the current intervention study run by the Social Cognition group (see below), further development of the prototype towards a fully applicable and adaptive training program is planned to be realized within the next years.

Quality information: With the mobile application Zirkus Empathico, the first IT-based realiation of a holistic and naturalistic concept to foster socio-emotional competencies in young children was implemented (Kirst et al. 2015). The concept is based on contemporary research findings demonstrating relationships between emotional, empathic, and social-cognitive competencies (Decety and Lamm 2006) and their trainability in clinical groups. Pilot testing of the app with 10 typically developed children revealed good usability and comprehensibility of the app. In the current intervention study (October 2015—October 2016), realized as a randomized, controlled trial, approximately 70 children with autism will be included and receive the training for 8 weeks to validate the app as a therapeutically applicable tool for autism-specific therapy.

Further information: For more information, please contact Isabel Dziobek (*isabel. dziobek@hu-berlin.de*) or Simone Kirst (*simone.kirst@hu-berlin.de*) for questions regarding the therapy concept and Ulrike Lucke (*ulrike.lucke@uni-potsdam.de*) for questions regarding app development.

12.4.8   SPARX—Mental Health Game for Youths & Adolescents

Authors: Mathijs Lucassen, Sally Merry, Karolina Stasiak, Theresa Fleming, Matt Shepherd, Karen Carter, Johan Strydom, Angela Chong, Chris Bullen

Title: SPARX (smart, positive, active, realistic, x-factor thoughts)

Application areas: serious mental health game; treatment of adolescent depression; assists young people who are feeling "stressed and down"

Target user group: SPARX was designed for use by young people 12 to 19 years old with depressive symptoms. SPARX can be used as a stand-alone self-help therapy, or as an adjunct to traditional face-to-face counseling/therapy. A version for all young people, with the aim of enhancing resiliency is in the development phase (SPARX-R). A version has been developed for sexual minority young people (e.g., homosexual and bisexual youth and those questioning their sexuality) called Rainbow SPARX.

Characterizing goal: Reductions in depressive symptoms and/or increased skills at managing low mood

Short description and gameplay: SPARX is a computerized self-help program (specifically a form of computerized cognitive behavioral therapy) for the treatment of depressive symptoms, and SPARX uses the medium of a fantasy world, where the user's avatar is faced with a series of challenges to rid a virtual world of gloom and negativity. The program uses appealing graphics and interactive exercises to engage users. Each of the seven modules takes approximately 30 min to complete, and modules have a direct teaching component—where skills from the fantasy world are applied to real life. SPARX is delivered online and can be supplemented with a paper-based user notebook (Fig. 12.29).

Distribution info: SPARX is freely available in New Zealand, where the Prime Minister's Youth Mental Health Project funded its rollout. Auckland Uniservices (the commercialization arm of the University of Auckland) manages the international distribution of SPARX. SPARX has been translated into Dutch and is in the

Fig. 12.29 SPARX—main characters

process of being translated into Japanese. Research projects utilizing SPARX have been completed in New Zealand, Australia, and the Netherlands.

Economic information: The initial development and evaluation of SPARX was funded by the New Zealand Ministry of Health. The subsequent rollout of the program in New Zealand has been funded by the Prime Minister's Youth Mental Health Project.

Quality information: Over a dozen peer-reviewed academic journal articles have featured SPARX. The seminal evaluation of SPARX, demonstrating its effectiveness, was based on a large randomized controlled non-inferiority trial published in the British Medical Journal (Merry et al. 2012). In this study, 187 adolescents aged 12–19 years seeking help for symptoms of mild-to-moderate depression, and deemed in need of treatment by their primary healthcare clinician, were randomly allocated to SPARX or usual care. Per protocol analyses (n = 143) showed that SPARX was not inferior to treatment as usual. Additional studies highlighting the acceptability and usefulness of SPARX have been completed with young people excluded from mainstream educational settings (Fleming et al. 2012), sexual minority youth (Lucassen et al. 2015), and Māori young people (Shepherd et al. 2015). SPARX has featured in several key reviews of computerized therapies for children and young people with mental health difficulties (e.g., Fleming et al. 2014). SPARX has also won several international awards, in particular a World Summit Award in 2011 (under the auspices of United Nations) for the best e-content in the category of health and education, and a digital award from Netexplo, a "global observatory on digital society," hosted by UNESCO. This award was presented for projects that Netexplo call "the 10 most innovative and promising digital initiatives of the year" in 2014.

Further information: For further contact go to https://sparx.org.nz/ or email *sparx@auckland.ac.nz*.

12.5 Societal and Public Awareness Games

12.5.1 Missio for Life—Exploring the World's Social Problems

Author: Clemens Hochreiter

Title: missio for life

Application areas: interactive learning course, augmented reality, global learning

Target user group: schoolchildren age 12 and over

Characterizing goal: According to global learning the purpose of the game is to give pupils an idea of the world's social problems, especially in India and the Philippines. At the same time, we outline the strength of solidary commitment is outlined.

Short description and gameplay: When entering the environment of the exhibition, each group gathers an iPad that guides them interactively through a set of sceneries and games and a compelling storyline (Fig. 12.30).

missio for life is much more than just another serious game or exhibition. It combines virtual and tactile worlds in complete new way never used for educational games before. Players find real sets with tactile experiences, which are connected to their experience on the iPad screen. They need to work together and interact with both worlds in order to succeed. A QR-Code scanner interface enables them to scan all the different exhibits right into their virtual inventory to solve puzzles. A sophisticated routing system enables storylines to be experienced by several groups simultaneously enabling a huge player throughput in a defined time frame. Special effects like artificial fire provide for even more involvement.

Through emerging the game world of Renu, Mercedes and Paulo the pupils are able to see the characters motives in a greater picture and discuss them. The three protagonists' lives question general things like social injustice and human dignity.

Distribution info: The exhibition targets German pupils above the eighth grade and is built directly on school grounds (100 m^2 required). Pupils are to explore the exhibition for 90 min, supervised by a pedagogical expert.

Fig. 12.30 *Missio for Life*—Props, like in the kitchen scene, extend the virtual world to the real world (*left*), kids virtually "cook" with the iPad in a "real" kitchen (*middle*), trust the police or try to escape? Finding the right path can be difficult (*right*)

The exhibition will charge 150 EUR plus running costs for catering and an overnight-stay. Missio München will provide teaching materials for further work, e.g., background information about the protagonists, or material for discussions about daily problems like gender (in)justice.

For more information concerning the exhibition and booking information, go to http://missioforlife.de/

Economic information: missio for life is a unique interactive exhibition developed by Reality Twist GmbH, in cooperation with benninger.eberle (http://www. benninger-eberle.de/) and produced by missio München. Missio has no financial interest with the project. It is sufficient if booking revenues pay for running costs. Funding has been achieved by education subsidies available at missio München. The business model is solely established on the fact to create a brand that is effective for the target group and roll out further brand activities later on. Development costs have been in the middle price region.

Quality information: Focus group tests have been highly successful. Students have gathered all necessary educational information after running through the exhibition, even the most difficult ones. Feedback has been positive throughout by both players and educators. It has been nominated for the German Developers Price.

Further information: Further information about the exhibition and educational materials can be downloaded on the website, as well as background information about the protagonist's countries. Booking and exhibition contact is Marion Roppelt. Information about missio München can be found on their website: http://www. missio.de/

12.5.2 Lotte—Holocaust Remembrance

Authors: Michael Geidel, Annekathrin Wetzel, Rolf Kruse, Kelvin Autenrieth

Title: [A] CHL Classroom App (Working title), [B] Friend Ship

Application areas: [A] education, [B] education, social game, group dynamics & tolerance training

Target user group: [A] school classes, age 12–16; [B] school version: school classes, age 11–18; Public version to be used by NGOs, public, and private institutions for all ages

Characterizing goal: [A] Reconstruct history, critical thinking, and teamwork; [B] Learn about social group dynamics, how to act in moral dilemma situations, reflect about the powers of individual decisions and responsibility in a repressing system

Short description and gameplay: Both games are part of a Transmedia-Project *Call her Lotte*, based on the multiple-award-winning 3D short film, but with a different focus:

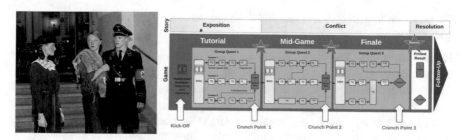

Fig. 12.31 Still from the short film: Maria and Lear are young actresses in the 1930s in Munich, one Jewish, the other not. Their friendship saves a young life from certain death despite the terror of Hitler's dictatorship (*left*). The quest structure of the Classroom App [A] (*right*)

[A] The *CHL Classroom App* is dedicated to school teaching. After being introduced to a comprehensive problem statement, students are assigned to teams. They have to accomplish three scenes full of quests before overcoming the final challenge (Fig. 12.31 right).

As the story is based on a concept called *Fragmented Storytelling*, many pieces of authentic analog and digital media are game elements. They are a source of information and also interactive items. Finding, interpreting, and deliberately using these elements are crucial for advancing in the game. The gameplay implements *Puzzle Solving Mechanics* known from adventure games on computers, which support educational aspects tied to critical thinking. They also are an instrument of engagement and motivation. Didactics are based on *Historical Thinking Competencies*, an educational state-of-the-art model used in school. It organically integrates into narration and gameplay, so it fulfills all requirements given by the different stakeholders.

The app itself is engineered as a multiplayer application for mobile platforms. It offers a client-server structure where the teacher can track progress and intervene (e.g., pause) if necessary. After the actual game, a result page for every team leads to critical discussions within the whole class to reflect the experiences made.

[B] The turn-based multiplayer strategy game is played within a class of 10–30 people and confronts the players with group dynamics like inclusion versus exclusion, belonging to a group versus being rejected, sacrificing friendships and loosing status. The players are put into a similar situation like the young protagonists in the short film—but in a non-WWII-related context. In an everyday life social situation they have to decide, what, and—more crucial—who will they sacrifice in order to gain status. The catch, however, lies in the fact that a player needs friends' support to win. Payers collect points by following tasks, solving challenges, and interacting with other players, thus gaining popularity, status, and hierarchy levels. But the higher the ranking, the more the individual has to sacrifice to reach further. Driven by seemingly arbitrary missions and by rule changes, player face moral dilemmas throughout. After the game, the group can discuss alternative options the players would have had, the aspects of tolerance, friendship, and civil courage, and how the game mechanics relate to the principles that were used in the

Nazi system to establish and keep their power. Also they can relate their findings to society today.

Distribution info: The games will be available online via the project website http://www.call-her-lotte.com/. [A] is distributed to schools directly and via publishers. The provided package optionally contains preconfigured hardware (tablets, notebook, WiFi access point) and printouts (maps, play cards, markers) for schools that don't have this equipment and resources. [B] is an online-based game that runs in browsers on desktops and most mobile devices. It will be available as free version for selected educational partners and as commercial version with a fee per game use. Additionally to the first version in German–English, French, and Spanish versions are planned.

Economic information: The transmedia project has been funded by *Medienboard Berlin-Brandenburg*, *Federal Government Commissioner for Culture and the Media*, *IHRA*, *Staatskanzlei Thüringen*, *Nordmedia*, *FFF Bayern*, *SLM* and *Bayerischer Rundfunk*. The concept for the CHL Classroom App [A] was developed by Michael Geidel as producer and Annekathrin Wetzel as author and director at MiriquidiFilm together with M.Sc. Kelvin Autenrieth, game designer, and Prof. Rolf Kruse with his team at Erfurt University of Applies Sciences.

Friend Ship [B] was developed together with Dr. Konstantin Mitgutsch, Research Affiliate at MIT GAME LAB Boston, Dominik Philp, teenage game player, Jaron Schulz, game designer, Dr. Martin Ganguly, expert for media in the German educational system, Adam Sigel, U.S. writer, and ItmattersGames company.

Quality information: At the time of this book, these games are currently in production. During development, we reached out to our target group to teachers and schools and worked closely with didacticians. The project was invited to present at *film festival de Cannes*, *Games Developer Conference* 2015 in San Francisco, *Quo Vadis Berlin* Games Conference, *Cross Video Days Paris*, *Medientage München*, and a *Gamescom Congress* 2015 panel.

Further information: For more information and playing requests, please contact us via the form on the website (http://www.call-her-lotte.com/) or by email: *game@call-her-lotte.com*.

12.5.3 Purpose—Racism and Sexism

Author: Helmut Hlavacs

Title: Purpose

Application areas: experiences, racism, sexism, zombie apocalypse

Target user group: no specific target audience

Characterizing goal: determine whether you have prejudices concerning race and sex

Short description and gameplay: In *Purpose*, the player manages a group of survivors after a zombie apocalypse. The player decides who can join the group, and who has to leave it. People thrown out have to die. Group members can have one of three roles: gatherers carry food, which is vital for survival. Fighters protect the group during the night. In case of a zombie attack, group members might die without protection. Finally, scouts find new camps the group can visit. Goal is to find Elysium, the only place not infected by zombies.

By deciding between ethnics and sexes, the player decisions reveal whether ethnicity of sex plays a role. After the game finished, a statistics presents whether there is cause to assume that there are racial or sexual prejudices (Fig. 12.32).

Distribution info: The game can be played free of charge at http://purpose.cs.univie.ac.at/

Economic information: The game was created as a bachelor's thesis.

Quality information: No experiments regarding effectivity have been carried out so far, but are planned.

Further information: The game was created at the Entertainment Computing research group in the Faculty of Computer Science at the University of Vienna (Austria). The game is available in German and English.

12.5.4 Utopolis—Democracy Simulation

Author: Clemens Hochreiter

Title: Utopolis—Aufbruch der Tiere (English: do you want to translate the latter part?)

Application areas: Multiplayer game, collaboration and communication training, democracy simulation

Fig. 12.32 *Purpose*: At the start, players must accept four members into their survival group (*left*). The group visits camps and searches for food (*middle*). Sometimes, while resting, the group is attacked by zombies (*right*)

Target user group: commuters and youth

Characterizing goal: The focus lies on collaboration and communication between players, as these skills are essential to master the game. It is a sophisticated democracy simulation, including a legal system to establish one's own community rules.

Short description and gameplay: A group of 15 or 25 players takes the dangerous journey to Utopolis. The players assume the roles of various animal species, each with different skills. Each individual has to contribute to the success of the single stages. The rules for this collaboration are set by the players: While in board games, unloved rules can easily be changed and be exchanged by house rules, this is usually not possible in video games. But in *Utopolis—Aufbruch der Tiere* the players establish the rules of their community and organize themselves according to democratic principles. With a law system, every player can propose a law, that is voted upon and that is effective for all players. Therefor not on the rules for resource management and other activities are determined, but also players can be punished for their illegal actions (Fig. 12.33).

Each player can create their own laws based on several templates and suggest them to the group. If the majority is in favor, the law becomes effective as a binding rule for everyone. That way for example, obligatory resource transfers to the camp can be determined as well as animals that hurt or kill other members of the group can be punished. Further, players decide in what way they want to perform the different tasks needed to survive: Whether *path of the commune* or *path of the warrior*, each of the six available paths offers advantages and disadvantages to players in attaining their goals, and their choice requires consideration and foresight.

Distribution info: Utopolis—Aufbruch der Tiere is available in German and runs on Android and iOS mobile devices. The game is free to play, and the Nemetschek foundation has no commercial interest concerning the game (no in app purchases, no advertising, and no merchandise products). The game is accessible for download at http://www.utopolis-online.de/, *and* in both GooglePlay and the iOS AppStore.

Fig. 12.33 *Utopolis*: It's crucial to work together as a team, otherwise the *red* glow can't be stopped (*left*). A core part of Utopolis is to introduce and pass bills. Players are defining the games rules with these laws (*middle*). Each species has its own skills, so only as team they will survive (*right*)

Economic information: Utopolis—Aufbruch der Tiere was developed by Reality Twist GmbH and financed by the Nemetschek Foundation. With prize money received by winning the German Computergame Award, an add-on of five new levels and a technical update was created. There is no further royalty concept behind Utopolis. Development costs have been in the middle price region.

Quality information: In 2015, the game won the German Computergame Award in the category Best Serious Game. It also won a Red Dot Design Award for best game design. Analysis by media educators approved great results in its effort to teach democracy and offer a valuable source for citizenship pedagogy.

Further information: Further information is available at the Nemetschek Foundation website http://www.nemetschek-stiftung.de/ in the project area. For direct questions, please contact Clemens Hochreiter, CEO of the serious game development studio Reality Twist GmbH.

12.5.5 Great Flu—Awareness Game for the Flu Virus

Authors: Roman Schönsee, Michael Bas, Rens van Slagmaat

Title: The Great Flu

Application areas: pandemic education, medicine

Target user group: Visitors of the exposition *H5N1—the evolution of a flu virus*, organized by Erasmus MC and Rotterdam Museum of Natural History; people who are interested in the risks of a virus and where it comes from

Characterizing goal: Introduce players to how a pandemic evolves

Short description and gameplay: In 2009, the 200th anniversary of Charles Darwin's birth was celebrated worldwide. The Erasmus MC and the Rotterdam Museum of Natural History organized the exposition *H5N1—the evolution of a flu virus*. ranj created *The Great Flu* in cooperation with well-known virologist Prof. Dr. Ab Osterhaus (Fig. 12.34).

The player chooses a virus, which determines game difficulty. The goal of the game is to control a possible pandemic. In the game, the player has a world map that is divided into regions. The player meticulously follows the outbreak of the flu pandemic. In a display, the player sees how many people have been infected and how many have died. The player has a budget and resources to control the virus. Beware: actions to control the virus cost money. This leads to some moral dilemmas, because conflicting opinions about fighting flu pandemics exist.

The player can control the pandemic by applying actions or assigning research teams to the regions. To help the player, there are global events that indicate what problems or solutions are found there. The game confronts players personally with these important choices, after which the effects immediately become clear. This creates a new understanding—and respect for the choices of others.

Fig. 12.34 *The Great Flu*—snapshot from the graphical user interface

Distribution info: The great flu is playable through a Web browser and needs Flash to run. The game is in English. http://www.thegreatflu.com/

Economic information: The game is free to play.

Quality information: The Great Flu has hundreds of thousands players worldwide as well as a widespread media coverage, among others including the front page of NRC Handelsblad (Dutch newspaper), TV spots at NBC (USA), a profile on the Dutch TV program Pauw en Witteman.

Further information: The game was initially built for the exposition of *H5N1—the evolution of a flu virus*. Two weeks after the release the Mexican flu, also known as Swine flu, broke out worldwide. Hundreds of thousands of players tried the game to get to know more about the virus—what the risks are and where it comes from.

12.5.6   Global Conflicts—A Serious Games Series for Social Studies

Author: Simon Egenfeldt-Nielsen

Title: Global Conflicts series (a game series, which includes *Palestine*, *Latin America*, *Child Soldiers*, *Sweatshops*, and *Afghanistan*)

Application areas: social studies, civic games, history games, RPG

Target user group: designed to fit school curriculum in history/social science and language courses for students 13–20 years old

Characterizing goal: *Global Conflicts* aims to illustrate the various perspectives present in a given conflict; through dialog and argumentation, the game provides players with the knowledge and experience to form their own opinion.

Short description and gameplay: Global Conflict is a series of role-playing games (RPG), which focuses primarily on dialogue. Through the game the player encounters a number of stakeholders, across a variety of locations. These locations are usually ordered in a narrative flow, which ensures that the player encounters all essential stakeholders during gameplay.

A game dialogue is initiated by clicking on the relevant stakeholder. Through the dialogues, the player tries to obtain information about the situation at hand—whether getting input to a news article about the tensions rising at check points in Jerusalem (*Check Points*), or the investigation of use of child labor at a leather mill in Bangladesh (*Sweatshops*). These pieces of information, or in some cases evidence, are ultimately used to either construct a newspaper article or confront the main culprit. This main stakeholder is always placed as the final encounter in the game, and all evidence gathering leads up to this crucial dialogue. During this "boss fight," the player is meant to use the arguments found during the game in order to try to convince the culprit to change his opinion or behavior (Fig. 12.35).

The core purpose of the games is to present various perspectives—each in the shape of a stakeholder—on the given conflict, and balance these in order to not favor one perspective over others. This in turn allows the player to (1) learn about the various perspectives that the conflict situation can be viewed through, and (2) form their own opinion about the conflict and about the various stakeholders. By talking to Gaza citizens, Israeli soldiers, a mullah in a small afghan village, or a child who works at a factory in Dhaka, the player is faced with these different perspectives. The perspectives might not always lead to one obvious solution, but helps to highlight the ambiguity of most such conflicts.

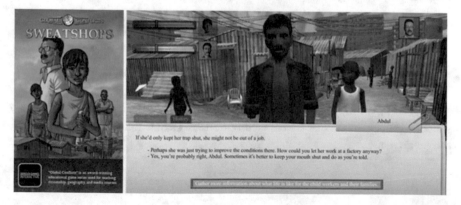

Fig. 12.35 Cover and snapshot (*right*) with a dialogue scene from *Global Conflicts: Palestine*

The games are single player, but can benefit from being played together by 2–3 students. The game packages are accompanied by an elaborate set of supportive material: Topic Overview, Teacher's Manual, and Student Assignments. The Topic Overview is meant to give the teacher a solid overview of the conflict area portrayed in the game. The content of the Topic Overview is derived from the extensive research that is part of every game production.

The Teacher's Manual helps the teacher structure curriculum around the game and ensures that the teacher is prepared for discussing game topics with the students. It also describes approaches to learning implemented in the game, and how to optimize this in a class setting. Student Assignments includes a number of specific tasks for students. These can either be used during game play by smaller groups or after concluding the game. The variety of tasks supports different learning styles that the teacher might use.

Distribution info: The games are available on https://school.seriousgames.net and all run on PC/Mac in the most commonly used browsers. The games were developed for English, Danish, Norwegian, and Swedish languages. The price of the games varies since there are different bundle versions and price ranges, depending on the requirements of the schools buying the games.

Economic information: The games are produced partly by sponsorship from Danida (part of the Danish Foreign Ministry, which heads development projects abroad) and by self-financing by Serious Games Interactive. The first game *Global Conflicts*: *Palestine* was quite expensive to develop, but today an episode is budgeted at around 80,000 EUR.

Quality information: The first game of the series, Global Conflicts: Palestine, received quite a bit of public attention (ex. https://www.youtube.com/watch?v= eKs1y2JDWF0) and also won a BETT award in 2010. The game was mentioned on CNN and several other news channels around the world. The game got noted as a new, groundbreaking way of combining computer games and education.

A study at Santa Clara University of *Global Conflicts*: *Sweatshops*, where 95 students played the game, showed some promising effects.

> Conclusion: Dogmatic students grew significantly less dogmatic about the child labor issue after playing Sweatshops. By confronting students with the complexity of the child labor issue from the perspectives of Bangladeshis, the game successfully encouraged students to see the nuances of this issue. The nature of this game forced users to question their strong beliefs and find a compromise with the views of Bangladeshis on child labor.
>
> (Chad Raphael, Christine Bachen, and Pedro Hernandez-Ramos performed the study)

Further information: More information can be gained by checking out https:// school.seriousgames.net or by contacting Serious Games Interactive at *info@seriousgames.net*.

12.6 Pervasive Gaming, Cultural Heritage and Tourism

12.6.1 FreshUp—Pervasive Gaming in a Campus Environment

Authors: Wiebke Köhlmann, Raphael Zender, Ulrike Lucke

Title: FreshUP

Application areas: pervasive game, campus introduction and orientation

Target user group: Freshmen at university in their first weeks of study

Characterizing goal: University freshmen face diverse problems in the beginning of their studies, such as organizing their courses and orientating in a new educational and personal environment. The pervasive game FreshUP (*Freshmen at the University of Potsdam*) aims at helping to overcome these initial difficulties by transforming a conventional scavenger hunt into a mobile pervasive game with real-world activities (Zender et al. 2014).

Short description and gameplay: FreshUP is a pervasive browser-based and platform-independent game that can be played on mobile devices as well as on a PC. It combines the card game foursome with a scavenger hunt. In order to get accustomed to previously identified main issues of student life (Lucke 2011)—like course registration, use of the cafeteria, library access, public transport etc.—the players have to solve tasks all over the campus and city of Potsdam. For each solved task, the player obtains a card. Every card is assigned to one deck of a certain topic (e.g., library, public transport, administration and e-learning) and each deck consists of four cards. The cards of one deck address four knowledge types: orientational, factual, actionable and practical knowledge (Zender et al. 2014) and consist of various types of tasks (e.g., single and multiple choice, GPS positioning, text input and selection of areas in an image) based on the IMS QTI standard (IMS Global Learning Consortium). The goal of the game is to complete as many decks as possible in order to gain the most points.

Currently there are overall 25 decks, where 12 can be solved in single-player mode. In order to encourage social contacts, players have to cooperate in teams in order to solve another 12 decks and can communicate by sending messages. Furthermore, bonus cards can be gained under certain conditions (e.g., certain time span or only available at a certain event) in order to complete 1 bonus deck. To increase the overall motivation, badges for certain numbers of solved knowledge types, sent messages etc. are awarded.

As each course of study has its specialties, course related decks have been developed in cooperation with the respective faculties. Thus players have to enter their course of study during registration (Fig. 12.36).

Distribution info: FreshUP is in use in the beginning of each winter term at the University of Potsdam, Germany. After a registration phase, the game phase lasts 4

Fig. 12.36 *FreshUP* active cards of different decks and knowledge types; task view; correctly solved task (from *left* to *right*)

weeks and ends with an award ceremony. A demo version is available at https://freshup.cs.uni-potsdam.de/freshupdemo.

Economic information: A prototype of the game was developed in the context of a computer science student's project in 2011 and enhanced in the context of a master's thesis in 2013. In the winter term of 2011, FreshUP was offered for computer science freshmen, and starting from winter term 2012, for all freshmen at the University of Potsdam. Since 2011, two student workers and one teaching assistant are entrusted with the further development, maintenance, advertisement and execution of the game. Prizes for the winners are kindly provided by local sponsors.

Quality information: The concept of the game FreshUP was derived from survey results (Lucke 2011) concerning e.g., technology in use and preferred game genres. An initial evaluation in 2011 (Köhlmann et al. 2012) evaluated, amongst others, the awareness level of the game in general and the experience with the game. Overall the questionnaire shows, that the game was well liked in terms of design, usability, concept and implementation.

Subsequent to the evaluation in 2011, the game was improved and the task catalogue was enlarged in order to serve all courses of study. A second evaluation (Zender et al. 2014) was conducted during the game phase in the winter term 2012/2013. 33 participants of FreshUP took part in the questionnaire before the game start and 19 at the end of the game phase. A control group consisted of 217 students who did not participate in the game. The general part of the survey concentrated on the general orientation on campus and the city of Potsdam, the knowledge concerning studies and university and the number of personal contacts among fellow students. The evaluation after the game showed that the general orientation, the familiarization with everyday life and university, and contacts to fellow students of the FreshUP players were better than of the control group. Additionally, the overall gaming experience was also rated positively.

Further information: FreshUP has been developed at the Chair for Complex Multimedia Application Architectures of the Department of Computer Science at the

University of Potsdam, Germany. A demo version is available at https://freshup.cs. uni-potsdam.de/freshupdemo. For more information, please contact Raphael Zender (*raphael.zender@uni-potsdam.de*) or Ulrike Lucke (*ulrike.lucke@uni-potsdam.de*).

12.6.2   REXplorer—Sightseeing Game

Authors: Steffen P. Walz, Rafael Ballagas, Jussi Holopainen

Title: REXplorer

Application areas: tourism, sightseeing, history, culture

Target user group: young adults visiting Regensburg, Germany

Characterizing goal: The main goal was to facilitate fun learning for young adults less interested in classical guided sightseeing, and help them to engage with the history and culture of their destination, in this case Regensburg.

Short description and gameplay: REXplorer was a sightseeing game set in Regensburg, one of the most visited tourist destinations in Germany and a UNESCO World Heritage site. Players assume the role of a researcher to uncover the secrets behind the paranormal activity linked to a secret language found in the Regensburger Dom Church in Bavaria, Germany. The symbols of this language have special powers: players can use them to summon historical spirits at 30 different sights. A special paranormal activity detector—a GPS enabled smartphone running the REXplorer application in kiosk mode, in a specially designed casing rented from the tourist information office—helps the players to detect and communicate with spirits living in the city; the device also allows the players to cast spells by gesturing with the detector, where each gesture mimics a symbol of the secret language. As the players walk around the town, they meet spirits that need help to deliver important messages to their counterparts. The players' mission is to solve these quests in order to score points, collect and document experiences with the detector's built-in camera, and gain knowledge about the history and culture of this medieval city.

In the game world of REXplorer, a spirit represents every historical site. These spirits are set in different historical epochs in order to convey the various ways of life and salient moments across the history of Regensburg. The cliffhanger stories are linked to other spirits through both space and time. Players must listen to a spirit's story, and then identify and find the corresponding sight to hear the resolution to the narratives and score points for solving quests.

Sightseeing in REXplorer is non-linear. Players are in control of the order in which sights are visited and quests are fulfilled. Players can accept up to three quests in parallel, and can delete unwanted quests to make room for others. This allows players to develop different strategies about fulfilling quests, such as collecting quest destinations that are spatially near, and eliminating quests that are too far (Fig. 12.37).

Fig. 12.37 *REXplorer* interaction principle, gameplay, map, information (from *left* to *right*)

Tourists rarely tour a city alone. Instead, they are most interested in shared experiences and memories, and REXplorer was specifically designed to support these goals (Ballagas and Walz 2007). In order to promote shared experiences, the paranormal detector contains a loud speaker so that the spirit's story can easily be heard in a small group of two or three—the group size also comes about because pupils under the age of 18 and unaccompanied by an adult in Germany can only tour an environment by themselves in a group of at least three. Additionally, the game requires multiple artifacts including the electronic detector, and a paper map with a gesture guide. These allow each player to participate by taking on a different role in the game, and the roles can be easily swapped during gameplay. To promote shared memories, the players' experiences and photos are automatically cataloged to a souvenir travel weblog, which uses an interactive map to show the users' path through the city and highlight points of interest they have visited. Players can express themselves through commenting on their blogs or taking pictures using the camera in their paranormal activity detector. After 2 weeks, and if a player leaves their postal address, they receive a print postcard from a game character, sending them "Greetings from Regensburg."

One of the lessons learned of REXplorer's commercial operating is that solo players of the game at times perceived spell-casting with the paranormal detector in a public setting as awkward. However, even the presence of one other player provides enough social support for the performative gesturing. The gestures are clearly not the easiest or most efficient way of interacting with the spirits, but this interaction fits best with the story and promotes engagement for the players, as expressed in interviews and surveys with the target group.

REXplorer provides a playful platform to explore the culture and history of Regensburg. The game helps build important associations between the historical characters and the buildings and changes the way visitors perceive and intervene with the city. These associations provide a springboard for learning more through the in-depth historical information linked on the travel blog that summarizes one's experience.

Distribution info: REXplorer was available in the UNESCO World Heritage protected Regensburg, Germany, during the tourist seasons of 2007 and 2008.

Regensburg ranks amongst the top sightseeing travel locations in Germany. Tourists could rent the paranormal activity detector from the tourist information office as a new service complementing existing services, such as guided sightseeing tours. The fee was designed to be competitive with the existing audio guide offering, 12 EUR for an hour of play. The *paranormal activity detector* was actually a Nokia cell phone and GPS receiver in disguise, so in today's market, one could imagine just allowing tourists to use their own cell phone. The rental model, however, allows the device to be skinned to look like a paranormal activity detector instead of a mobile phone. This is a key in promoting the atmosphere and adding to the mystery of how the gestures are recognized.

Economic information: REXplorer was created by Rafael "Tico" Ballagas from RWTH Aachen University and Steffen P. Walz from ETH Zurich (Ballagas and Walz 2009), in collaboration with the Regensburg Experience (REX) Museum (http://www.rex-regensburg.de/) and with generous support from, as well as input by, Nokia Research Center Helsinki and Tampere.

Quality information: The game was playtested (Ballagas et al. 2008) with sightseeing guides and other stakeholders throughout development, and also evaluated with target groups on site prior to the launch. The evaluation was structured as an interactive play session followed by a focus group interview; in the early stages, Wizard of Oz methods were used. Next to a school group study, there were 18 participants in the major study between the ages of 18–45. Two participants played REXplorer alone, and the rest played in pairs resulting in a total of ten playing sessions. The playing sessions were coordinated in such way that two playing sessions would happen concurrently and then the different groups of players would come together at the end for a focus group interview (consisting of three to four participants). All 10 play sessions and the corresponding five focus group interviews were videotaped, and the videos were analyzed using grounded theory affinity analysis. Participants expressed that, overall, they thought the game provided a unique and fun experience, once used to the new types interactions and spatial exploration the game offered. It should be noted that the game service was launched prior to the release of the Apple iPhone in 2007; several sensor and actuator-based functionalities that REXplorer offered had not yet reached a mass customer base.

Further information: A short trailer of the game and gameplay is available at https://www.youtube.com/watch?v=Mf7m97tF3Ls. The credits at the end of the video show all partners and cast involved in the commercial production of the game service. REXplorer is also a part of the permanent exhibition at the Computerspielemuseum Berlin (http://www.computerspielemuseum.de/). For further information see the reference list.

12.6.3   Jogging Over a Distance—Healthy, Pervasive Gaming

Author: Florian "Floyd" Mueller

Title: Jogging Over a Distance

Application areas: health game, exergame, jogging

Target user group: people who are interested in jogging with their friends but are not located in the same physical location, and/or do not have the same physical abilities (i.e., jog at different speeds)

Characterizing goal: *Jogging Over a Distance* supports the motivation to exercise coming from social engagement with the activity.

Short description and gameplay: Jogging Over a Distance connects two joggers in different geographical locations and different athletic abilities through the use of heart rate data. With Jogging over a Distance, two joggers plan to run at the same time, with mobile phones and wearing stereo headphones, a microphone and a heart rate monitor. Each jogger can hear the live audio of their jogging partner while they run. Relative to their target heart rate (which the joggers entered beforehand), the jogger's heart rate data affects the audio location in a 2D plane that is oriented horizontally around the jogger's head. If the other jogger is "in front," the sound appears to come from the front, and the further "in front," the softer the audio volume. When both joggers perform at their preferred heart rate (or have both slowed at the same percentage from their baseline), they hear the audio right beside them, as if they were running side-by-side. This way, the jogger is able to detect whether their partner is putting in more, the same, or less effort, based on their relative heart rates (Fig. 12.38).

Distribution info: Jogging Over a Distance is still a research project and as such not available for purchase yet. However, since the original development, systems that provide functionality similar to Jogger Over a Distance's features are now available in the Apple App Store, and also aim to support joggers and their desire for social engagement.

Economic information: Jogging Over a Distance was supported by the University of Melbourne, Australia, and Distance Lab, UK.

Quality information: Jogging Over a Distance has been evaluated with 32 social joggers, with some of them as far apart from each other as Europe and Australia. Joggers found the system suitable to balance their physical abilities and appreciated the social support coming from their jogging friends that the system facilitated. Participants saw the distance between each other not as a hindrance to go jogging anymore, but rather an opportunity to jog with their partner despite their different physical abilities. As such the system was not fixing a problem, but rather offering an opportunity for social exercise engagement, which joggers appreciated (Mueller et al. 2010).

Fig. 12.38 *Jogging Over a Distance*—connecting and motivating people to exercise "together"

Further information: More information on Jogging over a Distance is available at: http://exertioninterfaces.com/jogging_over_a_distance/

12.7 Marketing Games

12.7.1 Quest for Oil—Branding Game

Author: Simon Egenfeldt-Nielsen

Title: Quest for Oil

Application areas: Real-time strategy, branding games

Target user group: high school students and university entry level graduates

Characterizing goal: Maersk Group and Serious Games Interactive based the game design around the key messages, which the client wished to promote through the game experience. These messages were to:

- Visualize the interior of the Earth
- Understand the cutting edge techniques and technologies used
- Reinforce the very heavy focus on safety, which permeates the whole industry

Short description and gameplay: *Quest for Oil* is a serious game used for branding the Maersk corporation and for internal corporate communication. Maersk Group, Maersk Oil and Drilling invest annually in communication initiatives to create understanding in the general public about the types of work, people and technologies involved in prospecting for and extracting oil and natural gas. Over recent years, the prime medium of communication had been informational videos intended to be experienced via video hosting sites and other channels, and Maersk Oil and Drilling was keen to explore new digital forms of communication. They had a strong conviction that the means of communication needs to continually evolve so as to meet the rising expectations of the primary target audience, primarily high school age students and undergraduates.

The aim of the game is to explore the game world, prospect for oil reserves, extract the oil which is economically viable, and reach a target condition of one million barrels before the computer controlled opponent. It focuses on a combination of speed of action and the appliance of knowledge about the oil and drilling business communicated during the gameplay. At the beginning of the game, the player has a homebase and two exploration units; a ship and a helicopter. The map is concealed and it is necessary to move the exploration units around the ocean conducting geological analyses of the rocks beneath the sea. Once the geological report is received, the player is challenged to determine the most likely places to carry out exploratory drilling for oil reserves. During the drilling phase, the player controls the drill, avoiding hazards such as hidden gas pockets and ultra-hard rock layers until the potential reservoir is reached, and finally are able to confirm its economic viability. Should the results be successful, a production rig may be constructed and the oil extracted using unique injection technology used by Maersk Oil and Drilling in the field. Finally, oil is transported hone via ships or pipelines, revenue starts to be generated, and the player chooses how next to invest and explore.

Through the game experience, the expectation was to fire the imagination of the players such that they might consider a science educational path and possibly attract them to the opportunities present in the exploration and drilling business. In order to maximize the impact of the game, a large-scale media promotion campaign was carried out leading up to and subsequent to the game's release, including coverage on major TV news outlets, and support at a senior executive level (Fig. 12.39).

Fig. 12.39 *Quest for Oil's* main GUI (*left*) and scene (*right*)

Distribution info: Quest for Oil is a free, 3D multi-player real-time strategy game, which can be played in a browser or tablet app. An educational package was produced to support the use of Quest for Oil in the classroom.

Economic information: The game was developed over a period of 2 years for undisclosed budget.

Quality information: Quest for Oil is an interesting serious games for numerous reasons, not least the demonstrated positive effect that it had on the target audience. The primary metric by which communication initiatives have been measured at Maersk is time of engagement with the medium, and in this respect the game-based solution redefined what is possible in terms of deep engagement with corporate information. The game has currently been played over 1 million times by more than 300,000 players. As a result of this great success, the Maersk Group continues to invest in game-based solutions:

> New times calls for new measures, and we want to use the computer game to tell the story of an extremely innovative business, which the entire world depends on, in a new and engaging way. We wish to engage in dialogue about our oil and energy business through gamification and at the same time give all interested the best opportunity to experience the underground.—Claus V. Hemmingsen, CEO of Maersk Drilling

Further information: http://www.maersk.com/en/hardware/quest-for-oil

12.8 Serious Games Archives

Some of the best practice serious games described above—as well as numerous additional examples of serious games with high quality—are listed in serious games archives; but the majority are not. Hence, a big chance is missed for successful retrieval and access of the games via searching those archives in search engines or game portals.

Existing repositories for games and serious games differ not only in the amount of recorded games, but also both in terms of (the size of) the covered application spectrum and in terms of the granularity of underlying classification schemata.

The *Serious Game Classification System* (http://serious.gameclassification.com/) provided by the ludoscience group in France as the result of an academic research project launched in 2006 is more generic and covers the broad spectrum of application domains for serious games in general (3,076 serious games in total). Hereby, the research work and subsequently the structure of the underlying taxonomy for the serious games classification system are focused on the analysis and derived theoretical model of gameplay principles. Games are classified according to overall category, gameplay, purpose(s), market(s) and target audience, alongside with user-contributed keywords. The category is deduced from the kind of gameplay and the market of a title/game, e.g., *video game, video toy, serious game, retro serious game* (indicating that the game was published before 2002), as well as sub categories such as *advergame, edugame,* or *exergame,* following the market and purpose of a game. The gameplay distinguishes two types of gameplay types: *game-based* for games with clear goals to reach in the game, and *play-based* for games without clearly stated goals and corresponding scoring mechanisms to evaluate the performance of a player. Whereas the game purpose(s) (e.g., educative message broadcasting, training, goods trading, or storytelling) and targeting market (s) (e.g., entertainment, state & government, military & defense, healthcare, education, corporate, religion, culture & art, ecology, politics, humanitarian, media, advertising, and scientific research) are closely coupled, the target audience is classified in age groups ranging from *0 to 3 years old* to *60 years+*, as well as domain values like *general public*, *professionals*, and *students*. A quick search provided by the classification system offers a text field for keyword search as well as checkboxes for directly playable or downloadable games. The advanced search mode offers radio buttons for searching a video game, a video toy, or both. Further, the classification system provides different (database) views to browse the system and search for dedicated/a set of serious games: A *Thumbnail* view provides an preview image, the title and year of a game, a *Details* view lists the title, year, supported platforms, the creator, editor and country of a game, a *Taxonomy* view—as conceptual basis of the classification system—focuses on the gameplay, purpose, market and audience, a dedicated *Gameplay* view separates games according to the (gameplay) goals and means, and finally a *Keywords* view focuses on keywords in addition to the title and year of a game. Individual games in the classification system are attributed with all the categories mentioned above plus of a brief description of the game (including snapshots), a hyperlink, distribution information, and information about/links to related games with similar characteristics.

The Serious Games Association also provides a serious games directory covering nine serious games application areas (including *Corporate*, *Education*, and *Health Care/Medical*). Here, basic information for the games listed in the archive includes the game's title, platform(s), market, and a brief description. When selecting one particular game—as an example, let's visit the cognitive brain training game *Braingymmer* (available at http://www.grandmetropolitan.com/)—narrower information includes the link to the website of the game, a snapshot of the game (here: game platform), comprehensive developer information (including the address, contact information etc.), comprehensive publisher information (website, contact, available outlets, quantity order/pricing information, year developed, typical hours of play, awards/certifications/rankings, measuring performance/learning), and additional information such as a generic contact for any further questions.

Probably the biggest and most elaborated database (especially dedicated) for health games is provided by the Center for Digital Games Research at UC Santa Barbara (http://www.cdgr.ucsb.edu). This database originates from the former Health Game Research national program in the United States, which was funded by the Robert Wood Johnson Foundation (USA). As of October 2014, the database contains 432 games, 488 publications, 157 resources, 853 organizations, and 85 events. The games (http://www.healthgamesresearch.org/db/search/tab=games) are attributed by 37 categories/health topics from *Allergies* to *Visual Health*. Further attributes—also serving as search terms in the database—include information about the target population (target user group such as adults, children or healthcare professionals) of a game, publication or resource, the game platform (e.g., arcade, game console, PC, or internet), the publication type (book, journal, etc.) and resource type corresponding to publications and resources (e.g., archive, game engine, or online community), the organization type (e.g., game development studio, publisher, sponsors of institutions such as museums where games are running) and the event type (e.g., conference, festival or workshop) according to organizations and events and information how to obtain games (download, free, purchase, subscription, etc.). More concrete, individual games—illustrated by the outdoor exergame *Active Life Outdoor Challenge* (available at www. healthgamesresearch.org/games/active-life-outdoor-challenge) are described by the title of the game, an illustration, a set of keywords (*Adults, Children, Exergame, Nintendo Wii, Physical Activity, Racing, Sports* and *Teens*), the name of the publisher and developer of the game, website(s) where to find the game, a short free text description of the game (*"In this Nintendo Wii exergame, players move their upper and lower bodies by using the Wii remote and a game mat. This game involves more than a dozen fast-paced activities, such as log jumping, river rafting, and a minecart adventure."*), and further information about the topic (*Exercise and Fitness*), target population (*General Audience*), and game platform (*Game Console*).

The analysis of existing games and health game repositories shows a major overlap of generic description elements such as the title, a short description, keywords and (opt) a preview/thumbnail of the game, the target audience (users, players), supported platforms, distribution info (how to access the game) and information about the developer and publisher of a game. The main differences exist in the covered spectrum of games (serious games in general ranging from *Advergames* to *Edugames, Healthgames*, and *Exergames*) contrary to dedicated, application oriented game repositories such as health game repositories covering games related to health topics from *Allergies* to *Diabetes, Obesity*, or *Visual Health*) and varying perspectives for the establishment and use of game repositories: Whereas the serious games directory provided by the serious games association strives for a generic system, as broad and complete as possible, the serious games classification system provided by ludoscience has a more IT-related approach (with a focus on the formal description and classification of gameplay principles) and the health game repository by the Robert Wood Johnson Foundation clearly focuses on a user-centered perspective (i.e., users such as institutions, doctors, therapists, and patients as stakeholders in the healthcare arena).

12.9   Summary and Outlook

Serious games cover a broad spectrum of application areas, ranging from educational games and games for training and simulation to health games as well as games for societal relevant topics such as security or energy. The serious games in different application areas vary in its characteristics, including different funding, business, and distribution models as well as involved parties, used technology, and user acceptance. There are numerous serious games available, either as commercial products (typically with a focus on entertaining a broad user group), corporate games (usually realized as contractual work ordered by individual customers) or smaller serious games and game prototypes often resulting from research projects (typically tailored to a smaller user group with a specific characteristic). Compared to entertainment titles, serious games typically have much lower budgets, resulting in lower quality—and a significant discrepancy between user/customer expectations and the quality of gameplay and (complexity) of game environments.

The examples of *Re-Mission* or *SPARX* show that it is worth investigating high quality serious games—for the wealth of individuals and society in general. Nevertheless, the current state of play or serious games is still at its infancy, and a sustainable market breakthrough is missing (cf. Chap. 11 tackling economic and legal aspects of serious games). Especially in the area of health games, comprehensive (evaluation) studies could prove the benefit of serious games and subsequently could pave the way for a broader use of the games by health-care providers—resulting in "games as medical treatment."

A major drawback of existing serious games is that they are usually not very well described and attributed with (machine-readable, quantitative and qualitative) metadata such as the characterizing goal of the game, the target user group, expected serious game effects well-proven in studies, etc. Therefore it is quite hard or even impossible for end users/players (individuals, private persons) or intermediaries/customers (trainers and teachers, doctors and therapists) to find and select a most appropriate game for a specific situation (user characteristic, needs). For that—similar to catalog systems for libraries, hotel reservation systems, or friend scouts—the establishment of enhanced game archives, serious games portals, or metadata information systems as conceptual basis to describe, offer, and retrieve the best serious game that matches the interests, need,s and characteristics of individuals and groups would be highly valuable in the future. Initial conceptual approaches to a standardized metadata format of serious games is provided by Göbel et al. (2011a, b), Hendrix et al. (2012), Elborji and Khaldi (2014) specifically in field of educational games.

Check your understanding of this chapter by answering the following questions:

- What are the characteristics of the field of simulation and training games?
- What are the characteristics of the application field of educational games?
- What are the characteristics of the application field of games for health?
- What are the characteristics of the application field of awareness games?
- What are the characteristics of the application field of pervasive games?
- What are the characteristics of the application field of marketing games?
- Which databases provide information concerning serious games?

Acknowledgments Most of the best-practice examples are provided by members of the GAME association of Game Developers in Germany (http://game-bundesverband.de/) and the working group on "Entertainment Computing" of the German Society of Computer Scientists (https://www.gi.de/aktuelles/meldungen/detailansicht/article/fachgruppe-entertainment-computing-gegruendet.html). Further valuable input has been provided by different colleagues specialized in dedicated Serious Games application areas. Many thanks!

Recommended Literature

Aldrich C (2009) The Complete Guide to Simulations and Serious Games: How the Most Valuable Content Will Be Created in the Age Beyond Gutenberg to Google. John Wiley and Sons. *Focuses on educational games and offers an encyclopedic overview and complete lexicon for those who care about the next generation of educational media*

Aldrich C (2009) Learning Online with Games, Simulations, and Virtual Worlds: Strategies for Online Instruction. John Wiley and Sons. *Provides a simple and practical guide to identifying when and what kind of games, simulations, and virtual environments should be used, how to get them, how to deploy them, and how to measure their effectiveness*

Egenfeldt-Nielsen S, Smith JH, Tosca SP (2012) Understanding Video Games: The Essential Guide (Second Edition). Rouledge. *Provides a comprehensive introduction to the growing field of game studies*

Ma M, Oikonomou A, Jain L (2011) Serious Games and Edutainment Applications. Springer, London, UK—*provides a pragmatic approach to the research and application area of serious games and edutainment applications, including a number of best practice examples*

Magerkurth C, Röcker C. (Eds.) (2007a) Concepts and Technologies for Pervasive Games: A Reader for Pervasive Gaming Research, Volume 1. Shaker Verlag, Aachen, Germany

Magerkurth C, Röcker C (Eds.) (2007b) Pervasive Gaming Applications: A Reader for Pervasive Gaming Research, Volume 2. Shaker Verlag, Aachen, Germany. *Provides theoretical aspects and practical insights into the research and development of pervasive games*

Michael D, Chen S (2005) Serious Games: Games That Educate, Train, and Inform. Cengage Learning PTR in 2005. *Tackles the development of serious games*

Ritterfeld U, Cody M, Vorderer P (2009) Serious Games—Mechanisms and Effects. Routledge, New York and London. *Tackles the nature of serious games from a social science perspective, in the context of various best practice examples in the field of serious games for learning, serious games for development and serious games for social change*

Walz SP, Deterding S (2014) The Gameful World: Approaches, Issues, Applications. The MIT Press. *Provides numerous examples and illuminations how gaming and gamification examples (might) pervade our daily life*

Further entry points for in-depth research and analysis/game studies of serious games in different application areas include: Numerous conferences and journals (see Recommendations for Further Reading, Chap. 1), various game archives provided in Sect. 12.7, game magazines (with ratings for new titles), and game awards—rewarding innovative and effective serious games

References

Azadegan A, Baalsrud-Hauge J, Harteveld C, Bellotti F, Berta R, Riedel J, Bidarra R, Stanescu I (2014) The move beyond edutainment: have we learned our lessons from the entertainment industry. In: Proceedings of first international conference on games and learning alliance (GALA 2013)

Baalsrud Hauge J, Braziotis C (2012) Enhancing the student's learning on supply chain management through the application of a business game. In: Pawar KS, Potter A (eds) New horizons in logistics and supply chain management, proceedings 17th international symposium on logistics (ISL 2012), Nottingham University Business School, pp 683–689, 8–11 July 2012

Baalsrud Hauge J, Braziotis C (2013) Improving the understanding of on supply chain interaction among post graduate students through the application of a business game—a pilot study. In: Proceedings of international symposium on logistics (ISL 2013), Vienna, Austria, 7–10. July 2013

Baalsrud-Hauge J, Boyle E, Mayer I, Nadolski R, Riedel JCHK, Moreno-Ger P, Bellotti F, Lim T, Ritchie J (2013) Study design and data gathering guide for serious games' evaluation. psychology, pedagogy, and assessment in serious games. IGI Global 2014:394–419

Ballagas R, Walz SP (2007). REXplorer: using player-centered iterative design techniques for pervasive game development. In: Magerkurth C, Roecker C (eds) Pervasive gaming applications—a reader for pervasive gaming research, vol 2. Shaker Verlag, pp 255—284

Ballagas R, Walz SP (2009) Case K: REXplorer. In: Montola M, Stenros J, Annika W (eds) Pervasive games: theory and design. experiences on the boundary between life and play. Morgan Kaufmann Publishers, San Francisco, CA, pp 215–218

Ballagas R, Kuntze A, Walz SP (2008). Gaming tourism: lessons from evaluating rexplorer, a pervasive game for tourists. Pervasive computing. Springer Berlin Heidelberg, pp 244–261

Baller G, Kalbe E, Kaesberg S, Kessler J (2010) NEUROvitalis. Neuropsychologisches Gruppentraining. Prolog, Köln

Benford S, Crabtree A, Flintham M, Drozd A, Anastasi R, Paxton M, Tandavanitj N, Adams M, Row-Farr J (2006) Can you see me now? ACM Trans Comput-Hum Interact (TOCHI) 13 (1):100–133

Bingham PM, Meyer M (2011) Self determination and health behaviors in children with cystic fibrosis. Open Pediatr Med J 5:1–7

Bingham PM, Bates JHT, Thompson-Figueroa J, Lahiri T (2010) A breath biofeedback computer game for children with cystic fibrosis. Clin Pediatr 49:337–342

Bingham PM, Lahiri T, Ashikaga T (2012) Pilot trial of spirometer games for airway clearance practice in cystic fibrosis. Respir Care 57:1278–1284

Brown SJ, Lieberman DA, Gemeny BA, Fan YC, Wilson DM, Pasta DJ (1997) Educational video game for juvenile diabetes: results of a controlled trial. Inform Health Soc Care 22(1):77–89

Brown SJ, Lieberman DA, Gemeny BA, Fan YC, Wilson DM, Pasta DJ (1998) Educational video game for juvenile diabetes: results of a controlled trial. In: van Bemmel JH, McCray AT (eds) Yearbook of medical informatics 1998. Schattauer Publishers, Stuttgart, pp 490–502

Crawford C, Newberg S, Damon R, Arneson D, Bever E (1988) For of war. A clearer view. Comput Gaming World 46:24–26, 52–53

Davis SB, Moar M, Jacobs R, Watkins M, Riddoch C, Cooke K (2006) Ere be dragons: heartfelt gaming. Digital Creativity 17(3):157–162

De Vries PW, Knol E (2011) Serious gaming as a means to change adolescents' attitudes towards saving energy; Preliminary results from the EnerCities case. In: Accepted paper for 'EDEN annual conference', June 2011

Decety J, Lamm C (2006) Human empathy through the lens of social neuroscience. Sci World J 6:1146–1163

Dillon R (2010) On the way to fun: an emotion-based approach to successful game design. CRC Press

Elborji Y, Khaldi M (2014) An IEEE LOM application profile to describe serious games « SG-LOM» . Int J Comput Appl 86(13)

Fleming T, Dixon R, Frampton C, Merry S (2012) A pragmatic randomized controlled trial of computerized CBT (SPARX) for symptoms of depression among adolescents excluded from mainstream education. Behav Cogn Psychother 40(05):529–554

Fleming TM, Cheek C, Merry SN, Thabrew H, Bridgman H, Stasiak K, Hetrick S (2014) Serious games for the treatment or prevention of depression: a systematic review. Revista de Psicopatologia y Psicologia Clinica 19(3):227–242

Games P, Knight M (2002) America's army. Crown Publishing Group New York, NY, USA

Göbel S, Schneider O, Holweg D, Kretschmer U (2004) GEIST—mobile edutainment with GIS and interactive storytelling. Proc UbiGIS, Gävle, Schweden

Göbel S, Hardy S, Wendel V, Mehm F, Steinmetz R (2010a) Serious games for health—personalized exergames. In: Proceedings of the 18th ACM international conference on multimedia. ACM New York, NY, pp 1663–1666

Göbel S, Wendel V, Ritter C, Steinmetz R (2010b). Personalized, adaptive digital educational games using narrative, game-based learning objects. In: Entertainment for education. digital techniques and systems 5th international conference on e-learning and games, edutainment 2010, Changchun, China, August 16–18, 2010, LNCS, 6249, pp 438–445. Berlin: Springer

Göbel S, Gutjahr M, Steinmetz R (2011a) What makes a good serious game—conceptual approach towards a metadata format for the description and evaluation of serious games. In: Proceedings of 5th European conference on games based learning. Athens, Greece. Academic Conferences Limited, Reading, UK, pp 202–210

Göbel S, Hardy S, Steinmetz R, Cha J, El Saddik A (2011b) Serious Games zur Prävention und Rehabilitation. In: 4. Deutscher AAL-Kongress, 25.-26.01.2011 in Berlin: Demographischer Wandel—Assistenzsysteme aus der Forschung in den Markt, VDE Verlag

Hardy S, Göbel S, Steinmetz R (2013) Adaptable and personalized game-based training system for fall prevention. In: Proceedings of 21st ACM international conference on multimedia. ACM, pp 431–432

Hardy S, Dutz T, Wiemeyer J, Göbel S, Steinmetz R (2014a) Framework for personalized and adaptive game-based training programs in health sport. Multimedia Tools Appl 74(14):5289–5311

Hardy S, Kern A, Dutz T, Weber C, Göbel S, Steinmetz R (2014) What makes games challenging? —considerations on how to determine the "challenge" posed by an exergame for balance training. In: Proceedings of 2014 ACM international workshop on serious games. ACM, pp 57–62

Habgood J, Overmars M (2006) The game maker's apprentice: game development for beginners. Apress, 2006, ISBN 1–59059-615-3

Hendrix M, Protopsaltis A, Rolland C, Dunwell I, de Freitas S, Arnab S, LLanas J (2012) Defining a metadata schema for serious games as learning objects. In: eLmL 2012, the 4th international conference on mobile, hybrid, and on-line learning, pp 14–19

Hess M, Wiemeyer J, Hamacher K, Goesele M (2014) Serious games for solving protein sequence alignments—combining citizen science and gaming. In: Games for training, education, health and sports. Springer International Publishing, pp 175–185

Hunicke, R. et al. (2004) MDA: a formal approach to game design and game research. In: Proceedings of challenges in games AI workshop, 19th national conference of artificial intelligence, San Jose, California, 2004

Kato PM, Cole SW, Bradlyn AS, Pollock BH (2008) A video game improves behavioral outcomes in adolescents and young adults with cancer: a randomized trial. Pediatrics 122(2):e305–e317

Kickmeier-Rust MD, Albert D (2010) Micro adaptivity: Protecting immersion in didactically adaptive digital educational games. J Comput Assist Learn 26(2):95–105

Kirst S, Zoerner D, Schütze J, Lucke U, Dziobek I (2015) Zirkus Empathico: Eine mobile Applikation zum Training sozioemotionaler Kompetenzen bei Kindern im Autismus-Spektrum. In: Proc 13. e-Learning Fachtagung Informatik, Lecture notes in informatics. Köllen Verlag

Knol E, De Vries PW (2010) EnerCities: educational game about energy. In: Conference proceedings 'CESB10 Central Europe towards sustainable building', June 2010

Knol E, De Vries PW (2011) EnerCities, a serious game to stimulate sustainability and energy conservation: preliminary results. eLearning Papers, 25, pp 1–10

Köhlmann W, Zender R, Lucke U (2012) FreshUP—implementation and evaluation of a pervasive game for freshmen. In: Proceedings of 10th IEEE international conference on pervasive computing and communications (PerCom) workshops. Lugano, Switzerland. IEEE, pp 691–696

Korn O (2005) learn2work—Spiel der Arbeit. Eine spielbasierte Unternehmenssimulation zum Erwerb beruflicher Kompetenzen. In Spath D, Haasis K, Klumpp D (eds) Aktuelle Trends in der Softwareforschung. Tagungsband zum doIT Software-Forschungstag 2004, Stuttgart 2005, pp 188–200

Korn O (2006) Business process simulations—hands-on skill-development as a means to improve business performance. In: Karapidis, A (ed) Proceedings of ICL 2005 workshop and the professional training facts 2005 Conference, Stuttgart 2006

Kuhn JT (2015) Developmental dyscalculia: Neurobiologcal, cognitive, and developmental perspectives. Zeitschrift für Psychologie, Dyscaclia, pp 02–2015

Kuhn JT, Raddatz J, Holling H, Dobel C (2013) Dyskalkulie vs. Re- chenschwäche: Basisnumerische Verarbeitung in der Grundschule. Lernen und Lernstörungen 2:229–247

Kuhn JT et al (2015) Interventions for children with math difficulties—a meta-analysis. Zeitschrift für Psychologie, Dyscalculia, pp 02–2015

Liarokapis F, Debattista K, Vourvopoulos A, Petridis P, Ene A (2014) Comparing interaction techniques for serious games through brain-computer interfaces: a user perception evaluation study. Entertainment Comput Elsevier 5(4):391–399

Lieberman DA (2001) Management of chronic pediatric diseases with interactive health games: theory and research findings. J Ambul Care Manag 24(1):26–38

Lucassen MFG, Merry SN, Hatcher S, Frampton CM (2015) Rainbow SPARX: a novel approach to addressing depression in sexual minority youth. Cogn Behav Pract 22(2):203–216

Lucke U (2011) A pervasive game for freshmen to explore their campus: Requirements and design issues. In: Proceedings of IADIS international conference on mobile learning. Avila, Spain, pp 151–158

Magerkurth C, Cheok AD, Mandryk RL, Nilsen T (2005) Pervasive games: bringing computer entertainment back to the real world. Comput Entertainment (CIE) 3(3):4

Martin P (2011) The pastoral and the sublime in elder scrolls IV: oblivion. Game Stud 11(3)

Merry SN, Stasiak K, Shepherd M, Frampton C, Fleming T, Lucassen MFG (2012) The effectiveness of SPARX, a computerised self help intervention for adolescents seeking help for depression: randomised controlled non-inferiority trial. Br Med J 344:e2598

Moore ME (2011) Basics of game design. Taylor & Francis Group, Boca Raton FL

Moskaliuk J, Bertram J, Cress U (2013a) Impact of virtual training environments on the acquisition and transfer of knowledge. Cyberpsychol Behav Soc Netw 16(3):210–214

Moskaliuk J, Bertram J, Cress U (2013b) Training in virtual environments: putting theory into practice. Ergonomics 56(2):195–204

Mortara M, Catalano CE, Bellotti F, Fiucci G, Houry-Panchetti M, Petridis P (2014) Learning cultural heritage by serious games. J Cult Heritage 15(3):318–325

Mueller F, Vetere F, Gibbs MR, Edge D, Agamanolis S, Sheridan JG (2010) Jogging over a distance between Europe and Australia. In: Proceedings ACM symposium on user interface software and technology. ACM, 1866062, pp 189–198

Nieborg DB (2005) Changing the ruses of engagement—tapping into the popular culture of america's army, the official U.S. army computer game. MA Thesis, Utrecht University, The Netherlands. 238 p. http://www.gamespace.nl/content/MAThesis_DBNieborg.pdf

Oppermann L (2009) Facilitating the development of location-based experiences. Doctoral dissertation, University of Nottingham. http://eprints.nottingham.ac.uk/id/eprint/14215

Panzoli D, Qureshi A Dunwell I, Petridis P, de Freitas S, Rebolledo-Mendez G (2010a) Levels of interaction (LoI): a model for scaffolding learner engagement in an immersive environment. In: Intelligent tutoring systems, lecture notes computer science 6095 (2010), pp 393–395

Panzoli D, Peters C, Dunwell I, Sanchez S, Petridis P, Protopsaltis A, de Freitas S (2010b) A level of interaction framework for exploratory learning with characters in virtual environments. Intelligent computer graphics, vol 321. Springer, Berlin Heidelberg, pp 123–143

Petrelli A, Kaesberg S, Kessler J, Barbe MT, Fink GR, Timmermann L, Kalbe E (2014) Effects of cognitive training in patients with Parkinson's disease: a randomized controlled trial. Parkinsonism Related Disorders 20:1196–1202

Petrelli A, Kaesberg S, Barbe MT, Timmermann L, Rosen JB, Fink GR, Kessler J, Kalbe E (2015) One-year follow-up of cognitive training in Parkinson's disease. Eur J Neurol 22:640–647

Rahe J, Liesk J, Rosen JB, Petrelli A, Kaesberg S, Onur OA, Kessler J, Fink GR, Kalbe E (2015a) Sex differences in cognitive training effects of patients with amnestic mild cognitive impairment. Neuropsychol Dev Cogn B Aging Neuropsychol Cogn 22:620–638

Rahe J, Becker J, Fink GR, Kessler J, Kukolja J, Rahn A, Rosen JB, Szabados F, Wirth B, Kalbe E (2015b) Cognitive training with and without additional physical activity in healthy older adults: cognitive effects, neurobiological mechanisms, and prediction of training success. Front Aging Neurosci 7:187

Sawyer B, Smith P (2008) Serious games taxonomy. In: Game developers conference 2008. http://www.dmill.com/

Shepherd M, Fleming T, Lucassen M, Stasiak K, Lambie I, Merry SN (2015) The design and relevance of a computerized gamified depression therapy program for indigenous Māori adolescents. J Med Internet Re (JMIR)—Serious Games, 3(1)

Squire K, Barab S (2004) Replaying history: engaging urban underserved students in learning world history through computer simulation games. In: Proceedings 6th international conference on learning sciences, pp 505–512. International Society of the Learning Sciences

Unger T (2013) Berufliche Orientierungsangebote für Jugendliche in der Metall- und Elektroindustrie: "Techforce," "ExeriMINTe" und "Ichhabpower.de." Chapter on recruitment, pp 85–94. 10.1007/978-3-658-01570-1_6. Springer Fachmedien Wiesbaden

Wagner MG, Wernbacher T (2013) Iterative didactic design of serious games. In: Proceedings of FDG, pp 346–351

Wernbacher T, Pfeiffer A, Wagner M, Hofstätter J (2012) Learning by playing: can serious games be fun? In: European conference on games based learning. Academic Conferences International Limited, p 533

Wetzel R, Blum L, Broll W, Oppermann L (2011) Designing mobile augmented reality games. In: Handbook of augmented reality. Springer New York, pp 513–539

Wetzel R, Blum L, Oppermann L (2012) Tidy city: a location-based game supported by in-situ and web-based authoring tools to enable user-created content. In: Proceedings of international conference on the foundations of digital games. ACM, pp 238–241

Zender R, Metzler R, Lucke U (2014) FreshUP—a pervasive educational game for freshmen. In: Pervasive and mobile computing, vol 14, pp 47–56

About the Authors

Editors

Ralf Dörner is Professor for Computer Graphics and Virtual Reality at the RheinMain University of Applied Sciences at Wiesbaden. He is author or co-author of more than 80 peer reviewed publications as well as text books. Starting to work in the area of serious games in 1998, he has held numerous courses on this topic and also conducted several public and contract research projects in this area. His research interests lie in the areas of visualization and the usage of computer graphics for e-learning and entertainment where his focus is not only on the user but also on the author of these applications. URL: http://www.hs-rm.de/~doerner

Wolfgang Effelsberg is Professor for Computer Networks and Multimedia Technology at the University of Mannheim. In 1984, after three years as a post-doc in the United States, he became a research staff member at IBM's European Networking Center in Heidelberg. He joined the University of Mannheim in 1989. He is the author of 11 books and more than 230 other reviewed publications. URL: http://ls.wim.uni-mannheim.de/de/pi4/people/wolfgang-effelsberg/

Stefan Göbel is Academic Councilor and head of the Serious Games group at the Multimedia Communications Lab at TU Darmstadt. He has a long-term experience in Graphic Information Systems, Interactive Digital Storytelling, Edutainment applications and Serious Games. Stefan is the author or co-author of 150+ peer reviewed publications, the initiator and host of the GameDays and Joint Conference on Serious Games, and project leader of different collaborative research projects on a regional, national and international level. URL: http://www.kom.tu-darmstadt.de/people/stefan-goebel/

Josef Wiemeyer is Professor for Sport Science with special emphasis on Movement, Training and Computer Science at TU Darmstadt. Based on extensive work on e-learning and ICT-supported training (from 1997), he started research in Serious Games in 2010. He developed and evaluated several Serious Games for education, health, science and sport. He has published numerous reviews and single studies addressing Serious Games. He is reviewer and co-editor of several international journals. URL: http://www.sport.tu-darmstadt.de/sportinstitut/personal/professoren/wiemeyer_seiten/wiemeyer_profil.de.jsp

© Springer International Publishing Switzerland 2016
R. Dörner et al. (eds.), *Serious Games*, DOI 10.1007/978-3-319-40612-1

Authors of Main Chapters

Tom Baranowski, PhD, is Prof. of Pediatrics and Senior Member of the Behavioral Nutrition and Physical Activity group, within the Dept. of Pediatrics, Baylor College of Medicine, Houston, Texas, USA. Tom is principal investigator for two currently funded research grants involving games. He is author or co-author of over 340 peer-reviewed articles, 40 non-peer reviewed articles, 30+ book chapters, two editions of a textbook on methods of evaluation for health promotion programs. He is Editor-in-Chief of both the Games for Health Journal and Childhood Obesity, and on the editorial boards of 5 other professional journals.

Daniel Drochtert is a scientific employee at the University of Applied Sciences in Düsseldorf, Germany in the Mixed Reality and Visualization group. He received a BSc degree in Media Informatics from the University of Applied Sciences in Düsseldorf in 2011 and an MSc in Computer Science from the Chinese University of Hong Kong in 2013. His studies in Hong Kong were supported by a scholarship by the German Academic Exchange Service (DAAD).

Simon Egenfeldt-Nielsen is CEO and founder of Serious Games Interactive. He founded Serious Games Interactive in 2006. Today it has around 20 employees. He has studied, researched and worked with computer games for almost 20 years. Over the years he has been involved in developing +100 games for different clients like Maersk Group, LEGO, Opel, World Bank and Siemens Wind Power. He has been involved in developing several award-winning series like Global Conflicts and Playing History. URL: http://egenfeldt.eu

Jonas Freiknecht is an IT architect at IBM and a PhD student at the University of Mannheim, doing research in the area of game development, serious games and procedural content generation. After completing his Master's degree in 2012 at the Karlsruhe University of Applied Science he taught game design, wrote a book on game programming and is an active member of a small independent game development team. URL: http://www.jofre.de

Paul Gebelein holds a PhD in sociology from TU Darmstadt. His research interests include the interplay of technology and social practice and the possibilities of interdisciplinary research. After a PhD on the social practice Geocaching he was a Post-Doc at the Multimedia Communications Lab and the Collaborative Research Centre MAKI at TU Darmstadt where he did research on get-togethers mediated by technology like i.e., flashmobs. Since 2015 Paul Gebelein is with the Humboldt Institute for Internet and Society (HIIG) in Berlin. URL: http://www.hiig.de/en/staff/paul-gebelein/

Christian Geiger is professor for mixed reality and visualization at the Düsseldorf University of Applied Sciences. He works on advanced human-technology interfaces in the areas of creative health, public spaces and entertainment computing. He published over 90 peer-reviewed papers on computer entertainment, human computer interfaces, mixed reality, system design and AI-based techniques. URL: http://medien.hs-duesseldorf.de/personen/geiger/

Benjamin Guthier is a post-doctoral researcher at the University of Mannheim where he teaches courses on video processing, programming and game engine development. After completing his PhD in 2012, he did research on Affective Computing at the University of Ottawa in Canada. He is author or co-author of a number of several peer-reviewed papers on video signal processing and games. URL: http://ls.wim.uni-mannheim.de/de/pi4/people/dr-benjamin-guthier/

Oliver Hugo originally started his career with Procter & Gamble and recently served Nintendo of Europe as Director of European Market Analysis and Research. During nine years at Nintendo, he worked on the launch of the DS, the Wii and most of the major franchises. He holds a PhD and Master's degree from the University of Cambridge and specializes in qualitative methods, concept development and communications strategy. He teaches media, communication and marketing at the University of Applied Sciences in Aschaffenburg, Bavaria.

Michael Kickmeier-Rust holds a PhD in cognition and knowledge psychology. His research activities focus primarily on technology-enhanced learning, in particular intelligent, adaptive educational systems and human-computer interaction. Michael is looking into psycho-pedagogical frameworks and models for efficient, effective, and immersive learning together with smart personalization. A particular aspect, Michael is working on digital game-based learning. Since 2010 Michael is with the Knowledge Technologies Institute at Graz University of Technology. URL: http://kti.tugraz.at

Mela Kocher published her dissertation on aesthetics and storytelling in video games in 2007. During a 2 year post-doc project at the UC San Diego and the Mobile Life Institute in Stockholm she discovered her passion for pervasive and urban games. In her current employment as research associate and game designer at the Specialization in Game Design of the Zurich University of the Arts, she focuses on the cross-over of urban and serious games, in teaching as well as in R&D projects. URL: https://www.zhdk.ch/?person/detail&id=179325

Johannes Konert is Professor for Web Engineering at Beuth University of Applied Sciences in Berlin. With a scholarship of German Research Foundation (DFG) for the research training group "Feedback-based Quality Management in E-learning" he developed solutions to add peer education to single-player educational games. Supplemented with his insights gained from foundation of a social media company, he investigates the optimization of individual learning experiences in social media-based learning applications. You find his recent research results and activities easily via popular social media applications. URL: http://johannes-konert.de

Maic Masuch is Professor for Multimedia Technology at the University of Duisburg-Essen and head of the Entertainment Computing Group. The game design and development process, and the correlation between gaming and learning are core areas of the group's research. Researching and teaching digital games since 2001, Maic Masuch is considered to be one of the pioneers of German digital game research. He authored and co-authored more than 110 reviewed publications. URL: http://www.ecg.uni-due.de/

Anna Lisa Martin-Niedecken is Senior Researcher at the Specialization in Game Design of the Zurich University of the Arts. With her background in sports science her work mainly focuses on movement based Exergames, RehabGames and on GX Research. Since 2013 she leads a R&D project on "Exergame Fitness Training" and is responsible for the accompanying research and teaching in the field of Serious & Applied Games. During her PhD scholarship at the TU Darmstadt she researched the experience of space while playing digital sports games. URL: http://gamedesign.zhdk.ch; https://www.zhdk.ch/?person/detail&id=190381

Florian Mehm is a game programmer at Subiculum Interactive and a regular lecturer of "Game Technology" at TU Darmstadt. He worked in the Serious Games group of the Multimedia Communications Lab (KOM) at TU Darmstadt where he designed and developed the game authoring tool *StoryTec*. He was also involved in the creation of several serious games. He received his PhD from TU Darmstadt in 2013. URL: https://www.kom.tu-darmstadt.de/people/florian-mehm

Philip Mildner is a research assistant and PhD candidate at the University of Mannheim. His research area focuses on serious games and how to make the creation of such games more accessible. He developed several serious games, most of them for the educational sector, and he is author or co-author of various peer-reviewed papers on networked games and serious games. URL: http://ls.wim.uni-mannheim.de/de/pi4/people/philip-mildner/

Christiane Moser is a postdoctoral research fellow at the Center for Human-Computer Interaction (University of Salzburg). Since 2008, she is working in the field of Child-Computer Interaction, Player Experience Research, and Ambient Assisted Living. She has recently finished her PhD on Child-Centered Game Development, where she refined and adapted games user research approaches for the active involvement of children. In several projects, she gathered experiences in applying User-Centered Design in various contexts (i.e., she has extensive knowledge in the requirements analysis, design and development with users, or user evaluation studies). URL: https://hci.sbg.ac.at/moser/

Florian 'Floyd' Mueller directs the Exertion Games Lab at RMIT University in Melbourne, Australia. He investigates the design of exertion games. Floyd has most recently been a Fulbright Visiting Scholar at Stanford University. He has also worked at organizations such as the MIT Media Lab, Media Lab Europe, Fuji-Xerox Palo Alto Labs and Xerox Parc. Floyd has also been a Microsoft Research Asia Fellow, working with the research teams developing the Xbox Kinect. Previously in Australia, he was a principal scientist at CSIRO. URL: http://floydmueller.com/home/home.htm

Lennart Nacke is the Associate Professor for HCI and Game Design in the Faculty of Arts at the University of Waterloo with a focus on studying player experience, physiological interfaces, and gamification. He is working on projects that deal with the cognitive and emotional side of playing games. Using body sensor technology Dr. Nacke taps into some of video gaming's most motivating features to improve physical fitness and mental wellbeing. His research is funded nationally and internationally and his publications have won best paper awards at the premier human-computer interaction conferences. URL: https://uwaterloo.ca/stratford-campus/people-profiles/lennart-nacke-phd

Christina M. Steiner completed her Diploma in Psychology and received her Dr.rer.nat at the University of Graz, Austria. She is a researcher at the Knowledge Technologies Institute of Graz University of Technology. Her research interests include knowledge and competence modelling, technology-enhanced learning, adaptation and personalisation, self-regulated learning, and user-centred evaluation of information technologies. URL: http://kti.tugraz.at/css/team/christina-steiner/

Viktor Wendel is a post-doctoral researcher at the Multimedia Communications Lab at the Technische Universität Darmstadt where he focused on game mastering and collaborative learning in multiplayer serious games during his doctoral thesis. He is author or co-author of more than 30 peer-reviewed papers on serious games, collaborative learning, game mastering, and adaptation in games. Further, he teaches on serious games and multiplayer games. URL: http://www.kom.tu-darmstadt.de/people/viktor-wendel/

Authors of Best-Practice Examples

Jannicke Baalsrud Hauge is head of the BIBA gaming Lab and works as a senior researcher at Bremer Institut für Produktion und Logistik (BIBA) Bremen, Germany. She is also co-director of GaPSLabs at KTH; Stockholm, Sweden. http://gaminglab.biba.uni-bremen.de/de/unser-team/

Michael Bas is co-founder and CEO of Ranj serious games. Since 1987 he has been active as visual artist, designer, scriptwriter, researcher and game designer. Michael is an expert in the field of serious games for health care and education. Michael's main interest is uncovering new ways to influence human behavior.

Peter Bingham is founder of RespirGames, and Professor of Neurology and Pediatrics at the University of Vermont Medical Center. Research on patented spirometer games has been supported by the NIH and the Robert Wood Johnson Foundation, and focuses on asthma, cystic fibrosis, and muscular dystrophy.

Winfried Diekmann is the CEO and Co-founder of Aerosoft GmbH located at the airport of Paderborn/Lippstadt. He is in the games business since 1992. With more than 30 employees Aerosoft is today on of the leading publisher and developer in simulation games worldwide. URL: http://www.aerosoft.com

Tim Dutz is a computer scientist and a research associate at the Multimedia Communications Lab of the TU Darmstadt. His research interest lies in pervasive and persuasive (mobile) applications, most notably mobile exergames. URL: http://www.kom.tu-darmstadt.de/people/tim-dutz/

Lynn E. Fiellin, M.D. is an Associate Professor of Medicine at the Yale School of Medicine and at the Yale Child Study Center. She is the Founder and Director of the play2PREVENT Lab at Yale, developing and rigorously testing innovative effective and targeted interventions for risk reduction and prevention in youth and young adults. URL: http://www.play2prevent.org/

Michael Geidel is Media Economist, researcher and an award-winning film and games producer. Since 1999 in the media industry, at Germany's Babelsberg film university he created new media formats and games, at MIZ Media Innovation Center Babelsberg he lead a project on Interactive TV. He is member of film festival juries and lecturer at universities. URL: https://www.linkedin.com/in/michaelgeidel

Sandro Hardy is a researcher of the Serious Games group at the Multimedia Communications Lab at TU Darmstadt. His main interest and expertise is in the field of adaptive exergames for prevention and rehabilitation. His work includes the development of various prototypes such as "ErgoActive", "TheraKit" and "BalanceFit" for cardio, balance and coordination training. URL: http://www.kom.tu-darmstadt.de/people/sandro-hardy/

Martin Heß is a full time researcher and PhD student in the groups Graphics, Capture and Massively Parallel Computing and Computational Biology and Simulation at TU Darmstadt. His research interests include serious games for bioinformatics and computer graphics. URL: http://www.gris.tu-darmstadt.de/~marhess

Helmut Hlavacs is professor at the faculty of computer science at the University of Vienna where he heads the Entertainment Computing Research Group. He works on technology and application of computer games, including virtual reality, mobile games, and games for well-being and health. URL: https://cs.univie.ac.at/Helmut.Hlavacs

Clemens Hochreiter Since the mid 1990s, the producer duo, Clemens Hochreiter and Thomas Wagner, have worked on media projects in which the division between the virtual and reality becomes blurred. In 2008, they founded the Reality Twist company, which has since become one of the leading production companies for serious games and simulators and whose political, often documentary-like games have made it famous.

Markus Herkersdorf is founder and CEO of TriCAT, a leading company in the field of Virtual 3D Worlds for learning, training, coaching, meetings and collaboration. The former military helicopter pilot holds a university degree in aviation and aerospace technology. With more than 25 years of experience in technology based learning, he is a sought-after expert on learning in immersive environments.

Kimberly Hieftje is an Associate Research Scientist at the Yale University School of Medicine and Deputy Director of the play2PREVENT Lab where she is currently involved in the development and testing of several health behavior change and educational videogames for youth and young adults. URL: http://www.play2PREVENT.org

Jussi Holopainen is a games researcher working Games and Experimental Entertainment Laboratory in Centre for Game Design Research of RMIT University. His research interests include game design research, game user experience, and playful design. Currently he is mostly interested in different design strategies for supporting urban play.

Bruno Jordaan is Senior Game Designer at Ranj Serious Games. He holds a European Media Master of Arts (EMMA) degree in Game Design & Development from the Utrecht School of Arts. At Ranj he focuses on the design, development and implementation of serious game solutions for recruitment, assessment, leadership development, change management, risk management and project management for a broad range of clients and industries.

Elke Kalbe is Professor of Medical Psychology at the University Hospital Cologne. For her work on the topic of early neuropsychological diagnosis of dementia and cognitive training and other non-pharmacological interventions to prevent and treat cognitive dysfunctions in healthy elderly and patients with Parkinson's disease she received several research awards. URL: http:// psychosomatik-psychotherapie.uk-koeln.de/medizinische-psychologie/

Simone Kirst is a doctoral candidate in psychology at Humboldt-Universität zu Berlin. Her research focuses on socio-emotional competencies and empathy, and especially their trainability in children with autism spectrum disorder. She has been working with atypically developed children and their families for several years. URL: https://www.psychology.hu-berlin.de/en/staff/1687964

Oliver Korn is full professor for Human Computer Interaction at Offenburg University in Germany and CEO of the software company KORION. His main areas of interest are gaming and gamification, affective computing and assistive technologies. URL:http://www.oliver-korn.de

Wiebke Köhlmann is a PhD-student at the University of Potsdam concentrating on accessible virtual classrooms for the blind. She worked at the University of Potsdam as a research and teaching assistant in the area of e-learning and accessibility. In 2015, she gained a best paper award at the IEEE International Conference on Advanced Learning Technologies.

Fotis Liarokapis is an associate Professor at the HCI Laboratory at Masaryk University in Czech Republic. His research interests include: computer graphics, virtual and augmented reality, brain-computer interfaces and serious games. Fotis has contributed to more than 90 peer-refereed publications and is the co-founder of VS-Games international conference. URL: https://www.muni.cz/fi/people/235197

Ulrike Lucke is professor of computer science at the University of Potsdam. Her research is

focused on interoperability in heterogeneous IT environments, especially mobile IT. Being the CIO of the university she is responsible for strategic IT issues and E-Learning. Among other positions, she was speaker of the German SIG E-Learning for several years. URL: http://cs.uni-potsdam.de/mm/

Mathijs Lucassen is a lecturer in the Department of Health and Social Care at the Open University, and an honorary research fellow in psychological medicine at the University of Auckland. His PhD evaluated a version of SPARX for sexual minority youth with depression. URL: http://www.open.ac.uk/people/ml8646

Sally Merry is professor of child and adolescent psychiatry, director of the Werry Centre of Child and Adolescent Mental Health, and head of department (Psychological Medicine) at the University of Auckland. She has led the development and research on SPARX (computerized therapy for youth with depression). URL: https://unidirectory.auckland.ac.nz/profile/s-merry

Roman Schönsee worked for many years as project manager and international account executive in the market research industry. Since 2007 Roman works as project and account manager at Ranj Serious Games and has huge experience in Serious Games projects—both industrial and public funded projects—on national and international level.

Ulrich Schulze Althoff is founder and CEO of Kaasa health. He has worked over a decade in the video game industry and is considered a valued expert in serious gaming. He founded his first company in 2001, when he was one of the first game developers to bring popular video game classics to Europe on the mobile phone. URL: https://www.xing.com/profile/Ulrich_Schulze_Althoff

Markus Schütze is Senior Marketing Manager at Kaasa health. Before taking care of Meister Cody—Talasia he worked in marketing-positions for several games-publishers incl. Electronic Arts where he was responsible for the successful launch of best selling mobile games like The Simpsons Springfield and Real Racing 3 in Northern Europe. URL: https://www.xing.com/profile/Markus_Schuetze

Alexander Streicher is a senior scientist at Fraunhofer IOSB in Karlsruhe. His research is centered on adaptive assistance and e-learning systems for image interpretation. The latest focus is on interoperable adaptive serious games and computer simulations. Furthermore he developed serious games for the medical domain at the University Hospital of Freiburg. URL: http://s.fhg.de/streicher

Daniel Szentes is a senior scientist at Fraunhofer IOSB in Karlsruhe. He is researching in the field of technology based learning. He currently investigates motivation aspects in correlation to the learning outcome of serious games. He has managed several projects in the field of technology based learning. URL: http://s.fhg.de/szentes

Siavash Tazari has a bachelor degree in game design from the University of Teesside, UK. Currently he is studying computer science at TU Darmstadt and is a research assistant in the field of game design at the Multimedia Communications Lab. Siavash has been working in the games industry, both as an employee and as an independent developer.

Klaus-Dieter Thoben is professor at the University of Bremen and director of the BIBA, Bremen, Germany. He is mainly involved in is SG application for production and logistics as well as product development and lifecycle. URL: http://gaminglab.biba.uni-bremen.de/de/unser-team/

GAF van Baalen is co-owner and game director at Ranj for 16 years. GAF holds a BA in the Fine Arts from the renowned Willem de Kooning Academy. As a game director he is the creative lead in many of Ranj's projects. His expertise is in serious game concepts, advergame concepts, game consultancy and art-direction.

Rens van Slagmaat is a senior game designer at Ranj serious games. Since 2006 he is involved in the development of a large number of serious games. During this time he has gained a lot of experience with the use of games in education and health care. Since 2014 he is the team lead of the game design team within Ranj serious games.

Marcus Vlaar is a long time industry thought leader in serious gaming and the founder and co-owner of Ranj serious games. Since 1987 Marcus Vlaar has been active as visual artist, designer, scriptwriter and game designer. As creative director Marcus is responsible for the overall didactical and creative concepts of the projects.

Steffen P. Walz is an Associate Professor at RMIT University in Melbourne, Australia, where he directs the Games and Experimental Entertainment Laboratory, the GEElab. He is a co-editor of the book edition The Gameful World, published by The MIT Press. Steffen has worked with a wide variety of industry partners (e.g., Audi, Novartis Pharma, LG Display). URL: http://playbe.com

Annekathrin Wetzel, writer/director/producer for German Television network (ARD) & Cinema, won the 3D Creative Arts Award in Hollywood 2015. As Transmedia pioneer she presented at Filmfestival Cannes, GDC & Crossvideodays. She created multiplatform shows for ARD-Alpha and was project consultant at Strategy&Innovation, Bavarian TV. URL: https://de.linkedin.com/in/annekathrin-wetzel-360b0a76

Illustrator and Author of Best Practice Example

Rolf Kruse is Professor for Digital Media and Design at the University of Applied Sciences in Erfurt, Germany. Educated as architect he has a long experience in the ideation and implementation of innovative educative interactive media. Be it in the area of city planning (at Art+Com, Berlin), MR serious games for tradeshows, mediatecture installations (with Invirt GmbH) or the "Cybernarium Edutainment Center" (a Fraunhofer Spin-Off)–always using newest media technologies to transfer complex knowledge to empower people. His research focuses on human computer interfaces for multisensory "visualization" of and intuitive interaction with dynamic spatial information that are seamlessly integrated into our environment.

Index

© Springer International Publishing Switzerland 2016
R. Dörner et al. (eds.), *Serious Games*, DOI 10.1007/978-3-319-40612-1

Printed in the United States
By Bookmasters